ALTERNATIVES TO INCORPORATION FOR PERSONS IN QUEST OF PROFIT

CASES AND MATERIALS ON PARTNERSHIPS, LIMITED PARTNERSHIPS, JOINT VENTURES AND RELATED AGENCY CONCEPTS

Third Edition

By

Daniel Wm. Fessler

Professor of Law
University of California, Davis

AMERICAN CASEBOOK SERIES

WEST PUBLISHING CO.
ST. PAUL, MINN., 1991

To my partners, June, Ann, Jean, Edward and Cathy

Preface to the Third Edition

In the five years since publication of the Second Edition change continues to predominate the limited partnership. The original uniform legislation remains in but a handful of jurisdictions. Nearly all have adopted the 1976 Revised Limited Partnership Act. Yet these adoptions were hardly in place before the National Conference of Commissioners on Uniform State Laws proposed what they styled a new "Uniform Limited Partnership Act." The year was 1985. The proposal of new legislation caused massive confusion. In a strategic retreat, the Commissioners retitled their proposals as "1985 Amendments to the Revised Uniform Limited Partnership Act." Notwithstanding, the revisions contain radical departures from the terms of a social contract which has marked the limited partnership from the dawn for the nineteenth century. It should come as no surprise that these changes and trends are major themes of the third edition.

Students of the second edition will note significant changes in the arrangement of the material. There is expanded coverage of the concept of a partnership by estoppel and further attention to the joint venture. These changes merely reflect the dynamic nature of these alternative business vehicles. In all we have a mirror of a society beset with tension even as it is blessed with opportunity.

There are two technical matters worthy of mention. In the ongoing effort to keep these materials as brief as possible I have edited the cases rather severely. I have also removed citations to state codes and replaced them with citations to the uniform partnership or limited partnership acts. I would like to express gratitude to Doug Welsh, of the Class of '92, for research and editing skills which exceeded my high expectations. My secretary, Ms. Berta Lewin, was invariably one step ahead of me in our collaborative efforts to meet a tight publication schedule.

DANIEL WM. FESSLER

King Hall on Putah
Davis, California
February, 1991

Preface to the Second Edition

I have little to add to the earlier preface to what continues to be a terse treatment of the major alternatives to incorporation of a business vehicle launched in quest of profit. The degree to which the first edition has facilitated the reintroduction of these important choices to the "business law" coverage in many law schools has been a source of gratification. I have attempted to profit from the constructive criticism and helpful suggestions offered by many who used the first edition.

The major change is the substantial expansion of the treatment of the limited partnership. In part this has come from greater recognition of this vehicle in contemporary practice. There is also the matter of the Revised Uniform Limited Partnership Act which has supplanted the original uniform statute in nearly half of our jurisdictions.

Gratitude is especially due to Professors Stanley Siegel and William A. Klein for their good counsel during the course of an enjoyable visit at UCLA. Here at home my colleagues Robert Hillman and John Oakley have supplied many helpful suggestions. A special word of thanks is in order to Brent Logan, of the Class of '87, for his assistance in technical corrections to the final manuscript and preparation of the extensive index. Dean Florian Bartosic has been more than generous with his encouragement as has Dr. Robert Cello, the Vice Chancellor for Academic Affairs. Campus research funds have supported my efforts. I hope they have been well expended.

DANIEL WM. FESSLER

King Hall on Putah
Davis, California
November, 1985

Preface to the First Edition

———————

Two things are immediately evident about these materials: they revive classroom treatment of subjects given little attention in the modern curriculum; and they are very brief. The relationship between these two features tells the essence of the tale. Contemporary law schools turn out graduates who have only a vague memory of a passing mention of agency and partnership. That is a serious disservice to the client community. The key to the reintroduction of these subjects lies in the creation of manageable classroom materials permitting their integration as a preface to contemporary courses in business organizations or associations.

The following cases, statutes, notes and problems provide a survey of general and limited partnerships, the joint venture, and related agency concepts. The emphasis is upon those aspects which generate recurrent controversy. The materials teach well in twelve to fifteen hours. A hidden agenda is the introduction of the world of business, an area of human interaction and concern, which I am distressed to say, lies beyond the experience (and initial interest) of many. Time invested in this manner is partially recouped in an enhanced pace as one breaks into "corporations." Even if this were not so, room should be made for this study.

The demise of agency and partnership in the law school curriculum did not abolish recurrent client problems in this important area-it merely produced a generation of inadequately trained lawyers. It is strange that decades marked by a proclaimed interest in the legal problems of the individual and the disadvantaged would have witnessed a near total abandonment of formal study of the business vehicles most generally encountered by the average citizen. Even schools that nominally retained business organizations or business associations courses seem to assume that the problems of the publicly held corporation (with the attendant and fascinating issues of finance) should monopolize the attention of the classroom. Yet the problems of the non-megacorporation continue. They simply fare less well in a community increasingly populated by lawyers whose ingrained reaction to "business" is the recommendation to incorporate! While I cannot prove it, I suspect that the current vogue-the close corporation-is a natural result of this artificially narrow preparation. Lawyers will incorporate any entity short of the family itself. The fact that the corporate structure is ill-suited to the emotional needs of many business relationships results in suggestions that either judicial construction or legislative amendment tailor the corporate vehicle to associations which, in more enlightened times, were pursued within the context of partnership agreements.

There are sound pedagogical advantages to beginning with unincorporated business vehicles. The emphasis upon human behavior in a business setting quickly emerges in cases dealing with partnerships. Knowledge of the recurrent problems of human trust, competence, and conflicting visions of both means and ends, suggests a dimension of business "law" which students, in my experience, find irresistible. In contrast to the traditional first weeks on the problems of corporate promoters, students find themselves confronted by a junk man who wants to classify as an "employee" an individual with whom he shared the formative years of a now rather successful business. In the next case they encounter a lawyer who betrays a client while exposing his innocent "partner" to ruin via joint liability. Agency principles reenter the curriculum through the natural conduit of business fact patterns. Indeed, the risk of "vicarious liability" quickly emerges as a concern in the business planning which daily enters classroom discussion.

With a business background furnished through the study of the general partnership, the student is prepared to digest quickly the concepts of the joint venture and to appreciate the utility of the limited partnership. Only when these alternatives have been explored does it become natural to approach the use of a corporate vehicle. Extensive use of the Uniform Partnership and Limited Partnership Acts is an excellent way to introduce the interplay between statutory provisions and common law developments. Tax considerations arise in an unalarming context. The final dividend is the framework provided wherein the corporate "solution" can be critically examined against meaningful alternatives.

It would add unseemly length to a short manuscript were I to attempt to thank all of the persons who have influenced, encouraged and assisted in the preparation of this work. Louis Faust, Raymond King, Bruce Markell, Kenneth Olmsted, and Mark Perry of the Class of 1980, provided research and organizational assistance. Judith Andress of the Class of 1981 labored as an alchemist with matters editorial. Caroline Van de Pol, Helen Forsythe, and Carole Hinkle demonstrated, once again, that the University of California prospers because of its most talented secretaries. My colleagues Daniel Dykstra, Daniel Simmons, and Bruce Wolk commented upon various aspects of the manuscript. Dean Richard Wydick was a source of encouragement and good counsel. Finally, mention must be made of Professor Edwin Bradley of the law faculty at the Georgetown University Law Center who, more years ago than either of us would like to recall, kindled my interest in this subject.

DANIEL WM. FESSLER

King Hall
Davis, California
July, 1980

Summary of Contents

Page

Preface to the Third Edition   iv

Preface to the Second   v

Preface to the First Edition   vi

Table of Cases   xvii

Chapter 1 INTRODUCTION   1

  A. THE SOLE PROPRIETORSHIP   1
  B. THE GENERAL PARTNERSHIP: DEFINITION AND
      DETERMINATION OF EXISTENCE   7
      1. Partnership de facto and de jure: 8
      2. Partnership by estoppel   17
  C. AN OBJECT LESSON IN THE LAW OF AGENCY   22
      1. Agent in Wonderland—The Concept of "Authority"   24
      2. The Consequences of Fidelity and Faithlessness   39
      3. Liability After the Fact   41
      4. Liability in Tort   43
      5. The "Scope of Employment" Defense: A Concept of
          Proven Elasticity   55
      6. Frolic vs. Deviation—A Distinction Producing a
          Substantial Difference   56

Chapter 2 THE PARTNERSHIP   63

  A. VIEWING THE PARTNERSHIP FROM WITHOUT   63
  B. PROBLEMS PECULIAR TO A TWO-MEMBER
      PARTNERSHIP   83
  C. VIEWING THE PARTNERSHIP FROM WITHIN—THE
      QUEST FOR STATUS   87
      1. Control and management   88
      2. The issue of compensation   92
      3. The fiduciary quality of the partnership relationship   100
          a. How does one detect the faithless fiduciary?   111

    b. Once a partner has become aware of a "wrong" suffer-
ed at the hands of a co-partner, what may be done to
redress the relationship?   113

D. PROPERTY RIGHTS AND THE PARTNERSHIP:
QUESTIONS OF OWNERSHIP AND INTEREST   131
   1. Partnership Property: firm capital distinguished from
the property of individual partners   131
   2. The interest of each partner in property conceded to
belong to the firm   144

E. DISSOLUTION: THE DURATION OF THE PARTNER-
SHIP RELATIONSHIP   148
   1. Duration of the Association   149
   2. The fate of the withdrawing partner   154
   3. Post-dissolution agency status of partners   168
   4. The final accounting   174

Chapter 3 THE JOINT VENTURE   189

A. INTRODUCTION   189
B. AGENCY CONSEQUENCES OF DISTINCTION   190
C. RELATIONSHIP OF JOINT VENTURERS INTER SE   199
D. USE OF JOINT VENTURES TO SHARE TECHNOLOGY
AND FORM ALLIANCES OF CONVENIENCE IN THE
MARKETPLACE   210

Chapter 4 THE LIMITED PARTNERSHIP   211

A. INTRODUCTION   211
B. FORMATION   215
   1. The consequences of defective formation: 229
   2. The fate of an investor in a defectively formed limited
partnership   234
C. THE RELATIONSHIP INTER SE   236
   1. "No action at law prior to dissolution" rule   236
   2. Prerogatives of the general partner(s)   237
   3. Disciplining the general partner   243
      a. A conceptual basis for litigation against the general
partner(s)   245
      b. The fiduciary duties of general partners and the
analogy to corporate directors   251
      c. A class action seeking a direct recovery by dis-
gruntled limited partners   253
      d. Limited partner's interest as a security   254
      f. Ouster and replacement of the offending general

partner(s)   261
    4. Dissolution at the behest of aggrieved limited partners . . . 263
D. LIABILITY TO THIRD PARTY CREDITORS   271
    1. Predicate for reclassification—powers reserved or
       actually exercised?   273
    2. Structural participation   274
       a. Discord under the Uniform Limited Partnership Act   275
       b. Safe harbor under Revised Uniform Limited Partner-
           ship Act   282
Appendix   287
Index   335

Table of Contents

	Page
Preface to the Third Edition	iv
Preface to the Second Edition	v
Preface to the First Edition	vi
Table of Cases	xvii

Chapter 1 INTRODUCTION   1

A. The Sole Proprietorship   1
  Crane and Bromberg, LAW OF PARTNERSHIP   2
  Henn, LAW OF CORPORATIONS   3
  Rohrlich, ORGANIZING CORPORATE AND OTHER BUSINESS
    ENTERPRISES   5
B. The General Partnership: Definition and Determination of Existence   7
  Henn, CORPORATIONS   7
  1. Partnership de facto and de jure   8
    Zajac v. Harris   8
      Notes   10
    Crawford v. State Bar   10
      Notes   11
    Martin v. Peyton   11
      Notes   17
  2. Partnership by estoppel   17
    Dority v. Driesel   17
      Notes   21
      Problem   22
C. An Object Lesson in the Law of Agency   22
  1. Agent in Wonderland—The Concept of "Authority"   24
    Epstein v. Corporacion Peruana de Vapores   24
      Appendix   28
    Zummach v. Polasek et al.   29
      Notes   33
    Walker v. Pacific Mobile Homes, Inc.   34

		Notes	37
2.		The Consequences of Fidelity and Faithlessness	39
3.		Liability After the Fact	41
		Ratification	42
		Quasi-Contract	43
4.		Liability in Tort	43
		Stockwell v. Morris	46
		Notes	54
5.		The "Scope of Employment" Defense: A Concept of Proven Elasticity	55
		Balinovic v. Evening Star Newspaper Co.	55
6.		Frolic vs. Deviation—A Distinction Producing a Substantial Difference	56
		Joel v. Morison	57
		Note	58
		Kelly v. Louisiana Oil Refining Co.	59
		Palmer v. Keene Forestry Ass'n.	61
		Notes	62

Chapter 2 THE PARTNERSHIP — 63

A.		Viewing the Partnership from Without	63
		Blackmon v. Hale	63
		Notes	67
		Zemelman v. Boston Insurance Co.	67
		Notes	69
		Ellis v. Mihelis	70
		Notes	75
		Problem	82
B.		Problems Peculiar to a Two-Member Partnership	83
		National Biscuit Company v. Stroud, et al.	83
		Note	87
C.		Viewing the Partnership From Within—The Quest for Status	87
	1.	Control and management	88
		McCallum v. Asbury et al.	88
		Notes	91
	2.	The issue of compensation	92
		Busick v. Stoetzl	92
		Notes	97
	3.	The fiduciary quality of the partnership relationship	100
		Fouchek et al v. Janicek	100
		Notes	111
	a.	How does one detect the faithless fiduciary?	111
	b.	One a partner has become aware of a "wrong" suffered at the hands of a co-partner, what may be done to	

	redress the relationship?	113
	Pilch v. Milikin	114
	Notes	121
	Fuller v. Brough	121
	Notes	126

D. Property Rights and the Partnership: Questions of Ownership and Interest — 131
1. Partnership Property: firm capital distinguished from the property of individual partners — 131
Hillock v. Grape — 132
Notes — 135
In Re Estate of Schaefer — 137
Notes — 142
2. The interest of each partner in property conceded to belong to the firm — 144
Bynum v. Sands, Inc. — 144
Notes — 147
E. Dissolution: The Duration of the Partnership Relationship — 148
1. Duration of the Association — 149
George B. Page v. H.B. Page — 149
Notes — 152
2. The fate of the withdrawing partner — 154
Zeibak v. Nasser — 154
Notes — 161
Hunter and Haugen v. Straube — 162
Notes — 167
3. Post-dissolution agency status of partners — 168
Harley King et al. v. John L. Stoddard — 168
Notes — 171
4. The final accounting — 174
Blumer Brewing Corp. v. Mayer — 174
Notes — 179
Harris v. Klure — 179
Mundy v. Holden — 185

Chapter 3 THE JOINT VENTURE — 189
A. Introduction — 189
B. Agency Consequences of Distinction — 190
Stone-Fox, Inc. v. Vandehey Development Co. — 190
Notes — 198
C. Relationship of Joint Venturers Inter Se — 199
Lipinski v. Lipinski — 199
Gramercy Equities, Corp. v. Dumont — 206
Notes — 209

D. Use of Joint Ventures to Share Technology and
    Form Alliances of   210

Chapter 4 THE LIMTIED PARTNERSHIP   211
A. Introduction   211
B. Formation   215
        Klein v. Weiss   215
            Notes   227
    1. The consequences of defective formation   229
            Dwinell's Central Neon v. Cosmopolitan Chinook Hotel   229
            Notes   232
    2. The fate of an investor in a defectively formed limited
        partnership   234
            Vidricksen v. Grover   234
            Notes   235
C. The Realtionship Inter Se   236
    1. "No action at law prior to dissolution" rule   236
    2. Prerogatives of the general partner(s)   237
            Brooke v. Mt. Hood Meadows Oreg., Ltd.   237
            Notes   241
    3. Disciplining the general partner   243
        a. A conceptual basis for litigation against the
            general partner(s)   245
            Wyler v. Feuer   245
        b. The fiduciary duties of general partners and
            the analogy to corporate directors   251
        c. A class action seeking a direct recovery by
            disgruntled limited partners   253
        d. Limited partner's interest as a security   254
        e. Derivative litigation against the general partner(s)   254
            Moore v. 1600 Dowing Street, Ltd.   254
            Notes   257
        f. Ouster and replacement of the offending general partner(s)   261
            Lesesne et al. v. Mast Property Management, Inc.   261
            Notes   263
    4. Dissolution at the behest of aggrieved limited partners   263
            Block v. Dardanes, et al.   263
            Note   269
D. Liability to Third Party Creditors   271
            Holzman v. De Escamilla   272
    1. Predicate for reclassification-powers reserved or
        actually exercised?   273
    2. Structural participation   274
        a. Discord under the Uniform Limited Partnership Act   275

xvi

Delaney v. Fidelity Lease Limited   275
Frigidaire Sales Corp. v. Union Properties, Inc.   278
b. Safe harbor under Revised Uniform Limited
Partnership Act   282
Mount Vernon Savings and Loan Association, et al. v.
Partridge Associates, et al.   282
Note   286

Appendices

App.

A. The Official Text of the Uniform Partnership Act   287

B. The Official Text of the Uniform Limited Partnership Act   303

C. Revised Uniform Limited Partnership Act (1976)/1985 Amendments   313

INDEX   333

Table of Cases

The principal cases are in italic type. Cases cited or discussed are in roman type. References are to Pages.

Abeloff v. Barth, 251, 260
Adams v. Jarvis, 167, 168
Aisenberg v. Adams Company, 54
Allen v. Steinberg, 243
Alpert v. Haimes, 253
Andrews v. Hastings Mut. Ins. Co., 40
B.K.K. Co. v. Schultz, 162
Bailey v. McCoy, 144
Balinovic v. Evening Star Newspaper Co., 55
Bates & Springer Inc. v. Friermood, 209
Beller v. Murphy, 161
Blackmon v. Hale, 63, 67, 69, 78
Block v. Dardanes, 244
Blumer Brewing Corp. v. Mayer, 174, 179
Boner v. L.C. Fulenwider, Inc., 210
Bonney v. San Antonio Transit Co., 199
Borah v. Motor Company, 73
Boxer v. Husky Oil Co., 243, 251
Brooke v. Mt. Hood Medows Oreg. Ltd., 237, 251
Brooks v. Muth, 189
Brown, Matter of, 143
Bullard v. Kinney, 113
Burns v. Gonzalez, 80
Busick v. Stoetzl, 87, 92, 97, 98, 99
Bynum v. Sands, Inc., 144, 147
Caley Investments I v. Lowe Family Associates, Ltd. v. Walters, 257
Carlton, State ex rel. v. Triplett, 41
Clawson v. Pierce-Arrow Motor Car Co., 59
Commissioner v. _____ (see opposing party)
Cooper v. Cooper, 137
Cox v. F & S, 245
Crawford v. State Bar, 10, 13
Cyrus v. Cyrus, 135
Delaney v. Fidelity Lease Limited, 275
Dority v. Driesel, 17
Dwinell's Central Neon v. Cosmopolitan Chinook Hotel, 229, 233

Ellis v. Mihelis, 70, 81, 137
Epstein v. Corporacion Peruana de Vapores, 24, 40
Federal Garage, Inc. v. Prenner, 43
Feinberg v. Great Atlantic & Pacific Tea Co., 41
Ferrarell v. Robinson, 39
Fiocco v. Carver, 59
Fouchek v. Janicek, 100
Frigidaire Sales Corp. v. Union Properties, Inc., 278
Fuller v. Brough, 121, 126
Garrett v. Koepke, 232
Gibson v. Angros, 92
Gittings, Neiman-Marcus, Inc. v. Estes, 40
Glensder Textile Co. v. Commissioner, 273
Gluskin v. Atlantic Sav. and Loan Ass'n, 199
Gramercy Equities, Corp. v. Dumont, 206, 209
Harris v. Klure, 179
Haveg Corp. v. Guyer, 41, 42
Heritage Hills v. Zion's First National Bank, 229
Herr v. Brakefield, 81
Herring v. Offutt, 209
Hillock v. Grape, 132, 135
Holzman v. De Escamilla, 272
Hosking v. Spartan Properties, Inc., 114
Hunter and Haugen v. Straube, 162, 167, 168
In re (see name of party)
In re Estate of (see name of party)
Infusaid Corp. v. Intermedics Infusaid, Inc., 210
Joel v. Morison, 56, 57
Jones v. Atkinson, 42
Kauffman, Inc., Milton v. Superior Court, 189, 190
Kelly v. Louisiana Oil Refining Co., 57, 59
Kristerin Development Co. v. Granson Inv., 79
King, Harvey v. John L. Stoddard, 162, 168,

172, 179
Klein v. Weiss, 215, 227, 228, 236, 237
Kline v. Devcon Realty Corp., 199
Kline v. Orebaugh, 40
Knaus Truck Lines, Inc. v. Donaldson, 43
Lamb v. General Associates, 38, 39
Largent v. Ritchey, 39
Lehman, Commissioner v., 147
Lesesne v. Mast Property Management, Inc.,
261
Lewis v. Firestone, 114
Lipinski v. Lipinski, 199, 209
Lux Art Van Services, Inc. v. Pollard, 39
McCallum v. Asbury, 87, 88, 91, 92, 111
Mahon v. Harst, 263, 269
Martin v. Peyton, 13, 274
Matter of (see name of party)
Mervyn Inv. Co. v. Biber, 190
Micheli Contracting Corp. v. Fairwood Associ-
ates, 233
Milligan v. Wedge, 54
Moore v. 1600 Downing Street, Ltd., 254, 258
Mount Vernon Savings & Loan v. Partridge
Associates, 282
Mullich v. Brocker, 55
Mundy v. Holden, 185
National Biscuit Co. v. C.N. Stroud, 83, 87
Newberry v. Slafter, 41
Olsson v. Hansen, 39
Page, George B. v. H.B. Page, 149, 162, 174
Palega's Estate, In re, 137
Palmer v. Keene Forestry Ass'n, 57, 61, 62
People v. _____ (see opposing party)
Phillips v. KULA 200 II, p. 253
Phillips, People v., 111
Pilch v. Milikin, 114, 126, 236
Plasteel Products Corp. v. Helman, 274
Pollack, H. Clinton, 145
Quarman v. Burnett, 73
Rathke v. Griffith, 274
Rayonier, Inc. v. Polson, 197
Riveria Congress Associates v. Yassky, 213
Roper v. Thomas, 252, 253
Royal Bank and Trust v. Weintraub, Gold &
Alper, 21
Ruth v. Crane, 229
Sanders v. Wyle, 162
Sanderson v. Cooke, 112
Schaefer, In re Estate of, 98, 137
Schenk v. Lewis, 164, 165
Schnucks Markets, Inc. v. Cassily, 81
Seifert v. Union Brass & Metal Mfg. Co., 43
SEC v. W.J. Howey Co., 254
SEC v. Glenn Turner Enterprises, Inc., 254
Sheppard v. Carey, 209

Shinn v. Thrust IV, Inc., 254
Snively v. Matheson, 56
Stapley Co., O.S. v. Logan, 39
State ex rel. v. _____ (see opposing party)
Stockwell v. Morris, 46, 54
Stone v. Fouse, 114
Stone-Fox, Inc. v. Vandehey Development Co.,
190, 198
Stubblefield v. Federal Reserve Bank, 55
Summers v. Dooley, 61
Swanson v. Webb Tractor & Equipment Co.,
80
Tracy v. Tuffly, 232
Triplett, State ex rel. Carlton v., 38
University Computing Co. v. Lykes-Youngs-
town Corp., 210
Vidricksen v. Grover, 234
Voudouris v. Walter E. Heller & Co., 229
Wagner v. Etoll, 162
Walker v. Pacific Mobile Homes, Inc., 34
Weil v. Diversified Properties, 241
Wheeler v. Green, 83
Wheeler v. Northwestern Sleigh Co., 42
Whitney v. Citibank, N.A., 111
Whitney v. Wyman, 39
Whittenton Mills v. Upton, 190
Wood v. Holiday Mobile Home Resorts, Inc.,
236, 269
Wood v. Western Beef Factory, Inc., 199
Woolard v. Mobil Pipe Line Co., 199
Wyler v. Feuer, 245
Zajac v. Harris, 8, 10, 13
Zeibak v. Nasser, 154, 161, 167
Zemelman v. Boston Ins. Co., 67, 69
Zummach v. Polasek, 29, 33, 34

ALTERNATIVES
TO INCORPORATION
FOR PERSONS IN QUEST
OF PROFIT

CASES AND MATERIALS ON
PARTNERSHIPS, LIMITED PARTNERSHIPS,
JOINT VENTURES
AND RELATED AGENCY CONCEPTS

Third Edition

Chapter 1

INTRODUCTION

This course is entitled "Business Organizations." We are about to spend many hours in consideration of vehicles for the organization of human enterprise. In my view these vehicles are morally neutral. As with any tool they may be used to advance or impede the greater interests of society. On this point I shall have little to say, for ultimately each individual must decide whether a specific application is desirable. But there are two points which these materials will continually stress-your roles as counselor and draftsman. Neither of these aspects of the lawyer's daily responsibility is emphasized in the initial curriculum. They form the professional challenge of this course.

The vehicles for conducting business in quest of profit are: the sole proprietorship; the general partnership; the limited partnership; the joint venture; the closely held corporation; and the publicly held corporation. These materials deal with the alternatives short of incorporation.

A. THE SOLE PROPRIETORSHIP

We start with the sole proprietorship. The "law" peculiar to this alternative is listed in the footnote.[1] The sole proprietor stands in the glory of individuality amid the toils and triumphs of the world. The "law" does not add or detract a tittle from the individual's status.

The practice of law begins when a sole proprietor enters your office. The reasons for this visit are easy to imagine. This caller may need funds and seek what we shall term "nondebt capital." Perchance this sole proprietor has heard rumors of a more favorable tax treatment or better pension benefits. Or the prospective client may seek to protect a portion of personal assets from the grasp of business creditors or tort claimants. Your visitor may also be motivated by personal appreciation that death or illness threatens to deprive the business of its sole proprietor. What do you do with such an individual and her particular package of economic, emotional and regulatory needs? Read on.

1

CRANE AND BROMBERG, LAW OF PARTNERSHIP

2-3 (1968).*

A man may carry on business as a sole proprietor. No formalities are required. He has total management authority. If he needs the services of others, he may hire them, entering the relation of master and servant, or principal and agent. If he needs funds, he may borrow from others, creating the relation of debtor and creditor. If he needs real estate or equipment, he may rent from others, forming the relation of lessee and lessor, or bailee and bailor. He becomes personally liable to pay all these people for what they furnish him. If there are losses in the business, he must bear them alone, to the extent of his resources. If there are profits, they are all his. This is the simplest form of business enterprise, totally lacking in internal structure.

One or more persons may form a corporation to carry on business. To do so, they must secure from the state a charter or certificate of incorporation pursuant to a statute which authorizes the creation of corporations. They transfer assets to the corporation or perform services for it, and receive in return the evidences of ownership of the corporation, called stock or shares. As stockholders, they periodically elect a board of directors who are charged by statute with managing the business. The directors generally make policy and major decisions but do not individually represent the corporation in dealing with third persons. The latter function is performed by officers selected by the directors, and by persons to whom authority is delegated by the officers or the directors. The same persons may be stockholders, directors and officers; they usually are in small corporations. The officers and directors owe fiduciary duties to the corporation or its stockholders; so, to a lesser extent, do controlling stockholders. The corporation obtains services, funds and property from third persons the same way a sole proprietor does (or by issuing stock to them), and enters the same relations with them. The stockholders, directors, and officers are usually not parties to these relationships in their own right, and have no personal liability in connection with them; they thus enjoy limited liability. If there are losses in the business, the corporation bears them to the extent of its resources; the stockholders indirectly bear them in that the value of their stock declines more or less in proportion to the losses. If there are profits, they are distributed among the stockholders (in proportion to their holdings) or retained in the business, at the discretion of the directors. If distributed, the stockholders enjoy them directly; if retained, the stockholders enjoy them indirectly through some roughly corresponding increase in the value of their stock. The legal existence of the corporation is unaffected by deaths or retirements of officers, directors or stockholders, or by transfers of stock from one person to another.

Partnership lies somewhere between. It requires two or more persons, each of whom is a co-owner of the business. No formality is necessary to create the firm, unless it is to be a limited partnership. The partners have equal right to participate in management, and each has authority to deal with third persons. They owe fiduciary duties to one another or to the firm. The partners usually provide many of the services, funds and property needed for the business. But the firm may also acquire them from third persons, as can a proprietor or corporation. Like a sole proprietor, and unlike a corporate stockholder, each partner is personally liable on debts incurred for these purposes. If there are losses in the business, the partners bear them to the extent of their joint and individual resources. While they may agree among themselves to share losses or pay debts in particular proportions, third persons are not bound by the agreement and may recover in full from any one or more of the partners. If there are profits, they are shared by the partners in the proportions they have agreed upon; they decide whether the profits shall be distributed or retained in the business. The legal existence of the partnership is altered, if not destroyed, by deaths, retirements, or transfers of interests by partners, but this is largely a matter which they can control by agreement.

HENN, LAW OF CORPORATIONS

43-46 (2d ed. 1970).*

The individual proprietorship or sole proprietorship-the two terms being interchangeable-is the oldest, simplest, and most prevalent form of business enterprise. Rules of contract, torts, property, and agency law loom large in its legal character.

. . .

In short, the individual proprietor is the "boss"; he personally employs others-his employees or agents. The business contracts-those made by him personally or by his agents within their actual or apparent authority or, when made beyond the agency power, ratified by him-are his contracts. As to torts, he is responsible directly for those he personally commits and vicariously (respondeat superior) for those committed by his employees within the scope of their employment. His personal liability, therefore, is unlimited, subject to possible protection by contractual stipulation or insurance. To the extent that most of his personal assets might already be invested in the business, limited personal liability would not add much benefit as a practical matter. Credit can be had for the business to the extent of not only the business assets but also the proprietor's personal assets.

Not a form of business association, it can become one, thereby ceasing to be an individual proprietorship, by being incorporated (possibly as a one-man corporation) and/or by admitting others to the business (e.g., partnership).

There are no formalities involved in the organization of an individual proprietorship, and no expense beyond the capital needs of the enterprise need be incurred. These factors make this form of doing business especially suitable to small one-man enterprises. There is little restriction on his doing business in other jurisdictions, although such activity might make him amenable to process there.

Of course, if the proprietor is entering a licensed trade, he must obtain such license-just as he would if he were to operate his business under any other form. If he desires to conduct his business under an assumed name (e.g., John Doe d/b/a "College Shop"), statutes in many jurisdictions require that a certificate to that effect be filed in a public office. ...

The obtaining of credit by the individual proprietor is limited by his own solvency. On the other hand, he is not bothered by problems of management and control. Since there is a single owner, there are no problems of relations with co-owners and therefore no contract between the owners-often a difficult drafting task in the partnership and small corporation. The relation of master and servant or principal and agent or employer and employee exists between him and anyone else associated with the enterprise. He retains all the profits of the business and likewise must bear all the losses, and he remains fully liable for any business debts although the business is dissolved.

There is generally no continuity of existence because on the death of the proprietor, his proprietorship obviously ends. ...

The interest of an individual proprietor in his business is freely transferable with a few possible exceptions: dower or curtesy rights, if they still exist, the restrictions contained in the bulk transfers law, and fraudulent conveyance law. Generally the bulk transfers law prevents the defeat of the interests of business creditors by the sale of a going concern. Insofar as tax considerations are concerned, the individual proprietorship or proprietor is like any other person and treated accordingly. His business income and other income, business losses and other losses, etc., are treated together ....

On the other hand, the individual proprietor is not subject to double federal taxation as are the shareholders and their corporations absent Subchapter S election. At the state level, however, his business might be subject to an unincorporated business income tax.

Capital gains possibilities exist upon the sale of the business, with gains on inventory being taxed as ordinary income. The basis of any capital assets acquired from the deceased owner would be the fair market value of the property either at the date of the decedent's death or as of the alternative valuation date for federal estate tax purposes, thus permitting a stepped-up basis without income tax consequences.

For tax purposes, the sale of an individual proprietorship is the sale of the individual assets comprising the business, with gain or loss figured according to the classification of each asset.

Although the individual proprietor is not treated as an employee of the business (as are those employed by him) for purposes of deductions for employee benefit plans and the like given to corporations, tax advantages of qualified retirement plans have been made available to self-employed persons. Since 1968, full deduction can be taken on contributions to retirement plans up to a maximum of $2,500, or 10 percent of gross annual "earned income", whichever is less. Those who devote full time to their businesses will be able to take 100 percent of their net profits as "earned income."

On the whole, it may be said that as important as tax considerations are, the choice between incorporating and operating as an individual proprietorship generally hinges upon the choice between limited liability with greater government regulation and full liability (possibly limited by contractual provisions or covered by insurance) with a high degree of freedom and secrecy of operation.

ROHRLICH, ORGANIZING CORPORATE AND OTHER BUSINESS ENTERPRISES

§§ 2.04, 2.05, pp. 2-9 through 2-12 (5th ed. 1977).*

2.04 Advantages of Individual Proprietorship

The advantages of the individual proprietorship are patent:

1. Absence of formalities and fees upon organization.

2. Owner is "his own boss" and may come to decisions and take action without delay or formalities (such as board of directors meetings).

3. Owner is not subject to risks inherent in the existence of broad powers to obligate the business vested in all the members of a partnership and in the officers of a corporation.

4. The business is free to trade anywhere without the formalities of "qualification."

5. The owner (if a citizen) is entitled to all the constitutional privileges and immunities accorded to "citizens."

6. The individual proprietorship is not subject to as many regulatory and reporting requirements as are other forms of business enterprise, and more particularly the corporation.

7. The enterprise may receive credit not only to the extent that the balance sheet of the business would justify but also to the full extent warranted by the owner's entire resources-outside of, as well as in, the particular venture.

8. The "double tax" to which corporate earnings are presently subject after they reach the stockholders is avoided.

There is another possible tax advantage in the individual proprietorship. If the entrepreneur has a large income and it is anticipated that the new business venture will show a loss during the early stages of its development, it may be "tax wise" to start the business as an individual proprietorship thereby giving the owner the tax "benefit" of the losses. When the development stage is concluded and profitable operations appear imminent, the business can be incorporated if incorporation is otherwise indicated.

. . .

While as to matters of title to property and the conduct of litigation, the individual proprietorship is subject to the laws applicable to individuals, the business need not be done in the owner's name but may be conducted under an "assumed" or "trade" name, subject to compliance with statutory requirements as to the filing of certificates.

2.05 Disadvantages of Individual Proprietorship

The primary disadvantages of the individual proprietorship are inherent in its very nature and include:

1. No one, other than the owner himself, is in a position to act on behalf of the business-except as an "agent" of the owner, with all the limitations inherent in that status. A primary limitation upon such agency relationships is their automatic termination upon the death of the principal.

2. The owner is subject to unlimited personal liability for all the obligations of the business and he cannot limit his risk or investment in the business to a predetermined portion of his assets. It is theoretically possible to procure agreements limiting the contracting creditor to the assets of the business but this procedure is not generally feasible and affords no protection against tort claims.

3. The risk or equity capital in the business is limited by the resources of the sole owner.

4. The business is subject to disintegration upon the death or incapacity of the owner.

5. The total profits are taxed as income to the owner-thus (a) if he has other income, serving to raise his tax rate bracket, and (b) limiting, because of

the need to pay such taxes, the possibility of retaining earnings in the business for its expansion.

6. As the owner of the business, the individual proprietor has fewer advantages than corporate employees from the benefits that may accrue from a tax-privileged qualified pension fund. Self-employed persons and partnerships may adopt tax-deductible contributions to pensions and profit-sharing plans within limits ....

B. THE GENERAL PARTNERSHIP: DEFINITION AND DETERMINATION OF EXISTENCE

HENN, CORPORATIONS

p. 67 (1974).*

Partnership is the simplest form of business association of two or more persons. In structure, it is more like the sole proprietorship, except that there are several owners, than like the corporation with its elaborate formal division of roles.

Partnership is very easy to create. No written agreement is necessary, and many firms have no more than an oral understanding that persons will work together and split the profits. Thus, partnership is the residual form of business association, the one that is created when two or more persons join together to do business but do not take the trouble to adopt any other form.

Though easy to initiate, partnership is not a particularly simple form of organization. ... Perhaps the most important [feature] is malleability: the relations among the partners and the internal structure of the firm can be anything the partners want. Their agreement is determinative, and may produce a highly complex and sophisticated structure.

One cannot sensibly say, in the abstract, that partnership is better or worse than some other form of business organization. One can compare specific characteristics and make judgments about them. One can (and frequently must) decide what is the best form for a particular business.

. . .

Consider the Uniform Partnership Act's provisions (see Appendix) on the formation of a general partnership. In most cases the "association of two or more persons to carry on as co-owners of a business for profit" will be the deliberate product of the co-owners' mutually expressed desires. But, in circumstances which Moliere might have worked for amusement, one may become a partner in spite of ....

1. Partnership de facto and de jure:

ZAJAC v. HARRIS
Supreme Court of Arkansas, 1967.
241 Ark. 737, 410 S.W.2d 593.

SMITH, JUSTICE.

The appellee, George Harris, brought this suit to compel the appellant, Carl A. Zajac, to account for the profits and assets of a partnership that assertedly existed between the parties for some two years. Zajac denied that a partnership existed, insisting that Harris was merely an employee in a business owned by Zajac. The chancellor concluded that Harris had met the burden of proving the partnership relationship. The court accordingly referred the case to a master for a statement of the partnership accounts. The essential question here is whether the chancellor's recognition of the partnership is against the weight of the evidence.

At first blush the testimony appears to be in such hopeless conflict that the controlling issue at the trial must have been one of credibility. Upon reflection, however, we arrive at a somewhat different view of the case. The business association that is known in the law as a partnership is not one that can be defined with precision. To the contrary, a partnership is a contractual relationship that may vary, in form and substance, in an almost infinite variety of ways. The draftsmen of the controlling statute, the Uniform Partnership Act, tacitly acknowledged that fact by stating only in the most general language an assortment of rules that are to be considered in determining whether a partnership exists. [UPA §7].

In the case at bar there is the additional consideration that these two laymen went into business together without consulting a lawyer or attempting to put their agreement into writing. It is apparent from the testimony that neither man had any conscious or deliberate intention of entering into a particular legal relationship. When the testimony is viewed in this light the conflicts are not so sharp as they might otherwise appear to be. Our problem is that of determining from the record as a whole whether the association they agreed upon was a partnership or an employer-employee relationship.

Before the two men became business associates Zajac had conducted a combination garage-and-salvage company, filling station, and grocery store in the Marche community in Pulaski county. This dispute relates only to the salvage branch of the enterprise.

In the salvage operation now in controversy the parties bought wrecked automobiles from insurance companies and either rebuilt them for resale or cannibalized them by reusing or reselling the parts. Harris, the plaintiff, testified that he and Zajac agreed to go into business together, splitting the profits equally-except that Harris was to receive one fourth of the proceeds from any parts sold by him. Harris borrowed $9,000 from a bank, upon the security of property that he owned, and placed the money in a bank account that he used in buying cars for the firm. The profits were divided from time to time as the cars were resold, so that Harris's capital was used and reused. He identified checks totaling more than $73,000 that he signed in making purchases for the business.

Zajac, by contrast, took the position that Harris was merely an employee working for a commission of one half the profits realized from cars that Harris himself had bought. Zajac denied that he had ever agreed that Harris would spend his own money in buying cars. "I told him, when you go out there, when you bid on a car, make a note that I will pay for it." We have no doubt, however, that Harris did use his own money in the venture and that Zajac knew that such expenditures were being made.

Counsel for Zajac put much stress upon their client's controlling voice in the management of the business. Zajac and his wife and their accountant had charge of the books and records. No partnership income tax return was ever filed. Harris was ostensibly treated as an employee, in that federal withholding and Social Security taxes were paid upon his share of the profits. The firm also carried workmen's compensation insurance for Harris's protection. In our opinion, however, any inferences that might ordinarily be drawn from these bookkeeping entries are effectively rebutted by the undisputed fact that Harris, apart from being able to sign his name, was unable to read or write. There is no reason to believe that he appreciated the significance of the accounting practices now relied upon by Zajac. They were unilateral.

We attach much weight to Zajac's candid admissions, elicited by the chancellor's questions, that Zajac paid Harris one half of the profits derived from cars that Zajac bought with his own money and sold by his own efforts. Zajac has insisted from the outset that Harris was working upon a commission basis, but that view cannot be reconciled with Harris's admitted right to receive his share of the profits derived from business conducted by Zajac alone.

There is no real dispute between the parties about the governing principles of law. The ultimate question is whether the two men intended to become partners, as that term is used in the law. *Brandenburg v. Brandenburg*, 234 Ark. 1117, 356 S.W.2d 625 (1962). Harris's receipt of a share of the net profits is prima facie evidence that he was a partner, unless the money was paid to him as wages. [UPA §7(4)(b)]. Unlike the fact situation in *Morrow v. McCaa Chevrolet Co.*, 231 Ark. 497, 330 S.W.2d 722 (1960), Harris's position does not rest upon the bare fact that he received a share of the profits. He invested, as we have seen, substantial sums of his own money in the acquisition of cars for the firm. Zajac concedes that Harris was entitled to a share of the profits from transactions that Harris certainly did not handle on a commission basis. When the testimony is reconciled, as we have attempted to do, it does not appear that the chancellor was wrong in deciding that a partnership existed. Affirmed.

Notes

Can you reconcile the holding in *Zajac v. Harris* with the content of Section 7(1) of the UPA: "Except as provided by section 16 persons who are not partners as to each other are not partners as to third persons."? Should this language be interpreted to require an affirmative intention to assume the legal relationship defined by this Statute?

George Harris was willing to go to court to establish that his relationship with Carl Zajac was a de facto partnership. Sometimes individuals resort to litigation to establish that no such relationship was ever formed. Consider the role of "intent" in the following opinion.

CRAWFORD v. STATE BAR
Supreme Court of California, 1960.
54 Cal.2d 659, 7 Cal.Rptr. 746, 355 P.2d 490.

THE COURT. Petitioner seeks the annulment of a resolution adopted by eight of the thirteen members of the Board of Governors of The State Bar present and voting that he be publicly reproved for violation of rule 3, Rules of Professional Ethics (52 Cal.2d 896). The local committee had recommended that no disciplinary action be taken.

Petitioner, now 35 years old, was admitted to the bar in 1953, after which he practiced in Sacramento for approximately 14 months. His father, Howard G. Crawford, was admitted in 1923 and practiced in Lakeport continually thereafter. In May 1954, after the Board of Governors had recommended Howard's disbarment, petitioner and his father formed a partnership, the profits from which were to be divided equally. Formal announcements of the partnership were sent out at that time. Howard was disbarred on September 16, 1954. After his disbarment he remained in the same office, kept his secretary, and continued his practice as a tax consultant. His name was no longer used as an attorney, and he did not appear in court, but he did confer directly with clients with respect to the preparation of deeds and birth certificates, probate matters, escrows and real estate deals, mining claims, and the dissolution of a partnership. He also referred his tax clients to petitioner for other legal advice. Petitioner and Howard continued to divide the profits from the entire business equally.

Before the formation of the partnership, the legend on the office window had read "H.G. Crawford-Attorney at Law-Notary Public," the stationery bore the letterhead "Law Offices of H.G. Crawford," and the bank accounts were maintained in the name of H.G. Crawford. No change was made in any of these until after Howard was disbarred. The window sign was then changed to read "Crawford & Crawford-Attorney at Law-Tax Consultant." The new stationery bore the heading "Offices of Crawford & Crawford" with "Phil N. Crawford" designated as "Attorney at Law" and "H.G. Crawford" as "Tax Consultant" in the top left margin. The letterhead had only a single phone number and address. Letters relating to all matters in the office were mailed to clients on this stationery, and many relating to the tax practice, to billing in regard to the legal practice, and to escrows, mining claims and the like were signed by H.G. Crawford without any title or identification other than that on the letterhead. Envelopes, checks, and statements bore only the firm name without any identification as to its members.

In October 1954, new bank accounts in the name of "Crawford & Crawford" were opened by Phil and Howard acting jointly, and the old H.G. Crawford accounts were closed. The printed signature cards relative to the new accounts contained the following statement over the signature of both Crawfords: "(2) That it is mutually understood that the undersigned doing business under the trade or partnership name of Crawford & Crawford are owners as co-partners and constitute all the members of the partnership. ..." Although the form of the card provided for the alternative, Howard was not thereon designated merely as an authorized signer on the account of petitioner as sole owner.

All the receipts from petitioner's business and from Howard's tax consultations were deposited in these accounts. Firm costs were advanced and all operating expenses paid out of the Crawford & Crawford account. Each withdrew what he needed with the understanding that withdrawals would be kept as even as possible. Only one set of books was maintained.

On March 25, 1955, during the period of disbarment, Howard made a sworn statement before petitioner as notary public on a creditor's claim of "Crawford and Crawford" that "he is one of the members of the firm of Crawford and Crawford" [italics added]. On February 2, 1955, petitioner, before Howard as notary public, had made an identical sworn statement on a similar creditor's claim.

Howard had had a large practice in Lakeport. Assets connected with his law office, including accounts receivable, totaled approximately $41,265.28. Petitioner's position is that in keeping with his father's wish not to abandon his clients and to stay in Lakeport to rehabilitate himself, petitioner employed his father to work for him as a law clerk, bookkeeper, and office manager, and to conduct a tax practice. Petitioner testified that his father was to receive about $400 per month for these services and that his father's withdrawals beyond that sum were to constitute a partial payment for his assets. There was no written agreement of sale, however, nor was any agreement reached as to the valuation of these assets. It was not until March 1957, after petitioner was informed of the present investigation, that he undertook an accounting of past operations, a valuation of assets, and a definite fixing of Howard's salary including withholding tax. At about the same time petitioner's law office, bank accounts, letterheads and so forth became clearly identified, and Howard moved to another location to conduct an independent tax practice.

The local committee found that although petitioner may have acted imprudently in allowing his father to continue working under circumstances that might have the appearance of a partnership for the practice of law, he did so in good faith and there was no actual partnership; that his father did not practice law; that petitioner was indebted to his father for the physical assets; and that the fact that all proceeds went into a common fund did not necessarily prove a partnership. Petitioner contends that these are the only supportable findings. He further contends that the use of the name "Crawford & Crawford" was not improper.

Petitioner relies upon [UPA §7(3),(4)(a)and(4)(e)] to support his contention that no partnership existed and that the relationship was not improper and was undertaken in good faith.

Section 7 (3) in part provides: "The sharing of gross returns does not of itself establish a partnership. ..." Section 7(4), provides: "The receipt by a person of a share of the profits of a business is prima facie evidence that he is a partner in the business, but no such inference shall be drawn if such profits were received in payment:

"(a) As a debt by installments or otherwise.

"(e) As the consideration for the sale of good will of a business or other property by installments or otherwise."

We are of the opinion that the foregoing authorities do not justify the relationship between petitioner and his father in the present case and that petitioner has failed to sustain his burden of showing that there was no partnership within the meaning of [UPA §6(1)] "A partnership is an association of two or more persons to carry on as co-owners a business for profit." The use of a firm name, the declarations of co-ownership, the continuation of equal withdrawals of sums from the commercial account coupled with the complete failure to attempt an accounting or valuation until these proceedings were under way, and the sharing of profits from the tax business, even though petitioner was in no way responsible for the attraction of tax clients or the performance of that business, makes it apparent that petitioner and his father not only held themselves out as partners, but that they actually considered themselves to be partners.

The board was also justified in finding that the name Crawford & Crawford on the office window and letterheads gave and was intended to give the impression that petitioner and his father were partners. Petitioner invokes the practice of retaining the names of deceased partners in the firm name by 22 San Francisco law firms as justifying the use of the two names here. That practice, however, is proper only if local custom permits it and does not mislead. The use of the name here is not in accordance with local custom and it does mislead, even if, as petitioner testified, his father told all clients of his disbarment. There was evidence that clients came to Howard for services that could only be performed because of the arrangement with petitioner. There was also evidence that Howard's business served as a feeder for petitioner's practice. Whether or not there was an actual partnership, and whether or not Howard was actually practicing law, the acts encompassed by the board's findings are proscribed by rule 3. That rule prohibits a member of the bar from employing another to solicit and from "directly or indirectly" aiding or abetting the unauthorized practice of law. The unauthorized practice of law includes the mere holding out by a layman that he is practicing or is entitled to practice law. (Bus. & Prof. Code, § 6126.)

. . .

The board properly considered the fact that petitioner is young and had limited professional experience, that he has never been the subject of any disciplinary proceeding, that he has a good reputation in the community, and that the activities herein complained of sprang from a commendable but misdirected filial devotion to his father.

The State Bar correctly concluded that Phillip Neal Crawford should be publicly reproved, and this opinion shall serve as that reproval.

Notes

The primary utility of *Crawford v. State Bar* is the contribution of two alternative routes to the partnership conclusion beyond the de facto doctrine suggested in *Zajac*. Unfortunately, the court does not give these theories clear labels. It may assist your understanding to term a finding that persons consciously desired to form the Section 6 relationship as a "partnership de jure." *Crawford* contained the seed of the other theory in the conclusion that it violated the canons of ethics to hold out a layperson as engaged in the practice of law. The suggestion falls short of a "partnership by estoppel" conclusion advanced under Section 16. Kindly consult the statutory appendix and reread that section.

Does Section 16 have any application to the facts in *Crawford*? What about Section 16(1)? Assuming an apt fact pattern, is the liability created restricted to creditors of the supposed firm? Could this statute be interpreted as a road to disciplinary procedures against Phil Crawford?

Is Section 16(2) applicable?

MARTIN v. PEYTON
Court of Appeals of New York, 1927.
246 N.Y. 213, 158 N.E. 77.

ANDREWS, J. Much ancient learning as to partnership is obsolete. Today only those who are partners between themselves may be charged for partnership debts by others. Partnership Law [Cons.Laws, Ch. 39], [UPA §7]. There is one exception. Now and then a recovery is allowed where in truth such relationship is absent. This is because the debtor may not deny the claim. [UPA §16].

Partnership results from contract, express or implied. If denied it may be proved by the production of some written instrument; by testimony as to some conversation; by circumstantial evidence. If nothing else appears the receipt by the defendant of a share of the profits of the business is enough. [UPA §7].

Assuming some written contract between the parties the question may arise whether it creates a partnership. If it be complete; if it expresses in good faith the full understanding and obligation of the parties, then it is for the court to say whether a partnership exists. It may, however, be a mere sham intended to hide the real relationship. Then other results follow. In passing upon it effect is to be given to each provision. Mere words will not blind us to realities. Statements that no partnership is intended are not conclusive. If as a whole a contract contemplates an association of two or more persons to carry on as co-owners a business for profit a partnership there is. [UPA §6]. On the other hand, if it be less than this no partnership exists. Passing on the contract as a whole, an arrangement for sharing profits is to be considered. It is to be given its due weight. But it is to be weighed in connection with all the rest. It is not decisive. It may be merely the method adopted to pay a debt or wages, as interest on a loan or for other reasons.

An existing contract may be modified later by subsequent agreement, oral or written. A partnership may be so created where there was none before. And again, that the original agreement has been so modified may be proved by circumstantial evidence-by showing the conduct of the parties.

In the case before us the claim that the defendants became partners in the firm of Knauth, Nachod & Kuhne, doing business as bankers and brokers, depends upon the interpretation of certain instruments. There is nothing in their subsequent acts determinative of or indeed material upon this question. And we are relieved of questions that sometimes arise. "The plaintiff's position is not," we are told, "that the agreements of June 4, 1921, were a false expression or incomplete expression of the intention of the parties. We say that they express defendants' intention and that that intention was to create a relationship which as a matter of law constitutes a partnership." Nor may the claim of the plaintiff be rested on any question of estoppel. "The plaintiff's claim," he stipulates, "is a claim of actual partnership, not of partnership by estoppel, and liability is not sought to be predicated upon [§16] of the [Uniform] Partnership Law."

Remitted then, as we are, to the documents themselves, we refer to circumstances surrounding their execution only so far as is necessary to make them intelligible. And we are to remember that although the intention of the parties to avoid liability as partners is clear, although in language precise and definite they deny any design to then join the firm of K.N. & K.; although they say their interests in profits should be construed merely as a measure of compensation for loans, not an interest in profits as such; although they provide that they shall not be liable for any losses or treated as partners, the question still remains whether in fact they agree to so associate themselves with the firm as to "carry on as co-owners a business for profit."

In the spring of 1921 the firm of K.N. & K. found itself in financial difficulties. John R. Hall was one of the partners. He was a friend of Mr. Peyton. From him he obtained the loan of almost $500,000 of Liberty bonds, which K.N. & K. might use as collateral to secure bank advances. This, however, was not sufficient. The firm and its members had engaged in unwise speculations, and it was deeply involved. Mr. Hall was also intimately acquainted with George W. Perkins, Jr., and with Edward W. Freeman. He also knew Mrs. Peyton and Mrs. Perkins and Mrs. Freeman. All were anxious to help him. He, therefore, representing K.N. & K., entered into negotiations with them. While they were pending a proposition was made that Mr. Peyton, Mr. Perkins and Mr. Freeman or some of them should become partners. It met a decided refusal. Finally an agreement was reached. It is expressed in three documents, executed on the same day, all a part of the one transaction. They were drawn with care and are unambiguous. We shall refer to them as "the agreement," "the indenture" and "the option."

We have no doubt as to their general purpose. The respondents were to loan K.N. & K. $2,500,000 worth of liquid securities, which were to be returned to them on or before April 15, 1923. The firm might hypothecate them to secure loans totalling $2,000,000, using the proceeds as its business necessities required. To insure respondents against loss K.N. & K. were to turn over to them a large number of their own securities which may have been valuable, but which were of so speculative a nature that they could not be used as collateral for bank loans. In compensation for the loan the respondents were to receive 40 per cent of the profits of the firm until the return was made, not exceeding, however, $500,000 and not less than $100,000. Merely because the transaction involved the transfer of securities and not of cash does not prevent its being a loan within the meaning of section 11. The respondents also were given an option to join the firm if they or any of them expressed a desire to do so before June 4, 1923.

Many other detailed agreements are contained in the papers. Are they such as may be properly inserted to protect the lenders? Or do they go further? Whatever their purpose, did they in truth associate the respondents with the firm so that they and it together thereafter carried on as co-owners a business for profit? The answer depends upon an analysis of these various provisions.

As representing the lenders, Mr. Peyton and Mr. Freeman are called "trustees." The loaned securities when used as collateral are not to be mingled with other securities of K.N. & K., and the trustees at all times are to be kept informed of all transactions affecting them. To them shall be paid all dividends and income accruing therefrom. They may also substitute for any of the securities loaned securities of equal value. With their consent the firm may sell any of its securities held by the respondents, the proceeds to go, however, to the trustees. In other similar ways the trustees may deal with these same securities, but the securities loaned shall always be sufficient in value to permit of their hypothecation for $2,000,000. If they rise in price the excess may be withdrawn by the defendants. If they fall they shall make good the deficiency.

So far there is no hint that the transaction is not a loan of securities with a provision for compensation. Later a somewhat closer connection with the firm appears. Until the securities are returned the directing management of the firm is to be in the hands of John Hall, and his life is to be insured for $1,000,000, and the policies are to be assigned as further collateral security to the trustees. These requirements are not unnatural. Hall was the one known and trusted by the defendants. Their acquaintance with the other members of the firm was of the slightest. These others had brought an old and established business to the verge of bankruptcy. As the respondents knew, they also had engaged in unsafe speculation. The respondents were about to loan $2,500,000 of good securities. As collateral they were to receive others of problematical value. What they required seems but ordinary caution. Nor does it imply an association in the business.

The trustees are to be kept advised as to the conduct of the business and consulted as to important matters. They may inspect the firm books and are entitled to any information they think important. Finally they may veto any business they think highly speculative or injurious. Again we hold this but a proper precaution to safeguard the loan. The trustees may not initiate any transaction as a partner may do. They may not bind the firm by any action of their own. Under the circumstances the safety of the loan depended upon the business success of K.N. & K. This success was likely to be compromised by the inclination of its members to engage in speculation. No longer, if the respondents were to be protected, should it be allowed. The trustees, therefore, might prohibit it, and that their prohibition might be effective, information was to be furnished them. Not dissimilar agreements have been held proper to guard the interests of the lender.

As further security each member of K.N. & K. is to assign to the trustees their interest in the firm. No loan by the firm to any member is permitted and the amount each may draw is fixed. No other distribution of profits is to be made. So that realized profits may be calculated the existing capital is stated to be $700,000, and profits are to be realized as promptly as good business practice will permit. In case the trustees think this is not done, the question is left to them and to Mr. Hall, and if they differ then to an arbitrator. There is no obligation that the firm shall continue the business. It may dissolve at any time. Again we conclude there is nothing here not properly adapted to secure the interest of the respondents as lenders. If their compensation is dependent on a percentage of the profits still provision must be made to define what these profits shall be.

The "indenture" is substantially a mortgage of the collateral delivered by K.N. & K. to the trustees to secure the performance of the "agreement." It certainly does not strengthen the claim that the respondents were partners.

Finally we have the "option." It permits the respondents or any of them or their assignees or nominees to enter the firm at a later date if they desire to do so by buying 50 per cent or less of the interests therein of all or any of the members at a stated price. Or a corporation may, if the respondents and the members agree, be formed in place of the firm. Meanwhile, apparently with the design of protecting the firm business against improper or ill-judged action which might render the option valueless, each member of the firm is to place his resignation in the hands of Mr. Hall. If at any time he and the trustees agree that such resignation should be accepted, that member shall then retire, receiving the value of his interest calculated as of the date of such retirement.

This last provision is somewhat unusual, yet it is not enough in itself to show that on June 4, 1921, a present partnership was created nor taking these various papers as a whole do we reach such a result. It is quite true that even if one or two or three like provisions contained in such a contract do not require this conclusion, yet it is also true that when taken together a point may come where stipulations immaterial separately cover so wide a field that we should hold a partnership exists. As in other branches of the law a question of degree is often the determining factor. Here that point has not been reached. ...

The judgment appealed from should be affirmed, with costs.

CARDOZO, CH. J., POUND, CRANE, LEHMAN, KELLOGG AND O'BRIEN, JJ., concur.

Notes

Do you find the apparent lack of a factual record as to what, if anything, the defendants actually did with respect to the prerogatives reserved in the "agreement" of interest? In fact patterns of this nature which should be relevant to the partnership issue the steps which the defendants actually took with respect to the brokerage business, or the steps which they might have taken given the terms of their credit extension?

2. Partnership by estoppel:

DORITY v. DRIESEL
Court of Appeals of Oregon, 1985
75 Or.App. 180, 706 P.2d 995

GILLETTE, PRESIDING JUDGE. This case began as an action for damages for incomplete and faulty workmanship in a house. Plaintiffs assert that defendant Daon corporation (Daon) is jointly liable with its co-defendant Driesel for breach of express and implied warranties applicable to plaintiffs' newly constructed residence. The trial court found Daon liable. That liability rests solely on the trial court's determination that Daon was a joint venturer with co-defendant Driesel, the builder of the house. Daon appeals. We reverse.

Daon developed a residential lot subdivision in Lake Oswego for construction of custom built homes. It did not undertake any residential construction on its own. In 1979, it initiated a marketing scheme for its subdivision, utilizing a "Showcase of Homes" exhibition designed to illustrate the desirability of its development. The showcase project involved six Portland area builders, including Driesel, who purchased lots from Daon and built custom homes of their own design. The homes were to be open for public viewing over a period of several months. For its part, Daon was to promote and advertise the project, decorate and furnish the model homes and provide an appropriate landscaping plan to the builders. Daon had on-site personnel to discuss lot sales with prospective purchasers, and Driesel retained his own broker for the sale of the home he was building.

While the Driesel house was under construction, plaintiffs, one of whom is a self-described real estate speculator, visited and became interested in purchasing the house. After several visits, both before and after the opening of the "Showcase of Homes", plaintiffs entered into negotiations with Driesel for the purchase of the house. All negotiations and documentation for the sale were between plaintiffs and Driesel; Daon was not represented. Many defects and incomplete items were apparent at the time of the negotiations as a result of the rush to complete the home in time for the showcase project. Driesel assured plaintiffs that those defects would be remedied before the scheduled occupancy of the house, which was to follow the close of the showcase program. The sale was closed in July, with occupancy delayed until August, 1980. Despite his assurances, Driesel failed to correct the remaining defects. Plaintiffs then made demand on both Daon and Driesel for completion of the home, voicing for the first time an assertion of a legal relationship between Driesel and Daon. When the defects remained uncorrected, plaintiff was forced to hire an other contractor to complete the work at a cost of $20,000. A default judgment was rendered below against Driesel for $20,000; the only issue at trial was whether Daon was also liable to plaintiffs. The trial court found that in fact a joint venture existed between Driesel and Daon and therefore, under the law of partnership, Daon was also liable.

Simply stated, a joint venture is a partnership for a single transaction, and partnership law controls joint ventures. *Stone-Fox, Inc. v. Vandehey Development Co.*, 290 Or. 779, 626 P.2d 1365 (1981); *Hayes v. Killinger*, 235 Or. 465, 385 P.2d 747 (1963). A contract of joint venture need not be express but may be implied in whole or in part from the conduct of the parties. *Dean Vincent, Inc. v. Russells Realty*, 268 Or. 456, 521 P.2d 334 (1974). Whether express or implied, the intent of the parties is controlling.

In *Hayes v. Killinger, supra,* 235 Or. at 471, 385 P.2d 747, the court stated:

> "The essential test in determining the existence of a partnership is whether the parties intended to establish such a relation. Given the multiplicity of legal consequences that flow from a partnership, we should not surprise the parties into such a relationship against their will. However, a disinclination to assume the burdens of a partnership does not necessarily preclude the creation of that relationship, since the substance of legal intent rather than the actual intent may be controlling. In the absence of an express agreement codifying the relationship, the status may be inferred from the conduct of the parties in relation to themselves and to third parties."

The main earmarks of a partnership are the right of a party to share the profits and losses and the right to exert some control over the business. *Hayes v. Killinger, supra,* 235 Or. at 471, 385 P.2d 747. These key issues are central to our analysis of the case at bar.

Both Daon and Driesel denied any intention of creating a joint venture relationship when entering into the showcase project. Although the "Showcase of Homes" marketing agreement between them was not an express partnership agreement, the trial court felt that, when it was considered in combination with other factors, a joint venture relationship between Driesel and Daon was inferable. The other factors included what the trial court considered to be a sharing of the benefits and potential losses from the showcase program.

Plaintiffs argue, and the trial court agreed, that shared profits for purposes of finding a joint venture were not limited to the pooling and sharing of profits from the sale of the Driesel home and Daon lots. The trial court felt that each party would benefit in its own way from the showcase program-Driesel from the promotional activities of Daon and the chance to show its product, leading to future construction jobs; Daon from having a home constructed as a demonstration of the feasibility and desirability of its development, leading to further lot sales. Conversely, each stood to lose its anticipated benefit if the other failed to fulfill its obligation to the showcase program.

The profits anticipated by Daon and Driesel to be derived from the showcase were not to be shared jointly. Rather, each was hoping to enjoy a distinct form of gain independent of that of the other. Indeed, either one might profit from the showcase while the other failed to receive any benefit at all. The fact that parties act in concert to achieve some economic objective, while relevant to the inquiry, is not enough to create a joint venture. *Hayes v. Killinger, supra,* 235 Or. at 480, 385 P.2d 747. As stated in II Rowley and Sive, On Partnership, 476, 52.9 (2d ed 1960):

"Not every joint operation which results in benefit for the parties constitutes a sharing of profits which characterizes joint adventure. The profits, in whatever form earned, must be the joint property of the parties before division."

"The chief characteristic of a joint adventure is a joint and not a several profit. Profits which are severally earned, the parties merely having dealt with the same subject matter, but not for and on behalf of each other, do not meet this requirements of the existence of a joint adventure."

Concomitantly, any potential loss from the showcase joint effort would also be unique to each party. Daon might fail to sell more lots or Driesel might fail to obtain any future construction jobs, but the loss would not necessarily be a shared one. The marketing agreement and the joint control anticipated from it- a factor also considered by the court--was a compact to cooperate, not a true agreement to share the control and decision-making of a business venture. Those elements necessary to constitute a joint venture are matters of law; whether a joint venture exists under the evidence is a question of fact. *Fitzgibbon v. Carey*, 70 Or.App. 127, 688 P.2d 1367, rev. den. 298 Or. 553, 695 P.2d 49 (1985). We hold that the trial court, as a matter of law, misconstrued the nature of a joint venture and erred in its application of the law to the facts of the case at bar; there was no joint venture between Daon and Driesel.

Although we conclude that there was not a joint venture between Daon and Driesel, our review is not complete. Plaintiffs also argued that Daon should be held liable under the concept of partnership by estoppel.[3] While no mention was made of the estoppel theory or [UPA §16] in the trial court's bench ruling, the trial judge did discuss reliance, a necessary element of estoppel. With regard to the advertising done by Daon, the trial court concluded that, "[it] would lead reasonably prudent people to the conclusion that Daon was involved in not only the development of the building site but the building of the homes."

When a partnership by estoppel arises, liability attaches to anyone who holds himself out or allows himself to be held out as a partner, thereby causing another to reasonably rely to their detriment on the representation. *Murphy v. Jacobs*, 280 Or. 215, 570 P.2d 371 (1977); *see C.A. Babcock Co. v. Katz, et al*, 121 Or. 64, 253 P. 373 (1927). The representation relied on by plaintiff in the case at bar rests exclusively on the promotional and advertising activities by Daon for the showcase program. Those representations to the public did not

---

[3]ORS [UPA §16] reads in part:

"When a person, by words spoken or written or by conduct, represents himself, or consents to another representing him to any one, as a partner in an existing partnership or with one or more persons not actual partners, he is liable to any such person to whom such representation has been made, who has, on the faith of such representation, given credit to the actual or apparent partnership * * *."

claim that the project was a Driesel-Daon partnership. Rather, the advertising generally attempted to introduce the subdivision to the public and expound upon its unique advantages. The advertising directly relating to the showcase project indicated that several Portland area builders, including Driesel, were constructing quality, custom homes that were open for public viewing. The Daon corporate logo was affixed to the advertisements, and this fact is the nearest Daon came to holding itself out as a partner with Driesel.

Considering the severe consequences of partnership liability, the doctrine of partnership by estoppel should be applied only with great care. See *Sitchenko v. Diresta*, 512 F.Supp. 758 (D.C.N.Y.1981). We think the Daon advertising praising Driesel's, as well as the other builders', reputation for quality and expertise is too slim a thread upon which to hang the consequences of partnership by estoppel. General commendations for one of the participants in the showcase project are not on a par with representations of a business relationship on which persons might reasonably rely.

None of the negotiations for the sale of the Driesel house included Daon personnel. None of the sale documents refer to a Daon-Driesel partnership. There is no evidence that either Daon or Driesel ever expressly or intentionally represented themselves as being partners. We find no evidence in the record of a representation on which plaintiffs could have reasonably relied that a partnership relation between Daon and Driesel existed. Daon is not liable as a partner by estoppel.

Reversed on appeal; affirmed on cross-appeal.

Notes

For a recent case imposing liability on a partnership by estoppel rationale see, *Royal Bank and Trust v. Weintraub, Gold & Alper*, 68 N.Y.2d 124, 497 N.E.2d 289 (1986). Plaintiff, bank, was approached by one Allen who sought a short term loan of $60,000. The year was 1977. Allen advised the plaintiff that the proceeds of the loan would be kept in an escrow account belonging to his attorneys, the firm of Weintraub, Gold & Alper. Shortly thereafter, Allen produced a letter written on law firm stationery and signed by Alfred Weintraub. The letter confirmed Allen's representation. Prior to issuing the check, the bank took the precaution of checking with its New York attorneys who advised that they had not heard of the firm Weintraub, Gold & Alper. A credit officer then made a call to the telephone number listed on the stationery used by Alfred Weintraub. The receptionist answered "Weintraub, Gold and Alper." When the call was transferred to Weintraub the attorney confirmed the escrow arrangement. Thereafter the bank issued the check payable to the law firm and received written acknowledgement from Weintraub. The funds disappeared.

Plaintiff commenced an action under UPA §15(a) to hold Weintraub, Gold and Alper severally liable. Plaintiff's theory was that liability had been created under

Section 14(b). Defendants, Gold and Alper, responded by an offer of proof that the three lawyers had mutually agreed to dissolve the firm in 1975. The New York Court of Appeals responded:

> Defendants' private agreement in late 1975 to dissolve the partnership does not alter this result. Whether or not the partnership of Weintraub, Gold & Alper continued in 1977 despite the intent of its members is an issue we need not resolve, for a partner who makes, and consents to, continued representations that a partnership in fact exists is estopped to deny that a partnership exists to defeat the claim of a creditor. . . . Here, defendants, are estopped to deny their relationship as against plaintiff. Nearly two years after alleged dissolution, the public indicia of the partnership remained undisturbed. Where the firm space, telephone number, telephone book listing and stationery continued in use by the individuals, with no discernible sign of dissolution, we conclude that the partnership continued to be liable as such to a party reasonably relying to its detriment on the impression of a ongoing entity. While partnership by estoppel should not be lightly invoked and generally presents issues of fact, here the undisputed evidence submitted on the summary judgment motion leaves no question for trial. . . .

Problem

Your client is Blanche Baker, local real estate developer. She is "putting together a shopping arcade" in conjunction with a large urban renewal project on the north side of the city. Ms. Baker has reached a point in her plans where she should think out the provisions of the leases that she will offer prospective business tenants. She has consulted you in this matter. Ms. Baker asks you to draft a document which will oblige the tenant in the following particulars: (1) the monthly rent will be fifteen dollars per square foot plus a percentage of the gross profits; (2) all businesses in the arcade will maintain a uniform schedule of business hours (9:00-5:30, six days per week); (3) each Thursday each tenant will contribute fifty dollars plus display copy for a common advertisement touting Saturday specials which will run in the two local newspapers; (4) each tenant will conform to a uniform sign design and the copy of said signs will be subject to the landlord's prior approval; (5) each tenant will provide the landlord with a detailed written description of the nature of the business to be conducted in the demised premises; and (6) the business will be neither subcontracted nor altered during the term of tenancy without the landlord's prior written approval.

Given the factors debated in the cases covering the formation of a partnership, are there any problems with these provisions?

C. AN OBJECT LESSON IN THE LAW OF AGENCY

The common law of "agency"—An introduction. If you or a client decide to go into a business which will be conducted with the activities of more than one person, then you will confront the law of agency. Every employee, whether a messenger boy or an executive with her name on the door and a

Bigelow on the floor, is a potential agent.

An agency is defined as a consensual relationship between two persons whereby the Principal, upon whose behalf acts are to be performed, agrees to accept another person as a legal extension-an Agent. As a legal extension the agent can obtain legal rights and incur legal liabilities for the principal.

An employment contract may or may not create problems of agency. The question matters only when the employee will deal with third parties.

At common law two great classifications of agents were distinguished: servant and non-servant agents. "Servant agent" refers to someone who is both directed in his assignment and under the principal's physical dominion in performing that assignment. An "in-house counsel" is an example of a servant agent. Contrast this status to that of a "non-servant agent" to whom the principal may give assignments but over whom she exercises no actual or potential physical control in his performance of those assignments. If XYZ, Inc., retains the services of the law firm of Smith and Smith the firm's lawyers who handle that account are XYZ's non-servant agents. Many of the older cases refer to such agents as "independent contractors."

Every true agent, servant or non-servant, serves the principal's interest and is regarded as a fiduciary. As a fiduciary the agent must seek the principal's advantage and not his own in any dealings within the scope of the agency. Contrast this fiduciary duty to the status of an individual who may act on my behalf but does so in order to further her own interests. Suppose that in the course of my business I have become heavily indebted. Suppose, too, that the Last National Bank is willing to lend further funds to me but only upon the condition that I allow the bank's financial experts to supervise any investments made by my firm during the life of the loan. The bank's representatives are not the business-debtor's agents. Theirs is a power status. English terminology for such an arrangement is "an agency coupled with an interest." That term is useful for it suggests a critical distinction: in performing their duties holders of an agency coupled with an interest seek their own interests and only incidentally advance the interests of the person they appear to serve. There is a further distinction. The holder of an agency coupled with an interest may preserve that status even when the principal has had a change of mind. In a true agency, as principal I can terminate the agency at will. If there is a contract of agency I may risk liability for damages for breach; but the principal can still destroy the agency at will.

An agency relationship may generate both tort and contract liability for the principal. When a claim is based upon an alleged tort the key inquiry concerns the "scope of the agency." When the claim is based in contract the issues involve the "agent's authority" or the principal's conduct in creating an impression that the offending agent had authority. [Questions of tort liability will be considered after the following cases which explore the somewhat more complicated world of contract litigation.]

1. Agent in Wonderland-The Concept of "Authority"

Where an agency has been created the agent's ability to deliver the principal's liability in contract depends upon the concept of "authority." Ideally, the agent serves as the principal's legal extension, so that when he acts to bind the principal he manifests her true consent to liability. If the transaction is within the scope of the principal's true consent the agent has "real authority." There are two types of real authority-express and implied. The following cases explore the boundaries of real authority and the fate of an innocent principal betrayed by a faithless agent acting in the principal's name in an unauthorized transaction. If the third party is ignorant of this lack of authority, which of the agent's victims should bear the loss? The betrayed principal or the deceived third party?

In the two cases which follow the courts experience some difficulty in distinguishing between express or implied real authority on the one hand and the very different concept of "apparent authority" on the other.

EPSTEIN v. CORPORACION PERUANA de VAPORES
United States District Court, Southern District of New York, 1971.
325 F.Supp. 535.

CROAKE, DISTRICT JUDGE. This is a suit in admiralty brought by the plaintiff, Stratford International Tobacco Company, against the Corporacion Peruana de Vapores to recover a balance of $7,206.50 due on a $13,436.50 purchase of cigarettes and liquor made on May 6, 1965. The facts of the case are as follows.

I

Plaintiff is a corporation engaged in the sale of tax-free cigarettes and liquor to vessels in the Port of New York. Alfred Parodi is a salesman in plaintiff's employ. On May 4, 1965 and May 5, 1965, Parodi had conversations with Luis E. Saavedra, the Captain of the S.S. NAPO (one of defendant's ships). On May 6, 1965, pursuant to these conversations, Saavedra agreed to purchase 2,270,000 cigarettes totalling $12,251.50 and 40 cases of liquor totalling $1,185.00 from plaintiff. ...

These goods were delivered to the S.S. NAPO on May 6, 1965, and copies of the invoices for them given to the captain. However, contrary to its usual practice of cash payment at the time of delivery, plaintiff reluctantly consented to a sale on partial credit as the result of Saavedra's simply not having enough cash to pay for the cigarettes and liquor he had ordered. As Parodi himself later testified, "We were more or less forced into granting credit. ... I was not aware that credit would occur until the last moment when the captain did not receive the money that he was supposed to have received."

Following delivery of the goods, plaintiff made repeated demands of Saavedra for the $7,206.50 still due on the sale. However, these demands were met only by promises that the money would be forthcoming. When these promises were not met, copies of the original invoices were forwarded to defendant's home office in Peru with a demand for payment. Defendant received these invoices on November 2, 1965. Disclaiming all knowledge of the transaction, it refused to pay, and began an investigation into the conduct of Saavedra. On December 1, 1965, the captain was discharged by the company. He died shortly thereafter.

It is not disputed by either party that the master of a vessel possesses full authority to make purchases binding upon the vessel's owner for "necessaries" to be used on board his own ship unless the contrary is clearly stated to all concerned. In describing the origins of this authority, Benedict's The Law of American Admiralty states—

> "A ship is, of necessity, a wanderer. She visits shores where her owners are not known or are inaccessible. The master is the fully authorized agent of the distant owners, but is not usually of sufficient pecuniary ability to respond to unforeseen demands of the voyage. These and other kindred characteristics of maritime commerce underlie the practice ...." Benedict, The Law of American Admiralty, 6th Edition (1940), volume 1, pp. 19-20.

Also, it should be noted that cigarettes have been held to be "necessaries" within the meaning of maritime law. *Allen v. The M/V Contessa*, 196 F.Supp. 649 (S.D.Texas 1961).

However, the amount of cigarettes and liquor purchased by Captain Saavedra makes it clear that these supplies were not purchased for consumption by the S.S. NAPO alone. Indeed, plaintiff itself concedes that, in March of 1965 (some six weeks before the transaction in question), the same captain of the same vessel purchased 1,500,000 cigarettes, admittedly "more than what was necessary for the use of the ship."

However, while admitting that the sale in question did not constitute "necessaries" for the S.S. NAPO itself, plaintiff contends that the supplies were purchased by the captain as "necessaries" for other ships owned by the defendant corporation. These cigarettes and liquor, it is claimed, were to be carried by the S.S. NAPO to a home port in Peru where they were to be redistributed to other vessels which had no access to United States ports. Accordingly, it is argued, the captain had authority to make the purchase and defendant should be bound thereby.

Defendant, in turn, denies any knowledge of or authorization for the captain's conduct. It maintains that the captain was never authorized to purchase the supplies in question for his own or any other ship in defendant's fleet, and speculates that the real motive behind the purchase was the captain's participation in a scheme to smuggle tax free, contraband cigarettes and liquor totally outside the scope of his duties as ship's captain. Accordingly, defendant refuses to be bound by the obligation owing from the captain to the plaintiff, and will not pay the balance due unless so ordered by this court. This court rules as follows.

II

The key question before the court in the instant matter is whether or not the captain of the S.S. NAPO had any kind of authority to purchase the cigarettes and liquor in question and bind the defendant thereby. Clearly, the owner of a vessel is liable for contractual obligations incurred by its master where such obligations were incurred pursuant to either express, apparent, or implied authority. But whether such authority existed in the case at bar is not an easy matter for resolution.

It is the judgment of this court that the captain of the S.S. NAPO was clearly without express authority to make the purchases in question. Express authority is that authority which a principal intentionally confers upon his agent by manifestations to him. In the instant case, not only were such overt manifestations lacking; the captain was specifically forbidden to make purchases such as the one in question by the internal regulations of defendant company (See Appendix for English language translations of these regulations-defendant's exhibits A and B). This prohibition was furthered bolstered by defendant's policy of not supplying the captains of its ships with American cash except for that supplied by Hansen & Tidemann (its American agent) for payroll purposes.

The absence of express authority, of course, does not rule out the possibility of apparent or implied authority. Apparent authority is that authority which a principal holds his agent out as possessing or which he permits the agent to represent that he possesses. However, in the instant case, one is hard-pressed to find any such conduct on the part of defendant.

Defendant did nothing to encourage the idea that the captain had authority to purchase the supplies in question. Indeed, the testimony of plaintiff's sole witness, Alfred Parodi, reveals that plaintiff never received any requisition forms directly from the defendant corporation nor did it receive purchasing requests from Hansen & Tidemann. Rather, it always dealt directly with the ship's master.

To counter this, plaintiff argues that past transactions of a similar nature established a pattern of apparent authority in the captain to make these purchases. But the evidence fails to link these transactions to the defendant company itself. In most instances, payment was by cash and, in those few cases where payment was by check, the check was not drawn on the account of defendant, but rather by a bank in Peru upon the Chase Manhattan Bank in New York. Thus the court finds apparent authority in the captain also lacking.

Plaintiff also claims that the captain of the S.S. NAPO had implied authority to bind defendant to the purchases in question. Implied authority is that authority which comes in conformity either with law or the general business customs of a particular trade.

Where conformity with law is concerned, the captain of a vessel has, as previously noted, implied authority to bind the owner thereof to the purchase of "necessaries" for the use of his ship. However, in the instant case, the court is concerned not with the purchase of necessaries for the captain's own vessel, but with the purchase of necessaries for other ships. Thus, the crucial question becomes one of whether or not a captain has implied authority to purchase "necessaries" for a ship other than his own.

This court holds that he does not. A captain is master of his own ship, not of any other. And no definition of "necessaries" dating back one hundred years that this court has been able to uncover holds to the contrary. *Hazelhurst v. The Steamer Lulu*, 77 U.S. 192, 19 L.Ed. 906 (1870). ... For, while "no hard and fast definition of necessaries can be given, when supplies are furnished to a ship on the order of one in apparent authority, whatever comes within the reasonable requirements, not of a ship but of the ship to which furnished, are necessaries." *The Lord Baltimore*, 269 F. 824 (E.D.Pa.1921), reversed on other grounds, 273 F. 990 (1921). (Emphasis added.)

Thus, plaintiff is left with the contention that the captain had implied authority to purchase the supplies in question because said purchase was in conformity with general business customs. This proposition must also fail.

Plaintiff's witness, Alfred Parodi, testified to the custom of captains purchasing more than their own ships' necessary requirements of cigarettes and liquor and distributing them to other vessels which do not reach the United States. But there is little else before this court to support the proposition that such a custom actually exists-a proposition which this court declines to accept in view of its earlier finding that a captain does not have implied authority to purchase necessaries for ships other than his own as a matter of case or statute law. And, even if such a custom did exist, one must doubt its applicability to the case at bar. For there is little to show that plaintiff sold the cigarettes and liquor in question to Saavedra in the belief that they would be transferred to other ships belonging to defendant. Indeed, the evidence is to the contrary. Parodi himself testified that, once the goods were cleared with customs and tax agents, his job was at an end and he was "not concerned" with the fate of the goods.

It is the conclusion of this court then, that the captain of the S.S. NAPO was without authority-express, apparent, or implied-to bind defendant to the purchase in question. The record supports the belief that, whatever the purpose of Captain Saavedra in making these purchases, it was outside the scope of his employment by defendant, and plaintiff had no reason to think otherwise.

Furthermore, the record supports the inference that the main concern of plaintiff was to make as many sales of tax-free cigarettes and liquor as possible without regard to where said cigarettes and liquor would ultimately come to rest.

As previously noted, these transactions were virtually always cash transactions. The record indicates that it was just extenuating circumstances which forced plaintiff to extend credit on this particular occasion and, in all probability, it was not until the failure of Captain Saavedra to pay for the goods that plaintiff began to seek a rationale which would bind defendant to the purchases.

To this it should also be added that, even giving plaintiff the benefit of the doubt and conceding that some of the cigarettes and liquor in question were purchased as necessaries for the S.S. NAPO itself, the $6,220 cash payment made by Captain Saavedra would have more than covered the cost of these "necessaries." Also, because the record fails to support the claim that defendant itself ever received or benefitted from the supplies in question, there can be no cause of action for unjust enrichment.

The foregoing constitutes the findings of fact and conclusions of law reached by the court pursuant to Rule 52(a) of the Federal Rules of Civil Procedure. Judgment is hereby directed for the defendant.

So ordered.

APPENDIX

Chucuito-Callao, July 3, 1953

O/I No. 235-53

PERMANENT
FROM: Manager
TO: All Captains of the Fleet & Agents of C.P.V.
SUBJECT: Absolute prohibition of orders of materials or supplies or repairs outside Callao without the authorization of the Corporation.-Reiteration.

1. The reiteration of the orders by the Corporation in force to the Captains for that under no circumstances orders of materials or supplies or repairs may be made outside Callao, without obtaining the authorization of the Corporation.

2. First all Captains, after they have received instructions of the Corporation through a mediator, Maritime Superintendence, for the Vo. of the ship under their commend, will order all the Chieves of Department aboard to proceed to make the orders for their Vo. with a margin of security. Such orders, after they have been examined, will be signed by the Captains and sent to the Corporation for their approval.

3. The Chieves of Department on board are responsible that the totality of the orders delivered aboard ship by the Markets of Chucuito and if by chance the order was not completely delivered, they will inform the Captain so that he may request to the Corporation the authorization to purchase in a foreign port the remainder of

the order that was not delivered.

4. When a Captain receives the authorization of the Corporation for the purchase of such remaining items in a foreign port, he must present this order to the Agents of the Corporation with a copy of the authorization attached.

5. The Corporation strictly prohibits, under the Captain's responsibility the adoption of different procedures that contradict these regulations.

CORPORACION PERUANA DE VAPORES

Empresa Naviera del Estado

o.204-2/Gerencia   Chucuito-Callao, June 1, 1959
O/I No. 96-59

PERMANENT
FROM: Gerente
TO: Captains of the Fleet & Agents of C.P.V.
SUBJECT: Absolute prohibition of orders of materials, supplies, or repairs outside of Callao without the authorization of the Corporation and supervision of the Agents.
REF.:   O/I No. 235-53 July 3, 1953.

1. On July 3, 1953, the Gerencia issued the reference O/I(a) a copy is attached to this letter.

2. The Gerencia considers that it is necessary to reiterate the content of the O/I, specially paragraph No. 4, that states:

"When a Captain receives authorization from the Gerencia to purchase materials or goods in a foreign port, he must present his order to the Agents of the Corporation with a copy of the authorization of the Gerencia attached."

3. The Agents of C.P.V. are authorized to notify by letter the various shipyards and also the providers that only the payments of invoices for repairs, materials, goods, etc., that have been ordered by the Agents with authorization of the Gerencia, will be given attention to. If opposite, no payments will be made, and the Agents and C.P.V. will not be held responsible to payment of orders made in any other way.

4. The Captains will make reference to the receipt of this present order.

(signed) ERNESTO RODRIGUEZ

ZUMMACH v. POLASEK ET AL.
Supreme Court of Wisconsin, 1929.
199 Wis. 529, 227 N.W. 33.

Action by William F. Zummach against Vincent Polasek and others. From a judgment dismissing the complaint, plaintiff appeals. Affirmed.-[By Editorial Staff.]

Action begun October 15, 1928; judgment entered December 10, 1928. Power of agent to bind principal. The plaintiff is a manufacturer and dealer in store fronts, paints, oils, etc. One James T. Biersach was in his employ from 1919 to 1926. The plaintiff employed Biersach to call upon contractors and architects and endeavor to make and promote sales of the goods in which the plaintiff dealt. Biersach supervised to some extent the installation of store fronts, but had no authority to make collections for the plaintiff except in the case of overdue accounts. In such cases statements of accounts overdue were handed to Biersach with directions to endeavor to get the money. This is conceded to be the extent of his authority.

The defendants were contractors, and through the solicitation of Biersach commenced doing business with the plaintiff some time in 1919. It appears that, when the dealings of the parties first began, the defendant John Polasek was at the plaintiff's place of business, and some one took him to Mr. Biersach's office about 100 feet distant from the office of the plaintiff and told him that Mr. Biersach would take care of him. From that time on the defendants transacted all or nearly all of the business done through Biersach. These transactions are indicated by a brief statement as follows:

Date	Amount	Payable to Order of
January 14, 1922	$315.00	William F. Zummach
May 9, 1922	284.00	William F. Zummach
June 28, 1922	363.00	William F. Zummach
June 25, 1923	70.00	William F. Zummach
November 5, 1923	444.00	J.T. Biersach
December 5, 1923	303.00	William F. Zummach
December 26, 1923	532.00	Cash
February 9, 1924	283.00	William F. Zummach
April 16, 1924	295.00	Cash
June 24, 1924	700.00	Cash
July 16, 1924	12.00	William F. Zummach
August 18, 1924	14.80	William F. Zummach
September 24, 1924	648.00	J. Biersach
November 12, 1924	300.00	J.T. Biersach
January 20, 1925	4.55	William F. Zummach
April 24, 1925	100.00	J.T. Biersach
July 6, 1925	580.00	J.T. Biersach
October 15, 1925	210.00	J.T. Biersach
December 9, 1925	260.00	J.T. Biersach

It further appears that Biersach, along with two other employees, had authority to sign waivers of mechanics' liens for the plaintiff, and that he did sign and deliver such waivers in some cases at least to the defendants. That from time to time among the accounts given to Biersach for collection there were overdue accounts owing by the defendants to the plaintiff.

It appears from the testimony of the defendant John Polasek that the defendants had no system of bookkeeping, and their method of transacting business was very simple and elementary; that the items down to November 5, 1923, were paid by check, payable to the order of plaintiff; that on that day, at the request of Biersach, the check was made payable to him personally; and that thereafter checks were made out as Biersach directed, some to Zummach, some to Biersach, and some items were paid in cash as indicated in the statement. It also appears that, whether the checks were made payable to plaintiff or to Biersach, or the items were paid in cash, Biersach delivered waivers in each case.

The defendants further testified that, when Biersach came to their place of business to make collection, he had other statements of account with him, and that from time to time they made payments on account in accordance with such statements.

It appears that Biersach, about 1923, commenced systematically to defraud his employer. He procured orders, took these orders directly to the shop foreman, had the goods manufactured and sent out in regular course, procured the order from the foreman, took the order to the customer, and, upon payment, receipted the order and gave it back to the person from whom he received it. In this way no account of the transaction appeared upon the plaintiff's books in his office. When Biersach had collected the money, he apparently converted it to his own use. This was discovered by the plaintiff when he noticed that in the neighborhood where they were doing the most work more of his store fronts were going up than there were orders for, and an investigation disclosed Biersach's dishonesty. Thereupon plaintiff began this action to recover the value of the goods delivered to the defendants for which they had paid Biersach in cash or by check payable to the order of Biersach, which he claimed Biersach had no authority to receive, and which were therefore as to him not payments of the account.

The issues were submitted to a jury and the jury found that Biersach, in securing from the defendants their checks made payable to the order of cash for the items set forth in plaintiff's complaint, acted within the scope of his employment with the plaintiff; and, second, that Biersach, in securing from the defendants their checks made payable to the order of said Biersach, for items set forth in plaintiff's complaint, did not act within the scope of his employment with the plaintiff. Upon motion after verdict, the court changed the answer to the second question from "No" to "Yes," and gave judgment for the defendants dismissing the plaintiff's complaint, from which judgment the plaintiff appeals.

ROSENBERRY, C.J. The question presented is whether or not Biersach, the agent, had the power to bind his principal by the acceptance of payments from the plaintiff's customers which he was not authorized to receive. The authority of an agent to act for his principal is often said to be of two kinds, express and implied, and, having reference to its extent, is said to be general or special. The word "authority" is used in connection with the power of an agent to bind his principal in different senses. As used in some instances, it means the power which the principal has conferred directly upon the agent; in other words, express authority. Power to bind the principal may result also from consent of the principal manifested to third persons by formal or informal writings or by spoken words, or it may result from manifestations of consent on the part of the principal implied from authority to do other acts. This is called apparent authority. An agency resulting from apparent authority is often spoken of in the books as an agency by holding out or as an agency created by way of estoppel. The distinction between authority and apparent authority is important. A principal may direct an agent not to do a particular act; as to that act the agent has no authority. The principal may by words or conduct lead a third person to believe reasonably that the agent has authority to act for the principal with respect to the forbidden act. If under such circumstances the agent acts, the principal is bound, although the agent had no authority, because the agent had apparent authority. Am. Law Institute Restatement No. 1. While the principal is bound as far as third persons are concerned by the agent's exercise of apparent authority, as between agent and principal the legal consequences are quite different. It is apparent that, if the agent Biersach had authority to accept payment of accounts other than those which were overdue, it was by reason of apparent authority resulting from manifestations made by plaintiff to the defendants.

In *Voell v. Klein*, 184 Wis. 620, 200 N.W. 364, it was held that, where appearances for which a principal is responsible give third persons dealing with an agent reasonable ground to believe the agent possesses power to act for his principal in a particular transaction, the principal is as responsible as if the agent possessed the power he apparently possesses; and in that case it was held that an agent with authority to sell an automobile had apparent authority to receive an automobile in exchange in part payment for the one sold.

The question here is, Were there such manifestations on the part of the plaintiff made to the defendants as reasonably induced them to believe that the plaintiff had authorized Biersach to receive payment and that they made payment relying upon such apparent authority? The plaintiff put the agent Biersach in a responsible position in his business by virtue of which he was authorized to enter into contracts, to make prices, to waive liens, to oversee installation of goods sold, to make adjustments where the goods were not as ordered, and to collect accounts where accounts were overdue. In addition to that, the defendants had been advised that Mr. Biersach would take care of them, and for a period of six years during which they had dealt with the plaintiff their dealings were almost entirely through the agent Biersach. Biersach took the orders, pursuant thereto the goods appeared from the shop of the plaintiff, being delivered so far as defendants could see in the regular course of business. It probably never occurred to the defendants and would not occur to very many contractors that an agent could take an order for goods, have the goods manufactured in his principal's shop and delivered by the principal's teamsters in the regular course of business without the knowledge of the principal.

It is considered that the evidence fully warrants the finding of the jury in answer to the first question. The trial court correctly held that payments made to Biersach by check payable to his order, which checks were cashed by Biersach, were no different than payments made in cash or in checks payable to "cash" so far as the legal effect of the transaction was concerned. It is true that ordinarily an agent to collect has power to receive nothing but cash unless a general custom that something else may be taken in lieu of cash is shown, yet, where the checks are in fact cashed by the agent, the principal is bound.

The court was fully justified in changing the answer to question No. 2 from "No" to "Yes."

Judgment affirmed.

Notes

Zummach and *Epstein* articulate the major distinctions in a discussion of an agent's "authority." The concept of "real authority" is based on the principal's having given true consent to the agent's acts which have generated the contract claim. Real authority is broken into two classifications premised upon the manifestation of this consent. Thus the cases speak of an agent's *express authority* as well as *implied authority*. The terminology strongly suggests the distinction. Authority is express if the grant can be traced to the principal's words or deeds communicated to the agent, words or deeds which define the scope of the agent's assigned task. Suppose that the owner of the *S.S. Napo* had telegrammed Captain Saavedra: "Proceed at earliest possible date with installation of Falcon Navigation System." What would be the scope of the real authority conferred upon Captain Saavedra as agent? If he were to contact representatives of the Falcon Navigation System Corporation would he have real authority to sign a contract obligating Corporacion Peruana de Vapores to $200,000 as the purchase price? If Falcon's representatives informed Saavedra that structural modifications of the *Napo* were physically required before their navigation system could be installed would Saavedra have authority to bind the vessel's owner to a contract with National Marine to accomplish those modifications? The principal's telegram made no mention of such work. Nevertheless, would you advise National Marine that they could assert the principal's liability on a theory of *implied real authority*? How would you establish such a theory? Judge Croake defines implied authority as: "... that authority which comes in conformity either with law or the general business customs of a particular trade." Are there any other sources of implied authority?

If Captain Saavedra doubted that he could authorize the modifications and asked the ship's owner about the $75,000 expenditure for the structural changes proposed by National Marine the owner might decline to authorize such work. How would this express refusal affect a transaction which might otherwise be sanctioned by business custom or even physical necessity? Naturally we must assume that in violating his principal's instructions Captain Saavedra did not inform National Marine of this limitation on his authority. If Saavedra were to sign a contract for the modifications as "agent for Corporacion Peruana de Vapores" he would be a faithless agent. But by this hypothetical there would be two victims of his treachery: Corporacion Peruana de Vapores, as principal; and National Marine, as a party performing services under the impression that it has the owner's liability. National Marine's legal representatives should have great interest in the concept of *apparent authority* as articulated in *Zummach* and *Epstein* and more fully developed in the following decision.

WALKER v. PACIFIC MOBILE HOMES, INC.
Supreme Court of Washington, 1966.
68 Wash.2d 347, 413 P.2d 3.

HALE, JUDGE. Plaintiff left his trailer to be sold on consignment. One of the defendant's salesmen sold it and absconded. Defendant, disclaiming responsibility for the consignment, appeals the $1,290.51 judgment.

The case turns on whether the court properly found from conflicting evidence that defendant's salesmen acted within their apparent or ostensible authority. Plaintiff Walker owned a 25-foot, 1953 Mainliner trailer in Seattle. Deciding to sell it and return to his former home in Oregon, he went to several trailer lots to see if the dealers would handle it on consignment. He found no dealers interested in a consignment until he met Robert Stewart at the lot of defendant Pacific Mobile Homes at South 140th and Pacific Highway.

At the trailer lot where plaintiff first talked to Stewart, he noticed a large sign designating it as Pacific Mobile Homes, Inc., an office, a number of trailers on display, and observed that Mr. Stewart appeared to be the sole employee in attendance. Behind the lot was a large trailer park known as "Southgate Trailer Park." Plaintiff told Stewart he would sell on consignment if he could get a net price of $1,500, and Stewart told him that he was too busy moving the trailers around at the moment to complete the deal but would pick up the trailer in a few days.

A few days later, Stewart came with a truck to plaintiff's residence and towed the trailer to the Pacific Mobile Homes lot where plaintiff on several occasions saw it among the other trailers displayed there. May 27, 1959, plaintiff stopped at the trailer lot where he again found Stewart alone in the office, and suggested that, since he intended to go to Oregon for a while, some sort of writing should be made out. Thereupon, plaintiff says, Stewart got a blank form having the legend "Trailer Consignment Agreement" in bold-faced type across the top, filled it out in ink, but, in barely legible handwriting, designated thereon Southgate Trailers as consignee. Plaintiff signed the consignment agreement, stating at the trial that, being primarily concerned at the time with the provisions as to net price and the avoidance of storage charges if the trailer was not sold, he did not notice the name of the consignee.

About one month later, a Robert Henderson telephoned plaintiff in Oregon, asking if plaintiff had left his trailer on consignment with Stewart at Pacific Mobile Homes and explained that Stewart was no longer with the firm but that he, Henderson, was the new manager. Henderson then told plaintiff they still had the trailer and had lined up a possible buyer. A few weeks later, plaintiff returned to Seattle from Oregon and talked to Henderson at the trailer lot. Plaintiff saw his trailer on this occasion still on display among the others and testified that Henderson, like Stewart before him, was there alone at the office and trailer lot.

Henderson again told him that he had a likely deal pending, and plaintiff went back to Oregon to have the deal confirmed by mail. He received a letter on the business stationery of Pacific Mobile Homes, Inc., giving the corporation's main office address at Edmonds and the branch office at 140th and Pacific Highway South, and containing also an installment note signed by one Korsmoe as maker. The letter, handwritten by Bob Henderson, dated July 25, 1959, explained that, after four payments, the enclosed note would be discounted and balance thereof paid in cash. Each month for the next three months, plaintiff received a monthly payment in the form of a check signed by Henderson, and when these ceased he returned to the trailer lot to inquire about the unpaid balance.

He found that Henderson had actually sold the trailer not to Korsmoe but to one Anderson for $1,500 cash, and, save for the three payments totaling $209.41, had absconded with the balance. After more than a year spent in tracing him, plaintiff located Henderson in the penitentiary at Walla Walla.

Henry M. Shelly, president of Pacific Mobile Homes, testified that his company maintained a small one-room office on the South 140th street trailer lot; that the lot had a sign 28 feet high and 14 feet long with "Pacific Mobile Homes, Inc." on it; that he visited the lot to check it about three times a week. He said that Stewart worked at the lot from April to July, 1959, and Henderson started to work there in June, but ordinarily there would be only one salesman on duty at any one time.

He said that neither had authority to complete a sale without approval of himself or the company sales manager and that all sales documents had to be signed by himself personally. He said too that the company forbade its salesmen to take trailers on consignment; that neither he nor the company had any record or knowledge of either the plaintiff's trailer, the consignment arrangement, or any other phases of the transaction; that he had never, during his periodic inspections, seen plaintiff's trailer on the lot. Only on a few occasions, he said, had his company taken trailers for sale on consignment and that all salesmen were well acquainted with this company policy.

Although the agent's authority must be established through proof of the principal's conduct, representations or actions (*Charette v. American Surety Co.*, 49 Wash.2d 777, 307 P.2d 252 (1957)), and cannot be proved by the admissions of the agent (*Foote v. Grant*, 56 Wash.2d 630, 354 P.2d 893 (1960)), the trial court, in the present case, had before it substantial evidence from which to find apparent authority.

We believe the evidence warranted findings and conclusions that Pacific Mobile Homes had clothed Stewart and later Henderson with apparent or ostensible authority to take the trailer on to the lot for sale on consignment and to collect the purchase money therefor. The salesman's solitary presence in the company office and about the lot on several occasions, among numerous trailers on display, beneath a sign conspicuously proclaiming the whole to be an enterprise of Pacific Mobile Homes, Inc., and his towing plaintiff's trailer to the trailer lot and putting it on display there, allowed a person of ordinary business prudence to reasonably assume that the salesman had authority from Pacific Mobile Homes, Inc., to buy, sell, receive and deliver trailers for cash, on credit, consignment, or in exchange. Then, too, the salesman's untrammeled access to and use of his principal's letterhead, stationery and business forms, and his seeming control of the office and lot, fortify the idea of apparent authority.

Authority to perform particular services for a principal carries with it the implied authority to perform the usual and necessary acts essential to carry out the authorized services. *Larson v. Bear*, 38 Wash.2d 485, 230 P.2d 610 (1951). One dealing in good faith with an agent who appears to be acting within the scope of his authority is not bound by undisclosed limitations on the agent's power.

Our decision in *Lamb v. General Associates, Inc.*, 60 Wash.2d 623, 374 P.2d 677 (1962), succinctly declares the principles which govern the instant case:

> It is a general rule, and the rule in this state, that a corporation may be bound by the contracts or agreements of its agent if within the apparent scope of the agent's authority, although the contract may be beyond the scope of his actual authority. (Citing cases.)
>
> It is also the well-established rule that the apparent or ostensible authority of an agent can be inferred only from acts and conduct of the principal. (Citing cases.) The extent of an agent's authority cannot be established by his own acts and declarations. (Citing cases.)
>
> The burden of establishing agency rests upon the one who asserts it. Facts and circumstances are sufficient to establish apparent authority only when a person exercising ordinary prudence, acting in good faith and conversant with business practices and customs, would be misled thereby, and such person has given due regard to such other circumstances as would cause a person of ordi-

nary prudence to make further inquiry. (Citing case.)

A principal may be estopped to deny that his agent possesses the authority he assumes to exercise, where the principal knowingly causes or permits him so to act as to justify a third person of ordinarily careful and prudent business habits to believe that he possesses the authority exercised, and avails himself of the benefit of the agent's acts. (Citing case.)

Applying the foregoing principles to the proofs presented on behalf of both the plaintiff and the defendant compels an affirmance.

Affirmed.

ROSELLINI, C.J., and OTT and HUNTER, JJ., concur.

HILL, JUDGE (dissenting).

I dissent. To me it is clear that the plaintiff knew that he was not doing business with Pacific Mobile Homes, Inc., and that he knew he was doing business with Robert Stewart, and later Bob Henderson. This action is somebody's afterthought, which has certainly paid off well.

Not only did the consignment form, which the plaintiff received when he delivered his trailer to Robert Stewart, contain no reference to Pacific Mobile Homes, Inc., but the checks he received in payment on his trailer were the personal checks of Bob Henderson. It was only after he finally located, in the penitentiary, the man who had defrauded him and realized that there was no balm in Gilead there, that the idea that Pacific Homes, Inc., ought to share its wealth with him, was evolved.

I will assume with the majority that the evidence warranted a finding that Pacific Mobile Homes had clothed Stewart, and later Henderson, with apparent or ostensible authority to take a trailer for sale on consignment.

Where the plaintiff's case breaks down, is that there is no evidence to establish that he relied on that apparent or ostensible authority. Instead it establishes that he at all times believed he was dealing with Stewart or Henderson. For more than a year, he ignored Pacific Mobile Homes, Inc.,-all the time transacting business at the same locations, all the time readily available-and instead devoted his time and energies to locating Henderson.

For this hiatus in proof, I would set aside the judgment and dismiss the action.

Notes

It is evident that no member of the Supreme Court of Washington believed that Pacific Mobile Homes had consented to the activities of either Stewart or Henderson. There was no real authority, express or implied, covering this transaction. What are the elements of an action seeking the betrayed principal's liability on a theory that "apparent authority" supported the transaction? Note the importance of the burdens of pleading and proof and the risk of non-persuasion of the trier of fact. Is it sufficient for Walker, the classic "third party," to assert that he had in good faith believed in the authority of Stewart or Henderson? Twice the court asserts that a belief in the scope of an agent's authority may not be established "by [the agent's] own acts or declarations." Is this a sound rule? Suppose that, before signing, Walker had received Henderson's affirmative reply to the question: "Do you have authority from the owner to make this deal?" Does Judge Hale's opinion stand for the proposition that such evidence would be irrelevant in a determination of the principal's liability?

Does Judge Hill strike a mortal blow if he is correct that Walker never believed he was doing business with Pacific through an agent but instead believed himself to be dealing directly with Stewart and then Henderson? Assuming that Walker had a subjective, good faith belief that Stewart and Henderson were agents of Pacific, did the majority conclude that he met the test established in *Lamb v. General Associates*? *Lamb* goes beyond the "reasonable person" and permits recovery only if belief in the agent's real authority would have matured in the mind of a reasonable person "conversant with business practices and customs." Further, the reasonable, prudent person of business habits would have had to draw a belief in the agent's authority while taking into account not only indications of that authority but red lights warning that it might not exist. Stewart's use of Southgate Trailers as the consignee, and the fact that Henderson sent a check drawn on his personal account rather than that of the supposed buyer, Korsmoe, should have given Walker warning that his transaction was not authorized by Pacific.

Note that there is a distinction to be observed between these two warnings. The first (use of a consignment form by Stewart that did not name Pacific as the consignee) arose at the formation of the deal. The checks drawn by Henderson were after the fact. Should this make a difference?

The *Lamb* standard for the mind set of the reasonable person would not appear to protect a novice in the marketplace. Is this wise? *Lamb* picks a rather extreme position on the continuum with respect to the scope of third party protection extended by apparent authority. At the opposite extreme would be a subjective, good faith belief of this particular third party. Moving toward a centrist position, we would have the "reasonable belief of this third party." Moving further in the direction of protecting the betrayed principal, we would have the belief of that myth termed "the reasonable person." By definition we now flesh out the fair to middling abilities, education and performance of a creature who may exceed the potential of our particular third party or fall below the plaintiff's actual abilities. Finally, we arrive at the *Lamb* standard which structures the behavior of the reasonable person. That individual is charged with responsibility to gain knowledge of the customs and mores of the marketplace before attempting the transaction. Beyond that, in reacting to the facts as they evolve, this savvy, informed and reasonable person is to be wary of "red lights" which warn that authority might be exceeded or non-existent.

Selecting a position on this spectrum is a social decision involving the incursion of social costs. *Lamb* has the virtue of promoting behavior which will minimize the instances in which the faithless agent "gets away with deceiving a third party." To that degree it will reduce the incidence of litigation. All of this is good. But what of the neophyte trader? What of the consumer who has neither the time nor resources to "get an education" before making an isolated foray into the marketplace? Are these individuals fair game for the crooked agent? It seems evident that Walker is merely paying lip service to *Lamb*. A more honest majority would have repudiated the precedent or distinguish it in such a manner as to destroy its application to consumers. Yet there is a cost incurred if one moves to the opposite extreme. If we say that the law will take into account the specific, personal attributes of the plaintiff and protect one who has done "all that he could" (even if it was a rather miserable stab at self-protection), are we holding out a promise of rescue which an overworked judiciary cannot honor? It is clear that prior to Walker the Washington judiciary had applied the higher expectations of performance demanded in *Lamb* to both neophyte and experienced traders who had drawn erroneous conclusions respecting the authority of faithless agents. Compare *Largent v. Ritchey*, 38 Wash.2d 856, 233 P.2d 1019, 1022 (1951), with *Olsson v. Hansen*, 50 Wash.2d 199, 310 P.2d 251, 254 (1957).

2. The Consequences of Fidelity and Faithlessness:

If, in a given transaction, an agent acts within the scope of real authority the legal consequences are easily stated. The principal and the third party become directly bound by contract (or "privity," as the relation is called in the older cases). The agent, having acted as a transparent intermediary for the liabilities of the principal and the third party, has no personal liability for the terms or performance of that contract. *Whitney v. Wyman*, 101 U.S. 392, 396, 25 L.Ed. 1050 (1879). If the principal thereafter breaches a contract negotiated by an agent acting within the scope of real authority the agent has no liability. *Ferrarell v. Robinson*, 11 Ariz.App. 473, 465 P.2d 610, 612 (1970).

If there is no real authority, apparent authority may generate the principal's liability to the innocent third party. In such cases liability is on the terms of the executory contract to the same extent as if the agent had had real authority. *O.S. Stapley Co. v. Logan*, 6 Ariz.App. 269, 431 P.2d 910, 914-15 (1967). Such liability is imposed even though the principal has not consented to the transaction or its terms, but was betrayed by a faithless agent. "Accurately speaking, 'apparent authority' is not authority at all, but is merely a power to affect the principal's affairs. ... [I]t arises not by authorization in the consensual sense, but from the principal's negligent omission or his acquiescence in the agent's activities." *Lux Art Van Services, Inc. v. Pollard*, 344 F.2d 883, 888 (9th Cir.1965).

Naturally, the faithless agent is liable to the injured principal. At least two lines of authority support the principal's cause of action. The most simple rationale is that the agent is guilty of breaching the contract of agency when he acts beyond the scope of real authority. On the other hand there are cases which stress the fiduciary nature of the principal-agent relationship. Such reasoning moves the cause of action in the direction of the law of trusts.

In *Kline v. Orebaugh*, 214 Kan. 207, 519 P.2d 691, 695 (1974), the court reviewed an action brought by two aged parents against their son for misappropriation of property through a power of attorney:

> ... The relation of principal and agent is a fiduciary one, and if a wrong arises because of the conduct of the agent the same remedy exists against the wrongdoer on behalf of the principal as would exist against a trustee on behalf of the *cestui que trust* ....

While one cannot test this assertion without having studied the law of trusts, remedies pursued in the *cestui*/trustee context are draconian in effect upon the defendant.

What if a principal suffered judgment at the hands of a third party and those damages might have been reduced if the principal had acted quickly to dispel the faithless agent's apparent authority? In such circumstances should there be a reduction of the damages which the principal could then recover from the agent? The Court of Appeals of Michigan recently answered in the affirmative. In *Andrews v. Hastings Mut. Ins. Co.*, 40 Mich.App. 664, 199 N.W.2d 260, 263-64 (1972), an insured party pursued an action against a carrier for losses covered by a policy which the carrier's agent lacked authority to issue. Recovery was allowed upon a theory of apparent authority. In the same action the carrier cross-claimed against the agent who raised as a defense that if the carrier had acted promptly when it learned of the unauthorized issuance the carrier could have cancelled the policy before the disputed casualty loss. On appeal the agent asserted:

> ... the doctrine of avoidable consequences as a defense to an agent where the principal knows or should know of the agent's failure to obey instructions. Although the authorities are split on this question, the better rule is that for which Kanter [the agent] contends. The rule is best stated in the Restatement of Agency, 2d § 415, p. 273:
>
>> 'The liability of the agent to the principal can be avoided, terminated, or reduced by a breach of contract by the principal, his contributory fault, or his failure to mitigate damages.'
>
> This rule is consistent with the principal's duty to minimize his damages wherever possible.

If the primary concern is the welfare of the innocent third party, which approach is preferable on the "doctrine of avoidable consequences"?

Thus far we have assumed that the principal's liability on an unauthorized contract could be gained on a theory of apparent authority. What if the facts do not support this theory? Cases such as *Epstein* convey the bad news to the injured third party-the principal has no liability. The point is bluntly made in *Gittings, Neiman-Marcus, Inc. v. Estes*, 440 S.W.2d 90, 94-95 (Tex.Civ.App.

1969). But there is a consolation prize. While the principal totally escapes liability, the agent does not. In some jurisdictions the faithless agent who has acted without or beyond authority becomes personally liable on all of the terms of the contract. *State ex rel. Carlton v. Triplett*, 213 Kan. 381, 517 P.2d 136, 139 (1973). Nearly a century ago this result was rationalized on the theory that "the [agent] is presumed to know the extent of his authority." *Newberry et ux. v. Slafter*, 98 Mich. 468, 57 N.W. 574, 575 (1894). Other courts prefer the legal fiction that the faithless agent must have intended a present contract, and that if the principal was not bound then the agent's liability was pledged. Standing apart from these cases are those jurisdictions which adopt the view of the Restatement of Agency, 2d: that every agent gives an implied warranty as to both his bona fide status as his principal's legal representative and the extent of his real authority. When such an agent exceeds his authority the aggrieved third party has the agent's liability for breach of this implied warranty, rather than on the theory that the agent has become a party to the contract. See Section 329. The Restatement view is adopted and defended in *Feinberg v. Great Atlantic & Pacific Tea Co.*, 131 Ill.App.2d 1087, 266 N.E.2d 401, 404 (1971). From the third party's vantage point which is the preferable cause of action?

3. Liability After the Fact:

Even where an agent has no real or apparent authority at the formation of a contract, the principal may become liable through after-arising factors. Several distinct theories compete for application.

Estoppel. In *Haveg Corp. v. Guyer*, 226 A.2d 231, 234 (S.Ct.Del.1967), the court declared:

> The doctrine of equitable estoppel is that a person not otherwise liable as a party to a transaction may nevertheless become subject to liability on the transaction to a person who has changed his position because of the belief that the transaction was entered into when he carelessly permitted such belief [of the agent's authority] to exist, or when knowing of the belief, he did nothing to notify the other party of the erroneous belief ....

An example will distinguish this theory from the doctrine of apparent authority as well as reveal the major limitation on the third party's potential recovery. Recall the saga of Captain Saavedra and the *S.S. Napo*. If the ship's owner had instructed Saavedra not to engage National Marine's services such instruction would have precluded any form of real authority. If, in violation of these secret instructions, Saavedra had entered into an executory contract with National the betrayed principal would have no liability unless Saavedra had had apparent authority at the time of the transaction. Let us suppose that he did not. Nevertheless, National knew nothing of the limitation on Saavedra's authority. On January 10 an executory contract was signed by Saavedra as agent for Corporacion Peruana de Vapores. By its terms National was to make the modifications to the *S.S. Napo* by March 1, at a price of $75,000. On January 20, before National began any actual performance, Corporacion Peruana de Vapores learned of its agent's unauthorized act, but said nothing to National. Instead, it waited until January 30 to inform National that Saavedra had had no authority in the transaction. By that time no work had actually been done on the *Napo*, but National had spent $8,000 in the fabrication of items to be installed as part of its contract responsibilities. Using the theory advanced in *Haveg*, National could seek recovery of the expended funds. Thus the damages are reparatory in nature and will usually fall far short of the expectation interest generated by the executory contract.

If the principal assents to an unauthorized contract or knowingly receives its fruits a very different doctrine is invoked.

Ratification. Here we must establish that the principal is guilty of knowingly accepting what are realized to be the fruits of an unauthorized contract. It should come as no surprise that a principal who takes such a deliberate step cannot escape liability to the third party on the unauthorized terms of such a contract. In many instances ratification is the express reaction of a betrayed principal who does not wish to contest liability with a deceived third party. In other circumstances ratification may be implied from the conduct of the betrayed principal. In either situation it is vital that the third party be able to demonstrate that the principal embraced the fruits of what he knew to be an unauthorized contract. If the principal blunders into the consumption or use of what she does not realize are the fruits of an unauthorized contract she may be liable upon a theory of quasi-contract but cannot be guilty of ratification. For an opinion which delineates the elements of a ratification theory in a common law action of detinue for a "mouse colored mule" see, *Jones v. Atkinson*, 68 Ala. 167 (1880).

As suggested, ratification may be either express or inferred from the principal's conduct. Yet in either case it is essential that ratification was undertaken by a principal who was conscious of the fact that he had been betrayed. If the principal was unaware of the unauthorized nature of the contract his apparent assent does not ratify the contract. *Wheeler v. Northwestern Sleigh Co.*, 39 F. 347 (C.C.E.D.Wis.1889). If the principal has received the benefits of an unauthorized contract there is strong pressure to find liability. The point was stressed by the Supreme Court of Vermont:

> It does not take much to amount to a ratification of such a contract, especially where the person to be charged has taken and enjoyed the benefits thereof. Much less than an express approval or promise will warrant a finding of ratification in such cases. Indeed, in many cases, the acceptance of benefits alone amounts to an implied ratification. But here we have an express promise to pay made with full knowledge of the facts. No matter whose debt it was before, the defendant made it his own by that promise. A promise so made evidences a ratification; and the ratification relates back to the original transaction and

supplies the necessary authority for it ....

Federal Garage, Inc. v. Prenner, 106 Vt. 222, 172 A. 622 (1934).

Upon learning of an unauthorized contract the principal must elect between repudiation and ratification. He cannot ratify those provisions which confer benefits while repudiating those which impose burdens. *Knaus Truck Lines, Inc. et al. v. Donaldson et al.*, 235 Minn. 453, 51 N.W.2d 99, 102 (1952).

Quasi-contract. If a principal has received the benefits of an unauthorized contract in ignorance of these facts there arises an immediate threat of unjust enrichment if such receipt is without liability to the third party. Such a result would not be desirable and is not permitted. The Supreme Court of Minnesota approached just such a fact pattern and declared:

> Of course, there can be no recovery quasi ex contractu unless otherwise there will be unjust enrichment. But, without recovery, there would be such unconscionable enrichment of the party who gets money, property, or services from another in exchange for an apparently binding contractual promise, which is not binding in fact and successfully repudiated by the promisor. In such cases there is an obviously unlawful and unconscionable acquisition, attended by the obligation to disgorge the proceeds. That is the obligation enforced as it would be if bottomed on contract (which it is not), and hence called for convenience a quasi-contract ....

Seifert v. Union Brass & Metal Mfg. Co., 191 Minn. 362, 254 N.W. 273, 274 (1934).

4. Liability in Tort:

The agency concepts developed thus far have introduced the notions of "real" and "apparent" authority which form the foundation of primary contract liability. Secondary routes to contract liability include adoption, ratification, and estoppel. It is now timely to concentrate on the topic of liability in tort. The major premises were well stated by Professor Floyd R. Mechem:*

Basic proposition. Respondeat superior. Let the master respond (i.e., in damages). Or, to put the matter more specifically: the master is liable for the torts of his servant, committed in the course of employment.

This has been well-settled law for 250 years; if any trend is observable, it is in the direction of increasing the scope and vigor of the doctrine. In connection with it, three questions primarily suggest themselves. One is an important question of policy; two are difficult questions of legal analysis. The first: why

---

* Copyright © 1952 by Callaghan & Company. Reprinted with permission from Outlines of the Law of Agency (4th ed.), published by Callaghan & Company, 3201 Old Glenview Road, Wilmette, Illinois 60091. Footnotes in the original text have been omitted.

is the master liable for the torts of his servants, committed in the course of employment? The second: given a defendant who may be a master, what are the criteria that determine whether or not the actor was "his servant"? The third: when is a servant "in the course of employment"? ...

Notable dissenters from the proposition. A number of notable persons have been inclined to doubt that there is any good reason for the master's liability. Mr. Justice Holmes remarked in a well-known passage: "I assume that common sense is opposed to making one man pay for another man's wrong, unless he actually has brought the wrong to pass according to the ordinary canons of legal responsibility-unless, that is to say, he has induced the immediate wrongdoer to do acts of which the wrong, or at least, wrong, was the natural consequence under the circumstances known to the defendant ... I therefore assume that common sense is opposed to the fundamental theory of agency."

Mr. Baty, in his well-known book on Vicarious Liability says that the master's liability is based on no considered theory; in fact the real explanation is: "the damages are taken from a deep pocket."

Likewise, the author of the first edition of this book appears to have some doubts as to the propriety of the rule, remarking that "the actual results reached are often harsh, if not absolutely unjust." Nevertheless he concedes that "there seems to be no tendency to mitigate its application."

Some supporters of the view. On the other hand, some far from inconsiderable modern thinkers have approved the doctrine. Professor (now Mr. Justice) Douglas, the late Mr. Laski, and Professor Seavey have all written acutely of the doctrine and each, in his own slightly different way, has found it not only sound on principle but almost a necessity in our modern highly-commercialized civilization.

The present writer ventures to share this opinion and to believe that the rule is a sound and reasonable one, producing a far more just result than would be reached in its absence. The failure of common-law rules to give anything like adequate protection to employees injured in their employment led to the passage of the (as it then seemed) drastic legislation known as Workmen's Compensation Laws. It is believed that if the common-law rules of the master's liability to third parties had not developed as they did there would ultimately have been irresistible pressure for similar legislation to achieve the result.

Justifications. A number of explanations or justifications for the rule have been offered. Mr. Justice Holmes who, as seen above, thought the rule opposed to common sense, in his book on the Common Law expresses the view that it is largely a survival of the earlier liability of the master for the act of his slave. It is sometimes said that as the principal or master has the power of control, he should take the responsibility. It has been said that as he is to get the benefit of the act, he should bear the burdens of it. It is said that, although the principal or master may be personally innocent, so also is the person injured, and that even as between two equally innocent persons, that one should bear the loss who initiated the enterprise. It is said that making the principal or master liable will induce him to greater care, from which the public will benefit. It is said that since the principal or master is likely to be of greater financial responsibility than the agent or servant-although the latter is liable-and since public policy demands that injuries shall not go uncompensated, the best results are promoted by giving a remedy against the principal. (This is the deep-pocket principle, regarded by Baty as odious and socialistic.)

—None of these reasons is completely satisfying, though many of them contain elements of truth. ...

The Entrepreneur Theory. The explanation or justification of master's liability which undoubtedly finds the widest acceptance today is one that goes under the rather pretentious name of the Entrepreneur Theory. Every industry, it is suggested, takes a regular and more or less predictable annual toll, both in property and in flesh and blood. If, e.g., the records of the Shantytown & Southern Railroad were examined and subjected to a statistical computation, it could be predicted with considerable accuracy how many people would be killed and maimed in the coming year, how many cars wrecked, and the like. Restaurants doubtless have an accounting item named "breakage"; this is breakage, too, if on a bigger and more distressing scale. On whom should the replacement cost fall? Unlike the restaurant, the railroad can get new victims without cost; to do so, however, leaves a tragic list of innocent and uncompensated victims. Why not treat it as a cost of the business, as the restaurant does? If the railroad pays, it will easily be able to spread the cost by raising its charges. The expense then ultimately rests, like other expenses of running a railroad, on that part of the public which needs, patronizes, and presumably profits by the existence of, a railroad. The cost, to each individual member of the railroad-interested public, is, per accident, insignificant; if left to lie on the victim of the particular accident it may be ruinous.

Thus, in the light of the Entrepreneur Theory, respondeat superior achieves an allocation of the loss which is fair and reasonable; no better justification, it is thought, could be needed.

Should society as a whole share the loss? Why not, it might be asked, go a step further and put the burden on society as a whole; more specifically, on the state? The state is interested in the welfare of its citizens; it is interested in the industry without which it could not grow to be great. Why not say that industrial accidents are affected with a public interest, and that all persons injured shall be compensated from a fund to be raised by taxation, perhaps general or perhaps on industry as a whole?

Most people would regard this as going too far. The dreadful word "socialism" would be hurled, forgetful of the obvious truth that socialism is anything which is a little too social for the particular time or the particular speaker. After all, in the light of the Entrepreneur Theory, is not the law of Master and Servant a small piece of mild and well-accepted socialism? Labels aside, however, there seem practical reasons against such an extension. While the effect of respondeat superior may be in a broad sense to put the loss on the industry, as long as there is competition within the industry, there will be a strong profit motive in keeping the accident loss low. With a state-supported pool a particular entrepreneur would have so little to gain by accident prevention in his own plant that he would have little zeal in seeking to attain it. It is quite otherwise when the cost is important as a competitive item. One of the best things about respondeat superior is the pressure it exerts on the individual entrepreneur to keep his accident cost low. State insurance against injury by motor car may be a development of the next few years; however, there seems little probability of the extension of such an idea to industrial accidents in general.

‘ ‘ ‘

Classic defenses to these theories of tort liability have been developed. As Professor Mechem stated, the first defense denies that the wrongdoer was the employer's servant; the second admits the principal-agent relationship but denies that the tort occurred in the "course of the agency."

STOCKWELL v. MORRIS
Supreme Court of Wyoming, 1933.
46 Wyo. 1, 22 P.2d 189.

BLUME, JUSTICE.

In this case Morris, salesman for the Maytag Intermountain Company, was driving his automobile from Hudson to Lander and collided with the automobile of plaintiff. The latter sued the salesman, as well as his principal, for damages caused by the collision. The court directed a verdict for the company, and the sole question herein is-assuming the agent to have been negligent-as to whether or not the court's action was right. The testimony herein is uncontradicted.

Morris was a salesman for the company in selling washing machines, and had been working for it for some years. That was his only occupation. He received a commission on all sales made, and no further compensation. He made no collections, but occasionally seems to have delivered washing machines sold. He drove his own automobile in the performance of his work, and paid his own expenses. He appointed and discharged subsalesmen under him, receiving a commission on their sales, and he took them out from time to time to show them how to sell washing machines. He was assigned the central portion of the state as his territory, which, perhaps, was somewhat changed from time to time. In any event, there is some correspondence in the record with the company's manager in Denver as to some change to be made therein. The company furnished him with no rules or regulations as to his work, except as to the terms of the contracts to be made for the sale of washing machines. The details of the work were left to him. Contracts for sales, blank forms for which were furnished by the company, were, by the subsalesmen, delivered in triplicate to a girl in charge of an office, which the company kept at Casper, but Morris apparently sent contracts made by him to the company at Salt Lake. He seems not to have had anything to do with the office at Casper, though apparently he made that his headquarters. On May 27, 1930, the date of the collision above mentioned, Morris, in company with his wife, drove his automobile to Lander to see a Mr. Tyler, a salesman under him, to see if he could help him in his work. After reaching Lander, he, at the suggestion of Tyler, and in company with him, drove to Hudson, to see Mrs. Radovitch, who had a Maytag washing machine which was out of repair, though repairs of machines were ordinarily made by a special representative of the company. Tyler discovered the trouble, fixed the machine, gratuitously, and he and Morris then drove back to Lander, and the collision occurred while doing so. Morris wrote the Maytag Company as to that fact.

Counsel for appellant argue that the Maytag Intermountain Company was the principal and Morris was its agent, and that the former is, accordingly, liable herein, and they say that the cases which hold contrary to their contention deal with the relationship of master and servant, and that such cases have no application here. But an attorney is an agent. If, then, in attempting to manage his client's case, he, without specific directions, travels in an automobile to see a man who, in his opinion, might become an important witness in his case, is his client responsible? So we have "Ford agencies," "Buick agencies," and other similar "agencies," handling products of automobile manufacturers. While today the managers of these agencies, ordinarily, perhaps, buy such products, they might handle them tomorrow on commission. They are agents, in the broad sense of that term, but should the manufacturer be held responsible for all the torts that the former might commit in disposing of these products? The Curtis Publishing Company, located at Philadelphia, every week sends its Saturday Evening Posts throughout the country. If a boy in Cheyenne, while on the errand of soliciting subscriptions for the magazine, or delivering it, negligently runs into another with his bicycle, should the company be held responsible? The citation to these examples, which might be multiplied many times, shows that the solution of the problem before us is not as easy as counsel for appellant seem to think, and in view of the fact that the case before us is one of first impression here, we have deemed it expedient to give it more attention than counsel for appellant apparently have thought it necessary.

Prior to the latter part of the seventeenth century, a master was not responsible for the torts of his servants, unless committed by his express command or subsequent assent. But in the case of *Jones v. Hart*, 2 Salk. 441, 91 Eng.Repr. 382, decided in 1699, it was held that if a servant driving a cart negligently runs into another cart, the master is liable. And from about that time commenced to be developed the modern doctrine that a master is responsible for the torts of his servant committed within the scope of his employment. Prof. Wigmore in

7 Harvard L.R. 392-404. Voices against this doctrine were heard from time to time. As late as 1876 Lord Bramwell told a Parliamentary committee that he could not "see why the law should be so ... why a man should be liable for the negligence of his servant, there being no relation constituted between him and the party complaining." 26 Yale L.J. 11. But dissenting voices have been swept aside. Shaw, C.J., said in *Farwell v. Railroad Corporation*, 4 Metc. (Mass.) 49, 38 Am.Dec. 339, that the "rule is obviously founded on the great principle of social duty, that every man, in the management of his own affairs, whether by himself or by his agents or servants, shall so conduct them as not to injure another." The doctrine was carried to its logical conclusion. Independent agents or contractors were treated the same as servants. It was not until the second quarter of the nineteenth century that it was doubted that the doctrine of respondeat superior should be applied in all cases in which one man was employed to perform an act for another. 65 L.R.A. 624-631, note; note, 14 R.C.L. 79. Two decisions rendered in 1840, namely, *Milligan v. Wedge*, 12 A. & E. 737, and *Quarman v. Burnett*, 6 M. & W. 497, took a definite departure from the then generally accepted rule, and by the middle of that century it came to be recognized that there are many cases in which a man should not be held responsible for the acts of a representative, if the latter is not under his immediate control, direction, or supervision. Such representative has generally been called an independent contractor, a phrase that has acquired almost a technical meaning, originally, of course, applied to one who actually performed services under an independent contract. It is not altogether appropriate to apply the term in all cases, or in the case at bar, and various other terms have been sought to be substituted, such as entrepreneur or enterpriser.

Courts in cases of the character now before us have ordinarily ignored the difference between an agent and a servant, and have ordinarily merely attempted to determine in a particular case whether the person through whose instrumentality a negligent act was committed was a servant or ordinary agent on the one hand, or an independent contractor, or independent agent, pursuing a separate occupation, on the other. The controlling or principal test is generally stated to be as to whether or not the employer, using that term in a broad sense, has the right to control the details of the work to be done by the servant or agent, or whether the latter represents the former only as to the result to be accomplished. 14 R.C.L. 67; 39 C.J. 1316, and the cases hereinafter cited. The rules governing principal and agent are a later development in our law than those governing master and servant, and have branched off from the latter. And it is insisted in the restatement of the law of agency by the American Law Institute that it is important that the distinction be observed. A servant is defined as a person employed to perform personal service for another in his affairs, and who, in respect to his physical movements in the performance of the service is subject to the other's control or right to control, while an agent is defined as a person who represents another in contractual negotiations or transactions akin thereto.

The reason assigned for the importance of making the distinction is that an agent who is not at the same time acting as servant cannot ordinarily make his principal liable for incidental negligence in connection with the means incidentally employed to accomplish the work intrusted to his care. Draft 1, p. 8; draft 5, pp. 30, 31; pp. 99, 100. We think that the distinction mentioned may be drawn with profit. The control, or right of control, over physical movements generally exists when a person performs personal service for another, unless he is an independent contractor. That is not true, or not nearly as true, in the case of an agent. Moreover, actual control is ordinarily more immediate in the case of a servant than in the case of an agent. There can be no doubt that a salesman, such as Morris was, is an agent. Of course, an agent may, as to some work performed for his principal, be a servant. But no personal service, not even the delivery of washing machines, is involved in this case, unless the driving of the automobile may be called such. And the gist of the controversy herein is as to whether the principal is liable for its agent's negligence while engaged in a more or less necessary physical act which is incidental to the performance of his general duties, or, if we must use a special term, whether or not the agent, while engaged in that physical act, must be regarded in the nature of an independent contractor. The test which courts have generally adopted is that already heretofore stated.

The first case which we have found to be at all similar to that at bar, decided in the United States, is the case of *Pickens & Plummer v. Diecker & Bro.*, 21 Ohio St. 212, 8 Am.Rep. 55, decided in 1871. In that case the employer of Wright, a traveling agent, was held liable for negligence of the agent in letting a team of horses get out of control and causing damages to a third person. Wright was hired on an annual salary. His duties required him to stay in the employer's store, or to travel, soliciting orders for goods and making collections, as his employers might direct; when traveling, his expenses were allowed to him and paid by his employers. The team used at the time of the negligence in question was hired from a third person. The court, while recognizing the rule that an employer is not liable, if an agent is not under its immediate control, direction, or supervision, held that such control existed, since the agent could not, consistently with his duty, have refused to obey the employer's direction, and that the contract of employment did not bind the employee to produce any given result. The second case, at all similar to the case at bar, decided in the United States, appears to be the case of *Singer Manufacturing Company v. Rahn*, 132 U.S. 518, 10 S.Ct. 175, 33 L.Ed. 440, decided in 1889. In that case one Corbett was engaged by the Singer Manufacturing Company to canvass for the sale of its machines. Corbett agreed to give his exclusive time and best energies to the business of the company, and to pay all expenses; the company furnished a wagon, Corbett a horse and harness, and as compensation Corbett received a commission on the sales made by him. By careless driving of the horses, another was injured. It was held that Corbett was a servant and that the company was liable, the court remarking that it might, if it had seen fit, have instructed Corbett what route to take or even at what speed to drive. . . .

In *Natchez Coca-Cola Bottling Co. v. Watson*, 160 Miss. 173, 133 So. 677, the company engaged a truck driver to drive its truck over a designated route for the purpose of selling Coca-Cola along the route, being paid on a commission basis. The company was held liable for negligence of the driver. A similar case is *Dunbaden v. Castles Ice Cream Company*, 103 N.J.Law 427, 135 A. 886. These cases may be distinguished from the case at bar, whether logically or not we need not say, by the fact that the route to be driven was fixed and definite, showing, perhaps, more detailed control over the physical movements of the person employed.

There are, however, a number of cases which are hard to distinguish from the case at bar. Several of them were decided under the workmen's compensation laws, and there is, perhaps, in such cases manifest a tendency toward a liberal construction in favor of a claimant under such laws. *Marquez v. Le Blanc* (La. App.) 143 So. 108. And while it seems, at first blush, that there should, perhaps, be no difference of construction in workmen's compensation cases and damage cases, as held by at least some of the authorities, those from Massachusetts, for instance, still the former involve a principle of public policy different from that involved in this case, namely, that each industry should bear its own burdens, and since it is not necessary to decide the point herein, we refrain from doing so. ...

Somewhat peculiar are the cases of *Aisenberg v. Adams Company*, 95 Conn. 419, 111 A. 591, a workman's compensation case, and *Borah v. Motor Company* (Mo.App.) 257 S.W. 145, a damage case, because of the fact that in each of them the relation of master and servant was held to exist, mainly because the employer had the right to control the terms of the contract, rather than the manner or means of accomplishing the result. In each of them the person, held to be a servant or agent, disposed of his own time and traveled mainly in his own discretion, and the only distinguishing feature from the case at bar is the fact that in each of them the agent used the vehicle of his employer. . . .In so far as these cases base the right of control on the fact that the employer had the right to direct the terms of the contract, they are opposed to the great weight of authority. If that test were correct, then there would be few, if any, cases involving negligence by a salesman, in which the doctrine of liability of the master for the negligence of a servant would not be applicable. These cases treat the physical movements of the person employed as but a minor part or incident in the performance of the employment, when, as a matter of fact, it is the major factor so far as an automobile accident is concerned. The making of a contract, affected by an agent, would seem to be but the result which is sought. It is exactly during the time that the so-called minor part is performed when an accident with an automobile is apt to occur. It will not likely take place while the salesman is talking to a customer, trying to effect, or effecting, a sale. If, accordingly, the right of control is the test in connection with the question before us, and the courts apparently agree that it is, then, it would seem, it ought to be directed to that portion of the employment directly connected with the factor by reason of which liability is sought to be established. It would not do, we think, to pursue the shadow, leaving the substance out of consideration.

. . .

In all of these cases the agent used his own automobile. In nearly all of them, the principal knew of that use, in many instances contributing all or part of the expenses in using the automobile. In only two, the Oregon and Maryland cases, the court paid some attention to the fact that the employer did not know or did not direct the use of the automobile. In some of these cases only a commission was paid; in some of them a salary plus a commission. In *Pyyny v. Biscuit Co.*, supra, the Biscuit Company was sought to be held liable for the negligence, in an automobile accident, of its salesman, who had no regular hours of work, except that he was to see his customers at some time during the day; his sole business was to sell biscuits for the company; he was paid a salary and commission and the expense of operating his car; he carried a sample case and advertisements of the company in the back of his car. The Massachusetts court said: "On the above facts it is plain Bancroft was his own master in respect to the time he should devote to the business of the defendant, and to the place within certain designated territory where he should solicit sales. It is also plain that it was his duty and not that of the defendant to register the automobile and obtain a license to operate it. The defendant had no right on the reported facts to direct the manner in which Bancroft should control his car. It assumed no obligation to keep the car in repair other than is involved in its agreement to pay the expense of operating it. ..."

In *Barton v. Studebaker Corporation*, supra, an automobile salesman injured another in an accident. He used the storehouse of the defendant corporation to show automobiles, but used his own car in finding prospective purchasers. The court in holding the defendant corporation not liable said among other things: "The test of control in such cases means 'complete control,' or the full and unqualified right to control and direct the details of or the means by which the work is to be accomplished. ... In this case, as the undisputed evidence shows, the defendant Owen was not subject to the authoritative control of the Corporation in respect of the details of his work or as to how it should be performed. This was entirely up to him. He could work when he pleased and seek out and select such persons as he pleased as purchasers of the automobiles of the Corporation. Indeed, he was so far from being subject to the control or direction of the Corporation as to the means or mode of and the time for doing his work that he was under no obligation to give any particular time or service to the Corporation. When he brought a 'prospect' to the Corporation, he was acting for himself as well as for the Corporation, and if such prospect was transformed into a purchaser, he received his stipulated share of the money for which the machine was sold and nothing if a sale was not effected."

In *McCarthy v. Souther* it is said that the decisive inquiry is as to whether or not the employer has any control over the management of the automobile of the salesman. One of the best statements which we have seen, particularly applicable in a case of the character now before us, is that of Prof. Seavy in Tentative Draft No. 5 of the Restatement of the Law of Agency, page 100, where it is said: "A principal employing another to achieve a result but not controlling the details of his physical movements is not responsible for incidental negligence while such person is conducting the authorized transaction. Thus the principal is not responsible for the negligent physical conduct of an attorney, a broker, a factor or a rental agent, as such. In their movements and their control of physical forces, they are in the relation of independent contractors to the principal. It is only when to the relationship of principal and agent there is added that right to control physical details as to the manner of performance, which is characteristic of the relation of master and servant, that the person in whose service the act is done, becomes subject to liability for the physical conduct of the actor."

In this view, then, that the right of control of the physical movements-the automobile-is the decisive inquiry, it becomes important what the record discloses in that regard. The evidence shows that the Maytag Company furnished Morris no rules or regulations to govern him in the performance of the work but that the means and manner thereof was left to him. That, perhaps, does not definitely show that the right of control was not in the company. The fact that the company did not exercise control does not show that it did not have the right of control, though it may be some evidence thereof. It has been held that in the absence of a stipulation the existence or nonexistence of the right must be determined by reasonable inferences shown by the evidence. Among the points frequently taken into consideration is the fact of the right of discharge. But we take it that that right exists in the vast majority of cases of the character under consideration. And it has been said that it is not by the later cases, considered any decisive test.

In the case at bar there was no express reservation of control, and none can be implied. In fact it would seem that in view of the fact that actual control of an automobile driven hundreds of miles away from the place of the employer can at best be theoretical only, even though actual control has been reserved, the right of such control should, in a case of this character, be able to be implied only from reasonably clear evidence showing it.

We think, accordingly, that the employer in this case ought not to be held liable. Whether we should hold the same in a case similar to the instant one, but where the agent uses the automobile of his principal, in accordance with what seems to be the rule recognized in *Premier Motor Company v. Tilford*, 61 Ind. App. 164, 111 N.E. 645, we need not say. Some criticism has been leveled at courts for their disagreement on this subject and for not finding a more decisive and clear-cut test. But it must be remembered that the rule that a master is liable for the negligence of his servant committed in the course of his employment—which is at the basis of the cases holding the employer in cases of this character liable—is founded not upon a rule of logic, but upon a rule of public policy, and hence the digression, not constituting an abrogation of the rule, must necessarily also involve the question as to how far public policy requires the digression to be made, and it is not to be wondered at that one court answers the question one way, another another way. It is suggested in 28 Mich.L.R. 378 that the "independent calling" test is easier of application. We are not certain of that, unless we limit independent callings to those definitely known as such in the past. But why should we? If a factor is an independent agent, for whose negligence in his physical movements his principal is not liable, why should liability lie in a case like that at bar? The difference between a factor and a man traveling to sell washing machines, or an insurance agent soliciting insurance, is not vital. The latter's calling may, in this age of commercial activity, well be considered as independent as that of a factor.

Every rule should, of course, have a reason. Why should we depart from the ordinary rule applicable in the case of master and servant? Is that departure, in the case at bar, based on reason? We think it is. We have, it may be noted, laid some emphasis on the fact of the ownership of the automobile in question. It has been said that when a plaintiff has suffered injury from the negligent management of a vehicle, it is sufficient prima facie evidence that the negligence was imputable to the owner thereof, though driven by another. The converse of that proposition should, of course, be true. Nay more, it has often been said that ordinarily a person who is not the owner and is not in control of certain property is not liable for negligence in respect of such property. 45 C.J. 882. And surely that is in accordance with the plain dictates of justice, unless a countervailing reason appears in a particular case. A number of cases are found in notes to 57 A.L.R. 739 and 60 A.L.R. 1163, in which it was held that the fact that an employee drove his own car or other vehicle did not relieve the employer from liability for the negligence of the employee in driving such car. But generally speaking that ought to be limited, we think, to those cases in which the driver is a servant, as distinguished from an agent, or in which it clearly appears that the right of control is reserved to the principal, and it has, we think, been generally so limited except in the class of cases already heretofore mentioned. And if a departure from the doctrine of respondeat superior is at all justifiable in any case, as we think it is, and we resort to a consideration of broad public policy, reasons for the limitation mentioned are not altogether absent. Practically, in a case of the character before us, the agent has the sole power of control of his automobile. He, as owner, can distribute the risk of driving it by taking out insurance better than, or at least as well as, his principal. If he alone is held responsible for his negligence, that has a tendency to cause him to exercise care to prevent accidents. To put a man upon his own responsibility generally has that effect. And that prevention of automobile accidents is a matter of considerable, nay vital, importance today is, of course, attested by daily experience. And while this reason cannot be held to be controlling, or perhaps should not be even considered, in some cases, it furnishes at least some basis in the application of public policy.

The judgment of the trial court is, accordingly, affirmed.

Notes

Justice Blume indicates that the principal's exposure to tort liability based on an "agent's" negligence has gone through discernible stages. Review the classic distinction between a "servant" and an "agent." Why was such a distinction ever drawn? Initially, courts were inclined to hold the principal liable for any agent's torts. Justice Blume suggests that it was not until 1840 that the courts started to depart from this position. Why was a restrictive distinction drawn at that time?

The birth of the "independent contractor" resulted from the coupling of an "old" idea with a "new" social need. But once created, the independent contractor classification remained in doubt for nearly a century. Not all courts were sympathetic to the newly "felt need" which led to creation of the independent contractor status. Justice Blume clearly identifies the technique for limiting the pragmatic scope of this doctrine. The counterattack on this restrictive concept of the independent contractor emerged in several of the decisions reviewed in *Stockwell*.

This counterattack, in turn, summoned a brief rally represented by *Aisenberg v. Adams Company* and *Borah v. Motor Company*, also reviewed in *Stockwell*. What was the gist of these opinions? They almost killed the independent contractor by means of an exception. In 1933 the Supreme Court of Wyoming added its force to the idea first developed in *Milligan v. Wedge* and *Quarman v. Burnett*. The *Stockwell* opinion has been so influential in revealing the competing interests behind the "independent contractor" label that today we still speak of "servant" and "non-servant" agents. This modern terminology focuses on the factor which Justice Blume used to resolve questions of the principal's tort liability.

Another rationale for *Stockwell v. Morris* may be found in Professor Mechem's entrepreneur theory. A line of cases strongly suggests that the control test should not apply if the hirer acts within an industry which has added risks to society (when working in that industry has a greater harm-dealing potential than that experienced in everyday living). This idea has re-extended the principal's liability, not in quest of a deep pocket (though this is often found), but on the theory that it makes the hirer have a financial stake in minimizing risks to third parties.

If that rationale were urged in support of master-servant liability in *Stockwell*, would it render a judgment against Maytag? What was the employee, Morris, doing at the time of the injury? He was driving a car, hardly a peculiar instrument created or exploited for financial benefit by Maytag which society should specifically discipline. A car has long since become an instrument used so often by so many in such diverse pursuits that the entrepreneur theory does not counsel liability.

After examining cases which debate the servant/non-servant controversy, be aware that there are other theories of employer's liability which are not founded on respondeat superior. If the task set by the hirer is inherently dangerous the hirer will not be relieved of personal liability by using an independent contractor. *Stubblefield v. Federal Reserve Bank*, 356 Mo. 1018, 204 S.W.2d 718 (1947). Also, liability will arise if the hirer is guilty of selecting an unqualified independent contractor to carry out an inherently dangerous project. *Mullich v. Brocker*, 119 Mo.App. 332, 97 S.W. 549 (1905).

5. The "Scope of Employment" Defense: A Concept of Proven Elasticity:

BALINOVIC v. EVENING STAR NEWSPAPER CO.
United States Court of Appeals, District of Columbia Circuit, 1940.
113 F.2d 505.

EDGERTON, ASSOCIATE JUSTICE. Appellant Balinovic sued the Evening Star on the theory that its delivery truck, negligently driven by its driver, injured him in a collision. The question is whether the District Court was right in directing a verdict for the defendant because the driver had left his route, and his work of delivering papers, and was chasing a traffic violator at the command of a policeman who jumped on the running board and stayed there.

The accident occurred on June 23, 1933, before the passage of the statute which imposes liability on the owner of a car for the acts of any person who drives it with his consent, and the mere fact that the Star had entrusted its car to its driver did not make it liable.

Appellant urges that when an agent is sent out in charge of a car he is "impliedly authorized" by his principal to aid in law enforcement at the command of a policeman. This comes to saying that he may assume that his principal, if present, would authorize the act. That depends upon the principal's disposition, the agent's knowledge of it, and the other circumstances. Perhaps sympathy with law enforcement may be imputed to a newspaper. Perhaps this extends to a willingness to interrupt delivery of papers and risk damage to truck, driver and public in order to chase a criminal. But the fact remains that the Star's business is not chasing criminals but producing and selling papers. When its driver set out to catch a criminal he was doing the work of the District of Columbia.

When B, for his own purposes, borrows, controls, and directs A's driver, B is responsible for the driver's negligence and A is not. An express authorization from an employer to his employee to do another's work under another's direction does not make the employer responsible for the employee's negligence in doing the work; and no implied authorization can be more effective than an express one. "The master's responsibility cannot be extended beyond the limits of the master's work." Whose work it is depends on "who has the power to control and direct the servants in the performance of their work."

. . .

. . .[W]e need not discuss at length *Babington v. Yellow Taxi Corporation,* [250 N.Y. 14, 164 N.E. 726 (1928)] on which appellant relies. There a cab company's driver was killed while chasing a criminal on the order of a police- man, and the New York court sustained an award of compensation against the company. The cab, unlike the Star's truck, was subject to call for any lawful journey. Moreover, the limits of workmen's compensation and of tort liability are not necessarily identical. The Star, by putting the driver on the road and keeping him there, did not create the risk that the criminal-catching activities of the District would injure a bystander. Whether it created the risk that those activities of the District would injure the driver, with the result that an injury to him in the course of those activities might be regarded as arising out of and in the course of his employment by the Star, is a question which we need not decide.

Affirmed.

RUTLEDGE, ASSOCIATE JUSTICE (dissenting).

In my judgment the issue is not one of private, consensual agency. Not all vicarious liability rests on consent of the principal, express or implied in fact, whether to the existence of the representative relation or to the particular activi- ties of the agent which result in the claim of liability. Plaintiff does not contend that defendant consented in fact to the driver's criminal-chasing activities. He says that liability arises regardless of such consent and because, at the time of the injury, the driver was discharging a duty imposed by law upon the defen- dant, not merely as part of its newspaper operations in the narrow business sense, but as part of its broader obligation as a corporate citizen of the commu- nity. Such a duty, if it exists, is inescapable by mere failure to consent or by refusal to perform it.

6. Frolic vs. Deviation-A Distinction Producing a Substantial Difference:

The unidentified driver of the Star's delivery truck was compelled by a police officer's orders when he pursued the fleeing traffic violator. But what if he had given pursuit voluntarily? What if the driver had used the Star's truck to deviate from his route in order to pick up a pair of boots and in the course of that deviation he drove over your new shoes (which you were wearing at the time)? Would the Star be liable? What if, at the time the delivery truck ran over your foot, the driver were deviating from his route in order to find a shortcut and thus reduce the time and fuel consumed in keeping his appointed rounds? Would the Star be liable?

A nineteenth century classic, *Joel v. Morison*, provides a way to distinguish *Kelly v. Louisiana Oil Refining Co.* and *Palmer v. Keene Forestry Association.* The later cases stem from a vile habit.

JOEL v. MORISON
In the Exchequer
6 Car. & P. 501 (1834).

The declaration stated, that, on the 18th of April, 1833, the plaintiff was proceeding on foot across a certain public and common highway, and that the defendant was possessed of a cart and horse, which were under the care, government, and direction of a servant of his, who was driving the same along the said highway, and that the defendant by his said servant so carelessly negligently, and improperly drove, governed, and directed the said horse and cart, that, by the carelessness, negligence, and improper conduct of the defendant by his servant, the cart and horse were driven against the plaintiff, and struck him, whereby he was thrown down and the bone of one of his legs was fractured, and he was ill in consequence, and prevented from transacting his business, and obliged to incur a great expense in and about the setting the said bone, &c., and a further great expense in retaining and employing divers persons to superintend and look after his business for six calendar months. Plea-Not guilty.

From the evidence on the part of the plaintiff it appeared that he was in Bishopsgate-street, when he was knocked down by a cart and horse coming in the direction from Shoreditch, which were sworn to have been driven at the time by a person who was the servant of the defendant, another of his servants being in the cart with him. The injury was a fracture of the fibula.

On the part of the defendant witnesses were called, who swore that his cart was for weeks before and after the time sworn to by the plaintiff's witnesses only in the habit of being driven between Burton Crescent Mews and Finchley, and did not go into the City at all.

Thesiger, for the plaintiff, in reply, suggested that either the defendant's servants might in coming from Finchley have gone out of their way for their own purposes, or might have taken the cart at a time when it was not wanted for the purpose of business, and have gone to pay a visit to some friend. He was observing that, under these circumstances, the defendant was liable for the acts of his servants.

PARKE, B. He is not liable if, as you suggest, these young men took the cart without leave; he is liable if they were going extra viam in going from Burton Crescent Mews to Finchley; but if they chose to go of their own accord to see a friend, when they were not on their master's business, he is not liable.

58

His Lordship afterwards, in summing up said—This is an action to recover damages for an injury sustained by the plaintiff, in consequence of the negligence of the defendant's servant. There is no doubt that the plaintiff has suffered the injury, and there is no doubt that the driver of the cart was guilty of negligence, and there is no doubt also that the master, if that person was driving the cart on his master's business, is responsible. If the servants, being on their master's business, took a detour to call upon a friend, the master will be responsible. If you think the servants lent the cart to a person who was driving without the defendant's knowledge, he will not be responsible. Or, if you think that the young man who was driving took the cart surreptitiously, and was not at the time employed on his master's business, the defendant will not be liable. The master is only liable where the servant is acting in the course of his employment. If he was going out of his way, against his master's implied commands, when driving on his master's business, he will make his master liable; but if he was going on a frolic of his own, without being at all on his master's business, the master will not be liable. As to the damages, the master is not guilty of any offence, he is only responsible in law, therefore the amount should be reasonable.

Verdict for the plaintiff-damages, 30£.

Note

This charge to a British jury has long been cited for its distinction between those cases in which a servant-agent's unauthorized negligence will result in the principal's liability and those cases in which it will not. Is Baron Parke consistent? What distinguishes a "frolic" from a "deviation"?

The dissatisfaction which many exhibit when confronted with the conceptual distinction between a frolic and a deviation is likely to grow when one attempts to trace its application in case law. In a little game which may someday be peddled by Parker Brothers or, in a more contemporary setting, show up in a video arcade, we can develop some interesting hypotheticals.

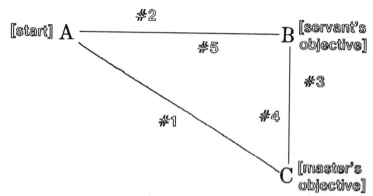

Hypothetical # 1: Accident between A and C although servant intended to go on to B. Liability on the part of the master. See, *Clawson v. Pierce-Arrow Motor Car Co.*, 231 N.Y. 273, 277, 131 N.E. 914, 915 (1921).

Hypothetical # 2: Accident between A and B although servant intended to go on to C. Cases are divided with a majority reaching a "deviation" or liability conclusion.

Hypothetical # 3: Accident between B and C. Having used the master's time and equipment to pursue his own ends, the servant is now on his way to the master's objective but is taking a route other than the one which would have been used (A to C) if there had been no personal detour. Cases generally find liability deeming this a deviation.

Hypothetical # 4: Accident between C and B. Having first performed the task of his master, the servant is now using the master's time and equipment to pursue some personal objective. This is the classic "frolic" resulting in a non-liability conclusion.

Hypothetical # 5: Accident happens between B and A. Having first performed his master's business and then taken a frolic, the servant's thoughts and travel have turned back to his master's office. While the cases are divided, the New York Court of Appeals has concluded that the employer is not liable. *Fiocco v. Carver*, 234 N.Y. 219, 225, 137 N.E. 309, 311 (1922). "... Whether we have regard to circumstances of space or time or of casual or logical relation, the homeward trip was bound up with the effects of the excursion, the parts interpenetrated and commingled beyond the hope of separation. Division more substantial must be shown before a relation, once ignored and abandoned, will be renewed and reestablished."

See generally, Annot. 51 A.L.R.2d 8 (1957). Deviation from Employment in Use of Employer's Car During Regular Work Hours.

KELLY v. LOUISIANA OIL REFINING CO.
Supreme Court of Tennessee, 1934.
167 Tenn. 101, 66 S.W.2d 997.

SWIGGART, JUSTICE. The plaintiff prosecutes his appeal in the nature of a writ of error from a judgment dismissing his suit on the defendant's demurrer to the declaration.

The suit is for damages for personal injuries sustained by reason of negligent conduct of defendant's servant, employed to deliver gasoline and oil.

Plaintiff was an employee of one Brockwell, a merchant, engaged partly in buying and handling cotton. The store contained quantities of "loose cotton samples and loose parcels and particles of lint cotton." Plaintiff's clothing "was pretty well covered with lint cotton, a very inflammable substance."

The declaration avers that the defendant knew, or had reason to know, that its servant was a smoker of cigarettes, and that he "constantly smoked while on duty, delivering gas and oil."

Defendant's servant came to the Brockwell store to deliver gasoline, and then entered the store to call defendant's office by telephone. While making the call, he struck a match to light a cigarette, and carelessly threw the match against plaintiff. Plaintiff's clothing was ignited and he was severely burned. The fire, thus ignited, spread, and consumed the store building.

Defendant contends, and the circuit court held, that the act of negligence of which its servant was guilty was wholly outside the scope of the servant's employment, so that the defendant may not be held responsible for the resulting injury. We are of the opinion that this contention must be sustained.

The question presented for our decision is the application to the stated facts of well-established principles of law. The principle we apply is stated in *Deihl & Lord v. Ottenville*, 82 Tenn. (14 Lea) 191, 197: "If a servant, wholly for a purpose of his own, disregarding the object for which he is employed, and not intending by his act to execute it, does an injury [to another] not within the scope of his employment, the master is not liable."

In the American Law Institute's Restatement of the Law, Agency (1933), § 235, the same principle is stated: "An act of the servant is not within the scope of employment if it is done with no intention to perform it as a part of or incident to a service on account of which he is employed."

The defendant's servant entered the Brockwell store and took his position at the telephone in furtherance of his service, and, was to that extent acting within the scope of his employment. But the act of lighting the cigarette was not incident to the telephoning and had no relation to it. It did not render the act of telephoning hazardous, nor did it create any causal relation between the service he was employed to render the defendant and the injury sustained by the plaintiff. Discussing a similar action and ruling as we do here, the Circuit Court of Appeals (4th Cir.), in *Adams v. Southern Bell Tel. & Tel. Co.*, 295 F. 586, 591, said: "If the defendant here is answerable, it must be because Heeney (the defendant's servant), at the moment he is said to have committed the negligent act, was in the service of the defendant and on duty for it, or because, if he had not been in defendant's employ and on its business, he would not have been at the place at which the alleged wrong was or could have been done; but it is clear that neither of these circumstances is in itself sufficient to impose liability."

. . .

In the Restatement of the Law, Agency, § 235, the rule above quoted is elucidated by the following "comment":

"Although an act is not done for the purpose of the master and hence is not within the scope of the employment, if it is accompanied by authorized conduct its performance may cause the servant to be negligent in the manner of doing that which is within the scope of the employment. The chief instances occur where the servant is the custodian of land or chattels which he is controlling on account of the master."

. . .

Nor is the plaintiff's case aided by the averment that the defendant knew its servant was a habitual smoker. This averment might have affected the result if the accident had occurred while the servant was in the act of hauling and delivering the inflammable oil and gas he was employed to deliver, ... but the duty in which the servant was engaged, when he threw the lighted match on plaintiff, was the simple and innocuous act of using a telephone, which he might have found it necessary to do if he had been delivering groceries instead of gasoline, and which contributed in no way to the accident. A general acquiescence in the servant's habit of smoking while on duty would not support a finding that the defendant was negligent in failing to instruct its servant not to light his cigarette in the event he should find it necessary to enter a place in which, for reasons wholly disconnected with the defendant's business, it might be unsafe to do so.

PALMER v. KEENE FORESTRY ASS'N
Supreme Court of New Hampshire, 1921.
80 N.H. 68, 112 A. 798.

The evidence tended to show that the plaintiff employed the defendant to set out in his field a quantity of trees; that it employed certain laborers to do the work, whom it sent to the field for that purpose, some of whom were cigarette smokers; and that while engaged in the work one of them carelessly dropped a lighted match into the grass, which was very dry, and that this caused the fire to spread over the field, burning other trees and destroying the plaintiff's building.

. . .

WALKER, J. One position of the defendant is that there is no evidence that it had knowledge or is chargeable with knowledge that its servants, whom it employed to set out trees in the plaintiff's field, were addicted to the use of cigarettes, the smoking of which when they were engaged in their work would be liable to result in setting fire to the dry grass and create a conflagration. If the defendant knew, or ought to have known, they were in the habit of smoking cigarettes, it also must have known that that habit, if practiced by them when setting out trees in a field which was abnormally dry and parched, might reasonably be expected to set the grass on fire and do serious damage to the property of others. The principal contention, therefore, relates to the sufficiency of the evidence in regard to the defendant's knowledge of its servants' smoking habits.

The evidence tended to show that the men, or some of them, including the foreman, smoked while doing their work; that they smoked at their boarding house and at the railroad station; that they were not forbidden to smoke while at work; that they, with one exception, had worked for the defendant doing the same kind of work in other places; and that they were young men. From this evidence it would be a reasonable inference that the officers of the defendant either knew, or that they ought to have known, that their men would probably smoke while working in the plaintiff's field. It was a custom for them to indulge in that habit, of which the jury might find the defendant was fully cognizant. *Curtis v. Car Works*, 73 N.H. 516, 63 Atl. 400. Moreover the jury would be justified in finding that the defendant ought to have known of this habit of its workmen, from the fact that it is common knowledge that most young men practice the habit when at work. Upon this view it would follow that the defendant would be chargeable with the knowledge that ordinarily prudent men would possess upon this subject, and ought to have provided by instruction or otherwise against the practice of the habit when it was liable to result in serious damage to third persons.

As from the evidence the jury might properly find that the defendant knew its men were habitual smokers, and that while at work as its agents or servants in the plaintiff's field they probably would indulge in the habit and carelessly drop lighted matches in the dry grass, setting it on fire, the duty to the plaintiff rested upon the defendant by reasonable means to prevent such a result. Its duty in this respect would not be different in principle than it would have been if its responsible officers and agents had been present at the time of the fire and had indulged in the smoking habit which caused the conflagration.

It is argued, however, that the men were not engaged in the defendant's business when the fire was set; that the smoking was no part of the work they were hired to do; and hence that the defendant is not liable. *Rowell v. Railroad*, 68 N.H. 358, 44 Atl. 488, and *Danforth v. Fisher*, 75 N.H. 111, 71 Atl. 535, 21 L.R.A.(N.S.), 93, 139 Am.St.Rep. 670, are cited in support of this contention. But the principle of those cases is not applicable to this case, since the defendant's liability depends on a finding that it had knowledge of the propensity of its servants to smoke, which habit they were likely to indulge in while at work in the plaintiff's field, and thus cause serious damage to the plaintiff's property. The question is, not whether the men in dropping lighted matches into the grass were acting within scope of their authority, but whether the doing of the act was reasonably to be apprehended by the defendant. *Searle v. Parke*, 68 N.H. 311, 34 Atl. 744. If it is, it is liable for the resulting damage; if it was not, it might not be liable.

Notes

Can you advance any theory which would reconcile *Kelly* with *Palmer*?

In the final analysis does the liability conclusion in Palmer have anything to do with the "scope of employment" rationale? Isn't the defendant held liable for his own direct negligence?

Chapter 2

THE PARTNERSHIP

A. VIEWING THE PARTNERSHIP FROM WITHOUT

BLACKMON v. HALE
Supreme Court of California, 1970.
1 Cal.3d 548, 83 Cal.Rptr. 194, 463 P.2d 418.

TRAYNOR, C.J. Plaintiff Blackmon appeals from a judgment in favor of defendants Hale, Lee, United California Bank, and Bank of America entered in an action to recover $23,500 plus interest. He sought to recover this sum from defendants on the ground that each of them was liable for the failure of defendant Adams to repay plaintiff $23,500 that plaintiff entrusted to Adams. A default judgment against Adams is not involved in this appeal.

In July 1961 James C. Adams, an attorney, undertook to represent plaintiff in the latter's proposed purchase of a note and mortgage on real property in Nevada, owned by H.H. Records. Plaintiff went to Adams at the suggestion of Records. At that time Adams practiced law in Lancaster in partnership with defendant Hale under the name of Adams and Hale. The two attorneys had been partners since 1952. From November 1958 to May 1961 they had a third partner, defendant Lee, and during that period the three practiced law under the name of Adams, Hale, and Lee. On May 31, 1961, Lee withdrew from the firm. Adams and Hale continued the practice under the name Adams and Hale until they dissolved the firm on August 31, 1961.

About the middle of July 1961 Adams told plaintiff that funds would be needed to make an offer for the Nevada note and mortgage. Plaintiff testified that he told Adams that he would put up the money, but he wanted the money placed in a trust account so that it would be available when needed. If the offer was not accepted, the money was to be returned. Adams instructed plaintiff to make a check payable to Adams and Hale Trust Account and said "in this manner that he could offer this money to these people and it would be available." On August 17 plaintiff purchased a cashier's check for $24,500 from the Bank of America, payable to the order of Adams and Hale Trust Account and mailed the check to Adams. On August 18 Adams endorsed the check "Adams and Hale Trust Account by J.C. Adams." Below that endorsement was rubber stamped "Pay to the order of California Bank; Adams, Hale and Lee Trust Account." The check was deposited in the Adams, Hale, and Lee Trust Account at the California Bank in Lancaster.

During the existence of the Adams, Hale, and Lee partnership the firm maintained a trust account at the California Bank, which later became the United California Bank, in the name of Adams, Hale, and Lee Trust Account. Withdrawals from the account were authorized on the signature of Hale alone or on the joint signatures of Adams and Lee. After Lee left the firm on May 31, Adams and Hale continued to use the same account under the same name for the deposit of trust moneys and did not open a separate trust account under the name of Adams and Hale. Before 1958 they had a trust account in the name of Adams and Hale at the same branch of the California Bank, but for several years that account had been either dormant or closed.

On August 31 Adams and Hale dissolved their partnership. On September 6 Adams asked Hale to sign a check for $21,386 drawn on the Adams, Hale, and Lee Trust Account and payable to the J.C. Adams Trust Account. Hale signed the check and delivered it to Adams. Adams used the check to open a new account at the Security First National Bank under the name of J.C. Adams Trust Account. Over the next four months he diverted this money to his own use.

Apparently plaintiff's proposed purchase of the note and mortgage was never carried out, and in due course plaintiff demanded the return of his $24,500. In April 1962 Adams paid plaintiff $1,000, leaving a balance due of $23,500.

[The court affirmed the judgment of non-liability as to the defendant banks, holding: "The bank is authorized to honor withdrawals from an account on the signatures authorized by the signature card, which serves as a contract between the depositor and the bank for the handling of the account. So long as the checks drawn on the account are signed in conformity with the signature card, and absent any knowledge of a misappropriation, the bank is free from liability for honoring a check drawn in breach of trust. ..."]

The trial court correctly concluded that plaintiff failed to establish any basis for imposing liability on either of defendant banks.

HALE'S LIABILITY

At the time Adams received the cashier's check for $24,500 payable to the Adams and Hale Trust Account he was practicing law in partnership with defendant Hale. Adams deposited the check in the firm's trust account, and thereafter secured $21,386 from that account by means of a check signed by Hale. Hale's liability for Adams' misappropriation of plaintiff's money must be determined in the context of the two capacities in which Hale acted, namely, as a partner of Adams and as a cotrustee of the funds deposited in the trust account.

Hale's liability as a partner is governed by the Uniform Partnership Act. (Corp.Code, §§ 15001-15045.) [UPA §14] provides that "The partnership is bound to make good the loss: (a) Where one partner acting within the scope of his apparent authority receives money or property of a third person and misapplies it; and (b) Where the partnership in the course of its business receives money or property of a third person and the money or property so received is misapplied by any partner while it is in the custody of the partnership." [UPA §15 provides that each partner is jointly and severally liable for everything chargeable to the partnership under [§14]. Accordingly, if Adams received plaintiff's money while acting within the scope of his apparent authority or the partnership received the money in the course of its business, Hale is jointly and severally liable for plaintiff's losses.

"Every partner is an agent of the partnership for the purpose of its business, and the act of every partner ... for apparently carrying on in the usual way the business of the partnership of which he is a member binds the partnership." [UPA §9]. The apparent scope of the partnership business depends primarily on the conduct of the partnership and its partners and what they cause third persons to believe about the authority of the partners. Ostensible agency or acts within the scope of the partnership business are presumed "where the business done by the supposed agent, so far as open to the observation of third parties, is consistent with the existence of an agency, and where, as to the transaction in question, the third party was justified in believing that an agency existed." (*County First Nat. Bank of Santa Cruz v. Coast Dairies & Land Co.* (1941) 46 Cal.App.2d 355, 366, 115 P.2d 988); .... The partnership will be relieved from liability for the wrongs of its partners acting individually when the third person has knowledge of the fact that he is dealing with the partner in his individual capacity. [UPA §9]

In the present case if Adams was acting only in his individual capacity and plaintiff knew that he was acting solely in that capacity, the partnership of Adams and Hale and Hale are not liable. Sound public policy dictates that a partnership must inform those who deal with its members in the course of the partnership's business of any special restrictions on a particular partner's authority. A person dealing with a partnership usually is in no position to know of special agreements between the partners and thus cannot be charged with knowledge of such agreements absent specific notice.

Adams and Hale practiced law in partnership under the name of Adams and Hale, Attorneys at Law. The firm did not conduct any business other than the practice of law. Plaintiff employed Adams to clear title to certain real property in Nevada and negotiate the purchase of the note and mortgage on that property. Adams was entrusted with $24,500 needed to make an offer to purchase the note and mortgage. In undertaking such responsibilities Adams was practicing law. ...

Although the firm's records indicate that Adams and Hale regarded plaintiff as a client of Adams only, there is no evidence whatever that either Adams or Hale ever informed plaintiff that Adams was not representing plaintiff as a member of the firm. Moreover, Adams and Hale held themselves out to the public and to plaintiff as partners. The partnership displayed a sign viewable from the street reading "Adams and Hale, Attorneys at Law." Such signs are commonly used by law firms to indicate a partnership. (See *Fletcher v. Pullen* (1889) 70 Md. 205, 213, 16 A. 887, 888, 14 Am.St.Rep. 355.) Plaintiff testified that he knew that the firm was called Adams and Hale and that he dealt with Adams in the firm's offices. Furthermore, Adams instructed plaintiff to make his check payable to the Adams and Hale Trust Account. In the absence of other evidence these facts would justify a reasonable man in believing that he was dealing with a partnership. ...

Hale contends, however, that plaintiff's own testimony supports the conclusion that plaintiff did not deal with Adams as a partner in the firm. Plaintiff testified as follows:

"THE COURT: Were you a client of the law firm of Adams and Hale at that time [at the time plaintiff first met Adams]?
"THE WITNESS: No, sir.
"THE COURT: Had you been at any time within the year 1961 a law client?
"THE WITNESS: No, sir.
"THE COURT: Were you at any time thereafter a law client?
"THE WITNESS: No, sir.
"THE COURT: Of either Adams, Hale or Lee?
"THE WITNESS: No, sir."

This testimony is inconclusive on the issue whether plaintiff knew he was dealing only with Adams individually. At most it reflects lay confusion and uncertainty as to what constitutes an attorney-client relationship. It does not show that plaintiff had any awareness of partnership law, let alone that he meant his transaction to be kept separate from other partnership business. It is therefore insufficient to establish that Adams did not act within the scope of his apparent authority.

. . .

LEE'S LIABILITY

Lee withdrew from the law firm of Adams, Hale and Lee and his name was deleted from the firm name on May 31, 1961, before plaintiff entrusted his money to Adams. Accordingly, Lee is not liable as a partner of Adams for the loss of plaintiff's money. [UPA §36].

[While he escaped liability as a partner of Adams, Lee was found liable to Blackmon in his capacity as co-trustee of the Adams, Hale and Lee trust account. ed.]

. . .

The part of the judgment in favor of defendant banks is affirmed. The part of the judgment in favor of defendants Hale and Lee is reversed. Defendant banks shall recover their costs on appeal from plaintiff. Plaintiff shall recover from defendants Hale and Lee his costs on the appeal from the part of the judgment in their favor.

McComb, J., Peters, J., Tobriner, J., Mosk, J., Burke, J., and Sullivan, J., concurred.

Notes

Given the plaintiff's very frank testimony, does this opinion permit Blackmon to reap where he did not sow? Is it a legal fiction to state that the sign on this office window held forth the promise that if Adams were to act dishonestly Hale would take up the loss? Does the court hold that Adams had apparent authority to steal Blackmon's funds or merely to take custody of them? Is the transition from one proposition to the other supplied at common law or by provision of the Uniform Partnership Act?

Does the opinion in *Blackmon* take proper account of the fact that the firm of Adams and Hale was dissolved on 31 August? What if Hale had raised as a defense to liability under Section 14 that the funds were not misapplied until after September 8 at which point they were no longer in the trust account? Nor, for that matter, were they in the custody of the firm. Would this dispose of the case under Section 14(b)? Respecting liability under Section 14(a), what if Hale contended that the misapplication did not take place until after dissolution and hence was not that of a "partner"? Before you answer these questions you would do well to read Section 35 of the UPA and to note the distinction between "dissolution" and "winding up."

ZEMELMAN v. BOSTON INS. CO.
California District Court of Appeal, Second District, 1970.
4 Cal.App.3d 15, 84 Cal.Rptr. 206.

Reppy, J. Appellants, who are copartners, brought this action against six insurance companies to recover the proceeds of policies of fire insurance and interest thereon claimed to be due after a fire damaged the partnership premises which were the subject of the policies. In their answers the insurance companies claimed that such policies were voided when one of the copartners, Irving Zemelman, made false statements on behalf of the partnership in its claim for the proceeds. Five of the insurance companies, who are the respondents herein, were granted summary judgments after both sides joined in a stipulation to the effect that Irving had been convicted of five counts of violating section 556 of the Insurance Code (willfully presenting to insurance company a false and fraudulent claim for the payment of a loss under contract of insurance).

Appellant's briefed contentions are as follows: (1) Willful misrepresentation made by one copartner should not be imputed to an innocent copartner to bar recovery under a policy of fire insurance, and, therefore, there is a triable issue of fact which precludes the court from granting summary judgment, to wit: did the innocent copartner, Hyman, in any way participate in or have knowledge of the fraudulent claim; and (2) even if Irving's acts can be imputed to Hyman, the clause relied on by respondents should not be allowed to void the contract because to do so would be against public policy.

I.

Appellants appear to mistakenly believe that Hyman has an independent claim to one-half of the insurance proceeds which is severable from the claim of his copartner, Irving. Such is not the case when a partnership is involved. Any proceeds which might be recovered become the assets of the partnership. [UPA §8], and so are owned by the partners as tenants in partnership having the incident of undivided ownership in the whole. [UPA §25] Thus, this action, while maintained in the individual names of the copartners, is an attempt to recover partnership assets. If the actions of Irving preclude the partnership from recovery, Hyman cannot recover separately.

The particular relationship between copartners which we focus on in the instant case is explained in an early opinion by our Supreme Court: "All the partners will be bound by the fraud of one of the partners in contracts relating to the partnership made with innocent third parties. That is to say, all are responsible for the injury occasioned by the fraud. ... whether they were cognizant of the fraud or not. The rule is the same as it is in respect to the responsibility of the principal for the fraud of his agent, while acting within the scope of his authority: and, indeed, a partner becomes liable for the fraud of his co-partner, because of the relation each bears to the other of agent in the partnership business." (*Stewart v. Levy*, 36 Cal. 159, 165).

If it can be said that Irving's acts were done within the scope of his authority as a copartner, then the partnership is bound to accept the legal consequences of such acts. [UPA §13] Acts within the scope of authority of a copartner are generally considered to be those which are "... for apparently carrying on in the usual way the business of the partnership of which he is a member. ..." [UPA §9(1)]

Appellants take the position that Irving's acts were not within the scope of his authority as a copartner, relying on *Nuffer v. Insurance Co. of North America*, 236 Cal.App.2d 349, 45 Cal.Rptr. 918. Such reliance is misplaced. In Nuffer an agent had a power of attorney and willfully burned down premises insured under certain fire insurance policies. The appellate court ruled (at p. 357) that a principal is not foreclosed from collecting the proceeds of insurance policies because his agent committed arson, an act not within that agent's apparent authority. In doing so, the court cited certain decisions which held that a principal is responsible for the results of his agent's filing of a false insurance claim even without the principal's knowledge, and distinguished them because in each the false filing was done with apparent authority.

Because the partnership is bound by the acts of Irving, and documentary proof of his conviction (after his plea of "not guilty" and trial before a jury for filing false insurance claims) was attached to respondents' motion for summary judgment, there was no issue of fact to be decided and the trial court was correct in granting the motion.

As a matter of law the insurance contracts were voided and the partnership was foreclosed from receiving any part of their proceeds.

II.

Appellants argue that the clause upon which respondents rely should be declared contrary to public policy when applied to the amount of damages actually brought about by a fire not caused by the insured. This contention was answered by the Fifth Circuit in *Chaachou v. American Central Ins. Co.* (5th Cir.1957) 241 F.2d 889, 892, 893: "The contract does not spell out that it is only false swearing, misrepresentation, concealment or fraud which is successful that avoids the policy. ... A judge-made policy which thus gives advantage to dishonesty will retard, not accelerate, the orderly adjustment of insurance losses." ...

The judgment is affirmed.

Notes

In both *Blackmon* and *Zemelman* an individual has been held liable for a partner's intentional wrongdoings. When one recalls that a "partnership" may be a de facto relationship, one can begin to appreciate the full profile of risk. The immediate rationale in *Blackmon* and *Zemelman* presents significant danger encountered by anyone who elects to conduct any business with more than his own efforts-the law of agency. It is important to understand that agency concepts haunt any business, be it a sole proprietorship (involving more than the sole proprietor's own activity), a partnership (limited or general), or a corporation (close or public). For the sole proprietor entanglements with the law of agency abound in the employer-employee relationship. A business conducted in any other organizational form encounters this problem and more.

Would a superior analysis of *Zemelman* strive for an application of Section 11 of the UPA?

Section 11. Partnership Bound by Admission of Partner

An admission or representation made by any partner concerning partnership affairs within the scope of his authority as conferred by this act is evidence against the partnership.

The partnership is bound by the representation made by Irving, a partner if the representation was within the scope of the partner's authority "... as conferred by this act." Where would we find the authority of Irving to file a claim with insurance carriers for damage to partnership property? Under Section 9(1). This section makes

Irving an agent by virtue of his status as a partner and defines what we might term the "default scope" of his real authority-acts for the purpose of its (the firm's) business. The insurance claim would fall within this definition of the real authority of a partner.

For the purpose of further exploring Section 9(1), let us assume that there were five partners in the firm of Zemelman Brothers. What if they all met in the wake of the fire and formally decided that only Hyman would have real authority to deal with the insurance carriers? Would such an internal decision deprive Irving of real authority to act in this matter? If he defied the decision, and filed the insurance claim, his action would raise the question explored in Ellis as to whether his deed would have been an act for apparently carrying on in the usual way the business of the firm.

ELLIS v. MIHELIS
Supreme Court of California, 1963.
60 Cal.2d 206, 32 Cal.Rptr. 415, 384 P.2d 7.

GIBSON, C.J. Herbert Ellis brought this action against Pericles Mihelis and Elias Mihelis to compel them to specifically perform a contract for the sale of real property and for damages resulting from their failure to convey the property to him. Defendants have appealed from the judgment decreeing specific performance and awarding damages. Plaintiff has cross-appealed on the issue of damages.

The principal contentions of defendants are (1) that plaintiff is precluded from relying on the contract because he was represented in the transaction by an agent whose action was not shown to have been authorized or ratified in writing before defendants refused to perform and (2) that the agreement can in no event be binding on Elias because he did not sign the contract and did not authorize Pericles in writing to enter into it on his behalf. If the first of these contentions is correct plaintiff has no cause of action against either defendant, whereas the second contention, if valid, would not, of course, be determinative of plaintiff's rights as against Pericles. We have concluded that the first contention is untenable but that defendants are correct as to the second point.

Defendants, who are brothers, own two ranches, both operated in the usual manner as ranch or farming property, one by Pericles in Stanislaus County and the other by Elias in Santa Cruz County. In 1948, following the death of a third brother, a judicial decree was entered declaring that both ranches had been owned by the three brothers in joint tenancy with right of survivorship and that upon the death of the brother the title vested absolutely in Pericles and Elias. All income and expense of the two ranches were lumped together for income tax purposes, partnership tax returns were filed with respect to income from the ranches, and the income derived from the two operations was divided equally between the personal income tax returns of the two brothers.

In 1957 the brothers decided to sell the Stanislaus County ranch and agreed that Pericles should handle negotiations for the sale and submit any prospective deals to Elias. Pericles listed the property with a real estate broker in Stanislaus County, George Moreno, telling him that he was the owner.

About this time plaintiff became interested in purchasing a parcel of real property in Alameda County owned by the Ratto family, but the Rattos did not want to sell for cash because of the capital gains tax. They were willing, however, to exchange their property for a ranch, and plaintiff orally authorized Antone L. Ratto, Jr., to act for him in locating and arranging for the purchase of a ranch to effect the exchange. An escrow was opened with an Oakland title company with respect to the Alameda County property, and plaintiff deposited $10,000 in that escrow. Ratto, learning that the Stanislaus ranch was for sale, contacted Moreno and told him of the arrangement between plaintiff and Ratto and of Ratto's interest in purchasing the ranch. Moreno, on the basis of what Pericles had said to him, told Ratto that Pericles was the owner. Ratto and Moreno thereafter informed Pericles of the trade arrangement and explained among other things that plaintiff, not Ratto, was to take title to the Stanislaus property initially.

On April 17, 1958, Pericles and Moreno with the assistance of Pericles' friend, the president of the Stanislaus County Title Company, prepared an instrument using a printed form denominated "Agent's Deposit Receipt." The instrument, bearing the above date, acknowledged receipt of $5,000 as a deposit on account of the purchase price of the described property and provided for a total purchase price of $165,000, the balance to be paid $30,000 within 30 days from date and $130,000 by note bearing interest at 5 per cent per annum, payable in specified installments, and secured by a deed of trust and crop mortgage. It also provided that "the amounts paid hereon" could be retained by the seller as consideration for execution of the agreement if the buyer failed to complete the purchase. On April 17 Pericles signed below a provision which recited, "I (or we) agree to sell and convey the above described property on the terms and conditions herein stated, ..."

Moreno informed Ratto that the agreement had been signed by Pericles. Ratto notified plaintiff, who thereupon instructed him to sign plaintiff's name to the agreement. Pursuant to plaintiff's direction the Oakland title company made out a check in the sum of $5,000 payable to the Stanislaus title company "for the account of Herbert E. Ellis, Jr." On April 19 Ratto delivered the check to Moreno, and the blank space in the agreement for the signature of the buyer was signed by Ratto as follows: "Herbert E. Ellis, Jr. By Antone L. Ratto Jr." Moreno showed the agreement and the check to Pericles who said he was "very satisfied on the whole thing." Pericles asked if he could keep the money, and, when Moreno said that it would have to be deposited with the title company Pericles made no objection. The agreement and check were placed in escrow with the Stanislaus title company and the check was cashed by the title company. Between April 19 and May 2, at the request of Pericles, one of the Ratto brothers and his family moved to Stanislaus County and did some cropdusting on the ranch.

On May 2, 1958, Pericles, Elias, Ratto, and Moreno met at the ranch. Until then, neither Ratto nor Moreno knew that Elias had an interest in the property. Pericles stated that he had changed his mind and did not want to sell, that he was not "going through with the deal," that as a result of a frost occurring a few days earlier which had damaged some vineyards in the area but left his grapes unharmed his crop had become too valuable for him to sell the ranch, and that he could get the same price after the harvest. He also stated, "I will probably have to sell you my half, but my brother doesn't want to sell; Elias doesn't want to wait 10 years." Elias said that he did not want to sell and that he did not want to wait 10 years for his money.

On May 12 plaintiff ratified in writing Ratto's acts in connection with the purchase of the Stanislaus ranch and placed in the escrow the additional $30,000 called for by the agreement, the note for $130,000, the deed of trust, and the crop mortgage.

The trial court found among other things that Pericles and Elias operated the ranch as partners, that the ranch was an asset of the partnership, and that each orally authorized the other to sell the ranch for the partnership. The court also found that Ratto, in executing the contract in plaintiff's name, acted pursuant to express oral authority given by plaintiff, that plaintiff accepted the terms of the agreement and entered into it on April 19, that the agreement was fair and equitable, and that plaintiff offered to perform all its conditions, but that defendants without just cause refused to perform.

Before discussing the principal questions involved, we should point out that we find no merit in defendants' contentions that the contract is too uncertain to be specifically performed and that equity should not enforce it because, assertedly, the arrangement between plaintiff and the Rattos was a scheme to avoid taxes.

[The Court rejected defendants' reliance upon the Statute of Frauds whereby they had sought to attack the authority of Ratto as agent to sign the plaintiff's name to the contract. The Court held that it would be "inequitable to allow the defendants to avoid the agreement because of a lack of written authorization by plaintiff."] ... The refusal of defendants to abide by the agreement was not based on the claim that Ratto lacked written authorization but on the circumstances that the grape crop had increased in value and that Elias did not approve of the agreement. Plaintiff ratified the contract in writing and tendered full performance within the time specified. So far as appears, the defense now urged was an afterthought, raised for the first time when defendants had already obtained everything for which the written authorization could have been important to them, namely, the certainty of full performance by plaintiff.

The claim of a lack of mutuality is likewise untenable. The old doctrine that mutuality of remedy must exist from the time a contract was entered into has been so qualified as to be of little, if any, value, and many authorities have recognized that the only important consideration is whether a court of equity which is asked to specifically enforce a contract against the defendant is able to assure that he will receive the agreed performance from the plaintiff. ...

We conclude that plaintiff was entitled to rely on the agreement whether or not he authorized or ratified Ratto's action in writing before defendants refused to perform.

Although plaintiff may rely on the agreement, it does not follow that he may hold Elias, who did not sign it or authorize Pericles in writing to act as his agent. In seeking to overcome the requirement of the statute of frauds that an agreement for the sale of real property must be signed by the party to be charged or by an agent who has authority in writing, plaintiff contends that there is an overriding provision in the Uniform Partnership Act which is applicable to the facts of this case and which empowered Pericles to bind Elias in the absence of written authority. It may be helpful in this connection to keep in mind that there is no evidence that defendants were in the business of buying and selling real estate or that the sale of the ranch was in the usual course of the partnership business.

The Uniform Partnership Act makes it clear that, unless it is otherwise provided therein, the usual rules of law and equity, including the law of agency, apply. [UPA §4(3), §5] As a provision overriding the statute of frauds plaintiff relies on [UPA §9], which reads in part: "(1) Every partner is an agent of the partnership for the purpose of its business, and the act of every partner, including the execution in the partnership name of any instrument, for apparently carrying on in the usual way the business of the partnership of which he is a member binds the partnership, unless the partner so acting has in fact no authority to act for the partnership in the particular matter, and the person with whom he is dealing has knowledge of the fact that he has no such authority. (2) An act of a partner which is not apparently for carrying on of the business of the partnership in the usual way does not bind the partnership unless authorized by the other partners. (3) Unless authorized by the other partners ..., one or more but less than all the partners have no authority to: (a) Assign the partnership property in trust for creditors or on the assignee's promise to pay the debts of the partnership. (b) Dispose of the good will of the business. (c) Do any other act which would make it impossible to carry on the ordinary business of a partnership. ..."

These provisions distinguish between acts of a partner which bind the partnership because of his status as a partner without any express authority being required and acts binding on the partnership only after express authorization by all partners. Under the express terms of subdivision (1) of the section all acts of a partner which are apparently within the usual course of the particular business bind the partnership. The effect of the provision is that the status of a partner, without more, serves as complete authority with respect to such acts, obviating the necessity of any express authority, either oral or written, from the other members of the firm. It necessarily follows that insofar as a partner limits his conduct to matters apparently within the partnership business, he can bind the other partners without obtaining their written consent. Subdivision (2), however, provides that there must be express authority for acts of a partner which do not appear to be in the usual course of the business. This subdivision does not concern the form of the required express authority, and, unlike the broad provision in subdivision (1), it contains no language which would justify a conclusion that written authority is not necessary in situations where the statute of frauds would ordinarily be applicable.

The distinction made by subdivisions (1) and (2) between acts which are apparently in the usual course of business and those which are not is in accord with the cases in other jurisdictions which have held, without mention of any statutory requirement for written authority of an agent, that a contract executed by one partner alone to sell partnership real estate is binding on the other partners provided the partnership is in the business of buying or selling real estate and the property covered by the contract is part of the stock held for sale. ... The distinction is also followed in [UPA §10] which provides that one partner may convey partnership realty or pass title to a partnership interest in realty depending, in some circumstances, upon whether the partner's act binds the partnership under subdivision (1) of [UPA §9].

Since it does not appear that the sale of the ranch was in the usual course of the partnership business, a contract to sell it would come within subdivision (2) of [UPA §9], not subdivision (1), even if the ranch were a partnership asset as found by the trial court. Accordingly, the statute of frauds would be applicable and Pericles could not bind Elias without authority in writing.

Moreover, the record does not support the finding that the ranch was property of the partnership. There was evidence that the ranch was operated by defendants as partners, but it is not unusual that property be used for partnership purposes and not belong to the partnership. There was no showing that the ranch was acquired for the partnership or with partnership funds or that the partnership existed at the time the ranch was acquired. (See [UPA §8], subds. (1) and (2).) Under circumstances like those involved here, the mere fact that real property belonging to individual partners is used in the partnership business is not sufficient to justify the conclusion that it becomes a partnership asset.

The finding that the ranch was partnership property is not aided by the statement in the memorandum opinion of the trial court that real property improvements, including grapevines, pipeline, and the remodeled portion of the home, were annually depreciated in the partnership income tax returns as assets of the business. Although copies of the tax returns were shown to the trial judge in connection with the amount of damages to be awarded, they were not introduced in evidence.

The statute of frauds precludes enforcement of the agreement against Elias, and the judgment must be reversed as to him. On the record now before us Pericles could be compelled as a joint tenant to convey his half interest in the ranch [citations], but the case was obviously not tried on that theory, and a reversal is also necessary as to Pericles. We, of course, do not know what evidence will be introduced or what remedy will be sought in the event of a retrial. Questions that may arise should plaintiff seek to recover damages against Pericles alone without specific performance or as incident thereto have not been briefed, and we shall not discuss them here. ...

Notes

1. What is wrong with this opinion? Has the court adequately taken into account the content of §9(1)? The court asserts that: ". . . the status of a partner, without more, serves as complete authority with respect to such acts [which are apparently within the usual course of that particular business], obviating the necessity of any express authority, either oral or written, from other members of the firm." What is questionable about this analysis? Is it sound to conclude that the UPA positively commands that "every partner" must have general agent status? If that point were conceded does it follow that the status of agency serves as complete authority with respect to any act which is (or appears to be in furtherance of the usual course of business? How could this court maintain that position given the final phrase in §9(1): ". . . unless the partner so acting has in fact no authority to act for the partnership in the particular matter, and the person with whom he is dealing has knowledge of the fact that he has no such authority."?

Questions such as these bring into sharp focus the need to determine the importance of §9(1) and the degree to which it expands the principal's potential liability for an unauthorized contract because the actor was a partner. To begin the analysis let us briefly recollect the common law position. If a third party seeks to hold an absent principal to a contract negotiated by a purported agent it is the burden of the third party to initially establish the fact of the agency. If the agent is an imposter, the purported principal eludes liability. Assuming proof of the agent's status, the third party must next establish a scope of real authority sufficient to cover the specific transaction. Real authority may be either express or implied. If the third party is unable to establish the real authority of the agent the principal eludes liability unless some doctrine operates to shift the loss from the deceived third party to the betrayed principal. The doctrine of "apparent authority" thus enters the picture only if the third party cannot establish the real authority of the agent. In fact it is an admission that the faithless agent has betrayed his principal. The grievance of the third party is that she was deceived.

The elements of common law apparent authority require more than that the third party establish personal, subjective, good faith deception. Repeatedly courts have insisted that the deception be traced to the acts or omissions of the principal before it even has the potential of shifting loss for the unauthorized transaction. That potential can be carried to recovery only if the third party can establish that a "reasonable person" would also have been deceived by the principal's acts or omissions into -forming a good faith belief in the real authority of the agent. Some courts go even further insisting upon a degree of skill or sagacity for the "reasonable person" which may well exceed that of a novice trader.

Now let us look at §9(1). "Every partner is an agent of the partnership for the purpose of its business. , . . " The irreducible " consequence of this provision is that partnership status confers a general agency upon every partner. It would appear impossible to have a partner who is not an agent. Who or what is the "principal"? Again, the statute supplies an answer, The principal is the "partnership" which means that every partner is both an agent of the firm and, in combination with the other partner or partners, the principal! Yet the terse introductory phrase of Section 9 goes even further. In default of any operative limitation, Section 9 defines the scope of each partner's real authority as the pursuit of firm business. What is to be made of the balance of §9(1)? Few things have been more confusing for courts. Yet isn't it clear that the balance of the section concerns itself with the consequences to the firm of *unauthorized* acts or transactions by a partner? Going beyond common law concepts of apparent authority, the firm is liable for any act by a partner ". . . for apparently carrying on in the usual way the business of the partnership of which [that partner] is a member . . . ." Here is a replacement "information predicate" upon which the third party may rely. If the partner's act appeared to carry on in the usual way the business of the firm the partnership is liable unless the partner in fact had no authority to act for the firm *and* the person with whom the partner dealt had *"knowledge"* of that lack of authority.

Please note that "knowledge" is defined by §3(1) of the UPA in a manner which is much closer to a subjective standard than the imputed knowledge of a "reasonable person" favored by the common law.

When all of these elements are put together are the chances that a partnership will be held liable for an unauthorized transaction enhanced if the actor was a partner? Clearly they are. In addition to the continued applicability of the common law theory of apparent authority, the third party may shift to the notion that the transaction appeared to carry on in the usual way the business of the firm of which that partner was a member and the third party was without actual knowledge of the lack of real authority.

2. A recent decision of the Supreme Court of Iowa re-examined the import of §9(1) as a liability shifting vehicle and also of the belated proof that the act of a partner defied undisclosed oral restrictions on his authority as an agent. In 1976 Kenneth L. Grandquist and two others formed a partnership known as Granson Investment. Shortly thereafter, the partnership purchased a small apartment building in Des Moines. Their written partnership agreement neither specified the business of the firm nor designated the number of partners required to execute conveyances

of partnership real estate. Four years later, the partners agreed to retain Meggison Real Estate to serve as agent in selling the building. Negotiations were commenced with one Peter Kaser. A sharp difference arose as to whether the obligation of the buyer would be limited by a non-recourse note. In the course of the negotiations Kaser joined with several individuals and a local corporation named Kristerin Development, to form a joint venture known as K J Joint Venture. It was the joint venture which was ultimately to be the buyer. A contract structured on a non-recourse manner was eventually prepared by K J and presented to the three partners in Granson. It is clear that two of the Granson partners signed this contract. Kenneth Grandquist did not. There was conflicting evidence as to his reasons including testimony that he informed Kaser that so long as two of his partners had signed his signature was unneeded.

Following the execution of the contract instrument by two partners in Granson negotiations and steps preliminary to performance seemed to occupy the parties for some six months. A title problem was discovered and this was eventually used by Granson in an effort to "cancel" the deal. When Kristerin commenced suit on behalf of the joint venture Granson raised a "no contract" defense. Specifically, the Granson partners asserted that an oral agreement among themselves required all three partners' signatures to bind the partnership on a real estate conveyance.

In reversing a trial court judgment for defendant, Granson, the Supreme Court of Iowa declared:

> Implicated here is the Uniform Partnership Act, Iowa Code chapter 544. Section 544.9 [UPA §9] provides:
>
> > 1. Every partner is an agent of the partnership for the purpose of its business, and the act of every partner, including the execution in the partnership name of any instrument, for apparently carrying on in the usual way the business of the partnership of which he is a member binds the partnership, unless the partner so acting has in fact no authority to tact for the partnership in the particular matter, and the person with whom he is dealing has knowledge of the fact that he has no such authority.

Further, Iowa Code section 544.10 [UPA §10] states that real property held by the partnership may be conveyed by any partner on behalf of the partnership. The partnership, however, may recover such property *'unless* the partner's acts binds the partnership under the provisions of section 544.9[1].'

> Under these provisions one partner can bind the partnership to a contract if he or she appears to act in the usual course of the partnership business. A contract to sell partnership real estate is no exception:
>
> > [A] contract executed by one partner alone to sell partnership real estate is binding on the other partners provided the partnership is in the business of buying or selling real estate. . . . .
>
> [UPA §9(1)] invites a two-step analysis in these situations. First, the fact finder must determine whether the partner or partners executing the agreement

apparently acted to carry on the partnership business in the usual way. An affirmative finding on this step ends the inquiry unless, in the second step of the analysis, it is shown the person with whom the partner was dealing knew the latter in fact had no authority to bind the partnership.

An act that is done "for apparently carrying on in the usual way the business of the partnership," [UPA §9(1)], is an act in furtherance of the partnership business. . . .Moreover, the "apparent scope of the partnership business depends primarily on the conduct of the partnership and its partners and what they cause third persons to believe about the authority of the partners." *Blackmon v. Hale*, 1 Cal.2d 548, 557, 463 P.2d 418, 423, (1970).

We already have noted that here the partnership agreement did not state the business of Granson. Nonetheless, there is substantial evidence in this record upon which the jury could have found Granson was in the business of buying and selling real estate. Netteland testified John Grandquist stated the partnership was in the real estate business. Partner Kenneth L. Grandquist conceded on cross-examination that Granson was formed to buy and sell the apartment building.

Granson suggests the transaction was not in the usual course of business because the 3707 Grand Avenue property was the only asset of the partnership during the relevant period. If, however, the business of Granson was selling this property, the jury could have found the two partners were carrying on business in the usual way when they executed the "offer." In short, the fact this apartment may have been Granson's only asset at the time of these events would not be fatal to Kristerin's claim.

In our analysis we next explore whether, as a matter of law, the two signing partners in fact did not have authority to bind the partnership and KJ knew of that lack of authority. Granson sought to show the three partners had an oral agreement that all partners would be required to execute a contract for sale of real estate in order to bind the partnership. There was scant evidence to show this agreement was communicated to KJ at any relevant time. Moreover, Kristerin produced direct testimony that two partners' signatures were sufficient to bind the partners to the contract. Pertinent here is the reasoning of the California Supreme Court:

> Sound public policy dictates that a partnership must inform those who deal with its members in the course of the partnership's business of any special restrictions on a particular partner's authority. A person dealing with a partnership usually is in no position to know of special agreement3 between the partners, and thus cannot be charged with knowledge of such agreements *absent specific notice.*

Blackmon, 1 Cal.3d at 558, 463 P.2d at 423, (emphasis added). . . .

We hold the contract count should have been submitted to the jury and trial court erred in directing a verdict for Granson on this cause of action.

Kristerin Development Co. v. Granson Inv., 394 N.W.2d 325, 329-31 (Iowa, 1986).

3. However construed, one might ask what relevance Section 9(1) had to the claim of Ellis against the Mihelis brothers? Unlike the facts in *Granson* in which the purchasers were aware that the seller was a partnership and knew the identity of each of the three partners, it seems clear from the record that at all material times Ratto, Moreno and Ellis assumed that Pericles Mihelis was the sole owner of the Stanislaus County ranch. If no one suspected that Pericles was a member of any partnership how could it be said that an impression had been formed that the agreement to sell the ranch was an act apparently carrying on in the usual way the business of the firm? Put another way, is it a minimum predicate to the use, of Section 9(1) to go beyond common law liability theories that the third party have believed that he was dealing with a *partner*?

Assuming that this question can be resolved we pass to the issue of what is apparently "usual". Here it seems that the fact patterns could range along a continuum from the strongest to the weakest case.

Suppose that a candy store, conducted as a partnership, bought and sold rare books from time to time. One day your client entered the store and formed an executory contract with an individual she recognized as one of the partners. Under the terms of the contract she was to sell the store a rare first edition of this book bearing the autograph of the author. The price was $10,000. Later, the other partners denied liability on the contract. They have produced the minutes of a partnership meeting held one week prior to the formation of the agreement with your client in which, by a vote of six to two, they have decided to abandon all future dealings in rare books. What would you deem the chances of recovery against the partnership? Consider the following further facts:

Variation f# 1: your client had sold rare books to this particular candy store on two prior occasions in the course of which she had dealt exclusively with the very partner who formed the disputed contract.

Variation # 2: your client had never had any direct dealings with the candy store but had heard from two friends that they had sold rare books to an individual who fit the physical description of the partner with whom your client eventually dealt.

Variation # 3: your client had no history of prior experience with the candy store nor had she ever heard that it dealt in rare books. It merely happened that she had the book in her possession on the day she wandered into the store in search of dietetic fudge.

Isn't it obvious that your client stands the greatest chance of success using a §9(1) theory in Variation # 1? On those facts your client could form a personal impression that the offer to purchase the book for $10,000 was an act for apparently carrying on in the usual way the business of the firm. Obviously she was not subjectively aware of the earlier meeting which had terminated the partner's real authority. In the second variation the client would lack any direct impression of what was "usual" but could rely upon her vicarious experience to form such an assessment. Again, she would be innocent of actual knowledge of the partner's lack of real authority. The third variation sees the client vulnerable to the accusation that she could have had no subjective impression of what was "usual" and thus no expectation worthy of protection under §9(1). But suppose that her expectation was premised upon conduct of other candy stores in the area which, from time to time in our hypothetical community, purchased and sold rare books. Could this information contribute to an impression of what was usual without doing violence to the language of §9(1)?

Several of these questions, along with issues surrounding the burden of proof, were before the court in *Burns v. Gonzales*, 439 S.W.2d 128, 131-132 (Tex.Civ. App. 1969):

> As we interpret Sec. 9(1), the act of a partner binds the firm, absent an express limitation of authority known to the party dealing with such partner, if such act is for the purpose of 'apparently carrying on' the business of the partnership in the way in which other firms engaged in the same business in the same locality usually transact business, or in the way in which the particular partnership usually transacts its business. In this case, there is no evidence relating to the manner in which firms engaged in the sale of advertising time on radio stations usually transact business. Specifically, there is no evidence as to whether or not the borrowing of money, or the execution of negotiable instruments, was incidental to the transaction of business 'in the usual way,' by other advertising agencies or by this partnership, InterAmerican Advertising Agency. It becomes important, therefore, to determine the location of the burden of proof concerning the 'usual way' of transacting business by advertising agencies.

> Sec. 9(1) states that the act of a partner 'for apparently carrying on in the usual way the business of the partnership' binds the firm. This language does not place the burden of proof on the non-participating partner to establish the non-existence of the facts which operate to impose liability on the firm. If the Legislature had intended to place the burden of proof on the non-participating partner, it could have done so easily. The statute could have been drafted to declare that the act of a partner binds the firm 'unless it is shown that such act was not apparently carrying on in the usual way the business of the partnership.' Actually, the liability-imposing language of Sec. 9(1) indicates that the burden of proof is on the person seeking to hold the nonparticipating partner accountable. . . .

> We conclude that, under a reasonable interpretation of the language of Sec. 9(1), and the provision of the Rule 93(h) [Texas Rules of Civil Procedure], the burden of proving the 'usual way' in which advertising agencies transact business was upon Burns.

4. Returning to a more substantive consideration, *Swanson v. Webb Tractor & Equipment Co.*, 24 Wash.2d 631, 167 P.2d 146 (1946), advances an interesting view on the apparent and implied real authority of partners as agents.

> The powers, actual or implied, of a special partner are much more limited than those of a general partner, and the presumptions which arise from the one relationship are in some respects the converse of those arising from the other. In

Snively v. Matheson, 12 Wash. 88, 40 P. 628, 629, 50 Am.St.Rep. 877, we find this statement defining the distinction between a general partnership and a special, or non-trading, partnership: "The general rule is that, so far as a general partnership, or, in other words, a trading or mercantile partnership, is concerned, each partner constitutes the other his agent for the purpose of entering into all contracts for him within the scope of the partnership business. This power rests in the usage of merchants, and grew out of the necessities of commercial business. Therefore the doctrine of implied liability received the sanction of the law, and has for a long time been, and now is, enforced by the courts. But this implied liability does not extend to partners in non-trading partnerships. In such cases the rule announced above is reversed, and the presumption is that one partner has no power to bind the other partners. Hence, before recovery can be obtained upon a contract entered into by one partner in a non-trading partnership against the other partners, it must be affirmatively shown by the party attempting to bind the noncontracting partners, either that the authority to bind was conferred by the articles of incorporation (co-partnership), or that authority had been specially conferred, or that it had been the custom of such partnership to recognize this right to such an extent as would give innocent dealers a right to reply upon the custom."

So far as third persons are concerned, the authority of a partner, whether he be a member of a general partnership or of a special partnership, must be found in the actual agreement of the partners, or through implication arising from the nature of the business or the actual or usual manner in which it is conducted by the particular partnership or by similar partnerships in the same locality, or else from a reasonable inference of its necessity or fitness for the successful operation of the particular partnership business.

Washington adopted the Uniform Partnership Act with an effective date of March 15, 1945. Is there any authority in the UPA for the court's perpetuation of a special/general partnership dichotomy? Why create a rule which distinguishes between "mercantile" and "non-trading" partnerships? Can the distinction be reconciled with the UPA's definition of a partnership or with the terms of §9.1? In 1987 the Missouri Court of Appeals concluded that, given the legislative adoption of the UPA in 1949, the "distinction between trading and non-trading partnerships is no longer relevant to the issue of partner agency authority." *Schnucks Markets, Inc. v. Cassilly*, 724 S.W.2d 664, 667 (1987).

For a more recent example of the Washington court's work see *Herr v. Brakefield*, 50 Wash.2d 593, 314 P.2d 397 (1957). The *Herr* opinion is an interesting contrast to *Ellis v. Mihelis, supra*, in that it finds liability for the partnership in a rural setting when one of the members sold a herd of cattle to the plaintiff. The court declared:

> While the evidence regarding the practice of selling entire herds of cattle would not lead to the inference that such a sale was necessary to the successful conduct of the cattle business and the farming operation, the showing was that such sales were not unusual and were appropriate and not ordinarily detrimental

to enterprises of this kind. Especially in view of the fact that the sale of this herd did not destroy the farming operation and the further fact that Brakefield had, in all of the plaintiff's dealings with him, acted as the managing partner with the tacit consent of Mrs. Stidham, we believe that the court was unjustified in concluding that he had no apparent authority to make the sale in question.

If Mrs. Stidham has been deceived by her partner, she has her remedy against him.

The court's statement that the sale did not "destroy the farming operation" suggests categorization under §9(3) of the UPA. The Act declares that real authority to deal with any of the enumerated transactions must be traced to express authority granted by the other partners. Does this provision preclude the possibility that liability on an unauthorized entry into one of these transactions could be sustained on a theory of apparent authority?

Problem

Suppose a partnership had tolerated Partner X's submitting a partnership claim to arbitration. Later, the other partners declared their displeasure to Partner X, but said nothing beyond the privacy of their immediate circle. Five months later a controversy arose with the same third party. Partner X again submitted the claim to arbitration. At that point the other partners seek to avoid the arbitration by citing certain proof of Partner X's lack of express real authority. Result?

Liability in tort: At common law a master was liable for the torts of a servant agent provided that they arose within the course of employment and not while the agent was engaged in a personal frolic. What of the tortfessor was a partner?

Section 13. Partnership Bound by Partner's Wrongful Act

Where, by any wrongful act or omission of any partner acting in the ordinary course of the business of the partnership or with the authority of his co-partners, loss or injury is caused to any person, not being a partner in the partnership, or any penalty is incurred, the partnership is liable therefor to the same extent as the partner so acting or omitting to act.

At a minimum it would appear that Section 13 resolves the first of the common law issues, sets the stage for determining the second, and is totally silent as to the third. The terms of the statute would appear to preclude the "servant vs. independent contractor" defense. If the tortfeasor is a partner there is an immediate potential of firm liability. The second issue surrounds the "scope of employment". Here the statute contributes the test which is to be employed. The firm is liable if the partner was acting in the "ordinary course of the business of the partnership or with the authority of co-partners." What of the "frolic vs. deviation" defense of last resort? The statute is totally silent. Should this silence be taken as an indication that the legislature intended to preclude such a defense?

For an interesting application of §13 see, *Wheeler v. Green*, 286 Or. 99, 593 P.2d 777, 792 (1979). Wheeler, a trainer of race horses, commenced an action for defamation against his former employers Green and Wassenberg, partners doing business as "Green Acres Appaloosas." Wheeler alleged that at a dinner party Green stated to his companion, another owner of appaloosas, that Wheeler had beaten a horse with a chain in an attempt to have the animal scratched from a race. Wheeler asserted that the statement was actionable as a tort to his reputation and that liability would extend beyond the orator, Green, to embrace the partnership. To the extent that firm assets would prove insufficient to cover any judgment, Wheeler claimed the several liability of Wassenberg under §15(a) of the UPA. In reversing a trial court judgment against Wassenberg the Supreme Court of Oregon declared:

> With respect to the statement of Green to Mr. Bates that plaintiff had beaten Bate's horse, the jury's verdict was against all defendants, and the trial court entered judgment accordingly. The trial court erred in refusing to direct a verdict on that cause of action in favor of all defendants except Green.
>
> The statement was made during a social occasion. There was evidence that Wassenberg was present at the time, but no evidence whatsoever that Wassenberg even participated in this part of the conversation. The jury could not have found, on the evidence before it, that he indicated agreement with Green's statement, or that he joined in any way in making it. There was clearly no evidentiary basis for finding him directly liable for this statement.
>
> There was evidence from which the jury could find that Green and Wassenberg were partners, under the name of Green Acres Appaloosas, in the business of racing horses. Partners are jointly and severally liable for the tortious acts of other partners if they have authorized those acts or if the wrongful acts are committed "in the ordinary course of the business of the partnership." ... Assuming the jury found the existence of a partnership, however, the evidence was still insufficient to warrant a finding that Wassenberg was vicariously liable for Green's statement. There was no evidence to support a finding that Wassenberg authorized Green to speak for the partnership in this way, and no basis for finding that this kind of dinner conversation was within the "ordinary course" of the partnership business. Wassenberg was entitled to a directed verdict.

B. PROBLEMS PECULIAR TO A TWO-MEMBER PARTNERSHIP

NATIONAL BISCUIT CO., INC. v. C.N. STROUD, ET AL.
Supreme Court of North Carolina, 1959.
249 N.C. 467, 106 S.E.2d 692.

The case was heard in the Superior Court upon the following agreed statement of facts:

On 13 September 1956 the National Biscuit Company had a Justice of the Peace to issue summons against C.N. Stroud and Earl Freeman, a partnership trading as Stroud's Food Center, for the nonpayment of $171.04 for goods sold and delivered. After a hearing the Justice of the Peace rendered judgment for plaintiff against both defendants for $171.04 with interest and costs. Stroud appealed to the Supreme Court: Freeman did not.

In March 1953 C.N. Stroud and Earl Freeman entered into a general partnership to sell groceries under the name of Stroud's Food Center. Thereafter plaintiff sold bread regularly to the partnership. Several months prior to February 1956 the defendant Stroud advised an agent of plaintiff that he personally would not be responsible for any additional bread sold by plaintiff to Stroud's Food Center. From 6 February 1956 to 25 February 1956 plaintiff through this same agent, at the request of the defendant Freeman, sold and delivered bread in the amount of $171.04 to Stroud's Food Center. Stroud and Freeman by agreement dissolved the partnership at the close of business on 25 February 1956, and notice of such dissolution was published in a newspaper in Carteret County 6-27 March 1956.

The relevant parts of the dissolution agreement are these: All partnership assets, except an automobile truck, an electric adding machine, a rotisserie, which were assigned to defendant Freeman, and except funds necessary to pay the employees for their work the week before the dissolution and necessary to pay for certain supplies purchased the week of dissolution, were assigned to Stroud. Freeman assumed the outstanding liens against the truck. Paragraph five of the dissolution agreement is as follows: "From and after the aforesaid February 25, 1956, Stroud will be responsible for the liquidation of the partnership assets and the discharge of partnership liabilities without demand upon Freeman for any contribution in the discharge of said obligations." The dissolution agreement was made in reliance on Freeman's representations that the indebtedness of the partnership was about $7,800 and its accounts receivable were about $8,000. The accounts receivable at the close of business actually amounted to $4,897.41.

Stroud has paid all of the partnership obligations amounting to $12,014.45, except the amount of $171.04 claimed by plaintiff. To pay such obligations Stroud exhausted all the partnership assets he could reduce to money amounting to $4,307.08, of which $2,028.64 was derived from accounts receivable and $2,278.44 from a sale of merchandise and fixtures, and used over $7,700 of his personal money. Stroud has left of the partnership assets only uncollected accounts in the sum of $2,868.77, practically all of which are considered uncollectible.

Stroud has not attempted to rescind the dissolution agreement, and has tendered plaintiff, and still tenders it, one-half of the $171.04 claimed by it.

From a judgment that plaintiff recover from the defendants $171.04 with interest and costs, Stroud appeals to the Supreme Court.

PARKER, JUSTICE.

C.N. Stroud and Earl Freeman entered into a general partnership to sell groceries under the firm name of Stroud's Food Center. There is nothing in the agreed statement of facts to indicate or suggest that Freeman's power and authority as a general partner were in any way restricted or limited by the articles of partnership in respect to the ordinary and legitimate business of the partnership. Certainly, the purchase and sale of bread were ordinary and legitimate business of Stroud's Food Center during its continuance as a going concern.

Several months prior to February 1956 Stroud advised plaintiff that he personally would not be responsible for any additional bread sold by plaintiff to Stroud's Food Center. After such notice to plaintiff, it from 6 February 1956 to 25 February 1956, at the request of Freeman, sold and delivered bread in the amount of $171.04 to Stroud's Food Center.

In *Johnson v. Bernheim*, 76 N.C. 139, this Court said: "A and B are general partners to do some given business; the partnership is, by operation of law, a power to each to bind the partnership in any manner legitimate to the business. If one partner go to a third person to buy an article on time for the partnership, the other partner cannot prevent it by writing to the third person not to sell to him on time; or, if one party attempt to buy for cash, the other has no right to require that it shall be on time. And what is true in regard to buying is true in regard to selling. What either partner does with a third person is binding on the partnership. It is otherwise where the partnership is not general, but is upon special terms, as that purchases and sales must be with and for cash. There the power to each is special, in regard to all dealings with third persons at least who have notice of the terms." There is contrary authority. 68 C.J.S. Partnership § 143, pp. 578-579. However, this text of C.J.S. does not mention the effect of the provisions of the Uniform Partnership Act.

The General Assembly of North Carolina in 1941 enacted a Uniform Partnership Act, which became effective 15 March 1941. . . .

[UPA §9] is entitled "Partner Agent of Partnership as to Partnership Business", and subsection (1) reads: "Every partner is an agent of the partnership for the purpose of its business, and the act of every partner, including the execution in the partnership name of any instrument, for apparently carrying on in the usual way the business of the partnership of which he is a member binds the partnership, unless the partner so acting has in fact no authority to act for the partnership in the particular matter, and the person with whom he is dealing has knowledge of the fact that he has no such authority." [UPA §9(4)] states: "No act of a partner in contravention of a restriction on authority shall bind the partnership to persons having knowledge of the restriction."

G.S. § 59-45 provides that "all partners are jointly and severally liable for the acts and obligations of the partnership." [Compare to UPA §15 ed.]

[UPA §18] is captioned "Rules Determining Rights and Duties of Partners." Subsection (e) thereof reads: "All partners have equal rights in the management and conduct of the partnership business." Subsection (h) hereof is as follows: "Any difference arising as to ordinary matters connected with the partnership business may be decided by a majority of the partners; but no act in contravention of any agreement between the partners may be done rightfully without the consent of all the partners."

Freeman as a general partner with Stroud, with no restrictions on his authority to act within the scope of the partnership business so far as the agreed statement of facts shows, had under the Uniform Partnership Act "equal rights in the management and conduct of the partnership business." Under [§18](h) Stroud, his co-partner, could not restrict the power and authority of Freeman to buy bread for the partnership as a going concern, for such a purchase was an "ordinary matter connected with the partnership business," for the purpose of its business and within its scope, because in the very nature of things Stroud was not, and could not be, a majority of the partners. Therefore, Freeman's purchases of bread from plaintiff for Stroud's Food Center as a going concern bound the partnership and his co-partner Stroud. The quoted provisions of our Uniform Partnership Act, in respect to the particular facts here, are in accord with the principle of law stated in *Johnson v. Bernheim*, supra; same case 86 N.C. 339.

In Crane on Partnership, 2d Ed., p. 277, it is said: "In cases of an even division of the partners as to whether or not an act within the scope of the business should be done, of which disagreement a third person has knowledge, it seems that logically no restriction can be placed upon the power to act. The partnership being a going concern, activities within the scope of the business should not be limited, save by the expressed will of the majority deciding a disputed question; half of the members are not a majority."

. . .

At the close of business on 25 February 1956 Stroud and Freeman by agreement dissolved the partnership. By their dissolution agreement all of the partnership assets, including cash on hand, bank deposits and all accounts receivable, with a few exceptions, were assigned to Stroud, who bound himself by such written dissolution agreement to liquidate the firm's assets and discharge its liabilities. It would seem a fair inference from the agreed statement of facts that the partnership got the benefit of the bread sold and delivered by plaintiff to Stroud's Food Center, at Freeman's request, from 6 February 1956 to 25 February 1956. See *Blackstone Guano Co. v. Ball*, 201 N.C. 534, 160 S.E. 769. But whether it did or not, Freeman's acts, as stated above, bound the partnership and Stroud.

The judgment of the court below is affirmed.

Note

Given this court's reasoning, what steps could Stroud have taken in the winter of 1955 to evade liability for an order of ten thousand crates of "people crackers" placed by Freeman on February 10, 1956?

Problems inherent in a two-partner firm were considered in *Summers v. Dooley*, 94 Idaho 87, 481 P.2d 318, 320-21 (1971). The result reached in Summers should be compared with that attained in *National Biscuit*. Summers and Dooley were partners in a trash collecting business. In the absence of an explicit partnership agreement the court presumed that they were "equal partners." In July 1966 Summers sought Dooley's agreement to hire a third person. Dooley refused. Despite his knowledge that his partner had refused agreement, Summers hired the individual and used his personal funds to pay him, eventually paying him more than $11,000. When Dooley continued to refuse to allow partnership funds to be used to meet this business expense or to reimburse Summers, litigation was commenced. The trial court refused to hold the protesting partner liable for any part of the "unauthorized expenses." On appeal The Supreme Court of Idaho declared: "The issue presented for decision by this appeal is whether an equal partner in a two-man partnership has the authority to hire a new employee in disregard of the objection of the other partner and then attempt to charge the dissenting partner with the costs incurred as a result of his unilateral decision."

The answer was "no." The court focused on §18(h) of the UPA [I.C. §318(8)], which provides that any difference arising as to ordinary matters connected with the partnership business may be decided by a "majority of the partners ...." This language was interpreted to mean that a change in the status quo could only be made by a majority vote. In a two-member firm a majority cannot be formed in a disagreement. Is this result consistent with *National Biscuit*?

C. VIEWING THE PARTNERSHIP FROM WITHIN—THE QUEST FOR STATUS

Review Part IV, §§18-23 of the Uniform Partnership Act. There are three topics to study in relation to the human problems covered by part IV of the UPA:

1. A partner's status in the control and management of the firm. Pay particular attention to §18 of the Act and the content of *McCallum v. Asbury* (Oregon, 1964), which follows.

2. A partner's standing to claim compensation from the firm for services rendered. Refer to §18 of the Act and the case of *Busick v. Stoetzl* (Cal.Ct.App., 1968), infra.

3. The concept that partners are fiduciaries one unto another. Examine §§19, 20, and 21. Two aspects of recurrent controversies in this area will be considered:

a. Access to the firm's books and records, and the ability to force a partner to yield information about knowledge and activities.

b. The question of what are "personal" business opportunities which a partner may exploit to his own advantage, in contrast to those opportunities which a partner must share or at least offer to share with his partners as a pre-condition to personal exploitation.

1. Control and management:

McCALLUM v. ASBURY ET AL.
Supreme Court of Oregon, 1964.
238 Or. 257, 393 P.2d 774.

GOODWIN, J. This is a suit between individuals practicing medicine as partners. The plaintiff sued to dissolve the partnership and for other relief. The remaining partners answered with a counterclaim for an injunction to enforce against the plaintiff a restrictive covenant contained in the partnership agreement. The covenant, if enforced, would prohibit the plaintiff for ten years from practicing medicine in Corvallis or within 30 miles of that city.

The trial court entered a decree denying relief to the plaintiff in his suit for dissolution, and also denying injunctive relief to the defendants. All parties appeal.

The plaintiff is a surgeon formerly associated with the Corvallis Clinic. The Corvallis Clinic was organized by three doctors in 1947. By 1962 seventeen doctors, ten of whom were partners, were associated with the clinic. After having been employed by the clinic for almost two years, the plaintiff became a partner in 1953. Some of the defendant partners had entered the firm before the plaintiff did, and others entered after the plaintiff had become a partner. The provisions of the partnership agreement material to this case were renewed each time a new partner came into the firm.

Growth and prosperity did not produce harmony. Differences about the proper management of the clinic arose between the plaintiff and his fellow doctors. The areas of disagreement between the plaintiff and his partners grew, and the working relationship among the partners began to suffer. The disagreements involved honest differences of opinion about the best way to run a business, and did not reflect adversely upon the professional abilities of any of the parties.

The defendants seek to enforce a provision of the agreement which permits a majority of the partners to expel a partner and buy his interest. They also seek to enforce a restriction upon the right of the departing partner to compete with the partnership. Neither provision is ambiguous.

The trial court held that the plaintiff was released from his obligation to comply with the terms of the agreement because the defendants breached the agreement before he sought to dissolve the partnership. The majority, over the protest of the plaintiff, had created an executive committee to:

"... manage generally all affairs of the partnership except that the committee shall have no authority to enter into any employment contract with a physician for services as a medical doctor, shall not take any action which is discriminating against any partner or partners, and shall exercise no power expressly reserved to the partnership by the Partnership Agreement."

The court reasoned that the majority of the partners had no right to form the executive committee and to delegate to that committee the management of the business affairs of the clinic.

Section 8 of the partnership agreement reads as follows:

"All partners shall have an equal share in the management of the business and all decisions pertaining to the partnership, not herein specifically provided for, including amendment of this contract, shall be decided by a majority vote of the partners. Provided that any amendments of this agreement shall not be discriminating against any partner or partners."

[UPA §18(h)] provides as follows:

"Any difference arising as to ordinary matters connected with the partnership business may be decided by a majority of the partners; but no act in contravention of any agreement between the partners may be done rightfully without the consent of all the partners."

The public statute and the private agreement must be examined together. See 1 Rowley, Partnership 500, §18h (2d ed 1960).

Fundamental changes in a partnership agreement may not be made without the consent of all the parties. This is true even though the agreement may provide that it can be amended by majority vote. The power to amend is limited by the rule that, unless unanimous, no amendment may be in contravention of the agreement. [UPA §18(h)].

The plaintiff insists that even though he had agreed in advance that the majority of the partners could amend the agreement, the executive-committee amendment was so broad that it was inconsistent with the agreement between the partners and was beyond the scope of the power of amendment under the agreement.

The defendants insist that the institution of an executive committee was well within the terms of the agreement. They further contend that even if the creation of the committee was not within the expressed grant of power to the majority to amend the agreement, the right to delegate routine functions to a committee would have to be implied from the purposes for which the partners had associated themselves. At the heart of this dispute is the question of the scope of the management powers delegated to the committee.

The amendment provided that any action taken by the committee could be altered or canceled by a majority vote of the partners. The majority of the partners retained the right to reconstitute the committee. All members of the partnership retained the right to attend all meetings of the committee. However, when attending a meeting, any partner who was not a member of the executive committee was not entitled to participate in committee deliberations unless given permission to do so.

A safeguard of the rights of all partners was provided in the requirement that ten days must elapse before any action, other than emergency action, taken by the committee would become effective. This delay gave a majority of the partners a power to override the committee at any time during the ten days that intervened between committee action and execution. There is no evidence that the emergency clause was intended to subvert the right of review. On the contrary, it is presumed that the clause was intended to be employed in good faith. We hold that these limitations upon the committee's power kept the delegation well within the scope and intent of the original partnership agreement.

The plaintiff for several years had not shared some of the views of the majority with reference to billing practices. These differences in views were expressed at various partnership meetings. It appeared likely that the differences would continue. The plaintiff's views were no less likely to prevail after the committee was formed than they were before it was created.

When it appeared to a majority of the partners that dissension was defeating the purposes for which the partners had associated themselves, they had a right to buy out the dissenting partner. The plaintiff understood this when he became a partner.

The plaintiff contends that, even if there had been no breach of the agreement by the defendants, the court should not enjoin him from practicing medicine in the city of Corvallis and the surrounding territory. The plaintiff says that the hardship to him would greatly outweigh any resulting benefit to the remaining partners. He also argues that the community will suffer if the injunction is allowed.

While it is true that courts of equity may refuse to enforce contracts if great hardship will be suffered on one side without a compensating benefit on the other, we do not believe this is a case that justifies the repudiation of the contract. In 1953 when the plaintiff was considering whether or not to accept the financial rewards offered by the partnership, he consulted counsel and delayed his decision for five months while he weighed the advantages and disadvantages of the partnership agreement. During these deliberations the restrictive covenant was his principal concern. In due course he executed the agreement and accepted the benefits thereof for several years. The benefits were substantial. As other young doctors came into the firm on the same terms, he renewed the agreement, binding the newcomers to the same covenant.

Obviously, it is a serious matter to uproot a professional man from the community in which he has developed his practice and served his profession. However, a breach of a covenant solemnly bargained for and entered into between thoughtful men of affairs is also a serious matter. *Cogley Clinic v. Martini*, 253 Iowa 541, 112 N.W.2d 678 (1962). If the plaintiff in this case can repudiate his agreement, then it would be idle to put such restrictions into similar partnership agreements.

Partnership under agreements which restrict future competition appears to be a common avenue of professional advancement. From the number of cases dealing with this kind of contract, it may be inferred that doctors, like other people, sometimes want to be relieved of contractual obligations. A young professional man may be willing to trade his future right to compete in a given community for an immediate and lucrative share in an established practice. Difficulties arise when one of the contracting parties changes his mind. ...

We do not believe the limitations as to space and time in this case are unreasonable. Relying upon the agreement, the partners invested substantial sums in the capital assets of the partnership. They have a right to the protection for which they bargained.

In view of the legitimate desire of the partners to provide realistic protection of their investment, the restriction of competition within 30 miles of Corvallis is not unreasonable. Because of the wide area from which the clinic draws its patients, the relocation of any former partner within 30 miles of Corvallis would defeat the purposes of the restriction. ...

The time limitation is not unreasonable. While ten years is a substantial portion of the active life of a professional man, it is not uncommon for medical practitioners to enter into such covenants. See 41 A.L.R.2d 15, supra at 212. Under all the circumstances of this case, there is nothing about the period of ten years that should render the covenant unenforceable.

The only evidence that the city of Corvallis will suffer by the removal of the plaintiff to another city came from the doctor with whom the plaintiff is presently sharing office space. The other evidence in the record indicates that surgical patients in Corvallis will not suffer undue hardship if the plaintiff is required to live up to the bargain he made when he became a partner in the clinic.

Upon the whole record, the defendants were entitled to the enforcement of the agreement. A decree should be entered in their favor.

Reversed and remanded; costs to none of the parties.

Notes

McCallum v. Asbury contains an important construction of §18 of the Uniform Partnership Act. It is often said that a partnership may be a de facto relationship with no formalities. But, obviously, a partnership need not be informal. Many detractors also note that it is difficult to centralize authority in a partnership. This is true in respect to limiting liability to third parties, as we have seen in §§9, 3 and 14 of the Act. Yet the rights of equal control and management of the partnership business, granted in §18(e), may be modified by agreement. Indeed, *McCallum* suggests that the partners may agree to any arrangement, including an executive committee, so long as they obey a single statutory command. Given this broad license, the attorney has a vital service to perform in drafting the terms of a partnership agreement. Begin by asking who your client is. Assume that ten physicians in your office announce their desire to form a partnership. What is the first thing you will want to warn them about the "law"?

Two other aspects of this opinion are noteworthy. Under §18(g) partners have a right to choose who may become new partners. What is the court's authority for the conclusion that a majority of the existing members may reserve the right to expel a partner? Not only do the remaining members gain a recognition of this right, but they gain an extraordinary equitable remedy in support of its effective exercise. Is there any reason why a court of equity should be more receptive to a "non-competition" clause in a partnership agreement than to such a clause in an employment contract? See *Gibson v. Angros*, 30 Colo.App. 95, 491 P.2d 87 (1971).

2. The issue of compensation:

BUSICK v. STOETZL
Court of Appeals, Fifth District, 1968.
264 Cal.App.2d 736, 70 Cal.Rptr. 581.

STONE, J. This is an appeal from an interlocutory judgment in a partnership dissolution action. Prior to July 19, 1950, Valley Feed & Fuel Company did business as a corporation. It then changed to a partnership, former shareholders taking an interest in the ratio to their ownership of corporate shares. The partnership business that emerged was composed of three husbands and wives: plaintiff, Anna Busick, then Anna Betters, and Walter, her deceased husband, Ralph E. and Rolline Stoetzl, and William and Cora Frey. The written partnership agreement vested management of the business in the three husbands, each of whom received a monthly salary, set from time to time by mutual consent of the partners. Inactive partners drew no salaries.

On July 1, 1957, the Stoetzls and the Betters purchased the interest of the Freys, each purchasing in proportion to his then interest in the partnership. Walter Betters and Ralph Stoetzl continued to manage the business and draw salaries. On November 21, 1959, Walter Betters died and Ralph Stoetzl assumed full management of the partnership affairs. Later, Ralph E. Stoetzl, Jr., joined the partnership by purchasing part of his parents' interest. The trial court found the partnership interests to be: Anna Rose Betters Busick, 33 percent; Ralph E. Stoetzl, Sr., 26 percent; Rolline Stoetzl, 26 percent; and Ralph E. Stoetzl,

Jr., 15 percent. Although no new written partnership agreement was executed after Mr. Betters' death, the trial court found that with each change in partner personnel the existing partnership terminated and a new one was formed, in part by express oral agreement and in part by implied agreement.

Perhaps the most critical finding insofar as this appeal is concerned is that under each agreement Ralph Stoetzl, the only active managing partner, was entitled to receive a salary. Stoetzl received yearly salaries, paid in monthly installments, as follows: $11,004 for the years 1960, 1961 and 1962. $14,117 for the year 1963, $14,400 for the years 1964, 1965 and January through March 1966, $20,000.04 April through December 1966 and for the year 1967. However, the court found that plaintiff agreed to the yearly salary of $11,004 only, that she did not agree to the increased amounts commencing with the year 1963. The court ordered Stoetzl to reimburse the partnership for all amounts received as salary over and above the sum of $11,004 per year, although it found that the increased amounts were justified, that Stoetzl properly managed the business, that he operated it at a profit each year, and that in each year the reasonable value of his services exceeded the amount he received in salary. Ralph Stoetzl has not appealed from the order to reimburse salary received in excess of $11,004 per year.

Plaintiff appeals from the judgment ratifying the annual salary of $11,004 contending that Stoetzl is entitled to no salary at all for his management of the business, upon the ground that she did not agree that the partnership should pay him a salary after the death of her husband terminated the original partnership agreement. She relies primarily upon [UPA §18], which provides:

"The rights and duties of the partners in relation to the partnership shall be determined, subject to any agreement between them, by the following rules:

"...

"(e) All partners have equal rights in the management and conduct of the partnership business.

"(f) No partner is entitled to remuneration for acting in the partnership business, except that a surviving partner is entitled to reasonable compensation for his services in winding up the partnership affairs."

Plaintiff argues the code section must be narrowly and literally applied and that absent a definite, express agreement a managing partner cannot be paid a salary. This contention is not new, nor is it the law.

The courts have not hesitated to find an implied agreement within the rationale of [§18] when fair play impels such a result. Not infrequently the rationalization has been a parallel between the efforts of a partner who devotes his time to the partnership business, keeping it operating successfully, on the one hand, and use of the capital investment on the other. Each is rewarded separately, as each constitutes a separate, distinct and necessary contribution to the partnership. Over a hundred years ago the Supreme Court held, in *Griggs v. Clark*, 23 Cal. 427, 430-431: "While all the parties are living, each is under obligation to devote his time and services to the partnership business, and there is therefore good reason for holding that neither should receive a compensation for such services. But, when, in consequence of the death of one partner, this equality no longer exists, it is but equitable that the surviving partner should be compensated for such services as he may have rendered in the business after the death of the deceased partner, to be deducted out of the profits realized by the continuance of the business; and the overplus of such profits, after deducting such compensation, to be divided between the partners."

Here, the business was operated profitably every year and each partner received his share of the profits. The capital investment also showed a considerable increase in value. Under the doctrine of *Griggs v. Clark*, supra, Stoetzl, who made this possible by devoting his time to the successful management of the business, was entitled to receive a reasonable salary.

Although Griggs was decided long before the enactment of [UPA §18], the Supreme Court followed the same reasoning in *Vangel v. Vangel*, 45 Cal.2d 804, 291 P.2d 25, 55 A.L.R.2d 1385, decided after the enactment of [§18]. The Supreme Court said, at pages 808-809: "[UPA §42] fixes the right of one retired from a partnership for cause, or the personal representative of a deceased partner, to recover compensation for the use of his assets in the continuing business pending an accounting. In such case, he is entitled to 'the profits attributable to the use of his right in the property.' As a practical matter, his share of the profits usually is computed on the basis of the ratio that his share of the partnership assets bears to the whole of them. (Citations.) However, that division may not be equitable when the contribution to profits from capital is relatively minor in comparison to the contribution from the skills or services of one conducting the business. In such a case, the managing partner may be entitled to a greater share of the profits."

In finding an implied agreement to pay a salary to a partner who has devoted his time and energy to the management of a partnership business, the courts lean heavily upon the principles of estoppel. For example, in Vangel a partner expelled from the partnership for cause and by judicial decree, continued to participate in the business in substantially the same manner as before the action for dissolution. As there was no protest by the other partners, the court held they acquiesced fully in his participation in management. Consequently, said the court, the partner who was active in the management of the partnership business was, absent objection by the other partners entitled to be paid for his services.

A parallel to the case before us is found in *Heck v. Heck*, 63 Cal.App.2d 470, 147 P.2d 110. The court was called upon to determine whether money withdrawn from a partnership business which was the separate property of the husband, was withdrawal of capital or was salary. An implied contract to pay

a salary was found from the following facts: the other partner did not participate in the management and control of the business and did not draw a comparable amount; the bookkeeping entries of the partnership reflected the payment
of salary; the other partner did not object, although he had knowledge of the
salary payments and of the bookkeeping procedure. The court said, at page 474:
"His failure to object to the withdrawal may be construed into his consent to it.
Failure to object to the act of an agent or manager, after full knowledge of it,
may be a ratification of such and may be considered a circumstance pointing to
prior authorization of it. Under these circumstances we may not disturb the
conclusion of the trial judge that the withdrawal of the $65,000 was salary paid
plaintiff by the partnership."

. . .

In light of the foregoing cases, we turn to the facts before us. Plaintiff was
never, at any time, an active partner. She knew that her husband and Stoetzl
managed the partnership and both drew salaries. After her husband died, she
agreed that Stoetzl should carry on the full management of the affairs of the
partnership. Plaintiff testified that she wanted to take her husband's place but
when Stoetzl demurred, she acquiesced. Under Stoetzl's management the business flourished. From the date of her husband's death, through the year 1965,
plaintiff withdrew $87,122.39 from the partnership in cash, and the value of her
equity in the assets increased $68,553.16. Plaintiff received copies of profit and
loss statements and copies of partnership income tax returns every year from the
time of her husband's death up to the time this action was commenced, and she
voiced no objection to Stoetzl's salary reflected in these documents. The books
and records of the partnership were open to her for inspection at all times.

According to plaintiff's testimony, she met with Stoetzl shortly after her
husband's death. They discussed a salary increase which he told her he intended
to make. She made no objection at the time, and later telephoned the bookkeeper to find out whether he had increased his salary, and was told that he had.
Subsequently plaintiff said to Stoetzl, "Well, you got your raise," without
making any objection.

The language of *Dugan v. Forster*, 104 Cal.App. 117, at page 120, 285 P.
384, appears to be applicable; there the court said: "As a general rule a partner
is not entitled to any compensation for services rendered by him to the partnership [citation]. It has been frequently decided, however, that the partners may
agree that a partner shall receive compensation, or such an agreement may be
implied, and the existence or nonexistence of such a contract is a question for
the court to determine from the facts and circumstances of the case, and its
inferences of fact which support its conclusions will not be disturbed on appeal,
though it might with equal propriety have found the other way (citation)."

There remains plaintiff's argument that the findings as to salary are contra-
dictory, or at least there is an incongruity. The court found:

"28. That all of the partners, with the exception of plaintiff, Anna Rose Busick, agreed to the amounts of salary that were received by the defendant, Ralph E. Stoetzl.

"29. That plaintiff, Anna Rose Busick, agreed to salaries received by defendant, Ralph E. Stoetzl, each year until 1963. That commencing in the year 1963, plaintiff, Anna Rose Busick, did not agreed to an increase in salary in excess of the amount of $11,004.00 per year."

Findings must be viewed in the light of the evidence; when we look at the record the alleged inconsistency disappears and the distinction between the approved salary of $11,004 and the salary increases becomes apparent. In a conversation between plaintiff and Stoetzl in a restaurant in the City of Madera shortly after the death of plaintiff's husband in 1959, she impliedly agreed that Stoetzl was to continue to manage the business and that he should be paid a salary. In 1963 plaintiff and her attorney met with Stoetzl and his attorney to discuss the partnership business. One of the items discussed was an increase in Stoetzl's pay. Plaintiff testified as follows:

"Q. All right. Now what was said about Mr. Stoetzl's salary at that time by you or what was said by him?

"A. I didn't say anything. Attorney Lindsey told me not to say anything, 'Don't you say a word in there,' so I didn't say a word.

"Q. What did Mr. Stoetzl say?

"A. He didn't say anything about his wages, but he said that, 'This man is worth that.'

"Q. By he-

"THE COURT: By he, I think you are indicating the senior Mr. Green.

"A. Sherwood Green.

"Mr. Say: Q. All right. What did Mr. Green say?

"A. He said, 'This is a valuable man. He should get twelve thousand - twelve hundred a month.'

"Q. And what did you say, if anything?

"A. I didn't say anything. I was mad, but I wasn't supposed to say anything.

"Q. And Mr. Lindsey told you not to say anything; is that correct?

"A. He said not to say a word."

However, in a letter written June 24, 1963, Mr. Lindsey said, in relation to the salary being paid Stoetzl: "The mere fact that he has seen fit to increase his salary is not to be construed as a consent on the part of Mrs. Betters for such increase, or increases."

Three years later, in April 1966, plaintiff and her attorney again met with Stoetzl and his attorney, and salary was again discussed. Mr. Stoetzl testified that at this meeting plaintiff said nothing about salaries, and that plaintiff's attorney, Mr. Lindsey, did not object when Stoetzl said he was entitled to at least $20,000 a year; as Stoetzl recalled, Mr. Lindsey said it was not unreasonable.

We conclude that the evidence is ample to support the separate findings that (a) Stoetzl was entitled, by implied agreement, to the original salary of $11,004 per year, and (b) plaintiff did not agree to any increase above that amount.

The judgment is affirmed.

Notes

Busick v. Stoetzl neatly illustrates the phenomenon of dissolution as well as testing the concept of the "agreement" which can supplant the default provisions of Section 18 of the UPA in governing the internal rights and responsibilities of the members of the firm.

DISSOLUTION:

Defined by §29 as the change in the relation of the partners caused by any partner ceasing to be associated in carrying on of the firm business.

Section 30 makes it clear that the partnership is not terminated by dissolution but continues until the affairs of the firm are wound up. "Winding up" is an important concept. It means the steps which must be taken to settle the firm's obligations to all third parties and, once this is accomplished, to divide whatever assets may remain between or among the partners.

Section 31 sets forth the causes of dissolution and develops the critical distinction between those circumstances where the dissolution does NOT violate the partnership agreement (they are listed under sub-section (1)) and the concept of a dissolution which does violate the agreement between the partners.

CONSEQUENCES OF DISSOLUTION:

Section 33: General Effect of Dissolution on Authority of Partner: In the wake of dissolution Section 9's grant of real authority is dramatically cut back by Section 33. From that moment on, the authority of a partner to act for the firm is destroyed except for those transactions necessary to wind up the affairs of the firm.

Section 35: Power of Partner to Bind Partnership to Third Persons after Dissolution: Again, we see a dramatic constriction of the circumstances in which a partner can bind the firm. This replaces the Section 9(1) liability shifting vehicle.

Section 37: Right to Wind Up: The right to wind up the partnership affairs belongs to the partner or partners who have not dissolved the partnership wrongfully.

Section 38: Rights of Partners to Application of Partnership Property: Again, a distinction is drawn between the rights of those partners who are not guilty of a dissolution in contravention of the partnership agreement (this is what is meant by the phrase wrongful dissolution) and those partners who have violated the partnership agreement by causing the dissolution. Under Section 38(1) the scheme is simple, the partners reduce all of the assets of the firm to cash and then apply those assets to the liabilities which the firm has to third parties. If there are assets in excess of those liabilities, they are distributed to the partners under Section 40.

In *Busick* we see the formation of three and the dissolution of two partnerships.

1950 partnership: Valley Feed and Grain formed as a partnership. In 1957 this partnership is dissolved when the third couple desires to quit the business and it is agreed that the two remaining couples, the Betters and the Stoetzl's, will purchase that interest.

At this point, the affairs of Valley Feed and Grain would have had to have been wound up under the terms of the act.

1957 partnership: when the business opened its doors, a de facto successor partnership was in place. This one was comprised of four partners.

The 1957 firm was dissolved with the death of Walter Betters. At this point, Anna, as the surviving widow was in a position to demand that the assets of the firm be reduced to cash under §38 and there be a settlement of accounts as among the three surviving partners and the estate of her husband, Walter. Had she done this she would have taken one-half of any assets which the firm possessed. But this step would also have destroyed Valley Feed and Grain as a business ... for all of its facilities and inventory would have been sold off in the course of the Section 38 winding up.

Anna may have found such a step imprudent ... to destroy the business following the death of her husband. But she could have used her undoubted right to demand this result as a bargaining chip with the Stoetzl's to seek preservation of her family's historical equal interest in the business.

1959 partnership: When Anna failed to insist upon a winding up and permitted the doors of the business to open without any explicit agreement as to the dimension of her interest in the firm a third, de facto partnership was created and under the terms of §18(e) her interest was reduced to one-third. The fate of her deceased husband's undistributed interest in the 1957 firm would be preserved under UPA §41, a concept which will be developed in *In re Estate of Schaefer*, infra.

THE PARTNERSHIP AGREEMENT AND THE ISSUE OF SALARIES:

It is clear that when the 1950 partnership was formed there was a formal written agreement existing as among the six partners. One of its features rebutted the presumption of Section 18(f) that no partner is entitled to remuneration for acting in the partnership business. The agreement was that the three husbands would be active in the business and that they should receive salaries. It also appears as a fair inference from the record that these salaries were equal in dimension and adjusted from time to time as to amount. The adjustments reflected the prosperity and nature of the evolving business.

In 1957, the successor four person partnership did not frame a written partnership agreement. But the record reveals that the behavior of the four partners was consonant with the terms of the agreement which had expressly governed the 1950 firm. In these circumstances is it fair to say that the 1957 firm had an agreement which supplanted §18?

The 1959 partnership: this de facto entity bears no functional relationship to the predecessor firms in that for the first time the interests in the firm are not equal. The Stoetzl's have a two-third's interest. Anna expressed an intention to become active in the business but Ralph Stoetzl vetoed her overture.

What is the status of the 1959 partnership on the issue of compensation for active partners?

Ralph will argue that by terms of an agreement which has never been repudiated, only the active partners receive salaries and that these salaries are to be treated as ordinary matters of partnership business under §18(h). If this view is sustained then none of the misery experienced from 1960-1966 need have arisen. Ralph could simply call a meeting of the members of the firm and put the matter of his salary to a vote.

Anna would argue that the absence of any formal action taken by the successor firm to adopt the writing means that Valley Feed and Grain operated under the default provisions of §18.

Does the statute settle this argument?

No, §18 makes a reference to "any agreement between them" language which clearly does not require the partnership agreement to be in writing. Does the agreement even have to be explicit? Could mere proof of custom within the operation of the firm constitute an agreement?

The problem in *Busick v. Stoetzl* is how to avoid an all or nothing answer to the question of whether there were to be salaries, and if so how they were to be set.

If there is no agreement, then how long can we expect Ralph to toil under the terms of §18(f)? Is it an answer to say that the other partners could become active? If there are no salaries what incentive do they have to stir themselves?

If we say that the terms of a prior agreement have, by conduct, been adopted by the 1959 firm, what about the issue of the amount of Ralph's salary?

If we deem it an ordinary matter then Ralph will simply put the question to his wife and son and they will out-vote Anna Busick 3-1. Note that in voting within a partnership, in the absence of an agreement that it is to be otherwise, each partner casts an equal vote notwithstanding that he may have a lesser equitable interest. Thus Ralph Jr. would have one vote just as would Anna.

If the salary issue is regarded as contravening the agreement of the partners then we require unanimous agreement and this would put Anna in a position to have an imperial veto.

Legal solutions to this impasse: Is there a middle ground? Anna brought this suit on the theory that §18(f) would preclude Ralph from any salary. Ralph's lawyer might have countered with a number of arguments:

* That as a successor to the 1950 firm, the 1959 partnership had an agreement that active partners were to receive salaries and the question of amount was an ordinary business matter. This is hardly a "middle ground."

* That if Ralph occupied the position of a third party, then under agency principles the firm would be liable on a theory of implied ratification. The gist of this argument is that the partners knew in advance that Ralph's services were not being rendered gratis but with the explicit expectation of a specific salary. (Recall the meetings at the restaurant in 1963 and 1966). When the firm received the benefit of those services it ratified the obligation. The problem is the nature of the firm and Ralph's position. As a partner he was 26% of the principal, by dent of UPA Section 9(1) he was its agent, and as the laborer he was the "third party." Can a single human play all three roles under agency law? Stranger fictions have been entertained by courts.

On the surface this looks like a fair solution. It isn't. If you follow this rationale Ralph could have a $50,000 salary by merely informing Anna in advance and then continuing to work for the firm.

* That there was an implied contract (quasi-K) to pay at least the fair market value of the services which were tendered in circumstances negating the possibility of a voluntary or gratuitous act.

Only this last solution commends itself as fundamentally "fair." It represents a middle ground because the claim would be limited to "market value."

3. The fiduciary quality of the partnership relationship:

FOUCHEK ET AL. v. JANICEK
Supreme Court of Oregon, 1950.
190 Or. 251, 225 P.2d 783.

WARNER, JUSTICE. This is a suit to establish a constructive trust in the hands of defendant and compel him to account for the profits arising therefrom.

Stephen J. Fouchek and Harry L. McBurnett, plaintiffs and appellants, allege that in 1946, they were copartners with Duane J. Janicek, defendant and respondent, doing business under the assumed firm name of Salem General Jobbing Company (hereinafter called the Salem Company). They claim that while that relationship subsisted, Janicek breached faith with them by turning to his personal account and profit a valuable business opportunity which properly belonged to the Salem Company. The transaction referred to springs from Janicek's alleged secret acceptance of an offer made to the partnership which carried the promise of $50,000 or more for the Company's use in buying war surplus supplies in a joint adventure arrangement wherein the Salem Company would be a party with an interest slightly in excess of fifty per cent. Janicek's espousal of the offer referred to (which we shall hereinafter call the Hickok offer) resulted in the formation of a joint adventure arrangement known as the Cascade Mercantile Co., Oregon, Ltd. (hereinafter called the Cascade Company) in which defendant owns a fifty-one per cent interest to the exclusion of plaintiffs. Plaintiffs pray that Janicek be decreed to hold two-thirds of his interest in the Cascade Company as a trustee for their use and benefit, and that he be required to account to them for all monies received by him in that capacity. Defendant's answer denies any partnership relation with plaintiffs. Janicek admits, however that the parties made what he calls a tentative agreement whereby at a future time, following August 10, 1946, he would associate himself with them as a partner but denies that the arrangements for the formation of that partnership were ever completed. He also denies that he breached faith with plaintiffs. After trial the circuit court entered a decree dismissing plaintiffs' complaint, from whence they appeal.

From March 28, 1946, to August 10, 1946, the plaintiffs as the sole partners operated the same business under the same name. It was a wholesale and retail enterprise with its principal office in Salem, Oregon, and from June 21, 1946, with a retail branch in Taft, Oregon. Then, as well as after August 10, 1946, the firm was engaged in the selling of sporting goods and substantial lines of war surplus items which they, as war veterans, were able to obtain on a preferential status.

The business, as operated by the plaintiffs, so prospered that it seemed to dictate the need for additional assistance in the operation of its affairs. This prompted them to solicit the services of the defendant, a fellow war veteran whom they had known before and who was then employed in Seattle, Washington. In response to plaintiffs' invitation, Janicek came to Salem, Oregon, in August, 1946. Here he surveyed plaintiffs' business establishment but declined to accept their invitation to join them as an employee. Instead, he offered to come if accepted as a full partner. This was readily agreed to by the parties on August 10, 1946. Indeed, the plaintiffs were so eager for his help and association that they included him as the owner of a one-third interest without demanding any present capital contribution on his part, agreeing that it might be made by withholding from his share of the future profits. On August 21, 1946, Janicek assumed an active place in the firm. This continued up to and including November 2, 1946, when the partnership between the three parties was terminated.

We have above referred to Janicek as being a member of the firm. We have done so advisedly, being persuaded that the record in this matter clearly sustains the conclusion that Fouchek, McBurnett and Janicek were copartners from August 10 to November 2, 1946. We deem it unnecessary, however, to extend this opinion by giving our reasons for that conclusion in view of the position taken and concessions made by the defendant in his brief. There we find the following statement: "... that so long as the business relations of the parties continued, whether those relations were as partners, joint venturors or otherwise, the parties each owed to the other duties similar to those owed in a partnership relation."

Thus by reason of our conclusion on the issue of partnership, we find that a fiduciary relationship existed between all the parties between the last dates mentioned and that their conduct as between themselves is amenable to and should be measured by the rules applicable to partners.

In 40 Am.Jur., Partnership, 137, §17, we read: "It is also a fundamental characteristic of partnership that the relation existing between the partners is one of trust and confidence when dealing with each other in relation to partnership matters. Each partner is, in one sense, a trustee and at the same time a cestui que trust."

Before proceeding to discuss plaintiffs' contentions respecting Janicek's alleged unfaithfulness as a copartner, we pause here to relate the circumstances giving rise to the Hickok offer and its content.

At all the times above referred to, Guy W. Hickok was the manager of the Salem Branch of the First National Bank of Portland (Oregon). It was the bank where the Salem Company maintained its deposits and where it occasionally borrowed money. Mr. Hickok, on or about October 3, 1946, and for some time thereafter, at least up to and including the time of the creation of the Cascade Company, was the agent for a group of investors who were anxious to enter the then attractive war surplus market. ...

Shortly before October 3, Hickok called the plaintiff, McBurnett, at his place of business and asked him to stop at his desk when he, McBurnett, was in the bank. This McBurnett did on October 3 and in the conference at the bank at that time, Hickok asked McBurnett if he would be interested in obtaining some capital funds with which to increase the scope of operation of the Salem Company. Upon receiving McBurnett's affirmative reply, he proceeded to tell him that there was "a considerable sum of money available, controlled by individuals that I represented, that they were interested in going into some sort of a joint venture deal and the Salem General Jobbing Company would conduct the business, with the profits to be divided approximately equally." He indicated that the available funds represented a "probable maximum of $50,000" but that "the amount of funds was not necessarily limited." If accepted by the Salem Company, the partners of that firm were to meet with Hickok's principals and work out the details. ...

Immediately after hearing Mr. Hickok's proposal, McBurnett carried the information to his copartners, Fouchek and Janicek. It was recognized as a real partnership opportunity and was seized upon with no small display of interest and avidity. We learn from Janicek that when McBurnett returned from the bank, he was "all steamed up" about what he had learned from Hickok and that "we all talked about it and decided that it would be a good deal. Any time anybody offered $50,000, we thought it would be a good deal to use." We learn from McBurnett that "the three of us agreed to accept it, and I went back to the bank and informed Mr. Hickok to that effect." This acceptance was transmitted to Hickok on the evening of October 3 or morning of October 4.

According to Janicek, the partners then proceeded to address themselves to the subject of appropriate ways to invest the funds when available. They inclined for a while to the purchase of rain parkas at a sale of war surplus supplies soon to be held by the Government at Salt Lake City; and Janicek, at the instance of his copartners, called Salt Lake City to learn more about the prospective parka sale. Although they concluded, after consideration, to abandon investment in the rain parkas, the Hickok offer, Janicek says, "was quite the subject of conversation for some time."

In the interim between the receipt of the offer and the termination of the partnership—a significant thirty days so far as the instant suit is concerned—McBurnett had further conferences with Hickok, who tells us that they numbered "two or three" over a space of "a week or ten days or two weeks." Coincident with these further conferences between McBurnett and Hickok, the partners were apparently preparing themselves to have some constructive and profitable plan of operation to present to Hickok's principals when the anticipated meeting for negotiation was held. This is borne out by Janicek's own recital of their activities prior to November 2, 1946. This valuable opportunity was never abandoned by the partners and was yet an active subject of concern up to the time Janicek left the firm on that date. ...

Paralleling the activities of the copartners after October 3, as outlined above, another force was set in motion which was destined to strip the Salem Company of the prospective benefits of the Hickok offer and make it a source of enrichment to Janicek alone. Just when Janicek surreptitiously began to put his self-serving design into operation, we do not know; but we are convinced beyond peradventure that it began not long after the Hickok offer was first unfolded by McBurnett to his business associates and was later brought to a point some time before November 2 where Janicek was definitely assured that he alone, and not his copartners in unity with him as the Salem Company, was to be the sole beneficiary of the funds available through Hickok's principals ... We emphasize that fact because in our opinion the reprehensible features of Janicek's activity took place before he made the plaintiffs farewell.

So well and certainly had Janicek operated prior to the closing of his partnership with plaintiffs that he was able to quickly and within four days thereafter bring his arrangements with Hickok's principals to the place where, on November 12, ten days after stepping out of the Salem Company, he was an active joint adventurer with them in the newly formed Cascade Company and the owner of a fifty-one percent interest in that company.

Those are the circumstances which form the basis for plaintiffs' claim against the defendant.

The last and principal question which remains unanswered is: Did Janicek's acts with reference to the Hickok offer constitute a breach of his obligations to his copartners so as to make him accountable to them as a constructive trustee?

> In 54 Am.Jur., Trusts, 167, §218, it is said: "A constructive trust, ... is a trust by operation of law which arises contrary to intention and in invitum, against one who, by fraud, actual or constructive, by duress or abuse of confidence, or by commission of wrong, or by any form of unconscionable conduct, artifice, concealment, or questionable means, or who in any way against equity and good conscience, either has obtained or holds the legal right to property which he ought not, in equity and good conscience, hold and enjoy. It is raised by equity to satisfy the demands of justice."
>
> . . .

We adopt as our own the forceful and terse words of the late Justice Cardozo, defining the obligations of joint adventurers and copartners as between themselves, which we find reported in *Meinhard v. Salmon*, 249 N.Y. 458, 463, 164 N.E. 545, 546, 62 A.L.R. 1, 5, where he says: "Joint adventurers, like copartners, owe to one another, while the enterprise continues, the duty of the finest loyalty. Many forms of conduct permissible in a workaday world for those acting at arm's length are forbidden to those bound by fiduciary ties. A trustee is held to something stricter than the morals of the market place. Not honesty alone, but the punctilio of an honor the most sensitive, is then the standard of behavior. As to this there has developed a tradition that is unbending and inveterate. Uncompromising rigidity has been the attitude of courts of equity when petitioned to undermine the rule of undivided loyalty by the 'disintegrating erosion' of particular exceptions. *Wendt v. Fischer*, 243 N.Y. 439, 444, 154 N.E. 303. Only thus has the level of conduct for fiduciaries been kept at a level higher than that trodden by the crowd. It will not consciously be lowered by any judgment of this court."

The essence of the fiduciary character of a partner as defined by Justice Cardozo and the remedies flowing from its breach, as stated in 54 Am.Jur., Trusts, 167, §218, are captured by and were succinctly written into [§21 of the UPA]. As far as pertinent, that section reads: "Every partner must account to the partnership for any benefit, and hold as trustee for it any profits derived by him without the consent of the other partners from any transaction connected with the formation, conduct, or liquidation of the partnership or from any use by him of its property."

The foregoing section is a part of the Uniform Partnership Law. So, too, are all the Code sections hereinafter cited.

Section [21] furnishes the standard by which we must determine whether or not Janicek's conduct is answerable to its provisions.

Before one can successfully invoke the penalty which [§21] imposes on an erring business associate, it must be demonstrated that: (1) the associate is a copartner-this we have already found in this suit; (2) the transaction is one of a kind that the partnership can legally embrace and act upon; (3) the transaction is connected with the formation, conduct or liquidation of the partnership or use of the partnership property by the accused copartner-in this suit our inquiry need go no further under this head than to determine whether the transaction is "connected with the ... conduct ... of the business"; (4) the transaction is of such nature that it may be said to be within the scope of the business of the firm; (5) the transaction complained of comprehends something of value to the partnership, whether or not it is of a present value or of a prospective value, which it is presently believed may accrue to the partnership in the future if and when it elects to act thereon; and (6) the transaction is one that the accused partner has acted upon to his apparent or sole advantage without the full knowledge or consent of his other partners.

We shall now proceed to weigh the Hickok offer and Janicek's actions with reference to it in terms of the elements just itemized, though not necessarily in the order above presented.

. . .

If, as we have shown, the Salem Company was legally competent to participate as a party to a joint adventure arrangement, then we must further inquire whether the Hickok offer involved a transaction within the scope of the partnership enterprise. We address ourselves first to consideration of the meaning of the word "transaction" as employed in §[21]. The word "transaction," it has been said, has never been the subject of any exact judicial definition nor given any very definite meaning by the courts. The courts have interpreted "transaction" as the justice of each case demanded rather than by any abstract definition, and have given the word a broad, comprehensive meaning whenever necessary to meet the intention and purpose of the statute in which it was employed. 63 C.J., Transaction, 770, § 1. "Transaction" in the ordinary and popular sense has been defined as signifying "the doing or performing of any affair; that which is done or *in the process of being done*", and again as "a matter or affair either completed or *in the course of completion*". (Italics ours.) *Chance v. Carter*, 81 Or. 229, 236, 158 P. 947, 949.

Within the boundaries of the foregoing definitions, we think the Hickok offer is a "transaction" in the sense that the word is used in [UPA §21].

Defendant in his brief argues that: "The partnership must have owned and held *tangible asset or property* and the withdrawing partner must have taken that valuable asset or property to the detriment of the preceding partnership."

(Italics ours.) We cannot accept that narrow construction. It is neither consonant with the provisions of [§21], nor can it be reconciled with the authorities.

The Hickok offer was a species of preemptive privilege or, better, a preemptive opportunity that was an incident of the enterprise known as the Salem Company. *Meinhard v. Salmon*, supra. It is not a sufficient answer to say that the chance which the offer presented to the Salem Company had no present value when made, because its acceptance would necessarily have to be followed by negotiations of uncertain result; and, if that stage was successful, the new joint adventure might not be profitable. "Such a calculus of probabilities is beyond the science of the chancery." *Meinhard v. Salmon*, supra. It is enough to constitute a given transaction, a business transaction under [§21] if it carries a reasonable prospect of future advantage, even though the anticipated values may be lost in subsequent negotiations designed to bring it to fruition. This is also true, even though it has no present market value in the hands of the partnership or cannot be made the basis of a legal claim against parties outside of the firm. Present value may be an incident of it, but not necessarily so.

Information belongs to a partnership in the sense of property in which it has a valuable right, if it is of the character which might be employed to the partnership's advantage. Such information cannot be used by one partner for his private gain. *Latta v. Kilbourn*, 150 U.S. 524, 550, 14 S.Ct. 201, 37 L.Ed. 1169; *Cassels v. Stewart*, 6 L.R.App.Cas. 64, 73.

The chance or opportunity of the Salem Company, as tendered by the Hickok offer, to make a profit by becoming a party to a joint adventure arrangement with prospective new capital up to $50,000, was an asset of the Salem Company in that sense until the offer was withdrawn or until repudiated by the copartners acting in concert. *Mitchell v. Reed*, 61 N.Y. 123, 129, 19 Am.Rep. 252; *Waller v. Henderson*, 135 Okl. 231, 275 P. 323.

One of the chief activities of the Salem Company was the purchase and resale of war surplus goods of divers kinds, depending in part upon the kinds which the Government offered from time to time. Hickok's principals were anxious to get into the war surplus business and the Hickok offer was made to the Salem Company with that in view. The Hickok offer was not only a transaction of the kind contemplated by §[21] but it was a transaction within the scope of the business of the Salem Company, as it was then constituted. Having thus concluded, it remains to determine whether Janicek's actions with reference to the Hickok offer were without the consent of plaintiffs and in derogation of his fiduciary obligations to them.

We again focus attention upon that period beginning with the receipt of the Hickok offer by McBurnett on October 3 and ending with the dissolution of the partnership on November 2. We have already reviewed it in terms of the response it conjured in the three partners acting in unison and noted their acceptance and plans for the ultimate use of the prospective new capital funds when received by them. Now, we give consideration to the separate and secret activities of the defendant with reference to the same subject matter and which, so far as we can determine from the record, ran more or less parallel in time to his ostensible gestures of cooperation with his copartners in the Salem Company.

When we approach this phase of the matter, we are at times confronted with some difficulty, for we find that Janicek's testimony is too often vague and equivocal, where we have reason to expect that it should be clear and positive. Taking his testimony as a whole, we cannot escape the inference that the defendant shortly after hearing of the Hickok offer from McBurnett, conceived the idea of becoming its sole beneficiary; indeed, referring to his conversations with Fouchek on October 31, he says: "I told him I was endeavoring to get into the war surplus business myself." We feel certain that those "endeavors" on his part began early in October and that he, with design and subtlety, promoted the various conferences that he had with Hickok at the bank during the month of October and with the purpose of destroying by suggestion and innuendo Hickok's faith and confidence in Janicek's copartners, Fouchek and McBurnett, and at the same time advance himself in Mr. Hickok's regard.

There were three conferences between Janicek and Hickok, and possibly more. The first, we are told by Janicek, was when he called upon Hickok and told him he "wanted a loan, to go into the war surplus business,-a GI loan," at which time, he added, "I said that the setup [referring to the Salem Company] was such that I couldn't see continuing on with it and that I wanted to break away and set up for myself." We think it is worthy of note that at the time it was not Mr. Hickok but Mr. Dempsie of the bank who handled the bank's loans to G.I. borrowers.

On the occasion of their second conference "a day or two later," Janicek went to Hickok to ask "what he thought of Mr. Fouchek and Mr. McBurnett," and for advice on whether or not it would be wise for him to continue as one of their copartners. This he did notwithstanding that only a day or two before he had at the first conference informed Hickok that he "couldn't see continuing" with the Salem Company and "wanted to break away." Just how far Hickok was unconsciously persuaded by Janicek at these times we cannot say; but we do note that more or less coincident with the time of these talks between defendant and Hickok, the latter was, as he expressed it, "losing confidence in their [Salem Company] setup" and "beginning to back away from them."

. . .

The third significant meeting between Janicek and Hickok was "four or five days or a week later," that is, after the second conference above referred to. This third conference in October was, as stated by defendant, "before I left Barb's Sporting Goods," (a retail outlet operated by the Salem Company). It was at this meeting that the scales were finally turned in favor of Janicek and against his copartners. It was then that Hickok offered him the opportunity which had previously been tendered the Salem Company through McBurnett. Upon its immediate acceptance by the defendant, the plaintiffs were out and Janicek was in, so far as the Hickok offer was concerned.

Success in the fulfillment of Janicek's ambition to go into the war surplus business on his own account appears to this Court to have been a matter of deliberate and careful previous consideration; first to dissuade Hickok from further traffic with his copartners; then to persuade Hickok to accept him in their stead as a potential joint adventurer with Hickok's principals; and then, after being thus first assured of a place to light, so to speak, in the war surplus market, to thereafter terminate his partnership relations with the very men who, so shortly before, had placed him in the position of vantage from which he could and did achieve, at the expense of their faith and confidence in him, the end he ultimately hoped for. In retrospect, the pattern of Janicek's departure from the ways of fiduciary rectitude now appears obvious and complete, although at the time of performance its deviousness and craftiness were not so apparent to those working closest to him.

Our conclusion that Janicek's efforts to supplant plaintiffs in the favor of Hickok, and by oblique and crafty approach win for himself the fruits of the Hickok offer, finds support in his secretive attitude toward them. His conduct in this respect does not meet the fiduciary standards of good faith required of a copartner, either in spirit or in fact.

Section [20 of the UPA] far as pertinent, reads: "Partners shall render on demand *true and full information of all things* affecting the partnership ***." (Italics ours.)

Good faith not only requires that a partner should not make any false statement to his partners, but also that he should abstain from any false concealment. ...

When we view Janicek's conduct in terms of the foregoing rules, we find in it the very antithesis to the standards which they mandate. The Government's sale of war surplus goods scheduled for the latter part of October, 1946, was an important event in the life of the Salem Company, made particularly so by its acceptance of the Hickok offer with its prospect for greater capital to invest at that time. The firm had planned to send Janicek as its representative. He later refused to go, without assigning any reason therefor. On October 30, 1946, while at the home of Fouchek, Janicek told him that "he had other irons in the fire and that he felt it was best for him to discontinue his relationship with the partnership," and was withdrawing, but he gave no hint as to his conferences with Mr. Hickok or his impending entry into what was later to be known as the Cascade Company. On the evening of October 31 or November 1, 1946, Fouchek, whose suspicions had been aroused in the meantime, confronted defendant concerning the reasons for his imminent departure from the firm. With reference to this meeting, Fouchek testified:

"Q. (Mr. Rhoten) What did you say to him? A. I said [to] him, 'Jan, Harry [McBurnett] and I want to know whether or not this other iron in the fire that you mentioned last night was in any way connected with Mr. Hickok, of the First National Bank, or obtained through him.' Those were almost my precise words, because I carefully phrased the question.

"Q. What did he say to that? A. He waited a while and then told me 'No.'"

Upon learning of Janicek's negative reply, McBurnett on the morning of November 2 called upon Hickok, who told him "that the money that had been available had been made available to Mr. Janicek." This was followed by a spirited conference of all the partners that day. Janicek, under the pressure of Mr. Hickok's disclosures to McBurnett, admitted for the first time his theretofore undisclosed dealings with Hickok. The dissolution of the firm was its natural aftermath.

Janicek's surreptitious trafficking with the Hickok offer, his evasions and concealment when questioned by the plaintiffs, evidence a flagrant breach of good faith and want of open-handed dealing with his associates warranting the condemnation of a court of equity and the application of the remedies provided by [§21]. We repeat from *Meinhard v. Salmon*, supra [249 N.Y. 458, 463, 164 N.E. 546]: "Not honesty alone, but the punctilio of an honor the most sensitive, is then the standard of behavior." The obligation of partners to act with the utmost candor and good faith in their dealings between themselves is not lessened by the existence of strained relations between them or the existence of any condition which might, in and of itself, justify the firm's dissolution. The fiduciary obligations of a partner remain until the relationship is terminated.

Respondent argues that the duty of a former partner to share profits with his former associates extends only to earnings accruing before the termination of the partnership. The true rule is: When a partner wrongfully snatches a seed of opportunity from the granary of his firm, he cannot, thereafter, excuse himself from sharing with his copartners the fruits of its planting, even though the harvest occurs after they have terminated their association. The stewardship of the erring member dates from the initial appropriation and continues until he is exonerated by a proper accounting. Or to put it otherwise: If a member of a copartnership avails himself of information obtained by him in the course of the transaction of partnership business which is within the scope of the firm's business, and thereafter applies it to his own account without the consent or knowledge of his associates, he is liable to account to the firm for any benefit he may obtain from the use of such information. ...

It follows that if Janicek came into possession of a partnership opportunity, which did not blossom into a thing of personal profit to him until some time after he retired from the Salem Company on November 2, 1946, the fact of such a delayed benefit to him does not exonerate him from accountability to his copartners thereafter, if his seizure and employment of that opportunity during the existence of the Salem Company was without the consent of his copartners in the Salem Company.

. . .

We hold that the information embodied in the Hickok offer was obtained by the defendant in the course of the transaction of the business of the Salem Company and was employed by him for his own use and benefit without the consent of his copartners; and by reason thereof he must, under §[21] account therefor to plaintiffs.

. . .

We come unavoidably upon a situation which strongly suggests to us the necessity for amplifying the accounting in the lower court beyond the scope of the prayer of plaintiffs' complaint. It will be recalled that plaintiffs alleged the existence of a partnership between them and defendant and that this was denied. We have found that there was a partnership. The record indicates that no accounting has ever been had between the parties growing out of their relations between August 10, 1946, and November 2, 1946. The importance of a final accounting between them is emphasized by plaintiffs' Exhibit No. 2, which is a letter under date of October 9, 1946, signed by Janicek as a partner and addressed to a San Francisco mercantile house. It enclosed a financial statement of the Salem Company as of August 25, 1946. This financial statement shows a net worth close to $60,000 as of that date and is signed by all the parties to this suit. This exhibit was offered as a part of plaintiffs' proof that Janicek was in fact one of their copartners at the times indicated. Whether or not the parties have made a satisfactory accounting between themselves or have in some way barred themselves from asserting a right to an accounting, we do not undertake to say from the record now before us. We feel, however, that it would be inequitable for a court to compel an accounting between defendant and plaintiffs as to defendant's interest in the Cascade Company and at the same time suffer the plaintiffs to retain the avails of the liquidation of the Salem Company, if any were realized as the result of its operations during the period from August 10, 1946, to November 2, 1946. Under the circumstances, we are of the opinion that the lower court should accord the parties hereto-if they so desire-an opportunity to amend their respective pleadings herein so as to encompass by appropriate allegations what they conceive to be their respective rights with reference to an accounting between them growing out of their operations of the Salem Company during the period beginning August 10, 1946, and ending November 2, 1946. Such amendments, if made, shall, of course, be subject to such terms as the lower court in its discretion may deem proper. This privilege to amend is predicated upon the familiar rule that where equity takes jurisdiction for one purpose, it will retain it to do complete justice between the parties.

The decree of the lower court is reversed and the cause remanded for further proceedings not inconsistent with this opinion.

Notes

It would appear from the record that banker, Hickok, knew, or as a reasonable person, ought to have appreciated that Janicek at some point was no longer representing the interests of Fouchek and McBurnett but was operating in a manner directly contrary to their economic future. Would Hickok have any potential liability to Fouchek and McBurnett on a theory that he had knowingly participated in the misconduct of Janicek? For a well reasoned affirmative answer see, *Whitney v. Citibank, N.A.*, 782 F.2d 1106, 1115-16 (2d Cir. 1986). The court found that the law of New York was well settled to the effect that "[O]ne who knowingly participates with a fiduciary in a breach of trust is liable to the beneficiary for any damage caused thereby." An attempt by defendant to invoke the status of an innocent third party under UPA §9.1 was rejected on grounds that the defendant's officers were, or should have been, aware that the relations among the partners had badly deteriorated and, from the paperwork, detected that the plaintiff was being deliberately excluded by his co-partners from vital information needed to protect his interest in the firm.

a.   How does one detect the faithless fiduciary?

A Partner's Right to Inspect the Firm's Books and Records

Unless the right to inspect is broadly recognized and easily enforced, a faithless fiduciary may conceal his wrongdoing. The basic response to this problem is §19 of the UPA:

Partnership Books—Right of Inspection

The partnership books shall be kept, subject to any agreement between the partners, at the principal place of business of the partnership, and every partner shall at all times have access to and may inspect and copy any of them.

Do the words "... subject to any agreement" modify merely the question of repository for the books and records? Does the Act permit the partnership agreement to bar or substantially restrict a partner's statutory right of inspection? Cf. *McCallum v. Asbury*, supra.

There appear to be but two cases on this question. The more recent, *People v. Phillips*, 207 Misc. 205, 137 N.Y.S.2d 697, 699 (1955), suggests that a partner's right to books and records may be restricted by agreement. The context is important in appreciating how limited is the import of this decision. Phillips was a partner in a firm under a grand jury investigation. He was served with a subpoena covering certain records of the firm. His co-partner took the books and fled the jurisdiction. *People v. Phillips* is a trial judge's opinion on whether Phillips was in criminal contempt for failure to furnish the books. The court merely makes the point that the people failed to state that the partner had an unqualified right to the books, and that unless it were proven that he had such a right the court would not issue the contempt citation.

Sanderson v. Cooke, 256 N.Y. 73, 80, 175 N.E. 518, 520 (1931), is far more authoritative, but it also fails to settle the question. New York had adopted the UPA in 1919. Thus while the court made no mention of §19, in Sanderson it must have had the statute in mind. Plaintiff, Sanderson, had been a partner in a brokerage firm. By 1921 he had withdrawn from the firm and received a settlement from his former partners. The firm's business was continued by a successor partnership. In 1928 Sanderson suddenly demanded surrender of the firm's books covering the period of his membership. His demand was denied on the express ground that the books had a continued utility to the brokerage house. Judge Crane stated:

> . . .He at no time had claimed, and does not now claim, that any of the partnerships owe him $1, or that the settlements were unfair or fraudulent. He never has made, and does not now make, any claim of any kind or nature upon any of his former associates or the partnership of Barney & Co. ...

> . . .[O]n the 15th day of November, 1928, or eight years after his final termination of all relationships ... [plaintiff] commenced his action, basing it solely upon the claim that the books belonged to him, were his property the same as a desk or a chair could be property; that he was entitled as a matter of right to see, inspect, and copy all or any part of the books in question, ... He has been sustained by judgments in the courts below, holding that the books, records, and papers of the various firms are the property of the plaintiff, with the other members of the firms, and the defendants are enjoined from removing or disposing of any of them. ... Has the plaintiff any such right, as a matter of law, on the conceded facts of the case?

> The general rule regarding business partnerships is that books should be kept, open to the inspection of any partner at all reasonable times, even after dissolution, subject, however, to special agreement .... Even under these broad statements of the law, a partner's rights are not absolute. He may be restrained from using the information gathered from inspection for other than partnership purposes .... The employment of an agent to make the inspection does not authorize the selection of anybody he may choose for the purpose. The agent employed must be a person to whom no reasonable objection can be taken, and the purpose for which he seeks to use the right of inspection must be one consistent with the main purposes and well-being of the whole partnership. ... *Howlett v. Hall*, 55 App.Div. 614, 67 N.Y.S. 267, recognizes that the right is not a strict property right the same as part ownership in other personal property, but is confined within limitations. Motive plays a part, which, of course attaches to the ownership of no other kind of property, for in this case it was stated that the application to examine the books may be refused, if it be made in bad faith.

In reversing the judgment of the lower courts the Court of Appeals was careful to point out that Sanderson was not seeking to enforce rights within an existing partnership or in conjunction with a demand for a formal accounting and dissolution. 175 N.E. at 520. Thus *Sanderson v. Cooke* does not seem to be authority for the proposition that a partnership agreement could restrict a partner's licit demands to inspect the books at any reasonable time.

While it is possible to distinguish the two cases which suggest that the UPA might permit a partnership agreement to qualify the right to inspect, it must be admitted that to date no case has held or even suggested that such a provision would be struck down under the Act.

Finally, if it is debatable whether the partnership agreement could qualify access to books and records, could a partner seeking information achieve that goal by invoking §20 of the UPA?

Duty of Partners to Disclose Information

Partners shall render on demand true and full information of all things affecting the partnership to any partner or the legal representative of any deceased partner or partner under legal disability.

Unlike §19, this provision does not suggest the possibility of modification by the partnership agreement.

> **b.** **Once a partner has become aware of a "wrong" suffered at the hands of a co-partner, what may be done to redress the relationship?**

Suppose that a partner has a grievance against a co-partner for an alleged violation of the partnership agreement. May that partner commence an action at law for damages? The answer is an emphatic "no." It is a common law rule, which seems everywhere to have survived the adoption of the UPA, that one partner cannot bring an action at law against a co-partner to recover an amount claimed by reason of partnership transactions until there has been a final settlement (dissolution) of the partnership, a winding up of its affairs, a discharge of all liabilities, the collection of all assets, and, in the event of a surplus, computation of each partner's final share. Until all of these steps have been taken the only remedy which may be had against a co-partner is by suit in equity for dissolution and an accounting. So under the general rule the price for resorting to litigation against a partner is the destruction of the partnership.

The classic reasons for this rule were bluntly stated by the Supreme Court of California in 1858, in *Bullard v. Kinney*, 10 Cal. 60, 63:

> ... This rule rests upon three grounds:
>
> 1. The technical ground, that a man can not, at the same time, in the same suit, be both a plaintiff and a defendant.
>
> 2. Because it would be useless for one partner to recover that which, upon taking a general account, he might be compelled to refund; and thus a multiplicity of suits be permitted, where one would answer.
>
> 3. The contrary rule would defeat the equitable right of the other partners

114

to set-off their advances against those of plaintiff, and would force them to first pay the amount, and then rely upon the individual responsibility of the partner for a return of his proportion.

The rule explained in *Bullard* had been laid down without explanation in *Stone v. Fouse*, 3 Cal. 292, 294 (1853), which also held that the partnership agreement cannot grant a right to bring an action during the life of the partnership:

> ... Although the written contract between the parties contains a covenant for stipulated damages, yet it is by this same contract that they are constituted partners, and partners cannot sue one another at law, in respect to any of the business or undertakings of the partnership.

> It can only be done in chancery, by asking a dissolution and account ....

Accord, *Lewis v. Firestone*, 170 Cal.App.2d 129, 137, 338 P.2d 953, 958 (1959), and *Hosking v. Spartan Properties, Inc.*, 275 Cal.App.2d 152, 156-57, 79 Cal.Rptr. 893, 895-896 (1969) [collecting authorities and applying the rule to associates in a joint venture].

But the rule is subject to exceptions.

PILCH v. MILIKIN
Court of Appeals, Second District, 1962.
200 Cal.App.2d 212, 19 Cal.Rptr. 334.

LILLIE, J. In June of 1946 plaintiff and defendant became partners in the operation of a meat packing plant in the city of Vernon. At the time of the events hereinafter related, each partner had an equal interest in the business. Disagreements developed in the early part of 1957, and during the next three or four months there were discussions respecting a severance of the partnership relation. Shortly after June 1, 1957, the defendant obtained an option (later exercised by him) to purchase or lease a meat packing plant in San Luis Obispo, California. He twice asked plaintiff to join him in that venture, but the latter on each occasion replied that he was not interested. Subsequently, defendant having indicated that he wished to do so, the parties orally agreed to terminate the partnership. Various steps were thereafter taken to effectuate such agreement; thus, the parties took inventory of their stock in trade and divided and distributed its monetary value between them; they also divided and distributed the physical assets of the business, including trucks, office equipment and furniture, stationery and the like. According to the plaintiff, these and other undertakings (referred to later) resulted in a dissolution of the partnership by mutual consent on or about June 28, 1957. Undistributed, however, after such asserted dissolution were two bank accounts (totalling $10,133.11) standing in the name of the partnership; funds therefrom could not be withdrawn without the joint signatures of both parties. Another uncompleted task, according to plaintiff, was defendant's obligation to reimburse him in the sum of $2,677.59, being one-half of $5,355.18 advanced by plaintiff for the benefit of the partnership.

The present action, admittedly one at law, was commenced on June 8, 1959, after defendant had failed to join in the execution of a withdrawal form for the sums remaining in the banks and after the further failure by defendant to make reimbursement for the money advanced by the plaintiff. Count one of the complaint entitled "Money Due" alleged that the parties, prior to June 28, 1957, were partners in a business under the name of Milikin Packing Company; that by both oral and written agreement the partnership was dissolved on June 28, 1957, by mutual consent; that following said dissolution there remained in the possession of the defendant Milikin assets in the total sum of $10,133.11, half of which belonged to plaintiff and was due, owing and unpaid from defendant to plaintiff; that said $10,133.11 was on deposit in the name of the Milikin company with certain described banks, which money could be withdrawn only upon the joint signatures of the parties; that defendant had refused to sign the necessary documents to secure such withdrawal. The concluding paragraphs alleged that plaintiff had advanced to the partnership the sum of $5,355.18, that defendant was indebted to plaintiff for one-half thereof and that no part of said one-half had been paid. Counts two, three and four were common counts for money had and received, account stated and open-book account respectively, being based upon the facts specifically pleaded in the first cause of action. Count five was predicated on an alleged oral agreement between the parties whereby defendant assertedly agreed to pay to plaintiff the sum of $7,744.15 in compromise and settlement of all disputes between them arising out of the partnership relation. The prayer, among other things, asked for interest from August 1, 1957, on any judgment rendered.

A demurrer, both general and special, was overruled, following which defendant by answer denied each and all of the material allegations of the complaint; he also affirmatively alleged that plaintiff and defendant were still partners. By way of cross-complaint, damages for the appropriation of the goodwill of the business were demanded, as well as an accounting and a determination of defendant's rights in and to said business.

The trial court found in plaintiff's favor, adjudging that plaintiff recover from defendant the sum of $7,744.15, together with interest thereon at 7 per cent from November 1, 1957; it was further determined that defendant take nothing under his cross-complaint. From such judgment defendant has appealed.

The several points on appeal have been ably and extensively argued pro and con.[1] Since they are controlled in great measure by the facts at bar, a rather detailed statement of such facts becomes necessary, particularly as they relate

---

[1]Neither side is to be commended, however, for the use of certain language, critical of his opponent's advocacy, which has no place in the lexicon of an attorney at this or any other level. Briefs should be confined to the facts and law of the case; a client's cause is not served by any departure, provoked or otherwise, from this recognized rule.

to plaintiff's claim that the partnership was dissolved prior to the institution of the present proceeding.

Two or three days prior to July 1, 1957, plaintiff received a phone call from the defendant, at which time the latter stated: "Charles, I have taken up the option on this plant up north. I am starting for myself effective Monday morning, or effective now, we are no longer partners, you are on your own beginning Monday morning." Plaintiff replied: "Fine." During the same conversation it was suggested by defendant that the parties take inventory the following Monday (July 1, 1957). On Monday, as arranged, the parties met at their place of business and took inventory of all the meats in stock. At that time the defendant suggested that there be a division and distribution of all of the company's physical properties on or before Wednesday (July 3, 1957) so that defendant could move his half thereof to San Luis Obispo over the coming holiday (July 4th). That same Monday defendant also called a meeting of the employees. According to plaintiff he told them: "Charlie and I have split up. I am going in business for myself. We are splitting up amicably, we have no hard feelings between us." (Under direct examination defendant furnished corroboration of the foregoing incident as follows: "We called a meeting of the employees and we told them the employees we were dissolving, any of the employees that felt that they were free-I told some of the employees that I would possibly ask some of them to go with me, and if they felt they wanted to, they were welcome to go with me.")

Two days later, pursuant to defendant's suggestion, the physical assets of the business were divided and distributed. Defendant's own testimony explains how this was accomplished: "We argued between ourselves that we would draw high card for any item that we chose, the man who drew high card, if there were two items of the same kind the man with the high card, he would have the pick or if there was one specific item, the man who drew the high card for that, he had the item. We divided all the equipment on that basis. ..." The next day or so defendant moved his share of the equipment thus distributed to San Luis Obispo.

Meantime, the accountant for the company, advised by defendant that the partnership had been terminated, was instructed to prepare a final audit and close the books as of June 30, 1957. He computed the book value of the physical assets received by the parties and struck a balance between them, plaintiff paying defendant $51.43 to make up the difference therein. Accounts receivable were likewise liquidated-the sums in due course received being split between the parties. The same accountant prepared an income tax return marked "Final" for the year ending June 30, 1957; defendant signed this return for the company.

We come now to an incident in the chain of events upon which defendant bases much of his case. It appears that following the taking of inventory and the division of assets, as noted above, the parties consulted an attorney for the purpose of reducing to written form the oral understandings theretofore had between them. Plaintiff says that the purpose of this document, subsequently drafted and entitled "Agreement for Dissolution of Partnership," was to "put into writing evidence of the prior termination of (the) partnership," while defendant argues that the dissolution of the parties' relation was not to become effective until the instrument in question was signed. This "Agreement" was never signed by either party. True, the instrument does provide that "The signing of this Agreement shall constitute and be deemed a mutual release and discharge of any and all obligations of each of the parties to the other ...," but it also recites (by preamble) that "a further continuance of the partnership is no longer desired, and the parties by mutual consent have agreed to a dissolution thereof." Pursuant to a further provision in the instrument, a notice of dissolution was thereafter published in a Los Angeles legal newspaper to the effect that the partnership "has been dissolved by mutual consent"-it was testified by defendant that he and the plaintiff signed a notice of dissolution "in blank" at the time of the meeting with the attorney who drafted the agreement under discussion.

During the same period, it further appears, defendant executed a "Consent to Assignment" pertaining to the lease on the Vernon premises from Milikin Packing Company, as lessee, to "Charles Pilch doing business as Delta Meat Company." There was also testimony that on July 18, 1957, defendant placed the following announcement in a Los Angeles weekly trade paper: "This is to announce that Milikin Packing Co. formerly of Los Angeles has moved its operations to San Luis Obispo," the exact location of the plant as well as its post office address and phone number being included in such announcement.

Defendant operated the San Luis Obispo business for about four months. In November of 1957 the plant closed; late that same year he met the plaintiff and (according to the plaintiff) stated: "Charles, things didn't go very well in San Luis Obispo. I am closing the plant" or "I have closed it ... and I want to be your partner again." Defendant's own testimony in this regard was as follows: "Q. Do you remember any time, after July 1, 1957, telling Mr. Pilch that you would like to come back as a partner in the business being operated by him? A. I told him I would like to come back. Q. What did he say to you? A. Turned me down."

In addition to the above admissions, the record reveals the following: "Q. What do you calculate you owe Mr. Pilch? A. (by Defendant) I claim I believe there is $5,066 in the bank and then there is $2,677.38, all these fund owing from a partnership. Q. What was that? A. $2,677.38 and then approximately $5,066. The sum of both of these, I believe are---Q. Due Mr. Pilch? A. That is right. Q. Do you know how many times Mr. Pilch has asked you to pay those from you to him? A. A few times. Q. Have you ever paid the whole or any part thereof? (An objection was overruled) A. I refused to make payment."

Plaintiff called nine witnesses to corroborate certain of his factual claims. We deem it unnecessary to detail their testimony. Defendant was the only witness to testify in support of his side of the controversy.

After all the evidence was in, and argument having been waived, the trial court immediately announced its oral decision as follows: "The Court is under the opinion that Mr. Milikin made a bad deal for himself and he is trying to back into a proposition that didn't exist and it will be the judgment of the Court that the corporation was dissolved by mutual consent. Mr. Katz: Partnership. The Court: Partnership was dissolved by mutual consent on or about June 30, 1957, and thereabouts for a few following weeks until the bills were collected, paid. Therefore, the judgment of the Court will be for the plaintiff ..." After defendant's counsel called attention to the cross-complaint, the trial court said: "Well, we have some $10,133.11 to dispose of according to Mr. Milikin. Mr. Smith: My findings will encompass both complaint and cross-complaint and answers to each. I assume your Honor was making full and complete disposition when your Honor announced the judgment. The Court: That is the thing the Court had in mind."

Findings of fact and conclusions of law, dispositive of the entire controversy, were duly signed; one proviso in the conclusions of law was to the effect that judgment be stayed for a period of 10 days so as to permit defendant an opportunity to execute the withdrawal form releasing the funds on deposit with the banks in question-this defendant failed to do within the prescribed period.

Consistent with the view taken below by way of demurrer, a motion to exclude all evidence and motion for a nonsuit, defendant relies on the general rule that until the affairs of a partnership are wound up, the claim of a partner is equitable and can only be enforced in an accounting action (*Hooper v. Barranti*, 81 Cal.App.2d 570, 578, 184 P.2d 688); further, that no personal judgment can be entered in such an action until all partnership assets have been converted into money, the debts paid and a final balance ascertained. Elaborately, and with considerable scholarship, his counsel has developed the asserted untenability of the following thesis: "Plaintiff seeks to recover from his partner in an action at law instituted after the alleged dissolution of the partnership, but before the winding up thereof and accounting between the partners, an amount equal to one-half the indebtedness owed to the partnership by the banks in which the partnership deposited its funds, and an amount equal to one-half of the sum allegedly owed to the plaintiff by the partnership for moneys advanced on its behalf." According to defendant, this is the gist of plaintiff's first cause of action; as for the common counts, he points out that where a common count follows a count in which all of the facts are specifically pleaded and the common count is based on the same set of facts, the latter is not to be considered as a different cause of action but as an alternative method of pleading the plaintiff's right to recover. (*Orloff v. Metropolitan Trust Co.*, 17 Cal.2d 484, 110 P.2d 396.) Citing *Smiths' Cash Store v. First Nat. Bank*, 149 Cal. 32, 84 P.

663, 5 L.R.A. N.S. 870, for the proposition that the sums on deposit with the banks are uncollected debts due to the partnership, defendant concludes an exhaustive discussion of the problem with these statements: "There is no allegation in plaintiff's purported first cause of action or in any count of the complaint that there has been a winding up of the partnership or an accounting between the partners. Indeed, assuming the averments of plaintiff's complaint to be true ... such allegation could not truthfully have been made. The very averments of the complaint establish that the partnership is still possessed of assets, has at least one liability yet outstanding, and that the assets have not been used to satisfy such liability."

. . .

... [D]efendant's insistence upon a reversal is without merit for the further reason that the general rule upon which defendant relies ... is not an inflexible one. In 37 California Jurisprudence 2d 676, section 78, the governing law is thus stated: "The general rule that an accounting is a condition precedent to an action at law by one partner against another is subject to exceptions. To begin with, it does not apply where there are no outstanding demands against the firm, all collectible debts due it have been collected, and the judgment to be rendered will effect a final settlement between the partners.... It has been held that where no complex account involving a variety of partnership transactions is involved, an accounting is not a prerequisite to suit .... After dissolution of a partnership and full settlement of accounts, one partner may bring an action at law against the other for contribution." (Emphasis added.) The principles above stated appear to be almost universal: "... practically all the courts have recognized an exception to the general rule that a partner cannot maintain an action at law against another partner based upon partnership transactions, without an accounting, where the facts are such that no complex accounting involving a variety of partnership transactions is necessary, and they have held that in such cases an action at law may be maintained, even though a partnership transaction was the basis of the suit. Naturally, the same exceptions apply in the case of a suit brought by one partner against another partner or against the partnership after the termination or dissolution." (168 A.L.R. 1110).

It is express statutory law that dissolution of a partnership may be accomplished by the express will of the partners [UPA §31(c)]. Decisional law also supports plaintiff's position that the subsequent conduct of either partner, or both, inconsistent with a genuine conviction that the partnership has continued is evidence of a voluntary dissolution.

This court declared in *Fisher v. Fisher*, 83 Cal.App.2d 357, 360, 188 P.2d 802: "'the partnership may be dissolved by agreement of the partners, or the will of one of them, where there is no fixed term of its existence. Such agreement, or the will of one, may be proven by all the circumstances of the case as well as by direct evidence. Complete cessation of partnership business and a division of all, or a major portion of its assets without any objection, express or implied, is strong evidence of an agreement to dissolve. If not explained or refuted, it is sufficient to force the conclusion of dissolution by agreement. (Citation.)'" The foregoing principles fit the facts at bar. Parenthetically, we wonder whether defendant would be persisting in his present position if the San Luis Obispo venture had proven to be successful. The trial court certainly felt otherwise, and understandably so, upon the record before us; defendant, it would seem, took a calculated business risk and now, as the trial court put it, "he is trying to back into a proposition that didn't exist."

In his argument for compliance with the general rule *(Hooper v. Barranti, supra)* defendant is also confusing the dissolution of a partnership with the liquidation of its affairs, as was the case in *Fisher v. Fisher,* supra. Partners may accomplish an accounting and final settlement without a formal judicial proceeding therefor. ...

Even if there had been no prior dissolution or accounting between the partners, the present action with its resulting personal judgment could well be sustained, at least with respect to the funds deposited with the two banks, on the theory of defendant's conversion thereof. *(Driskill v. Thompson,* 141 Cal.App.2d 479, 296 P.2d 834.) In the case just cited it was said, quoting from an earlier decision: "'Where, as in this case, some of the partners have excluded another and have appropriated the partnership property to their own use, the latter may treat the matter as a conversion and, without any accounting or disposition of the former partnership assets, sue the offending partners and recover against them a personal judgment in the amount of his damage.' (Italics added.)" (P. 482.) Conversion has been broadly defined as any act of dominion wrongfully exerted over another's personal property in denial of or inconsistent with his rights thereto. *(Gruber v. Pacific States Sav. & Loan Co.,* 13 Cal.2d 144, 88 P.2d 137.) It is not necessary that there be a manual taking of the property, since any wrongful assumption of authority over chattels, inconsistent with another's right of possession or, subversive of his vested interest therein amounts to conversion. *(McCaffey Canning Co. v. Bank of America,* 109 Cal. App. 415, 294 P. 45.) Too, it is immaterial that the property in question may be in the actual possession of a third party. *(Kessinger v. Organic Fertilizers, Inc.,* 151 Cal.App.2d 741, 312 P.2d 345.) Defendant, as mentioned earlier, admitted that one-half of the moneys on deposit belonged to the plaintiff and not to the partnership; what had been previously a valid assumption of authority over such moneys became wrongful in the light of defendant's continued refusal to execute the joint withdrawal form. A case of conversion was, therefore, made out.

We have examined the many authorities cited by defendant in his briefs, the latter encompassing almost 150 pages.[2] Some contain statements not applicable at bar; others are clearly distinguishable on their facts. For example, on "the law versus equity" aspect of the case, as plaintiff puts it, defendant cites *Martyn v. Leslie*, 137 Cal.App.2d 41, 61, 290 P.2d 58, to the effect that a partner is not entitled to sue the other members of the partnership "until an accounting has been had." Also cited is *Demattei v. Lagomarsino*, 123 Cal.App. 646, 11 P.2d 897, where the evidence showed "without conflict" that there had been no settlement of the partnership affairs. Despite counsel's urgings, we are not persuaded that his position has merit, and we accordingly pass to the remainder of the points on appeal.

. . .

The entire controversy was fairly and ably tried. No reversible error has been manifested.

Notes

It is often asserted that a partnership is an unstable form of business association because it is destroyed by the death or withdrawal of any partner. This is true. One factor which reduces the pragmatic impact of this dissolution is the evident ease with which a replacement partnership is formed de facto. If the remaining associates open the business the next day their actions cast them in the role of co-partners.

Against this inherent destructibility the cases reveal two aspects of the common law which reflect the courts' desire to preserve the partnership. The first is the rule that actions at law may not be maintained against a co-partner during the life of the partnership. In some circumstances a partner might resort to litigation but not desire a formal dissolution and accounting. By forcing all such disputes inter se onto the equity docket, courts may fashion remedies with due regard for the interests of employees and consumers-interests which might best be served by repairing rather than dissolving the partnership. The second important factor is a self-help measure which the partners can use to stabilize the partnership through built-in pressures to tough out their difficulties and preserve the firm. This tool is well illustrated in the following opinion.

FULLER v. BROUGH
Supreme Court of Colorado, 1966.
159 Colo. 147, 411 P.2d 18.

Mr. Justice McWilliams delivered the opinion of the Court.

---

[2]The table of authorities (pages V through X of appellant's opening brief) lists approximately 150 cases cited or discussed thereafter. As in Achen v. Pepsi-Cola Bottling Co., 105 Cal.App.2d 113, 115, 233 P.2d 74 (1951), "[W]e have literally been bombarded by having the 'law books thrown at us.' " A further example of the needless length of the same brief is a four-line footnote on page three devoted to advising us that there is a one-cent error in computation both in the complaint and the judgment.

This is a dispute between two professional persons who decided to form a partnership and for some six years thereafter engaged in the practice of public accounting. On December 1, 1958 Joseph Brough and Quintus Fuller, each of whom was a certified public accountant, entered into a partnership agreement whereby they formed a partnership to engage in the practice of public accounting under the name and style of Brough & Fuller with their principal office to be located in Greeley, Colorado. Brough had been a resident of Greeley for many years prior to 1958, whereas Fuller had resided in California from 1956 to 1958, although prior to 1956 he too had resided in Greeley.

The partnership agreement, which was prepared by the parties thereto without the benefit of counsel, provided that the partnership "shall continue until terminated as herein provided." The agreement then went on to provide that the partnership could be terminated either by "retirement" upon reaching the age of sixty-five, which provision has no application to the instant controversy, or by "voluntary liquidation of the partnership." As concerns "liquidation" of the partnership, the agreement reads as follows:

"b. *Liquidation. Either partner shall have the right to withdraw from the partnership at any time.* Written notice of intention to withdraw shall be served upon the other partner at the principal office of the partnership at least three months prior to his withdrawal. The withdrawing partner shall be entitled (or his estate in the event of his subsequent death) to receive his capital balance computed on a cash basis as of withdrawal date and 10% of the cash receipts for five years following withdrawal payable monthly." (Emphasis supplied.)

The partnership agreement also contains a so-called "noncompetition" clause and it is this particular proviso that triggers the present controversy. The noncompetition clause provides as follows:

"c. Noncompetition. The withdrawn or retired partner shall not engage directly or indirectly in the practice of accounting in or within 45 miles of the City of Greeley, Colorado, or such other towns or cities wherein the firm may have established an office, for a period of 5 years from the date of his withdrawal or retirement."

On August 21, 1964, after the partnership had been in existence for nearly six years, Fuller caused the following notice to be delivered to Brough:

"Please be informed that out partnership will be terminated prior to the end of 1964, in fact, as soon as details can be worked out together.

"This action on my part is due to the fact that you have violated the terms of our agreement in that

"1. you have not devoted your entire time and energy to the business of the partnership.

"2. you have engaged in other 'business' without first obtaining my written or verbal consent."

In response to this notice Fuller testified that Brough informed him as follows: "if you're going to withdraw from the partnership, then you withdraw on the basis of the agreement."

Thereafter, on September 4, 1965 [1964] Fuller caused a second written notice to be delivered to Brough. In this particular notice Fuller advised Brough as follows:

> "Please be informed that I'll do my utmost to complete all necessary arrangements by the end of the month to move by office to another location in Greeley."

On September 24, 1964 Brough brought an action against Fuller, attaching to his complaint a copy of the partnership agreement, and then setting forth in the complaint the two notices which Fuller had caused to be delivered to him on August 21, 1964 and on September 4, 1964. Based on information and belief, Brough then went on to allege that Fuller, as the withdrawing partner, intended on or about October 1, 1964 to open a separate office for the practice of accounting in Greeley, Colorado, all of which was contrary to the noncompetition agreement. Accordingly, Brough prayed that the partnership be declared terminated as of October 1, 1964 and that Fuller be restrained from practicing accounting in or within 45 miles of Greeley for a period of 5 years.

By answer and also by way of a counterclaim, Fuller denied that he had in anywise breached the partnership agreement or that he was *voluntarily* withdrawing from the partnership. Fuller then went on to affirmatively allege that it was actually Brough who was the voluntary retiring partner and that it was Brough-not himself-who should be restrained from the practice of accounting in and within Greeley for a period of 5 years. Fuller averred that Brough had theretofore breached the partnership agreement in that Brough had purchased a farm in January 1964, without first obtaining the consent of Fuller, and as a result of this purchase it was alleged that Brough was no longer devoting his full time to the partnership business, all of which was said to be in violation of the partnership agreement. It was also said that differences of opinion had arisen between Fuller and Brough concerning the operation of the business which could not be resolved. Accordingly, Fuller asked that the partnership be dissolved and that Brough be determined to be the voluntarily retiring partner and that Brough be compelled to comply with the noncompetition clause.

A trial of this matter was had to the court on November 6, 1964. Without going into great detail, it was Brough's general theory of the case that this was purely and simply a situation where Fuller had a change of heart and wanted to get out of the partnership, but at the same time wanted to be free from the noncompetition clause in the partnership agreement. To thus have his cake and eat it too, Brough claims that Fuller accused him of misconduct as to the partnership affairs in his efforts to make his own withdrawal appear to be an "involuntary" one, instead of a voluntary withdrawal. Conversely, it was Fuller's general position that Brough was guilty of such misconduct in regard to the partnership that under the circumstances his was an involuntary withdrawal from the partnership, and that accordingly he should not be bound by the noncompetition clause.

At the conclusion of the presentation of evidence, the court took the matter under advisement. On November 18, 1964 the court made its findings and conclusions and proceeded to enter judgment in favor of Brough. More specifically, the trial court found that Brough had not violated the terms of the partnership agreement between the parties. And though the trial court found that Fuller had not in anywise breached the partnership agreement, the court nevertheless went on to find that it was Fuller who was the voluntarily retiring partner. Noting that the partnership agreement required the withdrawing partner to give at least 3 months notice prior to his withdrawal, the trial court entered a judgment declaring that the partnership be deemed terminated as of November 21, 1964-which was 3 months from the date when Fuller sent his first notice to Brough. Finally, the trial court entered an injunctive order restraining Fuller from practicing accounting in or within 45 miles of Greeley for a period of 5 years from November 21, 1964.

On November 20, 1964, which was two days after the trial court made its finding and entry of judgment and one day before the partnership was to be deemed formally terminated, Fuller served a notice on Brough of his desire to withdraw his prior notice of that which the trial court had just determined to be a notice of intention to withdraw. Specifically, Fuller requested that his letter of August 21, 1964 be withdrawn, and requested that their partnership continue, with the promise that he (Fuller) would perform all duties required of him as a partner in accordance with the partnership agreement and in accordance with sound "business and moral practices." In this latter notice Fuller stated that he was motivated by a "careful consideration of all factors and matters involved in this controversy," including the serious damage both financially and to the reputation of the parties which would result if the litigation between them was continued.

Thereafter, Fuller filed a motion for new trial or to amend the judgment, averring among other things that the court was without jurisdiction to terminate the partnership as of November 21, 1964, inasmuch as on November 20, 1964 he had withdrawn his prior notice of August 21, 1964. On motion the trial court ordered that Fuller's "notice" of November 20, 1964 be stricken and thereupon denied the motion for a new trial. By writ of error Fuller now seeks to reverse the judgment of the trial court.

Although the general rule is that gross misconduct, want of good faith, wilful neglect of partnership obligations, and such other causes as are productive of serious and permanent injury to the partnership, or which render it impracticable to carry on the partnership business, are proper grounds for the dissolution of a partnership by a court of equity at the instance of the innocent partner, nevertheless a court of equity will not dissolve an existing partnership for trifling causes or temporary grievances involving no permanent mischief. See 40 Am.Jur. pp. 300-301. It should be noted, however, that in the instant case the trial court found in effect that neither Brough nor Fuller was guilty of any misconduct as concerns partnership matters and in this connection specifically found that Brough had in nowise violated the terms of the partnership agreement between the parties. At best, the evidence discloses only temporary grievances between the parties which tended to be of a trifling nature. In any event this finding of fact that there was no misconduct on the part of either Brough or Fuller was supported in the record, and hence cannot be disturbed by us on review. The trial court, not this court, is the fact-finding body.

Having determined that neither party was at fault, the trial court went on to determine that under the circumstances it was Fuller who was "voluntarily liquidating the partnership" and that inasmuch as he was the withdrawing partner he was bound by the noncompetition clause. Fuller argues that his was really an *in*voluntary liquidation on the premise that he was virtually compelled to do so because of the alleged misconduct on the part of Brough. However, in view of the finding of the trial court that Brough had not violated the terms of the agreement, this argument falls under its own weight.

It should be remembered that we are here concerned with a partnership which could be terminated at the will of either of the parties. In other words, the partnership could be terminated at any time by either party with or without reason. However, the same partnership agreement goes on to provide that he who voluntarily liquidates the partnership by withdrawing therefrom is to be bound by the noncompetition clause. This type of noncompetition clause has been upheld and enforced by this court in *Mabray v. Williams*, 132 Colo. 523, 291 P.2d 677 and also in *Freudenthal v. Espey*, 45 Colo. 488, 102 Pac. 280. It should be noted that the agreement in the instant case contains one provision which was not contained in the contracts under consideration in either the Mabray or Freudenthal case, namely the proviso that for the period of time that the voluntarily withdrawing partner is prohibited from practicing he is to receive 10% of the cash receipts of the partnership. Finally, Fuller's plea that to enforce such a restriction is unnecessary and tends to work an undue hardship upon him loses its appeal when it is remembered that he sought to fasten the same burden on Brough. The partnership agreement in this regard at least is quite clear, and under the circumstances the noncompetition clause cannot be ignored, but on the contrary must be enforced as it was written by the parties themselves.

One remaining issue relates to the effect of Fuller's action of November 20, 1964 when he attempted to withdraw his earlier notice of intention to withdraw which had been delivered to Brough on August 21, 1964. In this regard Brough urges that under the circumstances Fuller is estopped from so doing. On the strength of that notice, as well as the subsequent notice of September 4, 1964 wherein Fuller stated that he would open another office in Greeley by October 1, 1964, Brough changed his position by retaining counsel and instituting the present proceeding in order to enforce the noncompetition clause in the partnership agreement. It has been held that the incurring of the expense of employing an attorney and commencing suit is such a change of position as to invoke the doctrine of estoppel. ...

In the instant case the matter, however, does not end there. By his answer Fuller did not elect to withdraw his notice, but rather joined issue with Brough and affirmatively sought to have Brough declared to be the voluntarily withdrawing partner and to enjoin him from practicing accountancy within 45 miles of Greeley for 5 years. And even upon trial Fuller evinced no desire to withdraw his earlier notices and return peaceably into the partnership fold. Rather, it was only after he had suffered an adverse judgment at the hands of the trial court that Fuller had this belated change of heart. Under such circumstances we hold that Fuller's notice of his desire to withdraw his earlier notice is too late. The notice having been acted upon before it was attempted to be withdrawn, the equitable principle of estoppel in pais precludes this belated shift in position. ...

The judgment is affirmed.

Notes

Fuller v. Brough presents an excellent opportunity to preview the practice of law. Assuming that you were consulted by Fuller and told of his disappointment in Brough's plans and activities respecting the farm, what course of conduct would you have recommended? Before any advice is attempted it might be best to inquire about the existence of an express partnership agreement. Advised that there was one, you would study its terms. You will find a partnership at sufferance. The agreement did not set a term, nor did it define a task. Yet it was hardly a "fragile" association. The non-competition clause was a powerful deterrent to an exercise of the power to dissolve the firm. Recall *McCallum*, supra. *Fuller* is the second opinion showing considerable understanding of and tolerance for such arrangements. In a two person partnership the agreement could hardly have included an expulsion clause! In an attempt to render the non-competition clause reasonable note the five year period and forty-five mile sweep. A glance at a map of Colorado will show that this would oblige the withdrawing partner to practice no closer than Ft. Collins or Boulder. It was a sensible term. Also, the ten percent payout clause suggests moderation.

Our prudent interest in the non-competition clause has caused us to stray from our question. What do we advise Fuller? If dissolution by act of Fuller is very dangerous given the non-competition clause, what about seeking a declaratory judgment? Such a step would be on the equity side of the court and thus would not run afoul of the rules laid down in *Pilch*. What would we ask?

Section 32: How about seeking a declaration that Brough's activities merit dissolution by decree of court under UPA Section 32? As we survey the list of grounds specified in sub-section (1) which seem suited to the fact pattern? What about (c) and (d)? Of the two I would prefer (c), that a partner has been guilty of such conduct as tends to affect prejudicially the carrying on of the business. Sub-section (d) mixes the matter of "willfulness" or proof of "persistent breach." The first requires us to look into the mind of the opponent. The second requires that our grievance take on the dimension of a persistent pattern. Note that there is a third (d) ground: "... that [the targeted partner] so conducts himself in matters relating to the partnership business that it is not reasonably practicable to carry on the business in partnership with him."

As stated earlier, under certain circumstances courts prefer to treat an ailing partnership rather than simply preside over its dignified demise by a dissolution and an accounting. Note the case development discussed by Judge Byron F. Lindsley in the following excerpt of an article (brought to the editor's attention by my late colleague, Professor Brigitte Bodenheimer), *Beyond the Family: Conciliation as a Judicial Technique*, 10 CONCILIATION COURTS REVIEW 13 (1972):

I believe in the judicial function of putting controversies at rest by a trial process. I do not believe, however, that the process need always to be cold and calculatingly designed to ferret out a factual answer in the context of legal principles. When human needs and feelings are rooted in something other than evidentiary facts I believe the judicial function can serve its proper purpose most effectively by being prepared to do what can best meet the needs of the parties who, after all, are there before the court for help. Sometimes a decision by a judge is the best kind of help. Often, however, a judicial decision out of a justiciable controversy may still leave the parties bleeding and indeed may add to the wounds.

I had such a case some months past. It was a lawsuit between partners in a small business. They had been close friends and associates for many years. Before acquiring the business several years before they had been friends and co-employees struggling up the economic ladder at the same time. When they got a chance to buy the business at a bargain out of their employer's estate they did so, together, on a shoestring. Working hard together, each having a particular competence important to the business, they had built it into a lucrative small enterprise. They were now economically successful and the sequelae to success was, as it is so often in marriage too, personal conflict. Now the partners who had been so close personally over the years were in personal and bitter conflict. In that frame of reference they could not function properly as partners. So the lawsuit was filed to dissolve the partnership.

There was no way that the partnership could be dissolved by sale of the business profitably to someone else. Its assets were in its partners and not in its fixtures, equipment and inventory. To order a sale of the business would have been economic disaster to both. Yet there was no way the court could order them to get along or decide to let one of them take over the business against the consent of the other. After a few days of trial it became apparent to me that the only way I could as a court achieve substantial justice was to find a way to get the parties to attempt to reconcile their differences. It was truly like a marriage gone sour.

With the cooperation of the attorneys on each side, who were also frustrated by the realization that the traditional trial to judgment approach would ruin both of their clients, the partners were referred to Bill Brockley, Marriage Counselor of the San Diego Conciliation Court. Of course I talked to Bill first. The challenge was irresistible. Crisis counseling took place. Out of it came an agreement of the parties, executed by their attorneys in the form of a stipulation and order, which was patterned after and almost indistinguishable from the reconciliation agreements and orders entered into by husband and wife who are trying to work out their marital conflicts. With the names of the parties blacked out, I include herewith that stipulation and order.

And it worked!

The parties did not become reconciled as partners. But then conciliation counseling for husband and wife can be very successful even though a reconciliation to the marriage does not result. Helping couples dissolve their marriage on a more constructive and positive basis is also a hallmark of successful conciliation counseling. As a judicial technique it worked. They operated under the agreement and order for one year. By then, though they were not able to be partners again, they were able to work out a fair and equitable agreement between them whereby one, for a fair price that could never have been gotten from anyone else, bought out the other partner. It was the kind of solution that the traditional judicial process could not have commanded. The order that was made because the parties were now able to agree could not have been made by the court without agreement. Justice was done. But it never could have been done if I had remained a slave in this case to the concept that courts exist only to hear and decide justiciable controversies on principles of law.

. . .

While there is nothing great or even significant in the handling of this one case, it does, I think serve as an example of how the judicial process can adapt itself to the application of different techniques to meet the very human needs of that great sea of litigants who daily pass before it and through its sometimes over-rigid machinery.

SUPERIOR COURT OF THE STATE OF CALIFORNIA

FOR THE COUNTY OF SAN DIEGO

JAMES _____

    Plaintiff,

     vs.   NO. _____

                                       ORDER

CHARLES _____ and DOES I through X,

    Defendants.

On the motion of the plaintiff and the subsequent stipulation by the parties hereto and good cause appearing therefore, it is hereby ordered that:

1. Defendant and cross-complainant, CHARLES _____ shall and he is hereby authorized and directed to solely manage, operate, and conduct the partnership business of plaintiff and defendant, _____ COMPANY, subject to the judgments and orders of the court in the above-entitled matter, and the terms and conditions of this order.

2. Plaintiff and cross-defendant, JAMES _____, is hereby enjoined and restrained from taking any part in or interfering with the management, operation or conduct of said partnership business, _____ COMPANY, by said defendant, CHARLES _____.

3. After six months from the date hereof, plaintiff, JAMES _____, may resume activity in said partnership business as a full partner therein.

4. At the end of one year from the date hereof or earlier by stipulation of the parties, the parties hereto may either:

(a) At the sole discretion of defendant, CHARLES _____, resume their former joint operation of said _____ COMPANY business as co-partners.

(b) Continue the operation of said business solely by one of the partners, upon terms and conditions acceptable to the said partners, or,

(c) Resume the trial of the above-entitled case before this Court which shall retain jurisdiction of this matter.

5. Defendant and cross-complainant, CHARLES _____, shall be compensated at the rate of $20,000.00 per annum for the period set out in paragraph 3 herein, and any additional period thereafter prior to plaintiff's and cross-defendant's resuming his activity in said business, over and above his partnership interest in said business, as compensation for so managing, operating and conducting said business.

6. This stipulated order is made solely for the purpose of attempting a reconciliation of the parties as working partners, and is not in any manner to be taken as an admission of any matter or facts or a waiver of any rights by either of the parties hereto.

7. Neither of the parties hereto shall transfer, sell, hypothecate, encumber or assign any of the property or assets of _____ COMPANY, except in the usual course of business.

8. Until further order of the court, defendant and cross-complainant, CHARLES _____, shall remit the sum of $750.00 to JAMES _____ on the first and fifteenth days of each and every month hereafter, which sums shall be charged first against plaintiff and cross-defendant's share, if any, of the firm's profits, and last, if necessary, against plaintiff and cross-defendant's capital account. Said remittance shall be made by mail to: JAMES _____ San Diego,

California 92119, or such other address as plaintiff and cross-defendant shall notify defendant and cross-complainant in writing. Plaintiff and cross-defendant may make additional withdrawals in such amounts as he may request from time to time, such withdrawals to be charged as above. Neither party shall deplete his capital account below the level of the other party.

9. This order shall cease to be of any force or effect upon the death of either of the parties hereto.

10. Upon plaintiff and cross-defendant's return to partnership activity in accordance with paragraph 3 hereinabove, each party shall do his utmost to work in harmony with the other, shall keep the other fully informed of his activity with relation to the business, shall not interfere with the other's business activities nor his relationship with the partnership's employees or customers, shall attempt to share the workload of the business equally with the other and shall in no way harass the other party or otherwise attempt to create unpleasant working conditions.

11. Plaintiff and cross-defendant may undertake any business activity during the six months following entry of this order and such activity shall be for his own account. No profits made or liabilities incurred therein shall accrue to the partnership.

12. During the period of this order, monthly disbursement and "net quick" reports shall be prepared and each party shall receive a copy thereof, together with a copy of any other financial reports prepared for the business.

Stipulation

It is hereby stipulated by and between the parties hereto, acting through their respective attorneys, that the court may make the foregoing order.

DATED:

May 4, 1971.

_____

BY Attorneys for plaintiff and cross-defendant

_____

BY Attorneys for defendant and cross-complainant

SO ORDERED

DATED: _____

_____

/s/ BYRON F. LINDSLEY
Judge, Superior Court

D. PROPERTY RIGHTS AND THE PARTNERSHIP: QUESTIONS OF OWNERSHIP AND INTEREST

Since a partnership (unlike a corporation) is not a distinct legal person there are confusing questions about the ownership of personal and real property used in the firm's business. Stated most generally: either the property has been contributed to (or acquired as part of) the firm's capital or the property has remained a partner's individual asset while loaned to the firm. At the formation of a partnership the drafting lawyer can do much to avert these complications in the ownership of realty and personalty "brought into the business" by the new firm's members. During the life of the partnership the lawyer can perform a valuable service by urging the partners to put into writing their intentions respecting property ownership questions. The UPA sets up a series of presumptions to be used to resolve these issues in the absence of an express agreement.

A second set of problems arises in attempts to define each partner's interest in property conceded to belong to the firm. The law has created a hybrid ownership called "tenancy in partnership" which gives the firm some status without recognizing the partnership per se as a legal entity. The presence of "legal fictions" and indirect reasoning is a clue that the law of partnerships has been viewed as the proverbial square peg seeking a niche in a wall with only round holes.

The third thorny area is the nature of each partner's interest in the "firm" itself.

1. Partnership Property: firm capital distinguished from the property of individual partners:

As soon as a partnership is formed, and until its formal dissolution, the law is faced with the question of ownership of assets used in the business. Has an asset become partnership property or is it merely on loan from one of the partners? Section 8 of the UPA is the modern point of departure for analysis of this issue.

(1) All property originally brought into the partnership stock or subsequently acquired by purchase or otherwise, on account of the partnership, is partnership property.

(2) Unless the contrary intention appears, property acquired with partnership funds is partnership property.

(3) Any estate in real property may be acquired in the partnership name.

Title so acquired can be conveyed only in the partnership name.

(4) ...

HILLOCK v. GRAPE
Supreme Court of New York, Appellate Division, 1906.
111 App.Div. 720, 97 N.Y.S. 823.

NASH, J. This is an action to establish a copartnership and for an accounting. The copartnership is denied. The complaint alleges that on, or about the 1st day of March, 1901, at the city of Rochester, N.Y., the plaintiff and defendant entered into a general trucking and carting copartnership each to be an equal partner therein, the firm name to be Grape & Hillock; and the assets of the firm at the first were to consist of four horses and two wagons put into said business by said Grape, against the knowledge and experience Hillock had of and in trucking and carting business; they to own said property so put in and whatever other property bought thereafter for such business, jointly. That such copartnership has been carried on ever since such date, and has made about the sum of $2,900 for the year 1901, $4,800 for the year 1902, $6,250 for the year 1903, and $5,320 for the year 1904 to September 1st, 1904, making $19,270 received in cash by such copartnership since said 1st day of March, 1901, besides the trucks, carts, horses and harnesses now owned by such copartnership, namely, seven pairs of horses, wagons, sleighs, harnesses, and other property of the value of $6,000, and an established trade and business worth the sum of $2,000.

There was no written articles of copartnership. The witnesses who testified to the making of the alleged agreement on the part of the plaintiff, were Freckleton, a nephew of the plaintiff, and the plaintiff. Freckleton testified that Grape applied to him, and asked if he was a nephew of Hillock and if he knew whether his uncle would go into the carting business. That Grape said:

"I have got five horses and a little money in the bank, and two wagons and a small wagon or sleigh, and why can't Tom and I go into business together, and he put up his experience against what I have got?"

Afterward Grape and Hillock having met, and had some negotiations, they came together and in the presence of Freckleton, made, it is claimed, the partnership agreement. Freckleton's testimony is:

"I said: 'Now, Mr. Grape, what do you intend to do? What are your plans? Mr. Hillock wants me to be a witness to this copartnership.' Grape said, 'I have five horses, two large wagons, a small wagon, the running gear bobs or sleigh, and about $600 in the bank to pay any running expenses they might have when they got started.' Q. Tell what one said, then what the other said. A. Grape said they would take, each of them, so much money out of the business each week, as the business would warrant after the business was started. No specified amount was named at that time. Q. Anything else said there? A. They said, 'we will get together,' and he said, 'I think I know where we can get another wagon or sleigh, or a top for a sleigh.' Q. Who said that? A. Grape. He made arrangements for Hillock to meet him to go to some wagon or blacksmith shop. Hillock said one of the first things they ought to do was to get some blanks they could put in the freight house, for authority to receive freight. He said he wanted the cards so he could start out with people he knew, and see if they could get their business. They started out, and agreed to go to the printers to get some cards. I did not hear any further conversation beyond a general line. Q. Did they say what they were going to call the business? A. Grape said he wasn't particular whether they called it Grape & Hillock, or Hillock & Grape. They decided on Grape & Hillock before they went away. After the talk was over, I asked Grape if something hadn't ought to be done about drawing papers about the copartnership. Grape said he had a friend, Assemblyman Smith, and he would have him draw the papers. That was practically the end of that conversation."

Hillock testified that a few days after Grape first met Freckleton he saw Grape and they talked the matter over. He says that Grape said he had two teams and a single horse and two wagons and sleigh, and he would put them up against my experience in the business. That he afterwards went and looked at the property, and after some further negotiations, they met by appointment at a restaurant and made the agreement testified to by Freckleton.

Hillock's testimony:

"Q. What was said in the restaurant? A. Grape went over the same thing about the teams and the single horse and two wagons and sleigh and tools. He put them all up against my experience in the business, and he had money in the bank to pay freight bills. Then I made the agreement with him that I would go in with him. Q. How long after that did you start together in the carting business? A. About the 1st of March, 1901. Q. When you wanted any money did you draw it from the firm? A. Grape and I made arrangements that we would draw so much a week the first year, and go as light as we could till we got started. We made arrangements to draw $8 each. Q. And the next year? A. He said the next year we would draw $9 each, and in a few more years we could probably draw $15 a week."

The defendant admits that a partnership was proposed and that he had conversations with Hillock upon the subject, but denied that any partnership agreement was ever made. His claim is that Hillock entered into his employment in the carting business. That upon Hillock's representations as to his ability to get work among his friends by the use of his name, cards with the name of Grape & Hillock upon them were used, and the name Grape & Hillock was put on one or two of the wagons and a sleigh. The plaintiff worked with the employees during the three years and a half, rendering services as a laborer. On pay day he received his money in an envelope with the rest of the men, and was docked as they were for lost time. The business was all transacted by Grape in his own name. He employed, directed, and paid all of the men, and made all the additions to the property by purchase in his own name.

The court below found as facts: (1) That on the 1st day of May, 1901, at Rochester, N.Y., plaintiff and defendant entered into an agreement, in and by which they agreed to form and did form a copartnership between them for an indefinite period, to conduct and carry on the business of drawing and conveying for hire, goods, and merchandise, and to conduct a general carting business at said Rochester, N.Y., under the firm name of Grape & Hillock; (2) that in and by said agreement defendant agreed to contribute to the capital and assets of said copartnership four horses and two wagons, and said plaintiff agreed to contribute to the business of said copartnership the knowledge and experience, which plaintiff had acquired in the trucking business; (3) that in and by said agreement the said parties further agreed that each partner should divide his time and energy to the prosecution of said business, and that said partners should share equally all profits and losses of said business; (4) that said copartnership continued and said business was prosecuted by said partners from and including said March 1st, 1901, to September 3d, 1904, when said partnership terminated by plaintiff's election, and notice thereof given by plaintiff to defendant.

It is further found that the partnership sold property from time to time, and acquired divers articles of property; that all purchases and sales were made by the defendant; that the plaintiff demanded of the defendant that he account to the plaintiff, and pay over to him the portion of the copartnership assets to which he should be found entitled, which was refused. And as a conclusion of law, that the plaintiff is entitled to an accounting by the defendant of and concerning all the property, assets, receipts, and disbursements, and business of the copartnership, from the beginning of the same to the termination thereof. It is so adjudged by the interlocutory judgment. The contention of the defendant is that the finding that an agreement of copartnership was entered into is against the weight of the evidence. Without passing upon that question, we conclude that a new trial must be granted, upon the ground that the decision, to the effect that the plaintiff is entitled to a portion or share of the property and assets of the business, is entirely unsupported by the evidence.

The witness Freckleton, on his cross-examination, testified that it was his understanding the Hillock was to be a joint owner with Grape of all the assets of the copartnership, including the horses, wagons, sleighs, harnesses and the equipment, and the $600 in the bank, put in by Grape. The plaintiff was asked on cross examination:

"Q. You were to have half the money, and a half interest in the horses and wagons and sleighs, and the equipment? A. That was the agreement." These were mere conclusions; neither of them testified to any language of Grape to that effect. The language imputed to Grape by both Freckleton and Hillock on all occasions testified to by them, was that Grape would put up his property against Hillock's experience. The language attributed to Grape, as testified to by Freckleton and Hillock, that Grape would put up his property against Hillock's experience will not bear the construction put upon it by the decision. It implied, at most, only a partnership as to the profits, and not a community of interest in the property which Grape put up against Hillock's experience. Agreements by which one person contributes his labor and experience to the business of a copartnership for a share of the profits are often made. The rights of the parties are well understood by the persons concerned. The title to the property as capital put in against labor, remains in the owner; the profits only being shared by the parties. The construction put upon the alleged agreement by the plaintiff would work out a result which could not possibly have been intended by the defendant. The contract testified to, and as found, was for an indefinite period. If the title to an equal share of the horses, wagons, equipments, and money of Grape, passed to the plaintiff by virtue of the alleged agreement, Hillock could have terminated the copartnership at any time; at the end of a week he could have demanded that the defendant account to him for one-half of the property.

There is no evidence in the record that the additional property was purchased with the money or profits of the business. The purchases were all made by the defendant. The plaintiff did not participate in making them. Grape made the purchases, and paid for the property purchased, as far as appears, with his own money and means. At the time of the trial he was indebted to Hartung, of whom the additional horses were purchased, some 13 or 14 in number, upon his individual promissory notes, one for $800 and another of $500; and there was also an indebtedness of the defendant to the Hoffman Wagon Company on account, which had accrued in the course of the business, amounting to between $800 and $1,200.

Interlocutory judgment reversed, and a new trial granted, with costs to the appellant to abide the event. All concur, except SPRING and KRUSE, JJ., who dissent.

Notes

Could a modern court applying §8 of the UPA reach the result in *Hillock v. Grape*? Was Grape's property not "... brought into the partnership stock ..."? Under §8(1), is it a "price tag" for the formation of a partnership that assets made available to the business must become "partnership property"?

Consider the following excerpt from *Cyrus v. Cyrus*, 242 Minn. 180, 64 N.W.2d 538, 540, 543-544 (1954):

In 1934, Cecil Cyrus, Edna Cyrus (the plaintiff), and their children were living on a farm in North Dakota. In 1935 Cecil Cyrus served time in the penitentiary at Burleigh, North Dakota, and the plaintiff and children lived in Minot. During the years 1934 and 1935, both Cecil and the plaintiff received letters from Curtis, Cecil's brother, in which Curtis urged them to move to Minnesota and enter into a "partnership" for the building and operating of a tourist camp or resort on Lake of the Woods. In response to the requests of Curtis, the family moved to Minnesota in December of 1936 and entered into an agreement with a third person to live in a house situated on property close to the 60-acre tract which Curtis had purchased in his own name in 1935. Curtis's property was vacant except for one old "shack," and in accordance with the agreement to start a resort, Cecil and his father built a cabin on Curtis's land. Although there is evidence to the contrary, the trial court could reasonably find that this cabin, and all subsequent improvements, were thereafter paid for out of earnings derived from the operation of the resort. Curtis personally paid the taxes and paid for boats purchased, but it is plaintiff's testimony that for these and other expenditures made Curtis was reimbursed out of resort earnings. Sometime after 1936 an additional 40-acre tract was acquired in Curtis's name, but there is credible testimony that it also was paid for out of resort earnings. Although out of the resort earnings Cecil was allowed the living expenses for his family, he contributed his labor, and his wife did all the washing and ironing and cleaned and took care of the cabins. In addition Cecil's three children, especially the older one who was 18 years old when Cecil died, helped with the resort work.

During the entire period involved herein Curtis was regularly employed in Minneapolis and did not contribute any personal work to the operation of the resort other than to build an occasional cabin shelf while on his vacation. Every fall when Curtis visited the resort, the earnings were accounted for and Curtis was given his one-half share. This continued until Cecil died in December of 1944. At that time the value of the resort was estimated to be $10,000.

Before Cecil's death, Curtis had sent a copy of his will and a letter to Cecil in which he explained that he was protecting Cecil by his will until he could deed one-half of the property to him. After Cecil's funeral he told the plaintiff that he would deed half the place to her. Later Curtis sent two letters to the plaintiff in which he offered to deed one-half of the resort to her, and in one of these letters he remarked that "It's yours as much as mine and I'll make the deed over that way when I have the opportunity." From 1945 to the present, Curtis himself, or others renting from him, have operated the resort.

Plaintiff, as special administratrix of Cecil's estate, brought her action in November 1951 for an adjudication that a partnership existed and for the liquidation of such partnership and a division of its assets. Judgment was entered in favor of the plaintiff declaring that a partnership had been formed and that the same was dissolved when Cecil died on December 17, 1944, and that Cecil's interest therein was then of the value of $5,000. The judgment further provided for the appointment of a liquidating receiver to liquidate the partnership and to pay to plaintiff as an ordinary creditor the sum of $5,000 with interest thereon from December 17, 1944. Defendant's appeal is from said judgment.

. . .

It is uncontradicted that the original 60-acre tract was purchased by the defendant with his own money and that the title was taken in his own name. As already noted it was acquired prior to the creation of the partnership. If the 60-acre tract constitutes partnership property, it must be on the theory that it was contributed to the partnership by the defendant. Whether real property acquired by a partner individually prior to the formation of a partnership belongs to or has been appropriated to the partnership is a question of intent. The fact that such realty is used for partnership purposes is not of itself, when standing alone, sufficient to establish an intent to contribute it to the partnership assets. 40 Am.Jur., Partnership, §§ 100 and 105. In addition to the element of partnership use, we have, however, certain other evidentiary factors. Cabins, docks, and other improvements were built upon this land for the use of the partnership and were paid for out of partnership earnings. Improvements so made at partnership expense, although not of controlling significance, tend to show an intent that the land should be partnership property. As with the 40-acre tract, we have the salient fact that the evidence sustains a finding that the taxes were ultimately paid for out of partnership earnings. In the light of these factors, the court could reasonably attach considerable significance to the statements which defendant made to plaintiff by letter and otherwise after Cecil died. These statements clearly recognized plaintiff's legal right to one-half of the property, a right which could exist only if the parties believed the property belonged to the partnership. Under the circumstances we can only conclude that the evidence sustains the trial court's conclusion that the entire realty was partnership property.

The decision of the trial court is affirmed.

Affirmed.

Would the Supreme Court of Minnesota have agreed with the alternative holding in *Ellis v. Mihelis*, supra, page 70?

In re Palega's Estate, 208 Misc. 966, 145 N.Y.S.2d 271, 272 (1955) presents a trial judge's conclusion that where a sole proprietor converted his business into a partnership and expressly retained title to all tangible assets used in that business, such assets did not become partnership property despite constant use by the partnership. Also see *Cooper v. Cooper*, 289 Ala. 263, 266 So.2d 871 (1972).

IN RE ESTATE OF SCHAEFER
Supreme Court of Wisconsin, 1976.
72 Wis.2d 600, 241 N.W.2d 607.

DAY, J. The orders appealed from arise out of a single petition filed in probate court by Marilynn H. Schaefer, widow of the decedent, Ben G. Schaefer, concerning a large number of matters in the administration of the estate. As the result of a pretrial conference the issues raised by the petition were bifurcated for hearing. The principal issue concerns real estate inventoried as property of a business partnership between Ben Schaefer and his brother, Arthur Schaefer, and claimed by Marilynn Schaefer to have belonged to the brothers as tenants in common. Appeal No. 101 is taken from an order denying her petition in this respect. ...

Ben G. and Arthur E. Schaefer went into business together in 1933, each providing an equal capital share to start an automobile dealership in Racine, which came to be known as Schaefer Pontiac Sales. No written partnership agreement was ever executed. The brothers began acquiring real estate in 1944, making purchases through 1967 which included items 26 through 38 of the inventory, which are at issue here. The deeds to all 13 parcels are included in the record; nine of the deeds name the grantees simply as "Ben G. Schaefer and Arthur E. Schaefer;" three of the deeds name the grantees as "Ben G. Schaefer and Arthur E. Schaefer, as tenants in common," and one deed refers to "Ben G. Schaefer and Arthur E. Schaefer, a real estate partnership."

In 1947, the automobile sales activity was incorporated, and separated from the real estate business which became known as "Ben G. Schaefer and Arthur E. Schaefer, Real Estate Department." A separate checking account was maintained for the real estate business, titled "Ben G. Schaefer and Arthur E. Schaefer, Real Estate Trust Account, Partnership." The respondents introduced testimony by an accountant, retained to examine the business records, to the effect that all payments for real estate purchased, and all proceeds from real estate sold, and income from leases, came from or went into this checking account. When mortgage loans were obtained, the proceeds went into the "partnership" bank account, and the amortization payments came from that account. When improvements were made to property held by the business, they were paid for out of the "partnership" account. This testimony was uncontradicted, and was accepted as true by the trial court.

Various documents in the record provide additional evidence concerning the understanding of the Schaefer brothers as to ownership of the real estate. A mortgage on one of the parcels in question was given by "Ben G. Schaefer and Arthur E. Schaefer, as co-partners." Leases were introduced by the respondents as follows:

(1) Lease from "Ben G. Schaefer and Arthur E. Schaefer, d/b/a Schaefer Realty Company," signed by Arthur E. Schaefer alone;

(2) Lease from "Ben G. Schaefer and Arthur E. Schaefer," signed by Arthur E. Schaefer as "Partner," alone;

(3) Lease from "Arthur E. Schaefer and Ben G. Schaefer, co-partners," signed by Arthur E. Schaefer alone; and

(4) Lease from "Ben G. Schaefer and Arthur E. Schaefer, a partnership" signed by Arthur E. Schaefer as "partner," alone.

In an attempt to show that the real estate was not regarded as partnership property, Marilynn Schaefer introduced additional leases as follows:

(1) Lease with option to buy from "Arthur E. Schaefer and Colette Schaefer, his wife, and Ben G. Schaefer and Marilynn Schaefer, his wife," signed by all four lessors;

(2) Lease from "Ben G. Schaefer and Arthur E. Schaefer," signed by both of them;

(3) Lease from "Ben G. Schaefer and Arthur E. Schaefer," signed by Arthur E. Schaefer, alone.

Marilynn Schaefer also introduced documents relating to a condemnation proceeding which referred to "lands of Ben G. Schaefer and Marilynn Schaefer, his wife; Arthur E. Schaefer and Colette Schaefer, his wife," and a deed conveying some of the business property from the Schaefers and their wives, individually named. The proceeds of that condemnation, however (as well as prior rental income from that property), went into the "partnership" books, and were distributed to Ben and Arthur accordingly. Arthur testified that the wives' names were included "because the attorneys wanted them, not because they [the wives] had any interest," although he was referring to a deed not admitted into evidence.

Respondents also introduced testimony based on tax returns filed between 1948 and 1969 by the business on tax forms designed for partnerships, and by Ben G. Schaefer individually, showing that the income of the real estate operation was divided equally between Ben and Arthur, and that Ben's reported income coincided with the amount distributed by the business. This testimony was undisputed, except insofar as Marilynn extracted the concession that the partnership tax return forms might be used for nonpartnership business arrangements.

On this evidence, the trial court found that a partnership existed, and that the real estate was partnership property. Marilynn Schaefer challenges the sufficiency of the evidence to support that finding, and makes legal arguments based on the statute of frauds and the form of the deeds of conveyance.

The evidence overwhelmingly supports the trial court's finding that a partnership did exist. ...

Once the existence of a partnership is established, there is a statutory presumption that property purchased with partnership funds belongs to the partnership unless a "contrary intent" is shown. [UPA §8]. The evidence in this case is plainly insufficient to establish a "contrary intent." The only evidence of intent not to operate as a partnership are the references to "tenants in common" on three of the thirteen deeds conveying the lands in question to Ben and Arthur, and the inclusion of the Schaefers' spouses as grantors on the two conveyances introduced. Even if this would be sufficient to overcome the statutory presumption, it must be weighed against the overwhelming mass of evidence showing that the lands were purchased with partnership funds, managed as a partnership activity, and sold for partnership benefit.

Marilynn Schaefer attacks the probative value of the respondents' evidence, in particular the testimony concerning the "partnership" tax returns. Even assuming she is correct that "partnership" tax returns may be, and are, used for nonpartnership joint ventures of various sorts, the tax treatment of the income is not stripped of all probative value. This court has held that receipt of a share of business profits, as shown in tax returns, is *prima facie* evidence of partnership, under [UPA §7(4)] .... In any case, there is ample evidence independent of the tax returns to support the trial court's finding that a partnership existed and owned the real estate in question. In order for this court to overturn the trial court's finding, that finding would have to be "contrary to the great weight and clear preponderance of evidence." *Milbauer v. Transport Employees' Mut. B. Soc.* (1973), 56 Wis.2d 860, 862, 203 N.W.2d 135; in the present case, the great weight of the evidence supports the trial court's decision.

Marilynn Schaefer also argues that a partnership dealing in real estate is subject to the statute of frauds, and must be evidenced by a writing. It is true that this court has adopted the minority view that a partnership created to deal in real estate is void unless conforming to the statute of frauds:

> "In Wisconsin, contrary to the great weight of authority in this country, a joint adventure or a partnership to engage in the sale or purchase of real estate, is held to be a contract respecting an interest in lands, and void under the statute of frauds, unless in writing, or unless sufficiently performed to take the same out of the statute." *Goodsitt v. Richter* (1934), 216 Wis. 351, 257 N.W. 23.

There was admittedly no written partnership agreement in the present case.

However, an exception to the statute of frauds is made where all parties have performed the contract, indicating their acquiescence in its terms. In *Smith v. Putnam* (1900), 107 Wis. 155, 82 N.W. 1077, 83 N.W. 288, a claimed partnership had been formed to purchase land, money had been invested, and several transactions had been completed and proceeds divided among the partners, when some partners sought to withhold certain proceeds from another. In upholding the existence of an unwritten partnership, the court said (page 163):

> "In applying the statute of frauds, courts long since recognized an exception, or more properly a distinction, in cases where a contract void by the statute had been fully executed, and one party sought to retain the fruits of the dealing in defiance of his promises. Such situation was declared to be not within the purpose of, and so not sheltered by, the statute. It has therefore been held in a vast array of decided cases that where the parties have fully executed all parts of such a contract relating to or affecting interests in land, so that the courts do not need to enforce anything with reference to the land itself, the rights and duties of the parties resulting from their dealings may be enforced, and each of them prevented from using that statute, not as a protection against, but as an effective means of, fraud."

Similarly in *Huntington v. Burdeau* (1912), 149 Wis. 263, 270, 135 N.W. 845, where only an accounting of some amounts due from one real estate partner to another was necessary, the statute of frauds was not a bar to suit based on an unwritten partnership. ...

Marilynn Schaefer also argues that because the deeds to the properties in question conveyed them as estates of inheritance (to Ben and Arthur Schaefer and "their heirs and assigns forever"), Ben and Arthur received estates of inheritance, as tenants in common, and did not take the lands as a business partnership. Words of inheritance, however, refer to the extent of the estate granted-a fee simple-and do not define the grantee. This is apparent from statutes making words of inheritance unnecessary to pass a fee in general, sec. 706.10(3), Stats., and unnecessary to pass a fee to a partnership in particular, sec. 178.05(4). ... In *Weber v. Nedin* (1932), 210 Wis. 39, 46, 242 N.W. 487, as in the present case, it was argued that the words "heirs and assigns forever" created a tenancy in common, because they were inconsistent with the principle of survivorship inherent in a joint tenancy. This court rejected that argument, holding that a joint tenancy had been created because of other evidence of such an intent. In construing a deed, the purpose of the court is to ascertain the intent of the parties. *Flynn v. Palmer* (1955), 270 Wis. 43, 47, 70 N.W.2d 231. The words "heirs and assigns forever" manifest no particular intent to create an estate of inheritance. Moreover, here the words of inheritance were part of the standard printed form of deed. They cannot be said, in light of the evidence of intent to create a partnership, to demonstrate any intent whatsoever to take the property as tenants in common.

Apart from the words of inheritance, Marilynn Schaefer argues that the muniment of title should govern; since the bulk of the deeds name as grantees simply Ben G. and Arthur E. Schaefer, the deeds acted to create a tenancy in common between them. Whatever presumption the muniment of title may ordinarily carry, this court has long held to the principle, now codified in sec. 178.05, Stats., supra, that property purchased with partnership funds and appropriated for partnership purposes is presumptively partnership property, regardless of the manner in which title is formally held. *Kyle v. Carpenter* (1907), 130 Wis. 310, 316, 110 N.W. 187:

> "It is elementary that 'real estate purchased for partnership purposes and appropriated to those purposes, paid for by partnership funds and necessary for partnership purposes, always becomes partnership property. Nor does it seem to be material in what manner, or by what agency, the land is bought, or in what name it stands.' Parsons, Partn. (4th ed.) § 265. In the same section it is said:

> " 'We consider it an established rule in equity that any party holding the legal title to land, however it may have come to him, will be held as trustee for the partnership, if it be certain that the land was in fact a part of their joint property as partners.' "

. . .

In *Kyle*, a partner who had been bought out, but had failed to reconvey legal title, subsequently sold lands to a third-party purchaser with alleged knowledge of the situation. The case of *Thompson v. Beth*, supra, involved property purchased by one partner and held in his name, but purchased and used for partnership purposes. Citing *Kyle*, this court held that the manner of purchase and legal tenure were immaterial where the facts disclosed a partnership operation. In the present case, the evidence established both that the real estate was purchased with partnership funds, and that it was purchased and used for partnership purposes. The fact that legal title was in the individual partners is immaterial under these circumstances.

In summary, the partnership of the Schaefer brothers was not subject to the statute of frauds because it was sufficiently performed to establish its existence. The words of inheritance used in the deeds, and the form in which legal title was held, are immaterial to the determination of whether the real estate in question was partnership property, since the evidence conclusively shows the purchase of the real estate with partnership funds, and its use for partnership purposes.

Notes

Schaefer is unrivaled as a discussion of the §8(2) presumption or the variety of means whereby it may be challenged. Why did Marilynn Schaefer go to such extraordinary lengths to contend that the property in question was held by tenancy in common as opposed to a concession that her late husband and Arthur had been partners and the real estate, acquired with partnership funds, was partnership property? Full understanding of her motivation will have to await the materials on dissolution and its consequences. However it may be useful to preview the topic. UPA §24 establishes three property interests or rights of each partner: (1) that partner's rights in specific partnership property; (2) that partner's interest in the partnership; and (3) that partner's right to participate in the management of the firm. Section 25 defines the extent of the rights which each partner possesses with respect to "specific partnership property", while §26 gives a very clear definition of the meaning of "interest in the partnership."

Please examine §25(2)(d) and (e) from the perspective of Marilynn Schaefer. If her late husband and Arthur were partners, Arthur is the sole surviving partner of the now dissolved firm. If the real estate in question was specific partnership property does sub-section (d) mandate that upon Ben's death his §25 interest was vested in Arthur? Is this the intended consequence of §25(2)(e)?

The consequences of the death of a partner as to the decedent's right in specific partnership property are startling. It reminds one of the classical tontine! Would it trouble many persons doing business in the partnership form to learn that, in default of any explicit partnership agreement making other arrangements, they are participants in a race for death? What is the "social" justification for such a result? It is clear that during the life of a partner insulating specific partnership property from the claims of her creditors (even a disgruntled spouse) may be justified on the grounds that presumably indispensable assets are being protected in the hands of the other partners. Such a justification (an interest in the survival of the business entity and, incidentally, in the business careers of the other partners) may be asserted to justify keeping partnership assets at minimum risk when faced with claims of the passive survivors of a deceased partner. But even granting this why continue the advantage to the "sole surviving partner" who must now, of necessity, carry on as a sole proprietor?

This last point also has a statutory hook: note the final phrase in §25(2) (d) to the effect that the rights of the surviving partner or partners or the legal representative of the sole surviving partner are restricted in their right of possession to a "partnership purpose." In a partnership which was neither organized for a term nor a task (see, §31(1)(a)) what is the last partnership purpose? Is it not the marshalling of assets under §38 for a distribution under §40? If that step is now incumbent on Arthur isn't this complete protection for Marilynn?

The "property" status of good will: The partnership agreement provides an opportunity to anticipate many questions about property claims and to protect partners from costly litigation. Consider one further property concept. Suppose that five individuals form a partnership to conduct a retail hardware business. For twenty years the firm is successful. Excellent consumer relations plus a large advertising budget have made the firm a major retail force in the community. In 1990 one partner dies and the question of her share of the "partnership property" immediately arises. The cases reviewed (along with the UPA) suggest some guidelines for the segregation of property brought into the firm by members and the fate of property acquired by the firm with partnership assets. Thus one can deal with interests in fixtures, real property and even inventory. But what of the firm's "good will"? Is this an "asset" for which the surviving partners must account? If so, how is it is to be valued? [These same questions would arise if any partner withdrew from the firm.]

The leading case on the point is *In the Matter of Brown*, 242 N.Y. 1, 6, 150 N.E. 581, 582 (1926), wherein Judge Cardozo declared:

> Good will, when it exists as incidental to the business of a partnership, is presumptively an asset to be accounted for like any other by those who liquidate the business .... The course of dealing, however, can stamp it with a different quality. Partners may contract that good will, though it exist, shall not "be considered as property or as an asset of the co-partnership" .... The contract may "be expressly made," or it may "arise by implication, from other contracts and the acts and conduct of the parties" .... The implication will be drawn the more readily when the good will, if any, is tenuous or doubtful ....

It is clear that the better course for the drafting lawyer is not to leave such important matters to implication.

Further support for the proposition that "good will" should, absent an agreement, be seen as a firm asset is §9(3)(b) of the UPA, requiring unanimity for the disposition of a partnership's good will.

One idea in *In the Matter of Brown* is under attack. Cardozo suggested that, for public policy reasons, good will should not be recognized as an asset if the partners' relationship is "distinctly personal or professional." Does this suggest the broad proposition that professional firms do not have "good will" which may be valued as an asset? Consider *Bailey v. McCoy*, 187 Neb. 618, 193 N.W.2d 270, 273 (1971), which holds (respecting a partnership formed to render accounting and income tax services): "... A partnership engaged in performing services may possess good will ...." Also see Crane and Bromberg, Partnership, § 84(a) (1968).

2. The interest of each partner in property conceded to belong to the firm:

BYNUM v. SANDS, INC.
Supreme Court of Nevada, 1953.
70 Nev. 191, 264 P.2d 846.

EATHER, CHIEF JUSTICE. This is an appeal from the judgment of the Eighth Judicial District Court of the State of Nevada, in and for the County of Clark, based upon undisputed facts and the construction of a written instrument in an action brought by the appellant, Harvey A. Bynum, to recover possession of an undivided one-fifth interest in and to certain lands located in Clark County, Nevada, occupied by respondent, and for rents and profits received by the respondent from the use and occupancy of said premises. The trial court's judgment denied all relief asked by plaintiff.

The facts are substantially these: On the 21st day of November, 1945, a co-partnership consisting of George W. Frisby and Dave Anderson leased certain lands located in Clark County, Nevada, for a term of ten years. On April 1, 1946, the said Frisby and Anderson, co-partners doing business under the name "Club Kit Carson", entered into the following agreement with appellant, Harvey A. Bynum:

"AGREEMENT

'This Agreement made and entered into as of the 1st day of April, 1946, by and between George W. Frisby and Davie Anderson, co-partners doing business under the name of 'Club Kit Carson', Parties of the First Part, and Harvey A. Bynum, Party of the Second Part,

"WITNESSETH:

"Recitals:

'The Parties of the First Part have a lease dated November _____ 1945, from Nate Mack and wife, and James S. Fulcher and wife, covering on a portion of the Northwest Quarter of Section 16, Township 21, S., Range 61 E., M.D.B. and M., in the County of Clark, State of Nevada, upon which leased parcel of land they have constructed a club building consisting of bar room, casino and dining hall, known as 'Club Kit Carson'.

'The Party of the Second Part has rendered services to the Parties of the First Part and is to be compensated therefor.

"The Parties of the First Part have contributed to their co-partnership as capital therefor, the sum of Sixty-two Thousand Five Hundred ($62,500.00) Dollars.

"The Parties of the First Part desire to assign to the Party of the Second Part a twenty percent (20l) interest in said co-partnership, upon the terms and conditions hereinafter stated, to-wit:

"Now, Therefore, It Is Agreed Between The Parties Hereto, as follows:

"1. The Parties of the First Part do hereby sell, assign, transfer and set over to the Party of the Second Part, a twenty percent (20l) interest of, in and to that certain co-partnership existing between the Parties of the First Part and known as and called 'Club Kit Carson'.

"2. It is understood and agreed between the parties hereto that the party of the Second Part is not a partner with the Parties of the First Part in said 'Club Kit Carson', nor shall said Second Party be permitted to interfere in the management or administration of the partnership business and affairs or to acquire any information or account of partnership transactions, or to inspect the partnership books, but shall be entitled to receive, in accordance with this contract, twenty percent (20l) of the profits to which the Parties of the First Part would otherwise be entitled, and in case of a dissolution of said partnership, the Party of the Second Part shall be entitled to receive from the Parties of the First Part said twenty percent (20l) interest, and may require an account from the date of the last account agreed to between the Parties of the First Part.

"3. It is understood and agreed that before there shall be any division of profits between the Parties of the First Part and the Party of the Second Part, the said Parties of the First Part shall be entitled to deduct and retain the said sum of $62,500.00 so advanced by them as aforesaid, and said sum shall be considered as a loan from the said First Parties to the partnership, but that after said First Parties shall have received from said partnership said sum of $62,500.00, then all profits from the partnership shall be divided, twenty percent (20l) to the Party of the Second Part, and eighty percent (80l) to the Parties of the First Part.

"4. The Parties of the First Part have this day paid to the Party of the Second Part the sum of Two Thousand Dollars ($2,000.00), which shall be considered as an advance on said share of the profits, and the Parties of the First Part shall in any settlement hereafter made with said Second Party, be entitled to a credit of $2,000.00.

"5. It is understood and agreed that all other agreements between the parties hereto are terminated and cancelled as of the date of this agreement.

"In Witness Whereof, the parties hereto have hereunto set their hands as of the day and year first above written.

"Dave Anderson

"George W. Frisby

"Parties of the First Part.

"Harvey A. Bynum

"Party of the Second Part."

In November, 1949, the co-partnership was terminated and dissolved by a written agreement under the terms of which Anderson, for and in consideration of the sum of $10,000 sold all of his interest in and to the assets and property of said partnership unto Frisby, the said Frisby assuming all the outstanding liabilities and obligations of the said partnership.

On the 12th day of August, 1950, Frisby and his wife leased said property to respondent for a period of five years and three months.

Appellant strongly urges that the instrument in writing here under consideration was misconstrued by the lower court. He contends here, as he did in the lower court, that by the terms of the agreement he became vested with an undivided twenty percent interest in the leasehold held by the partnership, and that since he has never released or conveyed such interest, he is a tenant in common with respondent here in the leasehold heretofore assigned by Frisby, one of the co-tenants.

Such is not the effect of the agreement under the provisions of the Uniform Partnership Act, [§§24, 25, 26, and 27].

As to the property rights of a partner, [UPA §24] provides: "The property rights of a partner are (1) his rights in specific partnership property, (2) his interest in the partnership, and (3) his right to participate in the management."

It is to be noted that the assignment to appellant was of an interest in the partnership, the second property right specified by the quoted section. [UPA §26] defines this right as follows:

"A partner's interest in the partnership is his share of the profits and surplus, and the same is personal property."

With reference to an assignment of this right, [UPA §27] provides:

"(1) A conveyance by a partner of his interest in the partnership does not of itself dissolve the partnership, nor, as against the other partners in the absence of an agreement, entitle the assignee, during the continuance of the partnership, to interfere in the management or administration of the partnership business or affairs, or to require any information or account of partnership transactions, or to inspect the partnership books; but it merely entitles the assignee to receive in accordance with his contract the profits to which the assigning partner would otherwise be entitled.

"(2) In case of a dissolution of the partnership, the assignee is entitled to receive his assignor's interest and may require an account from the date only of the last account agreed to by all the partners."

The similarity in phraseology between this last quoted section and the agreement itself makes it quite clear that this was the extent of the assignment intended.

With reference to rights upon dissolution, [UPA §38(1)] provides in part: "When dissolution is caused in any way, except in contravention of the partnership agreement, each partner as against his copartners and all persons claiming through them in respect of their interests in the partnership, unless otherwise agreed, may have the partnership property applied to discharge its liabilities, and the surplus applied to pay in cash the net amount owing to the respective partners."

It is clear, then, that by the agreement appellant received a right upon dissolution limited to one-fifth of the partnership profits. See *State v. Elsbury*, 63 Nev. 463, 175 P.2d 430, 169 A.L.R. 364. No showing is made by him as to the winding up of the partnership or payment of partnership obligations. Specifically it does not appear that the $62,500 obligation provided by paragraph three of the agreement has been received by the surviving partner. Not only has appellant failed to establish any right to specific property of the partnership but he has failed to establish the existence of any surplus on which he is entitled to share.

Appellant strongly relies upon the case of *Johnson v. De Lay*, 63 Nev. 1, 158 P.2d 547, 161 P.2d 350. In that case it was conceded that Johnston and Ward were owners and tenants in common, each owning an undivided one-half interest in the land in question. As we have pointed out, such is not the case here.

. . .

We do not deem it necessary for us to consider here the rights appellant may have against Frisby and Anderson. Whatever these rights may be, if any, they in no wise involve the respondent.

For the reasons above stated, the judgment of the lower court is hereby affirmed with costs.

Notes

Bynum v. Sands, Inc. illustrates one aspect of the difference between an individual's interest in a partnership under the UPA and property concepts of joint tenancy and tenancy in common. Judge Learned Hand explored this difference and its connection with §25's "tenancy in partnership" in the following excerpt from *Commissioner v. Lehman*, 165 F.2d 383, 384-85 (2d Cir.1948):

> The Commissioner's first point is based upon the strict theory of the common-law that a partnership is no more than a joint ownership of the firm assets by the partners, and that, when a partner sells his interest in the firm, he sells his interest as joint owner of each firm asset. ... In a court of common law that would be true; just as it is still true today in the case of joint owners who

are not partners. A gain upon the sale of any asset held by such a group would be taxed as though it had been owned by a single person, the period during which each capital asset was held being reckoned from the date when the group acquired it. However, in equity and in bankruptcy the chancellors long ago imposed modifications upon the rights and liabilities of partners, as the common-law conceived them; and, while the firm never became a jural person, capable of being sued and of suing as such, in the administration of its affairs it did become for most purposes an entity; and it was upon this traditional structure that Congress fitted the taxation of partnerships, although it levied the income tax upon the separate distributive shares of the partners, whether they were distributed or not.

The modifications imposed upon the common law were of two kinds: not only were the individual partners not allowed to withdraw firm assets from the firm while the firm business continued; but it was a corollary that individual creditors, unlike firm creditors, were not allowed to levy upon and sell in execution their debtor's-the individual partner's-interest in firm assets. This was carried out also in bankruptcy by virtue of the doctrine that firm assets should first go to firm creditors and individual assets to individual creditors. The practical effect of these interpolations into the common law was to impound firm assets and deprive the individual partners of any control over them except in so far as they were dealing with them on behalf of the firm as a unit. The individual partner's beneficial interests as a legal joint owner were trimmed down so that he had nothing left save that the firm assets should be devoted to the firm business, that he should share in any profits they produced and in the surplus upon winding up, whether voluntary or by legal process.

The Uniform Partnership Law codified this congeries of rights and obligations as it had developed; and made no substantial change, when it declared in so many words that "a partner's interest in the partnership is his share of the profits and surplus." For that reason, we can, and for argument we will, accept the Commissioner's position that for tax purposes we should ignore the statute: we decide the case upon the basis of the law as it was before it was codified.

E. DISSOLUTION: THE DURATION OF THE PARTNERSHIP RELATIONSHIP

Review Part VI, Dissolution and Winding Up, §§29-43 of the Uniform Partnership Act.

Two issues dominate this material. The first deals with the duration of the partnership association. The partnership agreement should explicitly cover this point. Failure to do so invites trouble and litigation. The second issue is related to the first-the "rights" of the withdrawing partner in contrast to those of the partners wishing to continue the business. As Part VI of the UPA indicates, the provisions of the partnership agreement strongly influence the fate of the partners. Put most simply, a partnership may be formed to endure for a specified time; for the time required to attain a specified objective; or as a relationship at sufferance of the participants (a partnership at will). Whether a partner may "rightfully withdraw" from the association depends upon the duration of the partnership. Very different fates await the partner who rightfully withdraws and the partner who wrongs the co-partners by forcing a destruction of the partnership. Make no mistake about it-a partnership cannot technically survive a partner's withdrawal (see §29), but a drafting lawyer can serve a client's desire for stability by building in a considerable disincentive to any partner who might later contemplate withdrawal.

1. Duration of the Association:

Among the first things a drafting lawyer should ascertain is how long the prospective partners want their association to last. The law gives great latitude. Under §31 participants are free to define the duration of their partnership as for a term, for a task, or at will. If the partners do not express their clear choice litigation may be the only way to resolve this fundamental question.

GEORGE B. PAGE v. H. B. PAGE
Supreme Court of California, 1961.
55 Cal.2d 192, 10 Cal.Rptr. 643, 359 P.2d 41.

TRAYNOR, J. Plaintiff and defendant are partners in a linen supply business in Santa Maria, California. Plaintiff appeals from a judgment declaring the partnership to be for a term rather than at will.

The partners entered into an oral partnership agreement in 1949. Within the first two years each partner contributed approximately $43,000 for the purchase of land, machinery, and linen needed to begin the business. From 1949 to 1957 the enterprise was unprofitable, losing approximately $62,000. The partnership's major creditor is a corporation, wholly owned by plaintiff, that supplies the linen and machinery necessary for the day-to-day operation of the business. This corporation holds a $47,000 demand note of the partnership. The partnership operations began to improve in 1958. The partnership earned $3,824.41 in that year and $2,282.30 in the first three months of 1959. Despite this improvement plaintiff wishes to terminate the partnership.

The Uniform Partnership Act provides that a partnership may be dissolved "By the express will of any partner when no definite term or particular undertaking is specified." [UPA §31(1)(b).] The trial court found that the partnership is for a term, namely, "such reasonable time as is necessary to enable said partnership to repay from partnership profits, indebtedness incurred for the purchase of land, buildings, laundry and delivery equipment and linen for the operation of such business. ..." Plaintiff correctly contends that this finding is without support in the evidence.

Defendant testified that the terms of the partnership were to be similar to former partnerships of plaintiff and defendant, and that the understanding of these partnerships was that "we went into partnership to start the business and let the business operation pay for itself, -put in so much money, and let the business pay itself out." There was also testimony that one of the former partnership agreements provided in writing that the profits were to be retained until all obligations were paid.

Upon cross-examination defendant admitted that the former partnership in which the earnings were to be retained until the obligations were repaid was substantially different from the present partnership. The former partnership was a limited partnership and provided for a definite term of five years and a partnership at will thereafter. Defendant insists, however, that the method of operation of the former partnership showed an understanding that all obligations were to be repaid from profits. He nevertheless concedes that there was no understanding as to the term of the present partnership in the event of losses. He was asked: "[W]as there any discussion with reference to the continuation of the business in the event of losses?" He replied, "Not that I can remember." He was then asked, "Did you have any understanding with Mr. Page, your brother, the plaintiff in this action, as to how the obligations were to be paid if there were losses?" He replied, "Not that I can remember. I can't remember discussing that at all. We never figured on losing, I guess."

Viewing this evidence most favorable for defendant, it proves only that the partners expected to meet current expenses from current income and to recoup their investment if the business were successful.

Defendant contends that such an expectation is sufficient to create a partnership for a term under the rule of *Owen v. Cohen*, 19 Cal.2d 147, 150, 119 P.2d 713. In that case we held that when a partner advances a sum of money to a partnership with the understanding that the amount contributed was to be a loan to the partnership and was to be repaid as soon as feasible from the prospective profits of the business, the partnership is for the term reasonably required to repay the loan. It is true that *Owen v. Cohen*, supra, and other cases hold that partners may impliedly agree to continue in business until a certain sum of money is earned (*Mervyn Investment Co. v. Biber*, 184 Cal. 637, 641-642, 194 P. 1037, or one or more partners recoup their investments (*Vangel v. Vangel*, 116 Cal.App.2d 615, 625, 254 P.2d 919), or until certain debts are paid (*Owen v. Cohen*, supra, at p. 150), or until certain property could be disposed of on favorable terms (*Shannon v. Hudson*, 161 Cal.App.2d 44, 48, 325 P.2d 1022). In each of these cases, however, the implied agreement found support in the evidence.

In *Owen v. Cohen*, supra, the partners borrowed substantial amounts of money to launch the enterprise and there was an understanding that the loans would be repaid from partnership profits. In *Vangel v. Vangel*, supra, one partner loaned his copartner money to invest in the partnership with the understanding that the money would be repaid from partnership profits. In *Mervyn Investment Co. v. Biber*, supra, one partner contributed all the capital, the other contributed his services, and it was understood that upon the repayment of the contributed capital from partnership profits the partner who contributed his services would receive a one-third interest in the partnership assets. In each of these cases the court properly held that the partners impliedly promised to continue the partnership for a term reasonably required to allow the partnership to earn sufficient money to accomplish the understood objective. In *Shannon v. Hudson*, supra, the parties entered into a joint venture to build and operate a motel until it could be sold upon favorable and mutually satisfactory terms, and the court held that the joint venture was for a reasonable term sufficient to accomplish the purpose of the joint venture.

In the instant case, however, defendant failed to prove any facts from which an agreement to continue the partnership for a term may be implied. The understanding to which defendant testified was no more than a common hope that the partnership earnings would pay for all the necessary expenses. Such a hope does not establish even by implication a "definite term or particular undertaking" as required by section [UPA §1(1)(b)].

All partnerships are ordinarily entered into with the hope that they will be profitable, but that alone does not make them all partnerships for a term and obligate the partners to continue in the partnerships until all of the losses over a period of many years have been recovered.

Defendant contends that plaintiff is acting in bad faith and is attempting to use his superior financial position to appropriate the now profitable business of the partnership. Defendant has invested $43,000 in the firm, and owing to the long period of losses his interest in the partnership assets is very small. The fact that plaintiff's wholly owned corporation holds a $47,000 demand note of the partnership may make it difficult to sell the business as a going concern. Defendant fears that upon dissolution he will receive very little and that plaintiff, who is the managing partner and knows how to conduct the operations of the partnership, will receive a business that has become very profitable because of the establishment of Vandenberg Air Force Base in its vicinity. Defendant charges that plaintiff has been content to share the losses but now that the business has become profitable he wishes to keep all the gains.

There is no showing in the record of bad faith or that the improved profit situation is more than temporary. In any event these contentions are irrelevant to the issue whether the partnership is for a term or at will. Since, however, this action is for a declaratory judgment and will be the basis for future action by the parties, it is appropriate to point out that defendant is amply protected by the fiduciary duties of copartners.

Even though the Uniform Partnership Act provides that a partnership at will may be dissolved by the express will of any partner [UPA §31(1)(b)], this power, like any other power held by a fiduciary, must be exercised in good faith.

We have often stated that "Partners are trustees for each other, and in all proceedings connected with the conduct of the partnership every partner is bound to act in the highest good faith to his copartner and may not obtain any advantage over him in the partnership affairs by the slightest misrepresentation, concealment, threat or adverse pressure of any kind." (*Llewelyn v. Levi*, 157 Cal. 31, 37, 106 P. 219; [UPA §21].) Although Civil Code, section 2411, embodying the foregoing language, was repealed upon the adoption of the Uniform Partnership Act, it was not intended by the adoption of that act to diminish the fiduciary duties between partners.

A partner at will is not bound to remain in a partnership, regardless of whether the business is profitable or unprofitable. A partner may not, however, by use of adverse pressure "freeze out" a copartner and appropriate the business to his own use. A partner may not dissolve a partnership to gain the benefits of the business for himself, unless he fully compensates his copartner for his share of the prospective business opportunity. In this regard his fiduciary duties are at least as great as those of a shareholder of a corporation.

. . .

Likewise in the instant case, plaintiff has the power to dissolve the partnership by express notice to defendant. If, however, it is proved that plaintiff acted in bad faith and violated his fiduciary duties by attempting to appropriate to his own use the new prosperity of the partnership without adequate compensation to his copartner, the dissolution would be wrongful and the plaintiff would be liable as provided by subdivision (2)(a) of Corporations Code, section 15038 (rights of partners upon wrongful dissolution) for violation of the implied agreement not to exclude defendant wrongfully from the partnership business opportunity.

The judgment is reversed.

Notes

Is there any justification within the statute for either of the court's "protective schemes?" Are they different routes to the same result?

The two possible outcomes suggested by the court do not lead to the same pragmatic result. Under Traynor's first suggestion George Page would be forbidden to "gain the benefits of the business for himself unless he fully compensates his copartner for his share of the prospective business opportunity." Here George would have the sole dominion of the successor business venture but would be obligated to pay a stream of income to H.B.. Under the second suggestion, if George is guilty of violating the partnership agreement by the decision to dissolve the firm, then H.B. has all of the rights set forth in §38(2)(a) and these include the right to possess the partnership property during the agreed term of the partnership while securing their obligation to pay George (the wrong doing partner) the value of his §26 interest in the partnership (only profits and surplus) ... less any damages occasioned by his breach of the partnership agreement!

The idea that the decision to dissolve a partnership at sufferance is subject to fiduciary standards: Section 21 obliges every partner to "account to the partnership for any benefit, and hold as trustee for it any profits derived by him without the consent of the other partners from any transaction connected with the formation, conduct or liquidation of the partnership or from any use by [a partner] of its property." Does this include subjecting the decision to dissolve a partnership at sufferance and account as of that moment to the "fiduciary" standard?

An argument can be advanced in favor of this result with the justification sounding in a plea for "fairness." The issue, however, is one of statutory support in §21 for the California court's position that the statute impresses the decision to dissolve a partnership at sufferance with a "good faith" requirement. However desirable such a conclusion may be, it is not clear that it can be derived from the language of §21(1). Upon reflection need the court have strained beyond the rather obvious import of the statute?

The issue is one of appropriation of what would otherwise be the firm's business opportunity. Is that a "benefit" to the partnership in connection with its liquidation? Is the statutory term "liquidation" a more narrow concept than that of "winding up?" Does it merely mean that there is an obligation to account to the dissolved firm for all of the proceeds derived from transactions involving partnership property? However, one might argue that in the circumstances faced by this laundry (the newly formed Air Force Base) a fiduciary would be obliged to sell the business as a going concern and that the price would reflect an anticipation of the future stream of income. Yet even this premise does not support the conclusion that George was restrained from dissolving a partnership sufferance. H.B. seems quite well protected from exploitation by the terms of the UPA. If we recognize George's right to effect dissolution he has no more right than H.B. to wind up under UPA §§37 and 38(1). Thus H.B. could insist that the sale of assets be in the form of the laundry as a going concern to a third party ... and George would have no ability to veto this decision in favor of a dismantling of the laundry (thus surrendering its major "value" in the marketplace) ... especially so that he might act on a plan to start up the same business in the same locale!

The notion that dissolution of a partnership at sufferance could somehow be in contravention of the partnership agreement: in the last paragraph of its opinion the court suggests that if "... it is proved that plaintiff (George Page) acted in bad faith and violated his fiduciary duties by attempting to appropriate to his own use the new prosperity of the partnership without adequate compensation to his copartner, the dissolution would be wrongful and the plaintiff would be liable as provided by subdivision (2)(a) of [UPA §38] ... for violation of the implied agreement not to exclude defendant wrongfully from the partnership business opportunity." Can this result be squared with the language of §38(2)? The answer is "perhaps." The critical language which sets the stage for the application of sub-section (a)'s rights of "wronged" partner(s) is: "When dissolution is caused in contravention of the partnership agreement ...." Does this language reflect the content of §31 [Causes of Dissolution] wherein we find:

Dissolution is caused:

(1) Without violation of the agreement between the partners,

(a) ...

(b) By the express will of any partner when no definite term or particular undertaking is specified.

. . .

If the laundry was a partnership at sufferance under §31(1)(b), how could the dissolution by George be "in contravention of the partnership agreement?"

There is yet another element of §38(2) which suggests that the idea floated by Justice Traynor will only confuse matters. If H.B. avails himself of the option to continue the business [granted by §38(2)(b)] for how long may he possess the partnership property? There is no agreed term (as there would not be in a partnership at sufferance) ... so could he conduct the business for the balance of his life? What if he associated others ... would this even further extend the life of the partnership?

2. The fate of the withdrawing partner:

ZEIBAK v. NASSER
Supreme Court of California, 1938.
12 Cal.2d 1, 82 P.2d 375.

THE COURT. Plaintiff brought this action for dissolution of a partnership or joint venture, theretofore entered into between him and defendants, for an accounting, and if necessary, a sale of the partnership property.

The pertinent facts involved herein are summarized as follows: On or about December 12, 1931, and prior to January 11, 1932, plaintiff and defendants William N. Nasser, Elias Nasser, L.G. Dolliver and Central California Theatres Company (a corporation, organized and owned by seven Nasser brothers, among whom were William and Elias), entered into an oral agreement whereby they contracted to become joint venturers in the acquisition of a certain theatre business, consisting of the ownership and leasehold interest of the New Fillmore Theatre, the New Mission Theatre and the American Theatre, all of which were then owned by the Estate of Greenfield and located in the city of San Francisco. On January 11, 1932, the members of the venture submitted a written offer to purchase the business, and agreed therein to assume an outstanding indebtedness of the business, and also obligated themselves therein to expend certain sums of money thereafter and within specified times, as and for the repair and alteration of each theatre respectively. This offer was accepted by the estate, subject to the approval of the probate court. The parties further agreed that should they acquire the said theatres, immediately thereafter they would form a corporation under the laws of the state of California to take over the management and operation of the said theatres; that plaintiff would own an undivided one-half interest, Dolliver a 20 per cent interest, and the remaining defendants, jointly, a 30 per cent interest in the corporation; and that each of the parties would contribute his respective share of funds, if such were found to be necessary, for the maintenance and operation of the said theatres.

On January 28, 1932, the plaintiff and the defendants, other than Dolliver, entered into a written agreement entitled "Memorandum of Understanding Reached and to be Reached," wherein it was provided in part, that, "The General Management and Administration of the corporation, ... the scope of which shall be determined at this time to include management and supervision of the said Greenfield Houses and all activities directly and indirectly pertaining thereto, shall be entrusted to the Nassers, and their compensation for all of said services shall be fixed upon the basis charged to their subsidiaries for like services. ... Definite understanding shall also be had concerning the manner of and check upon the disbursement of funds, general policies, and the manner and extent to which Zeibak shall participate in the joint operation of the business of the corporation, subject however, to the primary general management and administration by the Nassers ... it being understood that when all details are finally ascertained, formal agreements evidencing the understandings between the parties shall be executed. ..." On the day following, Dolliver and the other defendants entered into a written agreement whereby Dolliver agreed that the exclusive management and control of the business should be lodged in the Nassers, and thereafter Dolliver appears to have assumed the status of a mere investor in the enterprise.

On February 1, 1932, the probate court having approved the sale of the Greenfield interest in the leaseholds and the business, the agreement of purchase was executed by the parties thereto. The amount of the initial payment, to wit, the sum of $50,000 was paid in equal parts by plaintiff on the one hand and the defendants on the other. Thereupon the venture entered upon the operation and management of said theatres. Each of two of the Nasser brothers, other than William and Elias, was given a position as theatre manager of one of the theatres thus purchased. The Nasser brothers also owned other theatres in the city of San Francisco, and the management of the three theatres thus acquired by the venture, was carried on by them in the offices used by Nasser brothers for the management and operation of the other theatres independently owned by them.

Shortly after the business was taken over by the venture, differences arose between plaintiff and the defendants Nasser with regard to the conduct of the business and the respective rights of the parties under the joint venture agreement. These differences continued practically from the date of purchase of the business to the time of the filing of the complaint. No corporation was formed pursuant to the evident intention of the parties, for the reason that the members of the venture could not agree upon certain terms and conditions which respectively they desired to set forth in the supplemental agreement contemplated by the terms of the agreement of January 28, 1932, above referred to. Numerous proposals and counter proposals were offered by the parties, each to the other, during this period of time, relating to the terms and conditions each sought to have incorporated in the said supplemental agreement. The parties could not agree, however, upon any certain draft of agreement submitted by plaintiff on the one hand, or by the Nassers on the other, with the exception of one certain draft of agreement, hereinafter mentioned, which was signed by plaintiff on or about October 3, 1932, and by the defendants on or about November 25, 1932, but the executed copies of which were never interchanged by the parties. Despite the lack of harmonious relationship between or among the members of the venture during this period of time, the record shows that the business (which had been operating at a substantial loss under its prior management) flourished to a marked degree, and that a very considerable profit was realized by the venture from the operation of the said business.

Plaintiff's action was founded upon the principal claim that the defendants had wrongfully taken exclusive possession and charge of the business against his will and without his consent, and had wrongfully excluded him therefrom; and particularly, that they had denied him access to the books of the corporation and had refused to give him sufficient information as to the details of the business to enable him to determine its condition sufficient to protect his interest therein; also that large amounts of money monthly had been paid by the venture as salaries to defendants' relatives, without adequate services having been rendered to the venture by such persons. The defendants, however, by way of affirmative relief, and upon the contention that plaintiff had caused the dissolution of the business wrongfully, asked that they be permitted to continue the business upon payment to plaintiff of the value of his interest therein, as contemplated by the provisions of [UPA §38(2)]. As the basis for this request they contended that plaintiff had refused to cooperate with them in the matter of carrying on the partnership business; that he had refused to comply with certain terms of the joint venture agreement and that contrary to the provisions thereof he had asserted rights and demands on his part not contemplated by the terms of said agreement.

During the course of a long trial, on the issues thus presented, defendant L.G. Dolliver died. With the permission of the probate court so to do, Marie Dolliver, his widow and special administratrix of his estate was thereafter substituted as a defendant in the action in the place of her deceased husband. At this time counsel for plaintiff, by motion, asked the court to enter an interlocutory decree of dissolution and to proceed with the winding up of the affairs of the joint venture upon the ground that the death of Dolliver *ipso facto* had dissolved the said joint venture. The court denied this motion and proceeded to hear the evidence in the case.

On July 20, 1934, the court made a minute order by which the joint venture was declared dissolved, and therein provided for the appointment of appraisers to appraise the property. It was further ordered that the defendants pay plaintiff the value of his one-half interest and indemnify him against all present and future liabilities; and the business thereafter should be conducted by defendants, including Marie Dolliver, during the remainder of the period of the leases; that an accounting be had and that the profits be divided between plaintiff and defendants. Thereafter it was further ordered that the appraisement be made as of the date December 11, 1932, as well as of July 20, 1934, and that neither of such appraisals should include the good will of the business. The final judgment was in accordance with these orders and recited that the dissolution of the joint venture occurred on July 20, 1934, "plaintiff having wrongfully caused the same by his conduct".

The parties hereto have filed cross-appeals. Defendants appeal from portions of the final judgment only. Plaintiff appeals from the whole thereof, and has also made a motion to dismiss defendants' appeal.

Each of the parties advances several asserted reasons why the judgment should be reversed or modified in accordance with his or their respective views, but the principal question before this court relates to the question of the sufficiency of the evidence to support the findings, which were favorable to the defendants in all material respects.

Plaintiff's first contention is that the evidence was insufficient to support the findings relating to the alleged wrongful conduct of plaintiff. These findings are substantially as follows: that during the period of negotiations following the acquisition of the theatres and while the parties were endeavoring to arrive at "definite understandings" prior to the organization of the proposed corporation, there was finally reached a point when a document purporting to be an agreement between or among the parties (and which had been signed by plaintiff prior thereto) was signed by defendants on November 25, but that "when the time arrived for the interchange of said agreement between the plaintiff and the defendants, the said plaintiff on or about December 11, 1932, failed, refused and neglected to deliver" the copy so signed by him, and has since refused to do so; and that "at all times since on or about December 11, 1932, in contravention of the terms of the agreements and understandings reached between December 12, 1931, and January 11, 1932, and in contravention of the terms and conditions of the agreement of January 28, 1932, the said plaintiff has wilfully and persistently failed and refused to proceed with the performance thereunder, but on the contrary ... has wilfully and persistently repudiated the aforementioned agreements and understandings" and has sought to revise the said agreements and understandings and to negotiate new terms and conditions under which the theatres should be maintained and supervised; and that "said plaintiff has been guilty of such conduct as has tended to affect prejudicially the carrying on of the business and has otherwise so conducted himself in matters relating to the partnership business that it is not reasonably practicable for the defendants to carry on the business in partnership with the plaintiff".

The record discloses the fact that the evidence was amply sufficient to support these findings, notwithstanding it was conflicting in some respects. ...

... The evidence also showed that plaintiff had refused to pay his proportionate share of a deficit incurred by the venture in 1932; and that he had failed to join the other members of the venture in the execution of plans for repairs and alterations to be made to the New Fillmore Theatre within the time agreed upon by them in their offer of purchase to the Greenfield estate. The court also found that "Defendants have at no time refused to give to the plaintiff sufficient or any information as to the details of the business so that he would be enabled to determine the condition thereof and protect his investment therein, but on the contrary the defendants have at all times supplied to the plaintiff all information which is available to the defendants themselves concerning the details of the business." In this regard the evidence showed that the venture had employed a firm of certified public accountants, which at regular intervals had audited the books, and that copies of such audits had been delivered to plaintiff; that in addition thereto he had made copious notes from the books and other memoranda relative to the business; that he was permitted to and did make frequent inspection of the books and records of the venture. The bookkeeper employed by the venture testified that the defendants had instructed her to give to plaintiff any and all information he might ask for relative to the business, and that she had complied therewith. The court further found that the defendants had been given the right, under the agreements of the parties, to the general management, administration and supervision of all activities pertaining to the theatres and to receive as and for their compensation a sum equal to the amounts charged to their subsidiaries for like services. These findings are likewise fully supported by the evidence. ...

[The court summarized the evidence of the plaintiff's unreasonable dissension from decisions necessary to the operations of the firm's theatres.]

Plaintiff also contends that [UPA §38] was erroneously applied to the facts of this case because, he asserts, that section relates to partnerships only, and not to joint ventures. That section provides as follows:

"... (2) When dissolution is caused in contravention of the partnership agreement the rights of the partners shall be as follows:

"(a) Each partner who has not caused dissolution wrongfully shall have:

"... II. The right, as against each partner who has caused the dissolution wrongfully, to damages for breach of the agreement.

"(b) The partners who have not caused the dissolution wrongfully, if they all desire to continue the business in the same name, either by themselves or jointly with others, may do so, during the agreed term for the partnership and for that purpose may possess the partnership property; provided, they secure the payment by bond approved by the court, or pay to any partner who has caused the dissolution wrongfully, the value of his interest in the partnership at the dissolution, less any damages recoverable under clause (2aII) of this section, and in like manner indemnify him against all present or future partnership liabilities.

"(c) A partner who has caused the dissolution wrongfully shall have:

"... II. If the business is continued under paragraph (2b) of this section the right as against his copartners and all claiming through them in respect of their interests in the partnership, to have the value of his interest in the partnership, less any damages caused to his copartners by the dissolution, ascertained and paid to him in cash, or the payment secured by bond approved by the court, and to be released from all existing liabilities of the partnership; but in ascertaining the value of the partner's interest the value of the good will of the business shall not be considered."

Plaintiff's contention that this section was not intended to apply to joint venture agreements, of the nature of the one in question here, cannot be upheld. The rule is that the rights and liabilities of joint adventurers, as between themselves, are governed by the same principles which apply to a partnership. (*Lerner v. Sanderson*, 126 Cal.App. 481, 14 Pac.(2d) 564, ...

Nor is the claim to be upheld that [UPA §38] is inapplicable to the situation here presented because it contemplates a partnership for a fixed term, whereas the joint venture agreement here involved failed to specify a certain length of time for its duration. Notwithstanding the fact that the trial court found the venture was not entered into for any specific period of time, but was to end, in so far as it was legally possible for it to end, upon the formation of a corporation, this was never done, and the parties voluntarily continued their status as joint venturers under the oral agreements between themselves, and those entered into by them with the Greenfield estate. The following authorities illustrate the rule that where a joint venture or partnership has leased property for the purpose of carrying on a particular business and no fixed period is set for the duration of the partnership, it will be deemed, by implication, to continue during the term of such lease. In the case of *Zimmerman v. Harding*, 227 U.S. 489, 33 Sup.Ct. 387, 57 L.Ed. 608, two persons entered into a partnership to operate a hotel under a lease. The agreement was never reduced to writing and there was no stipulation as to its duration. After the parties had taken possession difficulties arose between them, which resulted in an attempted dissolution of the partnership by one of the partners. There the court said, "... We agree with the court below that although there was no express stipulation as to the duration of the partnership agreement, it was by implication to continue during the term of the lease of the hotel property."

. . .

Plaintiff further contends that, assuming the application of section [UPA §] to joint ventures, it does not apply here because the venture was one which could have been lawfully dissolved by the "express will" of a member thereof, under [UPA §31(b)]. This section reads as follows: "Dissolution is caused: ... (b) By the express will of any partner when no definite term or particular undertaking is specified. ..." This contention likewise cannot be upheld for the reason that the venture here was not one which could have been lawfully dissolved by the express will of a member thereof. Here there was a definite, and "particular undertaking", voluntarily assumed by each of the partners, and as hereinabove stated, the term of the venture, at least impliedly, was of similar duration as the term of the leases under which the theatres were operated. In the case of *Bates v. McTammany*, 10 Cal.(2d) 697, 76 Pac.(2d) 513, this claim was also made. There the court found that the partnership was formed for the purpose of conducting a radio station "so long as the license therefor could be obtained from the federal government". The defendant contended that the partnership was one at will and that he was entitled to a dissolution under certain sections of the Civil Code, including section [§31 (b)]. The court there said, "The finding that the partnership was formed for a definite undertaking ... and so long as the federal license therefor could be procured, is fully supported by the record, and negatives any conclusion which otherwise might be drawn that the partnership was one at will."

. . .

Plaintiff also makes the claim that the death of L.G. Dolliver worked a dissolution of the partnership. We cannot concur in this view. Here the parties themselves had by their several agreements and undertakings created a situation wherein the death of Dolliver could not defeat the obligations voluntarily assumed by him and his copartners. In the case of *Beller v. Murphy*, 139 Mo.App. 663, 123 S.W. 1029, hereinbefore referred to, one of the partners died before the expiration of the term of the lease and it was there contended that his death had dissolved the partnership. The court said: "As a general proposition the death of one partner does dissolve the partnership; but, even in those cases, the dissolution caused by death does not affect existing contracts. (30 Cyc. 620; *Hughes v. Gross*, 166 Mass. 61, 43 N.E. 1031, 32 L.R.A. 620, 55 Am.St.Rep. 375.) Since this partnership had contracted to mine this land and pay royalties for ten years, its contract must be fulfilled." Here also, as above noted, Dolliver had but a twenty per cent interest in the business, and immediately upon his entry into the venture, he assumed the status of an investor, and took no active part in the affairs of the partnership. In the case of *Schenk v. Lewis*, 125 S.C. 228, 118 S.E. 631, the court, in considering the effect of the death of a partner stated that "While it is true, as a general rule, that the death of a partner effects an immediate dissolution of the partnership, it is not always so. If there was any special skill or capacity in the deceased partner, the partnership would, of course, cease to exist from the time of his death. But if the business was for the purpose of keeping the dead partner's capital invested in the partnership, there is no reason why his death would necessarily terminate the relation. (2 Story Eq.Jur. (14th ed.), sec. 916.) In this particular case the small interest of Lewis in the partnership does not indicate any special skill or capacity; and the course of dealing suggests the purpose of keeping his capital invested, in which event the Lewis estate would be entitled to his share in the profits of the continued business." (See, also, 47 C.J., p. 1112.)

Defendants and cross-appellants also contend that the trial court erred in not awarding them damages as prayed for. The trial court found that defendants had failed to show that they had suffered any damages by reason of plaintiff's conduct. The evidence fully supports this finding.

. . .

Judgment affirmed. Motion to dismiss appeal denied.

Notes

This case involves important construction of §§31(1)(c), 31(4) and 38 of the California version of the Uniform Partnership Act.

What is striking about the court's view on the effect of Mr. Dolliver's death upon the partnership? The causes of dissolution are enumerated in §31. Death is listed in sub-section (4). The uniform act adopted in California in 1929 contained the following language:

Dissolution is caused:

(4) By the death of any partner:

Given this statutory provision, how could the Supreme Court of California have decided that Dolliver's death was not a "... change in the relations of the partners caused by any partner ceasing to be associated in the carrying on ... of the business."? What definition of "dissolution" does the court seem to adopt in lieu of that found in §29 of the UPA?

Does the holding attributed to *Beller v. Murphy* support the result reached in *Zeibak*? *Schenk v. Lewis* was decided by the Supreme Court of South Carolina in 1923. The language quoted from that opinion seems to sustain the holding in *Zeibak*; yet there are two problems. First, South Carolina did not enact the UPA until 1950. It is misleading, at best, to cite Schenk for an expression of the law in a jurisdiction which had adopted the UPA. Second, the quoted language is pure dictum. Unfortunately, the author of *Zeibak* did not finish the quoted paragraph: "... But, as both parties have proceeded upon the theory that the partnership was dissolved by the death of Lewis, ... we will treat the matter as it has been treated." 118 S.E. 631, 636.

Section 15031(4) of the California Corporations Code was amended in 1963. It currently contains the following modification of §31 of the UPA which appears unique to that jurisdiction:

> (4) By the death of any partner unless otherwise provided in an agreement in writing signed by all of the partners before such death;

Is this statutory amendment harmonious with the holding in Zeibak?

For a judicial dictum in accord with *Zeibak v. Nasser*, see *Wagner v. Etoll*, 46 A.D.2d 990, 362 N.Y.S.2d 278, 280 (1974). New York has retained the original language of §31(4), so it is hard to account for the Appellate Division's suggestion that the partnership agreement might negate a dissolution caused by the death of a partner. For a holding that dissolution would result, see *Sanders v. Wyle*, 67 N.Y.S.2d 623 (1946).

California common law may have been redirected toward a better reading of the statute by the District Court of Appeal's decision in *King v. Stoddard*, infra. Beyond the language of the statute, what is the practical advantage in the Superior Court's determination in *Zeibak* that the plaintiff has wrongfully dissolved the partnership with the Nasser interests?

Turning to another aspect of the opinion, note the court's extraordinary position on the *duration* of this partnership. It seems that the partnership was originally formed for the accomplishment of a task. Once it became clear that the task would not be accomplished, what became of the life of the partnership? In light of the court's later opinion in *Page v. Page*, supra, would the "partnership for a term" result be reached today?

An important provision of §38 receives short treatment in *Zeibak*. In their cross-complaint the defendants sought damages for Zeibak's wrongful dissolution of the partnership. No relief was granted in the Superior Court. On appeal, this is affirmed with the common sense notation that under the statute the wronged partners take nothing absent specific proof of harm and consequent loss. Also see *B.K.K. Co. v. Schultz*, 7 Cal.App.3d 786, 797, 86 Cal.Rptr. 760, 767 (1970).

HUNTER AND HAUGEN v. STRAUBE
Supreme Court of Oregon, 1975.
273 Or. 720, 543 P.2d 278.

MCALLISTER, J. This suit was filed by the plaintiffs, Dr. Arthur F. Hunter and Dr. O.D. Haugen, to dissolve a three-man medical partnership in which the defendant, Dr. Kurt R. Straube, was the third member. The three doctors were radiologists practicing in Portland under the firm name of Lloyd Center X-Ray. The partnership was created by a partnership agreement dated July 26, 1969 and a written addendum dated November 24, 1971 which added the plaintiff Haugen to the partnership.

On September 11, 1974 the plaintiffs filed this suit in Multnomah County to dissolve the partnership and prayed for the appointment of a receiver and the winding up of the partnership. The defendant counterclaimed, alleging that he was entitled to continue the partnership business, to recover damages from plaintiffs for the breach of the partnership agreement, and to settle with the plaintiffs as withdrawing partners as provided by the partnership agreement.

The only regular pleading filed was the plaintiffs' complaint. Thereafter, the parties, at the request of the trial court, prepared a pretrial order stating the admitted facts and the contentions of the parties, which order was approved by the court on November 29, 1974. The case was tried on the facts admitted in the pretrial order and the issues framed by that order.

The pretrial order states the nature of the proceedings as follows:

"This is a suit of equity in which plaintiffs seek judicial supervision over the winding up of the affairs of a partnership they claim is dissolved and a liquidation of respective partnership interests in accordance with Oregon's Uniform Partnership Law and defendant seeks continuation of the partnership business, damages for breach of the partnership contract, and a distribution to plaintiffs in accordance with the partnership agreement."

The trial court found that by the filing of this suit the plaintiffs "did not cause by express will a dissolution of their partnership with defendant." The court further found that since "the partnership continues as an entity," the court had no jurisdiction to wind up the affairs of the partnership. The court also dismissed the counterclaims of defendant because "no dissolution had occurred."

The pertinent portions of the partnership agreement read as follows:

"3. *TERM:* The partnership shall continue until the partnership is dissolved as herein provided.

. . .

"16. *TERMINATION:* In the event of the death or retirement of any Partner or the voluntary liquidation of the partnership, the following procedure shall be observed:

"A. *Death:*

"(1) The death of any Partner shall not dissolve the partnership as to the other Partners, ..." (Emphasis added.)

"B. *Retirement:*

"The retirement of any Partner shall not dissolve the partnership as to the other Partners, and each Partner hereby does bind his estate, heirs or personal representatives to receive the sums as in this paragraph computed as full acquittance and payment of his interest in this partnership and all undistributed or uncollected earnings therein and does hereby agree to execute such receipts and bills of sale, deeds, or other instruments of conveyance or satisfaction as may be required to carry out the terms, conditions and stipulations herein set forth. (Emphasis added.)

"(1) Upon the voluntary or involuntary retirement of a Partner from the partnership, or upon the withdrawal of a Partner from the partnership, the books of the partnership shall be closed as of the first day of the month in which the retirement or withdrawal becomes effective, and such Partner shall be entitled to receive the following sums and no more, all subject to Paragraph 16B(2) hereof:

"(a) An amount equal to the capital account of the withdrawing or retiring Partner as of the close of the last fiscal year of the partnership, adjusted for additional capital investment subsequent thereto and reduced by any distributions during the current fiscal year of net profits in excess of said net profits. The capital amount, as so determined, shall be paid in forty-eight (48) equal monthly installments, with the first installment payable on the fifth (5th) day of the fourth (4th) month following the closing date and remaining installments on the fifth (5th) day of the ensuing months, all without interest.

"(b) An amount equal to the retiring or withdrawing Partner's share in the undistributed net profits, if any, of the partnership as of the closing date determined as provided in said Partnership Agreement reduced by any accounts payable relating to the collection of accounts receivable. The amount of such undistributed profits shall be paid as soon as reasonably practical.

"(c) A share in future income of the partnership, as evidenced by the accounts receivable for services of the partnership as of the closing date, computed as provided in this subparagraph. Accounts receivable shall be valued at 75%, except that accounts which were first billed more than one year prior to the closing date shall be valued at zero. The amount to which the retiring or withdrawing partner shall be entitled shall be computed on the basis of the following formula:

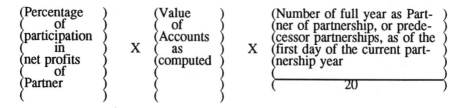

"For example, if the total value of such accounts receivable is $40,000 and the retiring or withdrawing Partner is entitled to 25% of the net profits on the closing date, such Partner would receive $500 for each of such full years as a Partner. The amount thus determined shall be paid as a distribution of income in forty-eight (48) equal installments, without interest, at the same times as provided for under subparagraph (a) above. (Emphasis added.)

"(2) Non-Competition:

"If a Partner shall voluntarily withdraw or retire and shall engage in the practice of medicine or participate in any association, group or clinic so engaged within a forty-mile radius of the City of Portland, Oregon, during a period of three years from the effective date of withdrawal or retirement, such Partner shall have no right to receive any distributions under Paragraph B(1) above, from the date he so engages in the practice of medicine. (Emphasis added.)

"(3) Procedure re Retirement:

"(a) Any Partner voluntarily resigning from the Partnership shall give six months' written notice to each of the other Partners of his desire to retire, and such retirement shall take effect six months from the date of delivery of such notice to the other Partners."

Plaintiffs contend that they expressed their will to dissolve the partnership by the filing of this suit, citing *Carrey v. Haun et al*, 111 Or. 586, 592, 227 P. 315 (1924). We agree with this contention. See *Clark v. Allen et al*, 215 Or. 403, 410, 333 P.2d 1100 (1959). However, we disagree with the contention of the plaintiffs that by the filing of this suit they are entitled to a dissolution in accordance with the Uniform Partnership Law. The plaintiffs ignore the provision of the partnership agreement that limits the dissolution to the withdrawing partners and expressly provides that "the retirement of any Partner shall not dissolve the partnership as to the other Partners".

The power to dissolve a partnership is governed by [UPA §31] and provides for dissolution both without violation of the partnership agreement and in contravention of the partnership agreement. In either case, it is clear that if the partnership agreement provides for the distribution of the partnership property the rights of the partners are governed by the partnership agreement rather than by the Uniform Partnership Law. See provisions in [UPA §§37, 40].[1]

In the case at bar the plaintiffs had the power to dissolve the partnership by electing to withdraw as partners, a choice which they made by filing this suit.

---

[1] All the provisions cited, relating to the rights and duties of the partners, make clear that they are subject to any agreement between the parties to the contrary. For example, [UPA §40] provides:

"Rules for distribution. In settling accounts between the partners after dissolution, the following rules shall be observed, subject to any agreement to the contrary:
...."

Plaintiffs, however, did not have the right to dissolve the partnership without complying with the terms of the partnership agreement. As was succinctly stated in *Straus v. Straus*, 254 Minn. 234, 94 N.W.2d 679, 686 (1959):

> "A distinction must be recognized between the power to dissolve a partnership and the right to dissolve a partnership. Any partner may have the power to dissolve a partnership at any time ... and this is true even though such dissolution is in contravention of the partnership agreement. ... If a partner exercises his power to dissolve a partnership, but does not have the right to do so, he must suffer the penalties ...."

The pertinent provisions of this partnership agreement have been set out earlier verbatim in the opinion. In brief, the agreement required the plaintiffs to give defendant, the remaining partner, six months' notice of their desire to withdraw and provided that the "retirement shall take effect six months from the date of delivery of such notice to the other Partners." The agreement also provided a specific plan of distribution to a withdrawing partner and contained a restriction on competition. It should be noted that Oregon law does uphold non-competition clauses if freely entered into by the partners and reasonable in effect. Such clauses are typical of professional partnerships. *McCallum v. Asbury*, 238 Or. 257, 263- 264, 393 P.2d 774 (1964).

The plaintiffs attempted by filing this suit to divest the defendant from his right to continue the partnership business, which he clearly had the right to do. They attempted to avoid the requirement of giving six months' notice. They also attempted to render nugatory the provisions of the partnership agreement governing the rights to the partnership property upon the withdrawal of a partner. We think the plaintiffs cannot, by merely calling their withdrawal a dissolution, escape from the liabilities which they assumed when they executed the partnership agreement. The plaintiffs have not cited a single authority in support of their contention.

A recent case from our sister state of Washington is in accord with our decision today. *Ashley v. Lance*, 75 Wash.2d 471, 451 P.2d 916, 920 (1969) and 80 Wash.2d 274, 493 P.2d 1242, 1245 (1972), in a very similar fact situation, held that the restrictive covenant in the partnership agreement would be enforced for the benefit of the remaining partner. The withdrawing partners could not avoid the covenant by devising "the legalistic theory that they would dissolve their partnership ... and not withdraw therefrom." 451 P.2d at 918.

In *Devlin v. Rockey*, 295 F.2d 266 (7th Cir.1961), the partnership agreement provided for termination upon a two-thirds majority vote of all the partners or upon the unanimous consent of all the partners. Two of the ten partners sought a decree declaring they had effected a dissolution of the partnership, alleging that the partnership was one at will and therefore subject to dissolution by any partner at any time. The court held that, despite use of the word dissolution by the plaintiffs, it was clear that they were to be treated as withdrawing partners under the agreement, the partnership was not dissolved, and distribution to the plaintiffs was to be controlled by the partnership agreement provisions pertaining to withdrawal of a partner. 295 F.2d at 269.

Similarly, in *Adams v. Jarvis*, 23 Wis.2d 453, 127 N.W.2d 400 (1964), the partnership agreement specifically provided that the partnership would not terminate upon the withdrawal of a partner. The plaintiff withdrew but contended this effected a dissolution under a Wisconsin statute identical to [UPA §29].[2] The court refused to construe the statute so as to invalidate an otherwise enforceable contract. In one sense plaintiff's withdrawal constituted a dissolution, the court, said, but the partnership was not wholly dissolved so as to require complete winding up. The partnership continued to exist under the terms of the agreement. 127 N.W.2d at 403-404.

Gibson v. Angros, 30 Colo.App. 95, 491 P.2d 87 (1971), involved a covenant not to compete upon withdrawal of a partner from the partnership. Plaintiff argued that his notice to resign from the partnership operated as a dissolution and he was therefore no longer bound by the restrictive covenant. The court held that plaintiff's actions constituted a voluntary retirement under the terms of the partnership agreement, and the terms of the agreement which became operative upon such retirement were not rendered nugatory by the dissolution of the partnership. 491 P.2d at 91.

We hold that the filing of this suit by the plaintiffs was an election by each of them to withdraw from the partnership in contravention of the partnership agreement. Under those circumstances the withdrawal entitles the defendant to continue the partnership business and to settle the affairs of the partnership in accordance with the terms of the partnership agreement. The defendant also has the right to any damages he may have suffered on account of the plaintiffs' breach of the provision for six months' notice of withdrawal.

This suit is reversed and remanded to the court below for further proceedings consistent with this opinion.

Notes

Hunter v. Straube, citing *Adams v. Jarvis*, dispels the confusion created by *Zeibak v. Nasser*, supra. The issue in all three cases is whether the co-partners could avoid the consequences of a partner's death or withdrawal under the original language of §31 of the UPA. *Zeibak* reached the remarkable conclusion that somehow §31 did not apply.

---

[2][UPA §20] provides:

"Dissolution defined. The dissolution of a partnership is the change in the relation of the partners caused by any partner ceasing to be associated in the carrying on as distinguished from the winding up of the business."

Since California revised the Act in 1963, co-partners can control the consequences of death or withdrawal.

Section 15031. Causes of dissolution

Dissolution is caused:

. . .

(4) By the death of any partner unless otherwise provided in an agreement in writing signed by all the partners before such death;

. . .

(7) By withdrawal of a partner or admission of a new partner unless otherwise provided in an agreement in writing signed by all of the partners, including any such withdrawing partner or any such newly admitted partner, before such withdrawal or admission ....

None of the provisions of any other section of this chapter shall prevent, or impair the effect or enforceability of any agreement in writing that a partnership will not be dissolved as provided for in subdivision (4) or (7) of this section.

It is important to note that the written agreement need not be the original partnership agreement, but may be a distinct covenant executed by all of the partners at any time before the event which would, otherwise, dissolve the firm.

The value of *Adams* and *Hunter* is their interpretation of the common law to mean that while the partnership agreement, as a contract, cannot avoid the statutory conclusion that a partner's death or withdrawal dissolves the partnership, that agreement can be drafted to prevent the winding up or liquidation of the business and to govern the accounting among the co-partners. In essence, the cases suggest that, subject to equitable limitations, an agreement can give the remaining partners who wish to continue the firm the same rights which the UPA gives wronged co-partners. See §38.

The next case deals with a different aspect of this topic.

3. Post-dissolution agency status of partners:

HARLEY KING ET AL. v. JOHN L. STODDARD
California District Court of Appeals, First District, 1972.
28 Cal.App.3d 708, 104 Cal.Rptr. 903.

BROWN (H.C.) J. This is an appeal from a judgment in the sum of $12,370 rendered in favor of respondents, Harley King and Stanford White, for accounting services performed for the Walnut Kernel, a newspaper. The action was brought against the executors of two deceased partners who owned the newspaper.

The question presented on this appeal is whether the continuation of the newspaper after the death of the partners was an act of winding up the partnership under Corporations Code section 15035 so as to render the estate of the partners liable for an accountant's bill incurred subsequent to the death of the partners.

The facts: Prior to 1962, the newspaper, Walnut Kernel, was operated as a general partnership in which Lyman E. Stoddard, Sr., and Alda S. Stoddard owned a 51 percent interest as community property, and their son, Lyman E. Stoddard, Jr., owned 49 percent. On January 3, 1963, Alda S. Stoddard died and her daughter, Nancy Gans, was appointed executrix. After the death of Alda S. Stoddard, no formal winding up of the partnership took place. On February 13, 1964, Lyman E. Stoddard, Sr., died, and his son, John L. Stoddard, was appointed executor.

The operation of the business continued after the death of Lyman E. Stoddard, Sr.; Lyman E. Stoddard, Jr., operated it as the sole surviving partner. John L. Stoddard, who was then acting on behalf of both estates, considered his duty was to obtain the winding up of partnership affairs as quickly as possible. He was not satisfied with the continuation of the business and when his brother, Lyman, Jr., did not wind up the business, John made some unsuccessful attempts to sell it himself. In 1965 he brought an action against his brother, Lyman, Jr., to force an accounting and liquidation of the assets of the partnership. The case was dismissed before trial upon agreement of the parties which became effective September 6, 1966. In the written agreement, the parties settled their accounts with each other. Lyman E. Stoddard, Jr., agreed to be responsible for all debts arising out of the business since February 13, 1964. The agreement was approved by the probate court. The business was in a weak financial condition after Lyman E. Stoddard, Sr.'s, death and was eventually discontinued.

For approximately 10 years prior to the death of Alda S. Stoddard, the respondents, King and White, and their predecessors had been accountants for the Walnut Kernel. They continued to do the accounting after the deaths of Alda and Lyman, Sr. The appellants were aware that respondents were continuing their work. One of the respondents, King, testified that he understood that respondents would be paid at such time as the estates were in a liquid condition allowing payment and that he would not have continued to render the services had he known that the estates would not be responsible.

John L. Stoddard and Nancy Gans, the executors, did not individually participate in the operation of the partnership business in any manner. The court concluded they were not individually liable.

The court found the estate of Alda S. Stoddard liable for the accounting services rendered by appellants during the period of time following her death-1963 to 1968. The court also found the estate of Lyman E. Stoddard, Sr., jointly liable with the estate of Alda S. Stoddard for the accounting services rendered by appellants following his death-1964 to 1968. The court disallowed any claim rendered prior to the deaths of Lyman E. Stoddard, Sr., or Alda S.

Stoddard as no claims were filed in those estates as required by section 700 et seq. of the Probate Code. The estate's liability was predicated upon the court's finding that the services were rendered during the process of winding up the partnership operation of the Walnut Kernel newspaper. We have concluded that the trial court erred and that the continuation of the business was not a winding up of the affairs of the partnership.

The partnership was dissolved by operation of law upon the deaths of Alda and Lyman E. Stoddard, Sr. [UPA §29] provides that dissolution of a partnership is "... caused by any partner ceasing to be associated in the carrying on as distinguished from the winding up of the business." Death is one of the causes of dissolution. [UPA §31(4)]. Dissolution, however, does not terminate the partnership which "... continues until the winding up of partnership affairs is completed." [UPA §30]. "In general a dissolution operates only with respect to future transactions; as to everything past the partnership continues until all pre-existing matters are terminated." (*Cotten v. Perishable Air Conditioners*, 18 Cal.2d 575, 577, 116 P.2d 603, 136 A.L.R. 1068; see also *Yahr-Donen Corp. v. Crocker*, 80 Cal.App.2d 675, 678, 182 P.2d 209.) Although the general rule is that a partner has no authority to bind his copartners to new obligations after dissolution (*Steinbach v. Smith*, 34 Cal.App. 223, 224, 167 P. 189; see also *Glassell v. Prentiss*, 175 Cal.App.2d 599, 605, 346 P.2d 895), [UPA §35(1)] provides that "[a]fter dissolution a partner can bind the partnership ... (a) By any act appropriate for winding up partnership affairs ...."

It is this latter provision upon which the court based its decision that the estates of the deceased partners were liable for the accounting services performed after dissolution. The court found that "LYMAN STODDARD, JR.'s continuation of the WALNUT KERNEL business was an appropriate act for winding up the partnership, since the assets of the business would have substantial value only if it was a going business. It was to the advantage of the partnership that the business be maintained as a going business."

Respondents, as accountants, had performed services both before and after the dissolution. The services, however, were a continuation of the accounting services pursuant to the ordinary course of the operation of the business. Respondent King testified that he was "... doing work for the activity of the newspaper, the financial activity of the newspaper" and that he was doing the same type of work as he had always performed for the Walnut Kernel. The exhibits which support his bill for services indicate that he did not, or was not able to, break down his services into categories which would separate ordinary accounting services from those related to a winding up of the partnership. The court, however, found that the continuation of the business itself was an "act appropriate for winding up partnership affairs."

We disagree with this finding. It is probably true that there might have been advantages to the partnership to sell the business as a going business, but the indefinite continuation of the partnership business is contrary to the requirement for winding up of the affairs upon dissolution. In *Harvey v. Harvey*, 90 Cal.App.2d 549, 554, 203 P.2d 112, the court disapproved a finding that the business and assets of a partnership were of such character as to render its liquidation impracticable and inadvisable until a purchaser could be found. The court stated: "In effect it [the finding] authorizes the indefinite continuation of the partnership after the death of a partner, a procedure not in accordance with section 571 of the Probate Code. Respondents counter with the argument that the business is such that it cannot be wound up profitably, and the estate given its share. But this argument overlooks the distinction between winding up a business and winding up the partnership interest in that business."

There are few cases which illustrate acts approved as "appropriate for winding up partnership affairs" under either the California Corporations Code or the identical section 35 of the Uniform Partnership Act. (See *Stump v. Tipps*, 120 Cal.App.2d 418, 261 P.2d 315 (assignment of partnership property to repay partnership debt); *Cooley v. Miller & Lux*, 168 Cal. 120, 142 P. 83 (disposition of partnership property); *Leh v. General Petroleum Corporation*, (S.D.Cal.1958) 165 F.Supp. 933 (maintenance of action for damages on behalf of the partnership); *In re Heller's Estate*, 319 Pa. 135, 178 A. 681 (execution of renewal notes after death of partner).)

Even if we assume that a situation might exist where continuation of the business for a period would be appropriate to winding up the partnership interest, such a situation did not exist here. The record reflects the fact that the surviving partner was not taking action to wind up the partnership as was his duty under Probate Code section 571, nor did the estates consent in any way to a delay. Rather, their insistence on winding up took the form of an effort to sell the business and a suit to require an accounting. There is nothing in the record upon which to base the argument made by respondents that appellants consented to their continued employment. The fact that they did not object is of no relevance. They had no right to direct and did not participate in the operation of the business. Therefore, the determination that the acts of the accountants were rendered during a winding up process is not based upon substantial evidence.

. . .

We conclude that the services of respondents were rendered after the dissolution resulting from the deaths of the partners, Lyman, Sr., and Alda Stoddard, and do not constitute services during the "winding up" processes of the partnership within the meaning of [UPA §35]. The claim for those services, therefore, are not chargeable to the partnership.

The judgment is reversed.

Notes

Whether a court recognizes that death or withdrawal dissolves the partnership or seeks some strained construction of the UPA, it is clear that dissolution of the partnership must be distinguished from the termination of the partnership affairs and the winding up (liquidation) of the partnership accounts. Section 30 states: "On dissolution the partnership is not terminated, but continues until the winding up of partnership affairs is completed." *King v. Stoddard* interprets this provision as well as that of §35 (respecting a partner's authority and liability for transactions after dissolution).

As the reader can now appreciate, few areas of partnership law are as troublesome as the topic of dissolution and its consequences. The following brief recapitulation of the Uniform Partnership Act may be helpful.

I. If the dissolution did not violate the partnership agreement (UPA §31(1)):

    A. If the dissolution did not violate the partnership agreement and was not pursuant to a judicial decree and none of the former partners wish to continue the business the following provisions of the UPA govern their respective rights and obligations:

        §30. The partnership is dissolved but not terminated. The firm continues until winding up of partnership affairs is completed.

        §37. The right to wind up the partnership affairs belongs to the surviving partner(s), when dissolution has resulted from the death of a partner, or to all partners who have not wrongfully dissolved the firm.

        §38(1). Each partner has a right to have partnership property applied to discharge liabilities to third parties and to have any surplus paid in cash in the net amount owed to each partner. This is an important provision for it grants to every partner the right to have the partnership property sold and thus reduced to cash. In some circumstances this may not be advantageous for the terms of a distress sale are rarely generous to the seller. Yet the alternative is to postpone the winding up of partnership affairs or to produce discord in the attempted division of the partnership property in specie (e.g., land to one partner, inventory to another, etc.).

        §40. In the absence of an agreement to the contrary, this provision determines the manner in which partnership assets will be marshalled with respect to liabilities to third-party claimants. Under §40(a) the assets of the partnership are the partnership property plus any contributions of partners necessary to increase those assets until they cover liabilities specified in §40(b). Section 40(b) governs the priority of claims to these marshalled assets. Section 40(c) commands that application of the §40(a) assets be set forth as in §40(b).

Compliance with these accounting and distribution provisions winds up the partnership.

    B. If one or more of the former partners desire to continue the firm's business.

        §41 of the UPA makes it clear that there is a right to continue the business without settlement of accounts and liquidation only in the event of expulsion [see §41(5) and (6)] or wrongful dissolution under §38(2)(b). If these provisions do not apply, then such continuation is not a matter of right, but of the consent of the retiring partner or a deceased partner's representative(s). This consent is an assignment of partnership property rights.

§42 assumes that there is a continuation under the consent required by §41. If this continuation is without settlement of accounts then ... subject to any contrary agreement among the partners ... the retiring partner or a deceased partner's representative is entitled to have the "value of his interest at the date of dissolution ascertained, and shall receive as an ordinary creditor an amount equal to the value of his interest in the dissolved partnership with interest, or at his option ... in lieu of interest, profits attributable to the use of his right in the property of the dissolved partnership ...."

This seems to mean that the retired partner or a deceased partner's estate stands in the position of a creditor with an immediate claim upon his "interest in the partnership" as defined by §26 (his share of the profits and surplus ...). He may, however, elect to renounce interest on that amount in favor of a continuing stream of income termed "profits attributable to the use of his right in the property of the dissolved partnership" ... which would continue throughout the term to which he had consented in the §41 assignment of his partnership property rights. When that term expired §40's provisions would apply and he would then have his claim to a return of assets attributable to his net share in the partnership property.

II. If the dissolution was "wrongful" being in contravention of the partnership agreement:

A. If the aggrieved partners do not desire to continue the business:

§37. The partners who are not guilty of wrongful dissolution have the right to wind up the partnership affairs and to exclude the partner who caused the dissolution from this process.

§38(2)(a). Each of the partners who has not caused dissolution wrongfully has the right to have partnership property applied to discharge liabilities to third parties and to have any surplus paid in cash in the net amount owed to each partner. (§38(2)(a)(I)). In addition, there is a cause of action against any partner(s) who caused wrongful dissolution for damages for breach of the partnership agreement.

§40. Here the rights and obligations are identical to those outlined above with the exception that the claims of the partner(s) guilty of wrongful dissolution may be discounted by the amount of their liability in damages for breach of the partnership agreement.

B. If the aggrieved partners desire to continue the business:

§38. The aggrieved partners have a cause of action for damages caused by breach of the partnership agreement [§38(2) (a)(II)]. If the aggrieved partner(s) should desire to continue the firm business they are given an extraordinary right to dominion over the partnership property. But in order to protect this right they must elect between two courses designed to protect the wrongful partner who still has a claim to the "value of his interest in the partnership at the dissolution": first, the aggrieved partners may secure such payment by court-approved bond or pay an amount equal to the wrongful partner's §26 interest less any ascertainable damages suffered under §38(2)(a)(II). In addition, they must indemnify the wrongful partner against all present and future partnership liabilities. These liabilities of the aggrieved partners are restated as "rights" of the partner who has caused the dissolution wrongfully under §38(c)(II).

How long may the aggrieved partners exert dominion over the partnership property under §38(2)(b)? For the balance of what would have been the "term of the partnership." (If the agreement expressly or implicitly set a term of years, then for that period; if it defined a task, then for such time as proved necessary for the accomplishment or manifest failure of that task.) But what if the partnership were at sufferance and the dissolution were "wrongful" due to violation of the fiduciary duties discussed in *Page v. Page*?

§40. This provision would govern when that term had expired. It is then that the wrongful partner would recover his share, if any, of the net assets.

§42. This provision appears to give this wrongful partner a right to interest or profits attributable if the aggrieved partners did not pay him the §26 interest less damages, but merely secured such payment with the judicially approved bond.

4. The final accounting:

BLUMER BREWING CORP. v. MAYER
Supreme Court of Wisconsin, 1936.
223 Wis. 540, 269 N.W. 693.

This action was begun on May 21, 1935, by the plaintiff, Blumer Brewing Corporation, against M.F. Mayer, administrator of the estate of Charles R. Einbeck and C.A. Roderick, administrator de bonis non of the estate of Hugo Einbeck, to wind up the affairs of a partnership known as Einbeck Bros., Monroe, Wis., and to procure an accounting between the various parties interested in the estates and for the appointment of a receiver. There was a trial, the court found against the plaintiff, and from the judgment entered on March 12, 1936, dismissing the action, the plaintiff appeals.

From some time prior to 1921, Hugo Einbeck and Charles R. Einbeck were doing business as partners under the firm name of Einbeck Bros., sometimes described, however, as the Monroe Bottling Works. On November 28, 1928, Hugo Einbeck died. The surviving partner, Charles R. Einbeck, was duly appointed administrator of the Hugo Einbeck Estate. He listed the partnership interest of Hugo Einbeck in his inventory of the estate filed June 3, 1929. As a part of the bookkeeping system of the partnership prior to the death of Hugo, separate accounts were kept of the investment of each partner and separate drawing accounts were also kept showing the withdrawals by the partners. To these accounts from year to year there was credited the net income from the partnership business and a charge was made for net losses.

After the death of Hugo Einbeck, the accounts were continued as before until December 31, 1931, when the Hugo Einbeck account was carried over to a new sheet headed Hugo Einbeck Estate. Charles R. Einbeck paid the expense of the funeral and claims against the estate of Hugo Einbeck by issuing checks of Einbeck Bros. In like manner there were issued to some of the heirs of Hugo Einbeck, during the years 1929 to 1934, checks aggregating $2,646.41. Charles R. Einbeck made income tax returns for himself personally, for Einbeck Bros. and as administrator of the Estate of Hugo Einbeck, all of which disclose that the partnership business was being continued as before the death of Hugo and that the estate of Hugo Einbeck was being credited with profits and charged with losses of the business.

The partnership had done business with the plaintiff corporation for many years and its claim against the partnership assets is based on sales of goods, wares, and merchandise made by it to the partnership between the 1st day of August, 1933, and the 23rd day of June, 1934, in the amount of $8,587.85. The trial court found that the plaintiff corporation knew of the death of Hugo Einbeck; that it made no inquiries as to the authority of Charles R. Einbeck to continue the business; that there were no written articles of partnership and no agreement between Hugo Einbeck and Charles R. Einbeck authorizing the continuance of the business after the death of Hugo; that no order was issued in the county court for Green county authorizing Charles R. Einbeck, as administrator of the estate of Hugo Einbeck, to continue the business; that the heirs of Hugo Einbeck other than Charles R. Einbeck knew nothing of the manner in which Charles R. Einbeck continued the business; that they had no information that the interest of Hugo Einbeck and the property owned by Einbeck Bros. was claimed as partnership property; that such heirs had no access to the books of Einbeck Bros.; that there was never filed in the county court for Green county any report by Charles R. Einbeck as administrator, from which the heirs could obtain any notice of the manner in which such business was conducted; that there was no holding out to the public that the estate was continuing such partnership after Hugo's death and no representation of such a fact to the plaintiff corporation; that Charles Einbeck died May 14, 1934, and C.A. Roderick was appointed administrator de bonis non of the estate of Hugo Einbeck.

The trial court directed judgment dismissing the action on the ground that Charles R. Einbeck was without authority to continue the business and that the assets of the estate of Hugo Einbeck were not chargeable with the liabilities of Einbeck Bros. incurred after the death of Hugo Einbeck.

ROSENBERRY, CHIEF JUSTICE. The principal question for decision is, Did Charles R. Einbeck as surviving partner under the circumstances of this case have authority to continue the partnership business after the dissolution of the partnership brought about by the death of Hugo Einbeck? The defendants contend that a partnership business may be continued after the death of a partner under the following circumstances and no other: (1) If it is provided by the partnership agreement and such agreement is binding on the estate of the deceased partner; (2) if it is so directed in the will of the deceased partner; (3) pursuant to order of the court first obtained; (4) by agreement by the surviving partner and legal representatives of the deceased partner, provided the legal representative has been given by the will of decedent the necessary power or the agreement is approved by the court.

The plaintiff does not seriously contest these propositions as matters of general law but contends that the propositions of general law have been modified by the provisions of the Uniform Partnership Act. ... It is to be noted in this case that the administrator did not assume, or attempt to assume, the duties of an active partner. All that was done in this case was to permit the interest of Hugo Einbeck, the deceased partner, to remain in the partnership business and to be thereafter administered by Charles R. Einbeck as surviving partner. The estate in no sense became a partner in the business and its liability under any theory of the law was limited to the interest of Hugo Einbeck in the partnership assets.

A determination of the issue raised in this case depends upon the interpretation given to [UPA §41(1), (2) and (3)] relating to rights and liabilities on continuing the business of a partnership after dissolution without liquidation.

The obvious purpose of this section is to continue the partnership business without the disruption and confusion which resulted at common law when a partner retired or died. Subsection (1) relates to the admission or retirement of partners and provides that "when any partner retires and assigns (or the representative of the deceased partner assigns) his rights" etc., the succeeding partners are liable both to old and new creditors. Subsection (2) provides that, when all but one partner retire and assign (or the representative of a deceased partner assigns), the person continuing the business shall be liable both to old and new creditors. Subsection (3), the one, if any, which is applicable to this case, provides that, when any partner retires or dies and the business is continued with the consent of the retired partner "or the representative of the deceased partner, but without any assignment of his right in partnership property," the continuing partnership business shall be liable as if such assignment had been made. Under subsection (3) when a partner dies and his personal representatives consent to a continuation of the business, the law takes hold of the situation and the consent of the personal representative has the same effect as if an effective assignment had been made and subjects the interest of the deceased partner in the partnership property to the claims of existing and future creditors.

Did Charles R. Einbeck, as administrator of the estate of Hugo Einbeck, have power to give such consent? The interest of Hugo Einbeck in the partnership property was personal property. [UPA §26]. *Mattson v. Wagstad* (1926) 188 Wis. 566, 206 N.W. 865. Charles R. Einbeck, as administrator of the estate of Hugo Einbeck, had power to sell and dispose of the personal estate without order of court, and to pass good title thereto. *Munteith v. Rahn* (1861) 14 Wis. 210; *Williams v. Cobb* (1916) 242 U.S. 307, 37 S.Ct. 115, 61 L.Ed. 325.

We are not called upon to consider here and do not consider to what extent if at all an administrator may make himself personally liable in dealing with the assets where he proceeds without an order of the court. It would seem to require no argument to show that an administrator who had power to sell and dispose of an estate-in this case, the interest of Hugo Einbeck in the partnership business-had power to consent to the retention of the assets by the surviving partner in the continuation of the business. While the Uniform Partnership Act deals with partnership law and we are unable to discover any intention on the part of the Legislature in adopting that act to enlarge or affect in any way the power of administrators and executors, the statute must be construed with regard to the purpose its framers sought to attain. In the past, there have been numerous instances in which the interest of the deceased partner in the partnership business has been allowed to continue. Where the partnership venture proved successful, of course no questions arose, every one concerned was benefitted. When, however, the partnership venture proved unsuccessful, many difficult questions were presented for solution growing out of the fact that at common law as under the statute the death of a partner dissolved the partnership. Claims of existing creditors were against the partnership as it then stood. Claims of future creditors were against the business as subsequently continued and the determination of the rights of the various classes of creditors presented problems very difficult of solution and upsetting to business transactions. The framers of the act said: "The neglect of the retiring partners or of the representatives of the deceased partner should not as at present create inexecrable confusion between the creditors of the first and second partnership in regard to their respective rights in the property employed in the business. Both classes of creditors should be ahead of the claim of such retired partner or the representative of the deceased partner, and both classes of creditors should also have equal rights in the property. This paragraph probably effects a change in the present law, though the same result is often now brought about by implying a promise to pay the debts of the dissolved partnership on the part of the person or partnership continuing the business."

It is considered that under this section it is not necessary for the administrator to be authorized by the court to give his consent. The situation which is dealt with by the statute is one where the knowledge and acquiescence of an administrator, the surviving partner is permitted to retain the interest of the deceased partner in the business and to continue it. When that happens, it operates as an assignment of the interest of the deceased partner to the surviving partner or partners. If the statute be not so construed, the principal purpose of its framers will be defeated. What is sought is not an enlargement of the power of an administrator but protection of the partnership creditors and a definition of their rights. That an administrator had such power even at common law is established by *Hoyt v. Sprague* (R.I.1881) 103 U.S. 613, 26 L.Ed. 585, and *Big Four Implement Co. v. Keyser*, 99 Kan. 8, 161 P. 592, L.R.A.1917C, 166. In cases involving this statute consideration must be given also to the manner in which the question considered by the court arose. The statute in question does not seek to define the rights of the beneficiaries of an estate as against the administrator of an estate who has consented. Most of the cases deal with a conflict of interest between the creditors of the partnership and the heirs of the deceased partner, although in *Hoyt v. Sprague*, supra, the liability of the administrator to the heirs of the deceased partner is adverted to.

The next question which arises is the power of Charles R. Einbeck to consent to the continuance of the business by Charles R. Einbeck, surviving partner. It is argued that Charles R. Einbeck had no power to contract with himself in different capacities. It is not considered that what happens in cases of this kind is a matter of contract. It was because there were so many cases in which no contract was made that legal consequences are given to the act of consent by [§41]. Certainly under the facts of this case the administrator must be held to have acquiesced and consented to the continuation of the partnership business and to the employment of the interest of the deceased partner in that business. We shall not at this time inquire what, if anything, the county court might have done either upon its own motion or upon petition of the heirs of Hugo Einbeck to require the partnership business to be liquidated, nor shall we deal with the question of estoppel which was dealt with and considered at length in *Hoyt v. Sprague*, supra. It may be said, however, that none of the heirs of Hugo Einbeck in any way protested against the continuation of the partnership business and the employment of the interest of Hugo Einbeck therein. While the trial court found that they had no knowledge of the manner in which the business was being conducted or the fact that the interest of Hugo Einbeck was in the business, certainly they must be charged with knowledge of the fact that Hugo Einbeck was dead; that he left as a part of his estate his interest in the partnership, Einbeck Bros.; that the estate has not been distributed, although payments had been made on account. They were certainly chargeable with knowledge that the estate was being administered in the county court for Green county. If no accounts were filed, the law provides a means by which they could require an accounting to be made by the administrator. Whether or not they are in fact estopped, a question not necessary to be decided here, their equities are greatly weakened by their failure to move within a reasonable time.

It is considered that the court was in error in holding that the interest of Hugo Einbeck in the partnership property was not liable for subsequent debts of the partnership business continued by Charles R. Einbeck in the name of Einbeck Bros. We perceive no reason why the court should not appoint a receiver for liquidation of the assets belonging to the partnership. Whatever the rights of the respective administrators may be, their interests are conflicting and it is in the interest of the heirs of both as well as the creditors of the partnership that the partnership assets be disposed of as such.

. . .

The judgment appealed from is reversed, and cause remanded for further proceedings as indicated in the opinion.

Notes

Why didn't the plaintiffs in *King v. Stoddard* pursue the tactic employed with such great success in *Blumer Brewing v. Mayer* and seek to charge the interest of the deceased partners with the after arising liability? Because in *King* there were no partnership assets! Recovery would be possible only if the personal liability of partners could be claimed under §15 of the UPA. In *Blumer* the creditor's claim could be satisfied by charging partnership assets although this was objectionable from the vantage point of the deceased partner's estate for it would diminish what would remain to be divided. Thus the cases are quite consistent from the vantage point of doctrine nor do they differ in terms of strategy. What does cause them to diverge is the condition of the firm with respect to assets. King faced a firm with no assets. Blumer did not.

HARRIS v. KLURE
California District Court of Appeals, Fourth District, 1962.
205 Cal.App.2d 574, 23 Cal.Rptr. 313.

COUGHLIN, J. The issues on this appeal primarily involve the interpretation of uncertain and ambiguous provisions of a written partnership agreement providing for the purchase by a surviving partner of the interest of a deceased partner in a partnership business, and the obligation of the former to account to the estate of the latter for any profits made while continuing the business after death and before purchase. No extrinsic evidence was introduced in the trial court as an aid to interpretation. Under these circumstances the meaning of the disputed provisions must be ascertained by this court as a matter of law in accord with applicable principles of construction....

This determination is made in adherence to the rule that the interpretation of an uncertain and ambiguous contract by a trial court, without the aid of extrinsic evidence, is not binding upon and will not be accepted by an appellate court unless the latter determines that it is reasonable, but if the interpretation by the trial court is reasonable, it will be accepted on appeal even though the contract in question is subject to other equally reasonable interpretations....

In construing a contract the court should strive to ascertain its object as reflected in the provisions thereof; should be guided by the intention of the parties as disclosed by those provisions ...; should endeavor to effect the intention and object thus ascertained ...; should adopt that construction which will make the contract reasonable, fair and just ...; should give it such interpretation "as will make it lawful, operative, definite, reasonable, and capable of being carried into effect, if it can be done without violating the intention of the parties" (Civ.Code, § 1643); should avoid an interpretation which will make the contract unusual, extraordinary, harsh, unjust or inequitable ..., or which would result in an absurdity ..., should reject language which is wholly inconsistent with its object ..., should consider the contract as a whole, using each clause thereof as a help to interpret the others ..., should give effect to every part thereof if reasonably practicable ..., and, if this is impossible, to favor an "interpretation which gives effect to the main apparent purpose of the contract"....

The plaintiff, Edward Harris, respondent herein, and Harry F. Klure, now deceased, owned and operated a business under a written partnership agreement dated June 22, 1949. This agreement contained provisions by which a surviving partner could acquire the interest of a deceased partner in the partnership business. After Klure's death, the plaintiff, as surviving partner, chose to acquire the decedent's interest in the business. A dispute arose respecting the price to be paid therefor. Thereupon, the plaintiff brought this action against the legal representative of Klure's estate, the defendant and appellant herein, to obtain a declaration of the rights and duties of the parties under the agreement, and to specifically enforce the same.

After Klure's death the plaintiff continued to operate the partnership business. The agreement provides that: "Upon the death of a partner, the books shall be closed immediately but the remaining partner may continue to operate the business under direction of the court until a sale has been effected as herein set forth." Thereafter the plaintiff orally indicated to the defendant, the administrator of Klure's estate, that he desired to purchase Klure's interest in the partnership business.

The partnership agreement is divided into numbered sections; one of these, i.e., section 23, consisting of six paragraphs, prescribes a method by which a surviving partner may acquire the interest of a deceased partner; contains many seemingly uncertain, ambiguous and repugnant provisions bearing upon this subject; and is the source of the controversy before this court. Specific provisions in this regard are:

(1) "... that in event of the death of one of the partners, all property herein-

before described, together with the furniture and fixtures and equipment and supplies may be purchased by the surviving partner upon his paying unto the heirs, executors or administrators of the deceased partner the sum of money which is equal to the appraised value of the share which belonged to the deceased partner at the time of his death ...";

(2) "The continuing partner shall have until thirty days after final appraisal of the partnership property to exercise his option to purchase"; and

(3) "Should the surviving partner make actual purchase of the share of the deceased partner in and to the assets of the firm, and should the appraisement of the State Inheritance Tax Appraiser for the estate of the decedent be not acceptable to either of the contracting parties, then such value shall be determined by arbitration, the surviving partner to name one arbitrator, the legal representative of the decedent's estate to name another arbitrator, and the third to be selected by them. The decision of a majority of such arbitrators shall be final, if such appraisement is likewise approved by the Court having jurisdiction over the estate of the deceased partner."

By these provisions the surviving partner is given the option to purchase the interest of the deceased partner at its appraised value which may be either the appraised value fixed by the appraisement of the inheritance tax appraiser for the estate of the deceased partner, if that value is acceptable to both parties, otherwise it shall be the appraised value fixed by arbitration. In the latter event the probate court must approve the appraisement. The surviving partner is given the option to purchase at the appraised value, but both the surviving partner and the legal representative of the estate of the deceased partner are given the option to require the appraised value to be fixed by arbitration.

Preliminarily the plaintiff and the defendant attempted to agree upon the value of the deceased partner's interest, but failed in this attempt. Thereafter, the inheritance tax appraiser made an appraisement and, on January 13, 1959, the defendant administrator caused it to be filed in the decedent's estate. Following this, i.e., on February 2, 1959, the plaintiff notified the defendant of his intention to purchase the decedent's partnership interest for the value placed thereon in the inheritance tax appraisement, i.e., $62,136. Thereupon, i.e., on February 18, 1959, the defendant advised the plaintiff that the appraisement in question was not acceptable to him and requested that the appraised value be fixed by arbitration. The plaintiff contended that the defendant theretofore had accepted the appraisement of the inheritance tax appraiser and, therefore, his attempted nonacceptance and request for arbitration was of no effect. This issue was presented in the present action and the trial court found in accord with the plaintiff's contention. On appeal the defendant claims that the conclusion of the trial court is not supported by the evidence which shows that all of the acts relied upon to establish acceptance took place before the inheritance tax appraisement was filed. The proof in this regard reflected the actions of the defendant at the time the inheritance tax appraiser was making his appraisal; showed purported agreement by the defendant with the appraisal placed on some articles and no disagreement with respect to the appraisal placed on others; consisted generally of evidence which the plaintiff claims establishes approval by the defendant of the amount which the inheritance tax appraiser proposed to include in the appraisement to be filed in the estate. The fact remains, however, that all of the evidence in question relates to a time before the appraisement of the inheritance tax appraiser actually was made and filed.

The provisions of the partnership agreement which prescribed the price for which the deceased partner's interest might be purchased by the surviving partner are concerned with the appraisement actually made and filed by the inheritance tax appraiser. Until filed, the appraisement is in an embryonic state; is subject to change by the appraiser; and his indicated conclusions in the premises, whether they be acceptable or not acceptable to interested parties, constitute only a proposed or contemplated appraisal. At some time in the course of the proceeding, the surviving partner must indicate his acceptance or nonacceptance of the appraisement as the method for determining the price he is to pay. In the instant case he did this after the appraisement was filed. Although there is evidence from which the trial court was entitled to find that he gave notice of his intention to exercise the option to purchase before the appraisement was filed, this evidence does not indicate that he offered to accept the appraisement of the inheritance tax appraiser as the price he was to pay. Until the surviving partner indicates his intention to accept the inheritance tax appraisement method for determining the appraised value of the property he is to purchase, the legal representative of the decedent's estate is not called upon to indicate his nonacceptance of that method. There is a distinction between the legal representative accepting the inheritance tax appraisement as such and accepting it as the price for which the decedent partner's interest shall be sold. There is nothing in the evidence which supports a finding that the defendant accepted the inheritance tax appraiser's proposed appraisal as the price to be paid by the plaintiff under his option. Merely agreeing that the proposed appraisal is correct for appraisal purposes, if it be assumed that this occurred, does not establish an acceptance thereof for sale purposes. The law required the defendant to file an appraisement in the subject estate (Prob.Code, § 600), and his doing so may not be considered an expression of his intention to accept that portion thereof appraising the decedent's partnership interest as the purchase price to be paid under the plaintiff's option to buy. We hold that the "appraisement" referred to in the partnership agreement is the appraisement filed by the inheritance tax appraiser in the estate of the deceased partner; that an interpretation of that agreement which would authorize the legal representative of that estate to accept the inheritance tax appraiser's appraisal of the decedent's partnership interest as the purchase price thereof prior to the filing of such appraisement, is unreasonable; and that under the circumstances, the evidence does not support the finding of the trial court that the defendant accepted such appraisal as the purchase price in question.

The trial court also ruled that the plaintiff was not required to account for any of the profits made in the business during the time he operated the same after the death of his deceased partner; that, under its interpretation of allegedly applicable provisions of the partnership agreement, the plaintiff should pay the decedent's estate interest from date of death at the rate of 5 per cent per annum on the value of the decedent's share, i.e., the purchase price under his option to buy, in lieu of any profits therefrom; and that, because of the delay resulting from the defendant's refusal to accept the appraisement figure as the purchase price, no interest should be charged for the time consumed by the instant litigation. The defendant contends that this was error; that the provisions relied upon by the court as the basis for its decision are inapplicable; that [UPA §42(1)][1] is controlling; and that the plaintiff is required thereby to account to the decedent's estate for any profit made during the period in question. Disregarding the subject agreement and applying the quoted section, the defendant, as legal representative of a deceased partner, would be entitled to interest on the value of the latter's partnership share or, in lieu thereof, the profits attributable to the use of that share. However, application of this code section expressly is conditioned upon the fact that the parties have not agreed otherwise. The plaintiff contends that, under the partnership agreement, the surviving partner who exercises his option to buy the share of the deceased partner is required to pay interest on the purchase price at the rate of 5 per cent per annum, and is not required to account for any profits made since death.

Reasonably construed, the various provisions of section 23, some of which by one standard are in conflict with others but by another standard are merely surplusage, all contemplate acquisition of the deceased partner's share by the surviving partner. At first blush, the paragraph in which the 5 per cent interest provision first occurs seems to refer to a method of acquisition by the surviving partner other than by purchase; directs that an accounting and statement of all of the assets of the partnership shall be made; by previous reference requires a

---

[1] Section 15042 of the Corporations Code [UPA §42] provides: "When any partner retires or dies, and the business is continued under any of the conditions set forth in Section 15041[UPA §41](1, 2, 3, 5, 6), or Section 15038[UPA §38](2)(b) without any settlement of accounts as between him or his estate and the person or partnership continuing the business, unless otherwise agreed, he or his legal representative as against such persons or partnership may have the value of his interest at the date of dissolution ascertained, and shall receive as an ordinary creditor an amount equal to the value of his interest in the dissolved partnership with interest, or, at his option or at the option of his legal representative, in lieu of interest, the profits attributable to the use of his right in the property of the dissolved partnership; provided, that the creditors of the dissolved partnership as against the separate creditors, or the representative of the retired or deceased partner, shall have priority on any claim arising under this section, as provided by Section 15041(8) of this act."

statement of the valuation of the partnership real and personal property "as it may be determined or agreed"; and provides that the amounts ascertained to be owing to the deceased partner shall be paid by the surviving partner within 12 months together with interest at 5 per cent per annum from date of death. However, the only method of determining the valuation of such property is that prescribed in connection with determining the purchase price thereof, i.e., the appraised value as fixed by the appraisement of the inheritance tax appraiser for the estate of the deceased or by arbitration. In this regard it is noteworthy that for the purpose of a similar account and statement during the life of the parties, the agreement by a separate section, i.e., section 24, provides for arbitration to ascertain such valuation in the event of dissolution "otherwise than by death." Inferentially, the requirement for an accounting and statement contained in section 23, i.e., that containing the option to buy, which directs that the valuation of the real and personal property to be included therein, shall be such "as may be determined or agreed," limits the determination feature to the method therein described, i.e., by appraisal through inheritance tax appraisement or by arbitration. Therefore, it is reasonable to conclude that the 5 per cent interest and time payment provisions refer to acquisition of the decedent's share by purchase. At the most, the paragraph in question adds to the foregoing concept the probability of an agreement respecting valuation, i.e., "the valuation as it may be ... agreed," in lieu of a determination on the basis of appraised value in accord with the formula heretofore noted. However, the existence of this probability does not conflict with the conclusion that the 5 per cent interest and time payment provisions refer to the acquisition of the deceased partner's share through the prescribed option to buy process.

In an immediately subsequent paragraph, provision is made for payment of "the aforesaid share" in monthly or yearly installments, with interest from date of death at 5 per cent per annum on the unpaid balance. The only prior mention of any "share" occurs in that part of section 23 which confers the option to purchase. This fact also supports the conclusion that all of the provisions in section 23 deal with the surviving partner's acquisition of the deceased partner's share.

Granted an agreement that upon the death of one partner the surviving partner may continue the partnership business, may purchase the partnership share of the deceased partner, and shall pay 5 per cent interest on the purchase price from date of death, it would be unreasonable to conclude that the parties did not thereby intend to dispense with the election provided by [UPA §42]. A surviving partner who continues the partnership business is not chargeable with both interest and profits for his use of the deceased partner's share in such undertaking. (*Robinson v. Simmons*, 156 Mass. 123, 30 N.E. 362; *Schneider v. Schneider*, 347 Mo. 102, 146 S.W.2d 584, 591.) To interpret the subject agreement so as to require the surviving partner to pay both interest on the partnership share purchased by him and also that portion of the profits attributable to such share after death, would render it oppressive and inequitable. We conclude that where a partnership agreement provides that a surviving partner may continue the partnership business after death, may purchase the deceased partner's share therein, and upon purchase shall pay interest on the value thereof from date of death, an election is made in the partnership agreement to accept interest in lieu of a share of any profits from the surviving partner's continued operation of the business in the event he makes such purchase.

However, there is no basis for the trial court's determination that the surviving partner should not pay interest during the time the instant litigation is pending; the partnership agreement makes no provision for nonpayment of interest in the event of such a contingency; and he has possession of both the business and the purchase money during that time.

The judgment is reversed with instructions to enter judgment in harmony with the views expressed in this opinion.

MUNDY v. HOLDEN
Supreme Court of Delaware, 1964.
42 Del.Ch. 84, 204 A.2d 83.

CAREY, JUSTICE. This is an appeal from a decree of the Court of Chancery for Kent County directing specific performance of a contract for the sale of a deceased partner's share in the partnership.

In 1945, William C. Holden and Gilbert H. Mundy entered into an informal partnership in Dover, Delaware, as an automobile agency. During subsequent years, the partnership continued to prosper, and the parties, on January 25, 1954, executed a formal written partnership agreement.

After recitals indicating that the partners shared equally in all assets and interests of the partnership, the agreement provided, inter alia:

"As a part of the consideration of this partnership agreement, IT IS MUTUALLY UNDERSTOOD AND AGREED that in the event of the death of one of the partners during the existence of the partnership, the surviving partner does covenant and agree to purchase from the estate of the deceased partner the share or interest of the deceased partner for the sum of Forty Thousand Dollars ($40,000) and to make settlement for the same within three months from the date of death of said partner, and the executor or administrator of the deceased partner is hereby authorized, empowered and directed to consummate said sale and to execute any and all papers necessary to be executed in order to carry out the provisions hereof to transfer and assign all of the right, title and interest of the partner so dying in and to the assets of said partnership, upon condition that the surviving partner shall assume and pay all of the then existing debts and obligations of said partnership. The surviving partner shall continue the operation of said business without interruption."

On April 14, 1959, the parties executed a written modification to the agreement which effected a change in the status of the financial reserves of the partnership but expressly reaffirmed the remaining terms of the original agreement. Following the death of Gilbert H. Mundy on May 31, 1963, William C. Holden, the surviving partner, tendered the sum of $40,000.00 to the Executor of the estate of the deceased partner, Holden having paid or assumed the debts due outside creditors. Tender of this sum was refused upon the ground that it was insufficient and, accordingly, plaintiff brought an action in the Court below seeking to compel an assignment of the interest of the deceased partner to him upon payment of $40,000.00. The Court below, finding no ambiguity in the agreement, granted plaintiff's motion for summary judgment, and defendants have appealed to this Court for review of that decision.

Before this Court, defendants urge that the tender of $40,000.00 was insufficient because they contend that plaintiff was also required to tender the amount of Mundy's share of capital and profits accumulated on the date of his death. In short, defendants urge that such capital investment is an "existing debt and obligation of said partnership" to be assumed and paid by the survivor.

. . .

Defendants initially contend that a material factual dispute exists, precluding the granting of summary judgment, because the words "debts and obligations" are inherently ambiguous. Specifically, defendants contend that the invested capital of a partner may properly be considered a debt or obligation of the partnership. As stated by the Missouri Court of Appeals:

> "It is the general rule that capital furnished by any partner, in the absence of agreement to the contrary, is a debt owing by the firm to the contributing partner, and necessarily is to be repaid him, if the firm assets are sufficient after paying the firm liabilities to outsiders ...".

Chapin's Estate v. Long, 205 Mo.App. 414, 224 S.W. 1012, 1013 (1920). ... Uniform Partnership Act, Sections 18(a), 40(b), 42; T. 6 Del.C.Ch. 15.

But the mere recital of this legal principle does not resolve the question presented by this appeal. The rule set forth in Chapin's Estate and the other authorities cited supra applies only in the absence of an agreement to the contrary. In the instant case, the parties have specifically provided for the manner of dissolution of the firm upon death of one partner and we must consider that entire agreement to determine whether the parties have expressed an intent not to treat capital as a "debt or obligation". See 12 Am.Jur. Contracts, Section 241. The first recitals of the agreement provided that:

> "The capital of the partnership shall consist of the present partnership assets including automobile agency, real estate located on South Governors Avenue, Dover, Delaware, improved with garage and repair shop, inventory of parts, accessories, supplies, automobiles, new and used, shop machinery and equipment, office furniture, accounts receivable, finance reserves, bank account and

farm, together with all income and profits arising from the operation thereof, except such amounts as shall be drawn from time to time from said profits by each partner as compensation.

"IT IS MUTUALLY UNDERSTOOD AND AGREED that the assets of said business and the partnership property shall be owned and held by said partners in equal shares, and the partners shall share equally in the profits and losses that may arise out of the operation of the business of the partnership and likewise shall share equally in the capital assets of the partnership".

Of course, the references in the death provision to the purchase of a "share or interest" for $40,000.00 must be read consistently with the quoted provision of the agreement indicating that each partner's "share" is one-half of the total capital of the partnership. When so read, the agreement is unambiguous and clearly means that the sum of $40,000.00 was intended to be full payment for all of the interests owned by the deceased partner, including his right to demand the return of capital from the partnership. In other words, the parties agreed upon a definite figure and said that this figure is designed to be compensation for all interests in the firm.

Secondly, defendants contend that there are facts and circumstances existing at the time the agreement was made which demonstrate a possible contrary intent, thus precluding the granting of summary judgment. That contention is predicated initially upon the fact that the partnership balance sheet as of December 31, 1953 lists the capital investment upon the liability side of the ledger. Obviously, in preparing the statement, the accountant simply carried investments on the liability side for purposes of achieving balance; the total is carried as "total liabilities and investments", and "liabilities" are listed separate from "investments".

Defendants then contend that since the book value of each party's interest was substantially in excess of the $40,000.00 figure at the time of the agreement, it is unreasonable to presume that the parties would have contracted for a sale of the share of each for $40,000.00. We do not know what the capital shares were when the parties reaffirmed their agreement in April, 1959; the excess was considerably smaller at the time of Mundy's death. In any event, this dissolution provision only applied upon the death of one partner, and neither partner could predict who would survive to enjoy the benefits of these provisions. As stated by the Supreme Court of Pennsylvania:

"Neither could know to whom the option to purchase would fall; and if, during the running of the agreement, because of large additions or reductions, the price might become inequitable, either party had the remedy in his own hands, as without his assent they could not be made". *In re Rohrbacher's Estate*, 168 Pa. 158, 32 A. 30, 31 (1895).

The decision of the lower Court is affirmed.

Chapter 3

THE JOINT VENTURE

A. INTRODUCTION

Earlier in the materials the Court of Appeals of Maryland and the Supreme Court of California suggested that the joint venture (or adventure) was a step-child of the law of partnerships. As the following passage from *Milton Kauff-man, Inc. v. Superior Court*, 94 Cal.App.2d 8, 17-18, 210 P.2d 88, 94-95 (1949), illustrates, this is generally true:

> The facts alleged in the amended complaint and stated in the affidavits of the plaintiff were sufficient to warrant the court in concluding for the purpose of the motion that plaintiff and petitioners were joint adventurers. ... A joint venture or undertaking may be formed by parol agreement or it may be inferred from the acts and declarations of the parties. ... While a corporation has no power to enter into a partnership, it may, under a joint venture with others, transact any business which is within the scope of its legal powers and thereby become liable on account of the fiduciary relation thus assumed. ... The relation-ship between joint adventurers is a fiduciary one. ... The resemblance between a partnership and a joint venture is so close that the rights as between adventur-ers are governed practically by the same rules that govern partners. Accordingly, a joint adventurer may sue in equity for an accounting of the profits flowing from the joint venture. ... "The receipt by a person of a share of the profits of a business is prima facie evidence that he is a partner in the business" with exceptions not pertinent here. (Civ.Code, § 2414) A fortiori a joint adventurer has the same rights and obligations. The parties are fiduciaries with a duty of disclosure. ... Whether the relations of joint adventurers existed was primarily a question of fact for the trial court to determine from the facts and the inferenc-es to be drawn therefrom. ... Having made a prima facie showing that the parties were joint adventurers and that he has not received his share of the profits plaintiff established prima facie that he is entitled to an accounting. ...

Similar broad statements may be found in *Brooks v. Muth*, 144 Cal.App.2d 560, 564, 301 P.2d 404, 407 (1956).

Before exploring the distinctions between a joint venture and a partnership, consider one of the "rules" recited in *Kauffman v. Superior Court*—that a cor-poration could not be a partner but could become a joint venturer. This rule was applied in California until 1977. Why should it ever have existed?

A corporation is a distinct person within the contemplation of the law. This simply means that a corporation is a debtor and a creditor of those who contract with it. Except in certain extraordinary circumstances, the corporate entity alone is liable to third parties. The enterprisers are not personally liable. Contrast this "limited liability" to the fate of partners and their personal assets. But there is a social risk in creating a corporation, the business organization defined by Ambrose Bierce as "an inglorious device for obtaining individual profit without individual responsibility." Since the human investors have limited liability, how can the corporation itself be compelled to behave responsibly? The legal response is the attempt to centralize authority and responsibility within the corporate structure. Thus there is the nearly universal statutory requirement that a corporation be controlled by directors elected by the shareholders (the beneficial owners). This centralization would be immediately threatened if the corporation were to become a partner. The villain is the law of agency. A corporate partner's assets would be at the mercy of co-partners ... individuals not selected by the shareholders and not in the legal position of corporate directors (who have duties of care and loyalty). For this reason, in many jurisdictions, "public policy" forbids a corporation to be a "partner." For an excellent statement of this public policy rationale see *Whittenton Mills v. Upton*, 76 Mass. (10 Gray) 582 (1858). Also see Annotation, 60 A.L.R.2d 918.

In California, cases like *Kauffman* simply assert the general prohibition. But see *Mervyn Inv. Co. v. Biber*, 184 Cal. 637, 194 P. 1037 (1921), holding that if the articles of incorporation authorize partnership affiliation, the shareholders have waived objection to compromise of control and the state will tolerate the corporation's partnership participation.

The new California Corporations Code, § 207(h), appears to put the matter to rest. It lists corporate powers as including the power to:

> (h) Participate with others in any partnership, joint venture or other association, transaction or arrangement of any kind, whether or not such participation involves sharing of control with or to others.

Still, in some jurisdictions the public policy prohibition on corporate partners is in full force. Yet almost all corporations may become joint venturers. Why? The answer may be in the doctrines discussed in the next case.

B. AGENCY CONSEQUENCES OF DISTINCTION

STONE-FOX, INC v. VANDEHEY DEVELOPMENT CO.
Supreme Court of Oregon 1981
290 Or. 779, 626 P.2d 1365

TONGUE, JUSTICE. This is a suit for specific performance of an earnest money agreement to sell a tract of land. Plaintiff contends that Vernon Vandehey and Jack Leonard were partners for the purpose of the development and sale of that tract of land and that, as such, the act of Mr. Vandehey in signing that agreement was binding upon Mr. Leonard even though he did not sign the agreement. The trial court held for the defendants based upon findings (1) that the evidence was insufficient to establish a partnership; (2) that an oral statement by Mr. Vandehey that he had authority to sell the property was insufficient to transfer the interest of Mr. Leonard in that to do so would violate the statute of frauds and, in any event, (3) that the earnest money agreement was not intended to be a final agreement.

Plaintiff appealed to the Court of Appeals, contending that the trial court was in error in each of these three findings. The Court of Appeals reversed the trial court, holding that there was a joint venture between Mr. Vandehey and Mr. Leonard for development and sale of the tract, and that "once a partnership or joint venture is established, agency need not be proved to show that one partner or venturer was authorized to act for another." 46 Or.App. 465, 470, 611 P.2d 1195 (1980).

We allowed defendants' petition for review because of our concern whether one party to a joint venture has the power to convey real property held in a tenancy in common with another joint venturer and whether partnership law was intended to govern joint ventures in this respect.

The property in dispute in this case is a 46 lot parcel in Washington County known as Family Acres. Late in 1977 Mr. Vandehey obtained a bank loan to finance development of the lots in Family Acres as homesites. In seeking the loan he informed the bank that Mr. Leonard would have an interest in the property and that Family Acres would be a joint venture between the two of them. The bank then required Mr. Leonard's guarantee on the loan, although the title to the property was then held in the name of Mr. Vandehey. Six months later, Mr. Vandehey deeded Family Acres to "Vernon L. Vandehey and Jack Leonard" as joint tenants.

On August 23, 1978, Mr. Vandehey called the office of Mr. Stone, president of plaintiff corporation, to inquire whether he was interested in purchasing the subdivision. Mr. Stone expressed an interest and invited Mr. Vandehey to meet him the next day to discuss the transaction. On August 24 Mr. Vandehey went to the office of Mr. Stone to discuss a possible sale of the property. The parties disagree as to what exactly was said during the ensuing discussion. According to Mr. Stone, however, Mr. Vandehey said that he had a "partner" in the transaction named Mr. Leonard, and that when Mr. Stone then offered to pay $15,000 per lot for the tract Mr. Vandehey said that his authority was limited to making a sale for $15,500 per lot and that "he would have to discuss" the offer of $15,000 per lot "with his partner, Mr. Leonard." Mr. Stone testified further that Mr. Vandehey called him the next morning and said that he had discussed the matter with Mr. Leonard, that they had agreed to sell the property at the price of $15,250 per lot, and that Mr. Stone then accepted that counteroffer.

Mr. Vandehey then signed on behalf of defendant Vandehey Development

Company (VDC) an earnest money agreement for sale of Family Acres to Stone-Fox Inc., the plaintiff. Four days later, Mr. Vandehey conveyed his undivided interest in Family Acres to VDC, a corporation owned entirely by Vandehey.[1] Mr. Leonard did not sign either the earnest money agreement or its addendum and those documents were not executed by Mr. Vandehey in the name of a partnership or joint venture. There was neither a written agreement between either Mr. Vandehey or VDC and Mr. Leonard governing their relationship, nor a written authorization by Mr. Leonard for Mr. Vandehey or VDC to sell the property.

On September 14, 1978, an attorney acting on behalf of Mr. Leonard returned the earnest money to Mr. Stone for the stated reason that at the time the earnest money agreement was signed VDC had no interest in the property. On September 20, 1978, defendants executed an earnest money agreement for the sale of Family Acres to a third party. The record does not reveal whether that sale was consummated. This lawsuit was filed on October 2, 1978.

1. The relationship between defendants was that of joint-venturers or partners.

[UPA §6(1)] defines a partnership as "an association of two or more persons to carry on as co-owners a business for profit." A partnership for a single transaction is a joint venture. *Hayes v. Killinger*, 235 Or. 465, 470, 385 P.2d 747 (1963). In *Hayes*, supra, this court held that "(t)he essential test in determining the existence of a partnership is whether the parties intended to establish such a relation"; that "in the absence of an express agreement * * * the status may be inferred from the conduct of the parties in relation to themselves and to third parties," and "when faced with intricate transactions that arise, this court looks mainly to the right of a party to share in the profits, his liability to share losses, and the right to exert some control over the business."

Defendants acknowledge that they shared in profits and losses and that each shared the right of control in the Family Acres project. They contend, however, that these factors also describe a joint tenancy, or tenancy in common, which alone is insufficient to establish a partnership; that they are, therefore, not partners or joint venturers, and that as co-tenants the act of one cannot bind the other.

. . .The existence of a joint tenancy or tenancy in common does not, however, preclude a partnership or joint venture from existing, as defendants seem to contend.

In this case defendants were clearly more than co-owners of land. They were

---

[1]VDC is 100 percent owned by Mr. Vandehey, who is its president and sole director. There is no vice president or treasurer and Mr. Vandehey's attorney is the secretary. At trial Vandehey acknowledged that he and VDC were "in fact one and the same."

engaged in a business venture for the development of a subdivision. That business venture required construction of curbs, grading of roads and installation of gas, electricity, sewer and water lines. The extensive development of property in such a manner, together with the intent to exert joint control and to share in the profits or losses, is sufficient to establish a partnership or joint venture. A. Bromberg and J. Crane, Law of Partnership 61 (1968). In addition, Mr. Vandehey told the banker that he and Mr. Leonard were engaged in a joint venture. In our opinion, the Court of Appeals was correct in holding that the relationship between defendants was more than one of joint tenancy or tenancy in common, but was either a partnership or joint venture.

It would further appear that the relationship of the defendants was that of a joint venture rather than a partnership. As stated in *Hayes v. Killinger*, supra, at 470, 385 P.2d 747:

"The principal difference between a joint adventure and a partnership is that a partnership is ordinarily formed for the transaction of general business of a particular kind while a joint adventure is usually limited to a single transaction." *Hayes*, supra, at 470, 385 P.2d 747.

Although defendants had engaged in some similar transactions before involving development and selling of real property, there is no substantial evidence that they had formed a partnership for the general purpose of carrying on such an enterprise. Instead, it appears that defendants joined together on isolated occasions, such as this, in enterprises of a more limited nature for the development and sale of tracts of land.

Having held, for these reasons, that the relationship between Mr. Vandehey and Mr. Leonard for the purpose of developing this tract of land was that of a joint venture, rather than a partnership, we must next consider whether the act of Mr. Vandehey in entering into an earnest money agreement for the sale of that real property was binding upon the joint venture, including Mr. Leonard as a member of that joint venture, without express written authority from Mr. Leonard.

2. Mr. Vandehey did not have authority to bind the joint venture under the facts of this case.

Partners are agents of the partnership, and the acts of a partner within the scope of the partnership business are ordinarily binding upon the partnership, with some exceptions. [UPA §9(1)]. It is contended by defendants, however, that a distinction exists between a joint venture and a partnership in cases involving the authority of a member of a joint venture to sell the real property which is the subject of the joint venture, and that in such cases the rules of agency governing partnerships should not apply to joint ventures.

This court has consistently held that partnership law controls joint ventures. See, e. g., *First Western Mtg. v. Hotel Gearhart*, 260 Or. 196, 203, 488 P.2d

450 (1971); *Wheatley v. Carl Halvorson, Inc.*, 213 Or. 228, 235, 323 P.2d 49 (1958). In recognizing this principle, we have applied various provisions of the Uniform Partnership Act (ORS Chapter 68) to joint ventures. See *Gearhart*, supra, [UPA §§29–42], regarding dissolution of a partnership, applied to dissolution of a joint venture); *Starr v. International Realty Limited*, 271 Or. 396, 403, 533 P.2d 165 (1975) [UPA §21(1)], making partners accountable as fiduciaries applies also to joint ventures).

We have not yet, however, had occasion to consider the application of ORS [UPA §9], regarding the agency authority of partners, to joint ventures. Applying that statute to joint ventures would seem to follow, however, from our previous cases in which we have held that partnership law governs joint ventures. Although it has been said that the decisions by other courts are divided on this question, we find that other courts which have addressed this question, at least in recent years, confirm this conclusion by holding that joint venturers are agents of each other and that the act of a joint venturer within the scope of the venture is binding on the joint venture. [collecting citations]

On the more specific issue of whether a joint venturer can bind the venture in a transaction involving the sale of real property, the authorities are more limited. Such authority as is available, however, follows the general rule, stating that the act of a joint venturer in such a transaction is binding on the joint venture if the transaction was within the scope of the venture. . . .

In light of the well-established rule in this state that the law of partnership governs joint ventures, including provisions of the Oregon Uniform Partnership Law relating to partnerships, as well as what appears to be the consistent recent authority from other jurisdictions applying that rule in cases involving the authority of one member of a joint venture to bind the joint venture and its other members, it follows that joint venturers are agents of each other in transactions within the scope of the joint venture in the same sense that partners are agents of each other in transactions within the scope of a partnership, even when the transaction in question involves the sale of real property. It must therefore be determined whether the act of Vandehey in entering into an earnest money agreement for the sale of Family Acres was within the scope of his agency authority as provided by Oregon partnership law. Defendants contend that because the Oregon statute of frauds provides that an agent cannot transfer real property unless his authority is in writing,[4] and because there was no writing

---

[4]ORS 41.580(6) provides:

"In the following cases the agreement is void unless it, or some note or memorandum thereof, expressing the consideration, is in writing and subscribed by the party to be charged or by his lawfully authorized agent * * *.
" * * *

"(6) An agreement concerning real property made by an agent of the party sought

as evidence of Mr. Vandehey's authority to sell the property, it follows that the earnest money agreement signed by him, but not signed by Mr. Leonard, is void. Plaintiff contends, however, that there are specific provisions in the Oregon Uniform Partnership Law which empower a partner and, therefore, a joint venturer, to bind the partnership or joint venture in the sale of real property without written authority. We must therefore examine these competing statutory provisions.

The Oregon Uniform Partnership Law, in addition to its provision to the effect that a partner is the agent of the partnership as to partnership business, with some exceptions (ORS [UPA §9]), includes a specific provision relating to the conveyance of partnership real property (ORS [UPA §10]). ORS [UPA §10](1) provides that:

"Where title to real property is in the partnership name, any partner may convey title to such property by a conveyance executed in the partnership name; * * *."

When, however, as in this case, title to the real property is not in the paship name, but is in the name of one or more of the partners or joint enturers, conveyances of such property are subject to the provisions of [UPA §10(4)] and [UPA §9(1)]. ORS [UPA §10](4) provides as follows:

"Where the title to real property is in the name of one or more or all the partners, or in a third person in trust for the partnership, a conveyance executed by a partner in the partnership name, or in his own name, passes the equitable interest of the partnership, provided the act is one within the authority of the partner under the provisions of subsection (1) of ORS [UPA §9]." (Emphasis added)

It is to be noted that ORS [UPA §10](4) includes no requirement that the authority of the partner to convey such property be in writing. Instead, it appears to require only that the partner be acting within the authority of a partner as provided in ORS [UPA §9](1).[5] ORS [UPA §9](1) provides as follows:

"Every partner is an agent of the partnership for the purpose of its business,

---

to be charged unless the authority of the agent is in writing."

[5][UPA §10](4) also requires that the conveyance be "executed by a partner in the partnership name or in his own name. * * * " In this case the conveyance was made in the name of Vandehey Development Co. and not Vernon Vandehey. As noted at footnotes 1 and 2 of this opinion, however, Vandehey and VDC are one and the same, and defendants have not contended that there is any difference between the two. Nor do defendants raise any contention that [§10](4) does not apply because VDC signed the earnest money agreement instead of Vandehey himself. They contend only that [UPA §10](4) is not applicable because the requirements of [UPA §9](1) are not met. It would therefore appear that the requirements of [§10](4) were met by a conveyance in the name of Vandehey Development Co.

and the act of every partner, including the execution in the partnership name of any instrument, for apparently carrying on in the usual way the business of the partnership of which he is a member binds the partnership, unless the partner so acting has in fact no authority to act for the partnership in the particular matter, and the person with whom he is dealing has knowledge of the fact that he has no such authority." (Emphasis added)

Subsection (2) of [UPA §9] goes on to provide that an act of a partner not within the usual course of business is binding only if authorized by the other partners. Subsection (3) lists certain acts of partners which are not binding unless expressly authorized by the other partners.

These provisions of [UPA §9] appear to distinguish between acts of a partner which bind the partnership because of his status as a partner and acts of a partner which are binding upon it only after express authority is given by the other partners. Under the provisions of [UPA §9(1)] all acts of a partner "for apparently carrying on in the usual way the business of the partnership" (i. e., which are "apparently" within the usual course of the partnership business) bind the partnership and the other partners. The effect of this provision would appear to be that the status of a partner, without more, serves as complete authority to bind the partnership with respect to acts within the apparent scope of the partnership business, obviating the necessity of any express authority, either written or oral, from the other partners. For the same reasons, it would appear to follow that the act of a partner in selling real property when in the apparent scope of the partnership business is binding upon the partnership and the other partners without obtaining their written consent, notwithstanding the provisions of the statute of frauds, ORS 41.580(6), requiring the authority of an agent to sell real property to be in writing. Conversely, it would appear that when a partner cannot act except by express authority from the other partners by reason of the provisions of [UPA §9] and [UPA §10], then the authority of such a partner is substantially the same as that of any other agent of the partnership in the sense that he must have express authority to act, with the result that when a partner undertakes to sell real property in such a situation his authority to do so must be in writing because of ORS 41.580(6).

. . .

Returning to the facts of this case, Mr. Vandehey was clearly acting within the apparent course or scope of the business of the joint venture when he undertook to sell Family Acres to the plaintiff. Indeed, the purpose of the joint venture was to develop and sell that property.[7] If, however, to paraphrase [UPA

---

[7]Normally the sale of all partnership assets is outside the usual course of business. See Crane, Law of Partnership 288 (1968). However, it is within the usual course of business for partners to sell real property that is held for the purpose of sale. . . .

In this case the property in question, Family Acres, was held for the purpose of sale and

§9](1), Mr. Vandehey had "in fact no authority to act for the partnership in (that) particular matter, and the person with whom he (was) dealing (had) knowledge of the fact that he (had) no such authority," then he could not convey title to that property in the absence of express authority to do so.

According to the testimony of Mr. Stone himself, as the president of plaintiff corporation, in his initial conversation with Mr. Vandehey, Mr. Stone made an offer to purchase the property at a price of $15,000 per lot and was told by Mr. Vandehey that he (Mr. Vandehey) did not have authority to enter into a sale for less than $15,500 per lot and that "he would have to discuss" that offer "with his partner, Mr. Leonard." Mr. Stone also testified that the next day Mr. Vandehey told him (Mr. Stone), that he (Mr. Vandehey) had discussed the matter with Mr. Leonard and that they had agreed to sell the property for $15,250 per lot, and that Mr. Stone then accepted that counter-offer. These facts, based upon testimony offered by the plaintiff, make it clear that on the first day of the conversations between Mr. Stone and Mr. Vandehey, Mr. Stone was informed of the fact that Mr. Vandehey's authority to sell the property was limited to a sale at a price not less than $15,500 per lot. In other words, Mr. Stone then "had knowledge of the fact" that Mr. Vandehey did not have authority as an agent of the joint venture, acting within the apparent or usual scope or course of the business of the joint venture under the initial provisions of ORS [UPA §9](1), to sell the real property being developed by it for the best price that he could negotiate. Instead, Mr. Stone then "had knowledge of the fact" that the authority of Mr. Vandehey was expressly limited to a sale at a price not less than $15,500 per lot. It follows, to again paraphrase the final provision of ORS [UPA §9](1), that Mr. Vandehey "had in fact no authority to act for the (joint venture) in the particular matter" (i. e., the proposed sale of the property at a price of $15,000 per lot as offered by Mr. Stone), and (Mr. Stone) "had knowledge of the fact that he (Mr. Vandehey) had no such authority." It also follows, in our opinion, upon application of the provisions of [UPA §9] and [UPA §10], that because of that limitation upon the authority of Mr. Vandehey to sell the property and because the title to that property was then held in his name, Mr. Vandehey had no authority to enter into an earnest money contract the next day for the sale of the property at a price of $15,250 per lot unless he had express authority from Mr. Leonard to do so as an agent of the joint venture and unless that express authority was in writing, as required by ORS 41.580(6) for agents selling real property.

. . .

---

thus conveyance of such property was within the usual course of business. Indeed, sale of the property was necessary for the venture's success, since it was by sale of the property that profit was to be made. Therefore, even though sale of Family Acres meant eventual termination of the joint venture, such termination was contemplated from the beginning as a usual and necessary part of the business.

For reasons previously stated, we are of the opinion that under these facts what plaintiff refers to as the "exception" provided by ORS [UPA §9](1) was not satisfied and that because Mr. Vandehey did not have express authority in writing when he entered into the earnest money agreement to sell Family Acres, that agreement was not binding upon the joint venture or upon Mr. Leonard, the other member of the joint venture. It follows, in our opinion, that the Court of Appeals erred in holding that Mr. Vandehey had authority to bind the joint venture when he entered into that agreement. For that reason we need not address the remaining issue of whether the earnest money agreement, by its terms, was an enforceable contract.

The decision by the Court of Appeals is reversed and this case is remanded to the trial court with instructions to reinstate its original decree dated May 14, 1979.

Reversed and remanded.

Notes

1. In a concurring opinion, Justice Peterson refused to equate Vandehey with his one person corporation, Vandehey Development Co.. Given this view, Peterson took the position that UPA §10(4) did not apply because the conveyance was not executed by "a partner in the partnership name" or "in his own name."

Peterson also refused to join the majority in disposing of the §9(1) liability of the joint venture for an unauthorized transaction:

[UPA §9](1) provides that the act of the partner binds the partnership "... unless [1] the partner so acting has in fact no authority to act for the partnership in the particular matter, and [2] the person with whom he is dealing has knowledge of the fact that he has no such authority." Vandehey's authority was unquestionably *limited* in that he could sell but only at $15,000; but that is not to say that he had "no authority to act for the partnership." I fail to see why Stone's knowledge as to Vandehey's stated lack of authority to sell for $15,000 per lot, on one day, puts Stone on notice under [UPA §9(1)] that Vandehey lacked authority to sell for $15,250 on the next.

. . .

However, in view of the fact that the conveyance did not meet the requirements of [UPA §10](4). . ., I concur in the result.

2. *Agency consequences of classification as a joint venture:* It is the organization for a single objective or transaction which distinguishes the joint venture from the partnership. Yet, since a partnership may be formed for the duration of a task, the distinction may not be obvious. In *Stone-Fox* the Oregon court quotes an earlier precedent which finessed the question by concluding that a partnership for a single task was a joint venture! Upon reflection, you may be able to arrive at a more discerning distinction. But why labor to make it? *Stone-Fox* hints that the difference is in the law of *agency*. Neither the majority nor concurring opinions in *Stone-Fox*

appear disturbed that §9 of the UPA would apply to hold a venture liable for an unauthorized contract. But do you get the impression that the limited nature of the venture's business may have led the majority to the rather questionable conclusion concerning the "knowledge" of Stone that Vandehey lacked real authority? If such a construction of the UPA is proper is it fair to a third party absent some sort of notice that she is dealing with a joint venture and not a partnership?

At least one set of commentators has sounded a warning respecting anticipation of any diminished liability exposure at the hands of a faithless venturer: ". . . It is a great mistake to think (as some businessmen do) that a joint venture offers significant protection from liability." Crane and Bromberg, LAW OF PARTNERSHIP, 194 (1966). The doubts expressed by Crane and Bromberg cannot overcome the many modern judicial opinions which suggest a more restrictive attitude toward the joint venturer's contract liability. Two factors influence this issue. First, do Sections 9 and 3 of the UPA govern the contract liabilities of joint venturers? Second, how does the more transitory and less committed quality of the joint venture affect exposure to vicarious liability? *Kline v. Devcon Realty Corp.*, 285 So.2d 641, 644 (Fla.App. 1973), has language typical of many opinions: "Generally, joint adventurers have the power to bind another in matters strictly within the scope of the joint enterprise. . . ." *Kline* makes no mention of the UPA. *Gluskin v. Atlantic Sav. and Loan Ass'n.*, 32 Cal. App.3d 307, 316-17, 108 Cal.Rptr. 318, 324-25 (1973), applies §9 of the UPA to determine a joint venturer's liability but then holds the joint venturer not liable on the facts of the case. The court emphasizes the other limiting factor: "... Assuming the existence of a joint venture, each joint venturer would have authority only to bind the others to contracts reasonably necessary to carry out the [specific] enterprise." *Rayonier, Inc. v. Polson*, 400 F.2d 909, 914 (9th Cir. 1968), holds that under Washington substantive law §9 of the UPA applies to determine contract liability at the hands of a joint venturer. The Tenth Circuit seems to take the same position in construing Colorado law, although the court cites no supportive Colorado authorities, in *Wood v. Western Beef Factor, Inc*, 378 F.2d 96, 99 (10th Cir. 1967). For an excellent discussion of these questions see Note, Apparent Authority and the Joint Venture-Reducing the Scope of Agency Between Business Associates, 13 U.C. DAVIS L.REV. 831 (1980).

3. *Liability in tort:* A joint venture seems to have the same risk of tort liability as that of a partner. See *Booney v. San Antonio Transit Co.*, 160 Tex. 11, 325 S.W.2d 117, 119 (1959); and *Woolard v. Mobil Pipe Line Co.*, 479 F.2d 557, 561 (5th Cir. 1973) (construing the substantive law of Texas).

C. RELATIONSHIP OF JOINT VENTURERS INTER SE

LIPINSKI v. LIPINSKI
Supreme Court of Minnesota, 1949.
227 Minn. 511, 35 N.W.2d 708.

GALLAGHER, JUSTICE. Appeal from an order of the district court denying a new trial in an action for the dissolution of a partnership and an accounting.

Prior to his death on June 15, 1943, Mike Lipinski, a commercial fisherman, was the owner of some real estate on the shores of Lake Pepin in Wisconsin. Situated on this land were a commercial fish pond, icehouse, packing shed, and dwelling used in connection with the business. On or about April 15, 1943, defendant Martin Lipinski, Mike's brother, and one Henry C. Jezewski entered into an oral agreement with Mike for the use of the property owned by the latter and for the commercial fishing of the waters of Lake Pepin and the furnishing of capital for the activity. Pursuant to this oral agreement, fishing operations were commenced and carried out during the summer of 1943, before as well as after Mike's death on June 15 of that year. It appears that Martin and a crew did most of the actual work of fishing; that Jezewski furnished some of the capital, but was not too active in the fishing operations, which consisted principally of seining carp, buffalo, and other commercial fish for the market.

The operations continued after Mike's death without a written agreement until November 24, 1943. On that date, plaintiffs, who are the heirs at law of Mike Lipinski, entered into a written agreement with Martin and Jezewski. Among other things, in this agreement plaintiffs demised and let to Martin and Jezewski, as parties of the second part, the real estate owned by Mike's estate, including the commercial fish pond, icehouse, packing shed, and dwelling, for a term of four years from April 15, 1943. The second parties agreed to keep and maintain the premises in as good condition as they were on April 15, 1943, and to pay all minor repairs and upkeep, which was to be an expense of the fishing operations. Mike's heirs were to make any permanent improvements to structures at their own expense. The second parties to the agreement agreed also to properly and aggressively fish the waters of Lake Pepin, to supervise and manage the fishing operations, to hire all necessary employees in the conduct of the business, and to deliver to and market from the leased premises all fish caught. They agreed also to sell such fish to the best advantage of all parties, to pay all expenses incurred in the operation of the enterprise, including wages, from the gross receipts of fish sold, and to keep accurate account books of fish caught or disposed of and disbursements made in the operations. It was also agreed that they were to furnish and use in the operations any nets or equipment they then owned without charge, but that any repairs or replacements should be paid as an expense of operation of the enterprise, and that at the expiration of the term all nets or other equipment on hand would become the property of all the parties in the proportions set forth in the agreement. It was also provided that on December 1 and April 15 of each year during the term of the agreement an accounting would be made, and that the receipts from the fishing operations, less expenses, should be divided one-fourth to plaintiffs and three-fourths to the second parties, except that $2,000 was to be retained in the business from such receipts for working capital. The agreement also contained certain provisions incidental to operation of the business and change of personnel, not particularly material in connection with this case.

For many years prior to 1943, a narrow strip of land adjoining the Mike Lipinski property and owned by one Bengtson had been used as a "haul" by Mike in connection with his fishing operations. This land is a narrow strip along the shore of the lake consisting of about 3.61 acres adjacent to and north of Mike's land, now owned by plaintiffs. In November 1943, about nine days prior to the time Mike's heirs entered into the agreement with Martin and Jezewski, Martin purchased this strip of land from Bengtson. This action arose, among other things, out of a dispute in connection with this purchase.

At the time Martin purchased the land from Bengtson, he drew a check for $200 out of the commercial fishing funds and charged the amount to himself. It had been Martin's practice to withdraw funds from time to time in advance of the division of profits, and any such advancements were deducted from his share of the profits at the next accounting. The withdrawal of the $200 was made on or about November 15, 1943, at which time Bengtson and his wife conveyed the strip of land in dispute to Martin and his wife, defendants in this action. The books of the fishing enterprise showed only that the check was drawn for Martin's personal use and did not show the purpose for which the money was used. The land purchased by defendants from Bengtson had been used from the time of Mike's death, and prior thereto in connection with the commercial fishing operations of the parties and continued in use up to the end of such operations in 1946. Martin contends in his testimony that at the time he bought this real estate he did not try to keep it a secret from anyone; that he had suggested several times to some of his associates that they should buy some of this land along the lake, because if they did not someone else would get it, but that "they didn't seem to pay any attention to it." However, he admitted on cross-examination that he did not say anything about acquiring this particular land from Bengtson at the time he signed the contract with plaintiffs on November 24, 1943. He explained that his reason for acquiring the land at the time he did was because some of the plaintiffs had suggested that one or more of the parties to the fishing operations be let out so that the profits would be greater for those remaining; that he was not in favor of such a change and feared that he would be the next one to be let out; and that he thought it would be desirable for him to acquire the land so that it would be less convenient for the others to oust him.

Plaintiffs contend that Martin purchased this land (which they claim was very desirable for use in connection with the business) without their knowledge, approval, or consent, and that he paid for it out of commercial fishing funds without disclosing on the books the purpose of the expenditure or that the check was made payable to Bengtson.

Plaintiffs raised the questions on appeal as to whether the relationship between the parties to the fishing enterprise was that of a partnership or joint venture; whether there was a fiduciary relation between the parties at the time of the purchase of the land; whether Martin purchased the land in violation of his obligations to his associates arising out of any relationship of mutual trust and confidence; and whether defendants are constructive trustees of the title to the land in question.

The trial court found that Martin became associated in a commercial fishing enterprise with his brother Mike in March 1943; that the enterprise was continued after the death of Mike under an informal arrangement with his widow and children for a time, and that on November 24, 1943, the rights and relations of the parties were defined and established by a written agreement; that defendants purchased the land in dispute from Bengtson on November 15, 1943, for $200; that the money was derived from the fishing enterprise, but was withdrawn by Martin for his own use; that although the land in dispute had been used for many years by Mike, and after his death by the parties to this action, in connection with their commercial fishing enterprise, none of these persons ever had any right, title, or interest in the land, nor had any of them ever claimed any right, title, or interest until title was acquired by defendants. Thereupon, the court concluded that plaintiffs were not entitled to any remedy or relief.

In its order of March 25, 1948, the court partially amended paragraph 4 of its findings, to the effect that a proper accounting of the $200 withdrawn by Martin had been made to his associates, and substituted a finding that an entry was made by him in the account books of the enterprise which showed that the withdrawal was charged to him; "that he made other withdrawals, both before and after said $200 item, and entered the same in like manner in said account book; and that all such entries were allowed and deducted from his share, without objection, when the parties examined the book at the end of each year."

In its memorandum attached to the order, the court said in part that it seemed clear that the relationship between the parties was fiduciary in character and that each owed to the others the highest degree of loyalty and good faith. "Such relationship and its obligations, however, were limited to the enterprise in which they were mutually engaged. The trial court then went on to say:

"... In determining their respective obligations, a court should always keep in mind the purposes for which the participants were associated and the manner in which the association was organized ...

"It should be remembered that the defendant contributed no land to the enterprise, and was to receive no interest in land upon its termination. This, alone, is not determinative; but it is an important consideration in discovering his duty toward the others, ... The defendant stood in the position of a lessee; the other parties were his landlords. The land was theirs to begin with, and it was to be theirs when the enterprise terminated.

"The defendant did not acquire any land that his associates owned. They had no right, title or interest in the disputed strip (called the haul), and they had made no plans to lease it, or buy it, or to acquire any easement or other right in it. ...

"... The agreement, by its terms, covered only land the record title of which was in the name of M.N. Lipinski."

The court further said in its memorandum that this was a fishing enterprise and not an undertaking to acquire land, or to improve or develop real estate, or to sell or lease land to others, and that the association was limited to a term of four years. It also said:

"The defendant did not buy the haul as the result of any information, priority, or advantageous position which he had obtained by virtue of the joint enterprise. He merely went up the hill and bought it. Any of the others could have done the same. He violated no confidence; he had no advantage in a race-the others were not intending to buy it. The vendors did not come to him because he was in charge. He sought them himself.

"The haul was not purchased with partnership funds. The defendant withdrew the sum of $200 and charged the withdrawal to himself on the partnership books. Other withdrawals, for his personal use, were made in the same manner. The amount was not large enough to impoverish or jeopardize the enterprise. It was deducted from the defendant's share, in the same manner as the other withdrawals, upon the annual accounting; and there was no objection. If he had used it for any other purpose, there would have been no complaint later. It was essentially his money. ..."

With reference to the issue raised by plaintiffs as to whether the relationship between the parties was that of a partnership or joint venture, it is somewhat difficult to determine from the agreement of November 24 just what kind of a deal the parties intended to make. It is somewhat in the nature of a lessor-lessee arrangement, in that plaintiffs demised and let to Martin Lipinski and Jezewski the real estate described in the agreement, and somewhat in the nature of a partnership or joint venture, in that Martin and Jezewski were to carry on, supervise, and manage the fishing operations, pay expenses from the gross receipts, and furnish certain equipment without charge. An accounting was to be made on December 1 and April 15 of each year, and receipts from the fishing operations, less expenses, were then to be divided one-fourth to plaintiffs and three-fourths to Martin and Jezewski, with certain exceptions unimportant here as to changes in personnel. Assuming, however, that it was the intention of the parties to make the deal a partnership or joint venture, we cannot see under the facts of the case how it can change the decision, because, as we see it, the real issue is whether the purchase of the 3.61 acres by Martin was a violation of a fiduciary duty which he owed plaintiffs so as to impose a constructive trust upon the property for the benefit of the parties to the agreement.

The action was tried to the court without a jury, and the court concluded that plaintiffs were not entitled to any remedy or relief.

...

[UPA §6(1)], defines a partnership as follows:

"A partnership is an association of two or more persons to carry on as co-owners a business for profit."

In discussing the question of the duties of partners toward each other, this court said in *Kitzman v. Postier & Kruger Co.* Inc., 204 Minn. 343, 346, 283 N.W. 542, 543:

"We may accept as valid plaintiff's statement of the law, that each of the parties to this cause occupies to the other a position of trust and as such 'must exercise the most scrupulous good faith toward each other.' Hence, 'in any dispute touching any transaction by which one partner seeks to benefit himself at the expense of the firm, he is required to show, not only that "he has law on his side, but that his conduct will bear to be tried by the highest standard of honor." ' *McAlpine v. Millen*, 104 Minn. 289, 300, 116 N.W. 583, 587. And we consider it immaterial whether the relationship was that of a general partnership or, as determined by the court, a joint enterprise. Obviously, the same rule should apply in either case. 'A joint adventure can arise only by contract or agreement between the parties to join their efforts in furtherance of a particular transaction or series of transactions. And in the absence of express limitations in that respect each party to such adventure is subject to all losses and liabilities, and entitled to share equally in the profits of the undertaking. The relationship is substantially that of a co-partnership.' *National Surety Co. v. Winslow*, 143 Minn. 66, 71, 173 N.W. 181, 183; Mechem, 'The Law of Joint Adventures,' 15 Minn.L.Rev. 644."

If we are to assume in the case at bar that the agreement of November 24, 1943, between the parties created a copartnership or joint venture relationship, it seems clear under the law that such relationship was fiduciary in character and that each of the parties to the agreement owed to the others the highest degree of good faith. [UPA §21(1)] provides:

"Every partner must account to the partnership for any benefit, and hold as trustee for it any profits derived by him without the consent of the other partners from any transaction connected with the formation, conduct, or liquidation of the partnership or from any use by him of its property."

In *Venier v. Forbes*, 223 Minn. 69, 74, 25 N.W.2d 704, 708, we held "that the relationship between partners is essentially one of mutual trust and confidence and that the law imposes upon them the highest standard of integrity and good faith in their dealings with each other."

It is true that a constructive trust will arise where an interest in property is purchased by one standing in a fiduciary relation to another where the scope of the former's obligation as a fiduciary is closely connected with the transaction. 3 Scott, Trusts, § 504. This rule is based on equity and good conscience, for a fiduciary should not be allowed to profit by exploiting those who have placed their trust and confidence in him, but the rule should not be interpreted so as to deprive the fiduciary of the power to invest his money in good faith in other profitable ventures. See, *Shrader v. Downing*, 79 Wash. 476, 478, 140 P. 558, 559, 52 L.R.A., N.S., 389. Consequently, it has been held that, while a lease held by a partnership and the right to renew it are partnership assets, the title of a landlord is not so adverse to that of his tenant as to prevent a partner from purchasing the fee to the premises which the partnership leased, provided he practices no fraud or deception upon his copartners and holds his fee subject to the lease for the duration thereof.

We now come to the question whether the 3.61 acres of land involved in this litigation should be considered partnership property and accounted for in the partnership assets. The trial court found that it was not; that defendants purchased the land from Bengtson with money withdrawn by Martin Lipinski for his own use; and that a proper accounting of such money had been made to his associates. The trial court further said in its memorandum that it seemed clear that the relationship between the parties was fiduciary in character and that each owed to the others the highest degree of loyalty and good faith, but that such relationship and its obligations were limited to the enterprise in which they were mutually engaged. It is our opinion that this is correct.

It must be considered in reviewing the agreement of November 24 that the purpose for which the parties entered into it was to conduct and continue to carry on a fishing enterprise consisting primarily of fishing the waters of Lake Pepin for commercial purposes with the object of making a profit. We can find nothing in this agreement to indicate that the acquisition of additional real estate was one of the objects or purposes of the business. The land described in the contract of November 24 was that belonging entirely to plaintiffs, and it was to remain theirs at the termination of the agreement. The undertaking involved was definitely that of a fishing enterprise and not one involving the acquisition, improvement, or development of real estate. It was limited to four years, and there was no provision for any renewal. It is true that the land acquired by defendants, referred to as the "haul," was used in connection with the fishing enterprise, but it appears from the record that some of the parties to the agreement at least had been familiar with the fact, for a long time before this action was commenced, that Martin had acquired this land, and that they had shown no interest in acquiring it for themselves, either before or for some time after Martin received title.

. . .

Plaintiffs particularly emphasize in their brief that the property involved should be accounted for in the accounting and dissolution because it was purchased with partnership funds, and they cite the case of *State v. MacGregor*, 202 Minn. 579, 279 N.W. 372. It appears to us that that case is not in point. In that case it was held that indictments for forgery against a partner for making false entries in the partnership books for the purpose of defrauding a partner by concealing a misappropriation of partnership funds stated public offenses under the statute. Here, there is no showing that the $200 used by Martin was misappropriated. The record shows that it was charged to his account and deducted from his share of the profits, and that this information was available to all the parties.

After carefully reviewing the record and under our rules in previous cases, we find it necessary to sustain the findings and conclusions of the trial court.

Affirmed.

GRAMERCY EQUITIES, CORP. v. DUMONT
Court of Appeals of New York, 1988
72 N.Y.2d 560, 531 N.E.2d 629

KAYE, JUDGE.   Where one joint venturer, managing the business of the joint venture, alone commits an intentional fraud against third parties resulting in the recovery of damages by them, he is not thereafter entitled to be indemnified by the other joint venturer.

This appeal—involving solely the allocation of damages between coventurers inter se—arises out of the conversion of a Manhattan building from commercial lofts to a residential cooperative. In early 1978, Paul Dumont (plaintiff) and Anthony Russo (defendant) entered into an oral agreement to sponsor conversion of the building. Russo, a hairdresser by trade, was not expected to take an active role, but only to provide the cash then needed to buy the building. Dumont, who had experience in cooperative conversions, was to contribute his expertise and do the actual work required to form a cooperative corporation and convey the building to it. The two agreed that after the conveyance was complete, Russo would receive the proprietary lease for the eighth floor of the building as well as half the net proceeds.

In 1979, a cooperative corporation known as Gramercy Equities Corporation was formed and acquired title to the property. Dumont, sponsor of the plan, began selling shares in the cooperative; Russo took no part in this activity. Dumont ultimately sold all other floors but two which he retained-- the ground floor (intended for a commercial tenant) and the sixth floor. It was understood that proprietary leaseholders, including Dumont, each would renovate their own "raw" space, so that the apartments could meet New York City Building Code requirements. Until those renovations and certain other repairs were complete, no certificate of occupancy could be obtained for the building. Dumont represented to the purchasers that the cooperative corporation would undertake to secure a tax abatement pursuant to "J-51" of the Administrative Code of the City of New York.

After a number of floors had been sold, Russo brought suit against Dumont, alleging in essence that he had failed to accord him his rights as a joint venturer, and demanding that Dumont account to him for the profits of the joint venture. Dumont denied the existence of any joint venture, and claimed that Russo was a mere subscriber to the offering plan. In August 1981, judgment was rendered declaring Russo a joint venturer with Dumont in the cooperative conversion and therefore entitled to half the profits. The court found, moreover, that Russo was not expected to take an active role in the business, but only to contribute the cash required to take title to the building. Supreme Court ordered that the moneys received by Dumont from the sale of shares be held in trust, and that an accounting be rendered. Meanwhile, trouble brewed between Dumont and the other cooperative tenants. In order to qualify for the "J-51" tax abatement, a certificate of occupancy for the building had to be issued no later than September 30, 1981; all renovations required to bring the building up to code standards had to be completed before that date. While work was well underway on other floors, Dumont had repaired none of the violations on the sixth floor, owned by Dumont but at the time occupied by a tenant-in-possession. Ultimately, the September deadline passed without a certificate of occupancy, and the cooperative failed to qualify for a "J-51" tax abatement.

The tenants sought damages against Dumont for loss of the tax abatement, alleging that he had breached his contract as proprietary leaseholder to complete his renovations in a timely fashion so that the building could qualify for the tax benefit. Additionally, they separately charged Dumont with fraud, contending that although he had promised to complete certain renovations in time to obtain the tax abatement, he never had any intention of doing so. Dumont in turn served a third-party complaint on Russo, alleging that if he were found liable to the tenants, Russo, as joint venturer, had to indemnify him for half the damages, as they arose directly out of the business of the joint venture.

Dumont and Russo agreed that, as between themselves, there were no facts in dispute--only the legal consequences of their relationship. Dumont's indemnification claim was therefore severed from the main action, to be later decided by the trial court.

At trial, the tenants' evidence of damages consisted of the testimony of their tax attorney as to the amount of the rebate they would have received had Dumont timely completed his renovation. At the conclusion of the evidence, a large portion of the court's instruction was devoted to the fraud charge, which was thereafter reread at the jury's request. The jury found Dumont guilty of both breach of contract and intentional fraud--specifically answering in the affirmative the question, "Did the Defendant Paul Dumont commit a fraud against the plaintiffs?" The court awarded damages to the cooperative tenant plaintiffs in the amount lost as a result of their failure to obtain the "J-51" tax abatement, and then allowed Dumont indemnification for half that judgment against Russo, based upon its interpretation of partnership law principles. While the jury found that Dumont had defrauded the tenants by making a promise with no intention of fulfilling it, the court made no finding that Russo in any sense participated in that wrongdoing or that Dumont's fraud profited the joint venture. Noting that the earlier action had determined both that Russo was a joint venturer and that he was not intended to take an active role, Supreme Court simply rejected Russo's claim that his exclusion from management foreclosed Dumont's right of indemnification arising out of his unilateral management of the joint venture. Based upon its finding that the damages were liabilities incurred in the ordinary conduct of the joint venture, Supreme Court held that, pursuant to Partnership Law § 40(2), Dumont was entitled to be indemnified, and the Appellate Division affirmed, without opinion. 136 A.D.2d 975, 523 N.Y.S.2d 331. We now reverse.

. . .

A joint venture is a "'special combination of two or more persons where in some specific venture a profit is jointly sought'" (*Forman v. Lumm*, 214 App. Div. 579, 583, 212 N.Y.S. 487). It is in a sense a partnership for a limited purpose, and it has long been recognized that the legal consequences of a joint venture are equivalent to those of a partnership (*see, Pedersen v. Manitowoc Co.*, 25 N.Y.2d 412, 419, 306 N.Y.S.2d 903, 255 N.E.2d 146). Thus, the trial court properly looked to partnership law principles to resolve the dispute between Dumont and Russo.

In New York, the right of a partner to be indemnified for personal liabilities is governed by Partnership Law § 40(2) [UPA §18(b)], which provides that "[t]he partnership must indemnify every partner in respect of payments made and personal liabilities reasonably incurred by him in the ordinary and proper conduct of its business, or for the preservation of its business or property." The question before us, simply put, is whether acts that have been determined to constitute the intentional fraud of only one of the coventurers--not shared by the other--may be considered to constitute "the ordinary and proper conduct" of the partnership business.

It is undisputed that the cooperative tenants could have brought suit for Dumont's fraud against the joint venture, or even against Russo individually, and recovered their damages. As agents for each other, partners and joint venturers are jointly and severally liable to third parties for "any wrongful act or omission of any partner acting in the ordinary course of the business of the partnership". (Partnership Law 24, 26 [1]; see also, *Royal Bank & Trust Co. v. Weintraub, Gold & Alper*, 68 N.Y.2d 124, 506 N.Y.S.2d 151, 497 N.E.2d 289. . . .) The sale of cooperative shares, during which Dumont made the fraudulent statements to purchasers, constituted the "ordinary" course of the business of this joint venture: it was formed for the very purpose of selling cooperative shares in the building. However, the tenants sued only Dumont, and the issue is whether as between the two joint venturers Dumont can shift a portion of the liability that has been imposed on him to his joint venturer, Russo. The fact that a charge may have been incurred in the *ordinary* course of partnership business—as the trial court found here—does not conclude the inquiry as to whether indemnification is necessarily recoverable. Partnership Law § 40(2) contemplates something more.

The principle that a partnership must indemnify a partner who has incurred liabilities in the ordinary course of the partnership business is not determinative where the liability is the result of unauthorized, intentional wrongdoing. Although the public interest requires that the partnership or even innocent partners be held answerable to third parties for unlawful actions of their agents apparently taken on their behalf (*see, Royal Bank & Trust Co. v. Weintraub, Gold & Alper, supra*, at 128-129, 506 N.Y.S.2d 151, 497 N.E.2d 289; . . .), there is no comparable interest in imposing liability on innocent partners when the suit is between the partners themselves (see, Reuschlein & Gregory, Agency and Partnership § 185 [1979]; Lindley, Partnership, at 460 [10th ed. 1935]; Restatement [Second] of Agency § 440[a]). Indeed, this distinction is codified in the Partnership Law, which imposes partnership liability for injury to third persons caused by "any wrongful act or omission of any partner acting in the ordinary course of the business" [UPA §13], but requires indemnification only for liabilities incurred in "the ordinary *and proper* conduct" of the partnership business [UPA §18(b)][emphasis added]).

In matters of indemnification between two joint venturers, the unauthorized fraud found to have been practiced against third persons by only one venturer obviously is not the "proper conduct" of the partnership business. That Dumont was vested with sole managerial control of the business does not alter that result in the absence of a finding that Russo in any way shared in Dumont's fraud. Partnership Law §40 is expressly "subject to any agreement" between partners (*see, Kraemer v. Gallagher*, 18 A.D.2d 676, 235 N.Y.S.2d 874), but without any finding of complicity, the unauthorized fraud of one venturer cannot be said to be pursuant to the "agreement" of both. Finally, we note that this result comports with the public policy of discouraging intentionally wrongful conduct. To permit a joint venturer to shift a portion of the liability for independent fraud to a partner not found to have had any complicity in it significantly diminishes the incentive to refrain from such conduct (*see, Rosado v. Proctor & Schwartz*, 66 N.Y.2d 21, 26-27, 494 N.Y.S.2d 851, 484 N.E.2d 1354). Such a policy has particular force in the case of joint venturers who--apart from their responsibilities to third persons--owe each other a duty of "finest loyalty" and honesty. (*Meinhard v. Salmon*, 249 N.Y. 458, 463-464, 164 N.E. 545.)

Accordingly, the Appellate Division order should be reversed, with costs, and the third-party complaint dismissed.

Notes

It is evident from *Lipinski* and *Gramercy Equities* that in their relations inter se joint venturers fall within the principles of partnership law. Like partners, they share the profits and losses of their enterprise. *Bates & Springer of Arizona, Inc. v.*

Friermood, 16 Ariz.App. 309, 492 P.2d 1247 (1972). Joint venturers can vary the matter by contract, but absent a contrary agreement they share equally in the control and management of their enterprise. *Sheppard v. Carey*, 254 A.2d 260 (Del.Ch. 1969). The fiduciary quality of their association attaches at the formation of the enterprise. *Herring et al. v. Offutt*, 266 Md. 593, 295 A.2d 876 (1972). Obviously, it dominates the relationship during the conduct of the joint venture. *Sheppard v. Carey*, supra. These same qualities discipline dissolution and any attempt to appropriate what would otherwise have been venture opportunities. *University Computing Co. v. Lykes-Youngstown Corp.*, 504 F.2d 518 (5th Cir. 1974). Absent an agreement, joint venturers receive no compensation for their effort but are expected to look to a distribution of profits for their reward. *Boner v. L.C. Fulenwider, Inc.*, 32 Colo.App. 440, 513 P.2d 730, 732 (1973).

For tax purposes a joint venture's profits and losses are treated as if generated by a partnership, There is presumptive "non-association" status under the Internal Revenue Code.

Finally, the Uniform Partnership Act is used to govern dissolution, liquidation and winding up of the joint venture. *University Computing*, supra, and *Zeibak v. Nasser*, 12 Cal.2d 1, 82 P.2d 375 (1938).

D. USE OF JOINT VENTURES TO SHARE TECHNOLOGY AND FORM ALLIANCES OF CONVENIENCE IN THE MARKETPLACE

Anyone who has followed the relations between domestic and foreign auto producers in the last decade will realize that the joint venture is the literal "vehicle of choice" for many transnational arrangements designed to share technology and form specific, as opposed to all encompassing, business alliances. For an illustration of the use of a joint venture to share technology see, *Infusaid Corp. v. Intermedics Infusaid, Inc.*, 739 F.2d 661 (1st Cir. 1984). Why would General Motors and Toyota prefer a joint venture to a partnership or corporate vehicle for their joint production for the North American market of a subcompact car? Does part of the answer lie in *Stone-Fox* and *Lipinski*? What about domestic *antitrust law* considerations? Does the less committed, specific quality of the joint venture pose a seemingly less threatening combination to attorneys at the United States Justice Department who worry about enforcement of the antitrust laws?

Whatever the consequences to agency exposure, fiduciary qualities, and antitrust implications, joint venturers risk everything to both tort and contract claimants. As with the partner, the exposure to liability is defined by §15 of the UPA. If a client wants to limit this liability there are but two choices: a limited partnership, or incorporation.

Chapter 4

THE LIMITED PARTNERSHIP

A. INTRODUCTION

If a general partnership is regulated by a uniform statute, the limited partnership is a creature of statutory law. Absent compliance with an enabling act, a limited partnership cannot be created nor can it be maintained. In the early part of this century a movement was begun to convince states to adopt identical or nearly identical statutory schemes for limited partnerships. The effort was largely successful. Revision of that uniform statute has currently cast the law into a state of transition. Depending upon the preference of individual legislatures, states may elect from no fewer than three "uniform" acts to govern the formation, conduct and dissolution of limited partnerships.[1] The choices are the 1916 Act, the 1976 Act or the 1985 Amendments to the 1976 Act. At present only seven of the fifty-three jurisdictions[2] have retained the original 1916 uniform act.[3] We will refer to it as the "Uniform Partnership Act" or "ULPA." The forty-five states which have opted for revision do not present a united front. Seven have adopted the 1976 Revised Uniform Limited Partnership, or "RULPA," and have thus far declined to embrace the 1985 Amendments.[4] This statutory transition is a clue to even more fundamental questions which remain to be fully answered in this area.

The Uniform Limited Partnership Act [ULPA]. The ULPA was proposed for adoption by the legislatures of the several states in 1916. By 1967 it had become the law in forty-four states and the District of Columbia. (The text of the ULPA is reproduced as Appendix B and should be read at this point.) A brief history of this unique business vehicle and a business rationale for its assump-

---

[1]Louisiana is the one American jurisdiction which has refused to date to enact any version of the uniform act. Such a position is consistent with its view as a civil law jurisdiction bordered by the Gulf of Mexico and the common law.

[2]In addition to the fifty states, the jurisdictions active in this regard include the District of Columbia, Guam and the Virgin Islands.

[3]As of January, 1990, the jurisdictions electing to retain the 1916 Uniform Limited Partnership Act are: Alaska, Guam, Maine, New York, Utah, Vermont, and the Virgin Islands.

[4]Alabama, Arkansas, Idaho, Michigan, Missouri, Wisconsin and Wyoming.

tion were presented in the official Comment appended to §1 of the original uniform act:

> The business reason for the adoption of acts making provisions for limited or special partners is that [individuals] in business often desire to secure capital from others. There are at least three classes of contracts which can be made with those from whom the capital is secured: One, the ordinary loan on interest; another, a loan where the lender, in lieu of interest, takes a share in the profits of the business; third, those cases in which the person advancing the capital secures, besides a share in the profits, some measure of control over the business.
>
> At first, in the absence of statutes the courts, both in this country and in England, assumed that one who is interested in a business is bound by its obligations, carrying the application of this principle so far, that a contract where the only evidence of interest was a share in the profits made one who supposed himself a lender, and who was probably unknown to the creditors at the times they extended their credit, unlimitedly liable as a partner for the obligations of those actually conducting the business.
>
> Later decisions have much modified the earlier cases. The lender who takes a share in the profits, except possibly in one or two of our jurisdictions, does not by reason of that fact run a risk of being held as a partner. If, however, his contract falls within the third class mentioned, and he has any measure of control over the business, he at once runs serious risk of being held liable for the debts of the business as a partner: the risk increasing as he increases the amount of his control.
>
> The first Limited Partnership Act was adopted by New York in 1822; the other commercial states, during the ensuing 30 years, following her example. Most of the statutes followed the language of the New York statute with little material alteration. These statutes were adopted, and to a considerable degree interpreted by the courts, during that period when it was generally held that any interest in a business should make the person holding the interest liable for its obligations. As a result the courts usually assume in the interpretation of these statutes two principles as fundamental.
>
> First: That a limited (or as he is also called a special) partner is a partner in all respects like any other partner, except that to obtain the privilege of a limitation on his liability, he has conformed to the statutory requirements in respect to filing a certificate and refraining from participation in the conduct of the business.
>
> Second: The limited partner, on any failure to follow the requirements in regard to the certificate or any participation in the conduct of his business, loses his privilege of limited liability and becomes, as far as those dealing with the business are concerned, in all respects a partner.

. . .

The practical result of the spirit shown in the language and in the interpretation of existing statutes, coupled with the fact that a man may now lend money to a partnership and take a share in the profits in lieu of interest without running serious danger of becoming bound for partnership obligations, has, to a very great extent, deprived the existing statutory provisions for limited partners of any practical usefulness. Indeed, apparently their use is largely confined to associations in which those who conduct the business have not more than one limited partner.

One of the causes forcing business into the corporate form, in spite of the fact that the corporate form is ill suited to many business conditions, is the failure of the existing limited partnership acts to meet the desire of the owners of a business to secure necessary capital under the existing limited partnership form of business association.

The text of the ULPA and the official comment by the drafting committee present the image and structure of a social contract. Some, but not all, of the terms of that bargain were articulated in *Riveria Congress Associates v. Yassky*, 25 A.D.2d 291, 294, 268 N.Y.S.2d 854, 857 (1966): ". . . A limited partnership is exclusively a creature of statute . . . the general purpose being to encourage persons with capital to become partners with those having skill, with a limitation on liability upon the limited partner so that he is not responsible for the general obligations of the partnership. Only his capital is imperiled.. . ." Unstressed in the *Riveria* court's summary was the statutory expectation that the limited partners would adopt a posture of passivity, leaving the conduct of the affairs of the limited partnership to the general partner or partners. The final dimension of the bargain pertained to the general partner or partners. They faced the world with all of the liability potential provided in the Uniform Partnership Act. If the limited partnership was dissolved at a time when assets were insufficient to meet the claims of third party creditors. the consequences to the general partner or partners were set forth in the grim provisions of §15 of the UPA.

The Revised Uniform Limited Partnership Act [RULPA]. In 1916 the framers of the ULPA were worried that the then accelerating trend toward incorporation would obscure the utility of a business entity formed with general and limited partners. Whatever the success of their statutory proposals in rescuing this vehicle, it was the structure of the federal income tax laws in the thirty years preceding the second Reagan Administration which guaranteed a modern relevance for the limited partnership and generated most of the problems with the ULPA. The essence of the strategy was simple: if economic activity was projected to produce near certain "tax accounting losses," it was to the advantage of participants that it not be pursued in the context of a corporation. This is because of the federal tax law presumption that a corporation is an "association," a taxpaying entity separate from its shareholders. Association status meant that the corporate taxpayer had a tax loss. The owners of the corporation, who might have had substantial income from non-corporate sources, were unable to offset their personal income against the corporate tax accounting losses. By contrast, partnerships were not regarded as distinct taxpaying entities. They were viewed as mere aggregations of individual partners, so that income or loss derived from such vehicles was included by the participants in reckoning their individual tax liability. While there were techniques for achieving "non association" treatment of certain corporations, the easiest way for individuals to combine their energy in quest of tax minimization was to form a partnership. Yet the fear of unlimited personal liability deterred those who preferred to define "loss" on a tax form rather than to experience the potential of uncapped liability to third parties.

The potential utility of the limited partnership was apparent but its adaptation to the needs of persons united for what are essentially tax planning purposes only has proven problematic. Questions of formation of partnerships frequently organized against the urgency of tax deadlines and the sought inclusion of last minute participants may, if successfully surmounted, yield to unease with respect to the presumed passivity of individuals who have invested substantial sums of cash in a scheme which may be branded a bogus tax shelter if mismanaged by the general partner or partners. The respective rights and obligations of general and limited partners, which might have tolerated lack of precise definition in other contexts, have been pressed for resolution by individuals with markedly divergent goals and agendas. The dimensions of fiduciary duties in this context were not clarified by the terms of a statute never intended for its dominant modern use.

In 1976 the National Conference of Commissioners on Uniform State Laws proposed a sweeping revision. At first there was a hesitancy to adopt the Revised Uniform Limited Partnership Act [RULPA] because of doubt as to the "association" or "non-association" treatment of partnerships formed under its terms by the Internal Revenue Service. That important tax issue was clarified in 1983 with the consequence that twenty-two states quickly repealed the ULPA in favor of the RULPA.

The 1985 Amendments [RULPA/85]. In 1985 the Commissioners on Uniform State Laws proposed what they termed a new "Uniform Limited Partnership Act." The step was taken at a point in time when nearly half of the states had yet to digest their 1976 reform! The resulting confusion produced a quick strategic retreat. The Commissioners retained the proposed significant changes which would have warranted designation as a "new act" but styled them "1985 Amendments to the 1976 Act." The prefatory note to the 1985 Amendments contained the following characterization of and justification for the proposals:

> The Uniform Limited Partnership Act (1976) with the 1985 Amendments (the 1985 Act) follows the 1976 Act very closely in most respects. It makes almost no change in the basic structure of the 1976 Act. It does, however, differ from the 1976 Act in certain significant respects for the purpose of more effectively modernizing, improving, and establishing uniformity in the law of limited

partnerships. The 1985 Act accomplishes this, without impairing the basic philosophy or values underlying the 1976 Act, by incorporating into the structure, framework, and text of the 1976 Act the best and most important improvements that have emerged in the limited partnership acts enacted recently in several states. Most of those improvements were considered by the draftsmen of the 1976 Act but were not included because of uncertainties as to the possible consequences of such inclusion under the applicable Federal income tax laws. Those uncertainties have since been resolved satisfactorily, and no impediment to incorporating them in the 1985 Act remains at this time.

The 1976 Act as amended by the 1985 revision is Appendix C and should be read at this point. The framers claim that the 1985 Amendments do not impair "the basic philosophy or values underlying the 1976 Act. . . ." Could they make the same claim with respect to the spirit and content of the 1916 Act and the surrounding century and one half of society's experience with limited partnerships? It is undoubted that the 1985 Amendments go far toward completing some agenda, but it is for you to determine the dimension of that goal and the direction in which it would take the society.

As you ponder these questions, the continuing relevance of the 1916 legislation will be manifested in three other factors. First, it is the basis for the statutory revisions. Second, a substantial number of the states which have adopted the revised act have continued the application of the ULPA to all limited partnerships formed prior to the effective date of the revision. Finally, and perhaps of the greatest importance, the 1916 Act is the foundation upon which nearly all decisional law in this area rests. It will be decades before those decisions will cease to cast a substantial shadow over business planning and litigation under the revised act.

B. FORMATION

Reread §2 of the ULPA and §201 of the RULPA with particular heed to the 1985 Amendment. In the cases which follow consider the liability consequences to participants and third party creditors of failure to comply with these statutory steps.

KLEIN v. WEISS
Court of Appeals of Maryland, 1978.
284 Md. 36, 395 A.2d 126.

[The following is a highly condensed statement of the elaborate fact pattern detailed by the court at 395 A.2d 129-145. ed.

Appellant, Klein, was appointed a receiver on behalf of creditors of Seventy Sixth Street Limited Partnership. Defendants agreed to purchase seven of what were to be twenty-five limited partnership units in a real estate investment scheme concocted by John Fulton, an Ocean City real estate broker, and Victoria Rinaldi, his associate. For a variety of reasons considered in this appeal, it is the contention of the defendants that no limited partnership was ever formed; that they were the victims of bad faith dealing on the part of the supposed general partners; and that as such they have no liability to creditors of the still born limited partnership.

In October, 1972, Fulton and Rinaldi were aware of an opportunity to purchase a tract of bay front land owned by the Seventy-Sixth Street Joint Venture. They contracted to purchase the property from the Joint Venture for $450,000. This contract was signed by Fulton and Rinaldi styling themselves as general partners of the Seventy-Sixth Street Limited Partnership, a partnership which did not then exist. A ten thousand dollar downpayment was tendered by Fulton. The contract stipulated that closing was to take place in six months at which time the limited partnership was to tender $175,000 to the Joint Venture, assume an existing mortgage on the property and execute a purchase money mortgage to the Venture.

Having formed this contract, Fulton and Rinaldi set about finding investors who would purchase twenty-five limited partnership units for $9,000 each. In this manner sufficient cash would be generated to meet the partnership's obligation to pay $175,000 to the Joint Venture. The excess capital would provide working funds. Fulton and Rinaldi hired an attorney who prepared a partnership agreement and certificate as well as a subscription agreement to be used in the solicitation of prospective limited partners. The original partnership agreement and certificate required each limited partner to make an initial capital contribution of $9,000 per unit and a future contribution of $15,298 representing the per unit share of the mortgage debt to be created on the property to be acquired from the Joint Venture. The proposed partnership agreement provided that a maximum of twenty-five units would be sold and restricted the right of any limited partner to withdraw capital already contributed or pledged to the partnership. Further provisions of the proposed agreement granted broad powers to the general partners to execute any documents on behalf of the partnership whether before or after the filing of the certificate.

> The agreement also provided that the limited partners consented to any mortgage by the general partners of the partnership's assets ... on such terms and conditions as may be determined by the General Partners, and to any contract agreement ... or arrangements with ... [others] as the General Partners may deem necessary to accomplish the purposes of this partnership. ... The general partners were empowered, in their absolute discretion, 'to borrow money and as security therefor to mortgage or subject to other security device any part of the property of the Partnership; to ... refinance, recast, increase, modify ... or extend any such property ... upon such terms as they deem proper ... [and] to execute, acknowledge and deliver any and all instruments to effectuate the foregoing.' The agreement designated the general partners as attorney and agent for the limited partners to execute and record on their behalf 'all certificates or other instruments ... which the General Partner deems appropriate to qualify or contin-

ue the Partnership as a Limited Partnership ... [and] all instruments which the General Partner deems appropriate to effect a change or modification of the Partnership in accordance with the terms of this Agreement.

The evidence at trial indicated that both the proposed agreement and certificate had been circulated with the subscription agreement to each of the defendants as a prospective limited partner. In varying degrees these formal instruments were not read. Nor was the subscription drive a success. Only seven units were subscribed with the consequence that Fulton and Rinaldi were unable to meet the obligations assumed in the name of the partnership on the settlement date with the Joint Venture. A one week extension was secured during which Fulton arranged for a two year loan in the amount of $309,000 from Commercial Credit Development Corporation. By its terms this loan ran to the limited partnership. This loan substantially increased the mortgage debt of the limited partnership beyond the projections in the original partnership agreement and certificate. Fulton instructed the attorney to make changes in these documents to reflect the economic reality.

On the day the extension was to expire Fulton and Rinaldi met with representatives of the Joint Venture and Commercial Credit. Counsel accompanied all participants. In the trial court it was not clearly established to what degree, if any, attention was paid on the part of the lender or the Joint Venture to the partnership agreement or certificate. It is clear that no disclosure was made that these instruments had been revised and did not reflect the content which had been presented to the holders of the seven subscribed units. In these circumstances the Limited Partnership executed mortgages in favor of the Joint Venture and Commercial Credit. On that same day the limited partnership certificate was recorded with the clerk of the court and a copy of the recorded certificate furnished to Commercial Credit.

It was not until after the closing of the real estate transaction and the filing of the certificate that the attorney who had prepared the modifications to the partnership agreement and certificate become aware that the limited partners had not been notified. When this fact was discovered, he prepared an informative notice and formal offer of rescission which was circulated to each subscriber. Two of the subscription units were rescinded and the subscribed funds refunded. One subscriber claimed never to have received the notice and rescission offer, and the remainder did not avail themselves of the opportunity to rescind.

Within a year the partnership defaulted on the mortgages and Commercial Credit foreclosed its first mortgage and obtained a deficiency judgment. Klein was appointed receiver and both Commercial Credit and the Joint Venture filed creditor claims with Klein who thereupon sued the limited partners on behalf of the creditors. The holders of all seven of the subscribed units were named as defendants with relief sought on the basis of the revised partnership documents. The receiver sought to recapture the initial $9,000 contributions refunded on the rescinded units and to assess each unit an additional $23,428.

The trial judge denied all claims for relief against any or all of the supposed limited partners. In the view of that court the defendants were subscribers to a limited partnership which could not be formed until twenty-five units had been subscribed. This was never accomplished and thus they were not limited partners. The revision of the partnership agreement and certificate established the defendants as victims of fraud at the hands of the general partners.]

MURPHY, CHIEF JUDGE.

Limited partnerships were unknown at common law; they are exclusively a creature of statute, their main purpose being to permit a form of business enterprise, other than a corporation, in which persons could invest money without becoming liable as general partners for all debts of the partnership. 2 R. Rowley, Rowley on Partnership § 53.0 (2d ed.1960); 60 Am.Jur.2d Partnership § 371 (1972). "The general purpose of [limited partnership] acts was not to assist creditors, but was to enable persons to invest their money in partnerships and share in the profits without being liable for more than the amount of money they had contributed. The reason for this was to encourage investing." *Gilman Paint & Varnish Co. v. Legum*, 197 Md. 665, 670, 80 A.2d 906, 908 (1951).

The first limited partnership statute in the United States was enacted by New York in 1822; Maryland adopted a similar statute by ch. 97 of the Acts of 1836. These early statutes required the recording of a partnership certificate giving notice to the public of the exact terms of the partnership, including the amount of the capital contributions of the limited partners, so that the public could deal with the partnership "advisedly." *Lineweaver v. Slagle*, 64 Md. 465, 2 A. 693 (1886). The fundamental difference between the liability of general and limited partners under these statutes was "that the former are responsible in solido for the debts and obligations of the firm, as in the case of ordinary partnerships, without regard to the amounts contributed by them to the social capital; whilst the latter is not personally liable if the statute has been complied with, because his cash contribution is substituted for a personal liability." *Safe Deposit Co. v. Cahn*, 102 Md. 530, 546, 62 A. 819 (1906). Strict compliance with all statutory provisions was deemed essential to create a limited partnership under these early statutes, since they were in derogation of the common law. As a consequence, even minor or trivial infractions of the statute were held by some courts to subject the limited partners to unlimited liability as general partners.... Because the strict construction of these statutes inhibited the effective accomplishment of the purpose for which they were intended, the National Conference of Commissioners on Uniform State Laws proposed the adoption in 1916 of a Uniform Limited Partnership Act. Maryland enacted the Uniform Act by ch. 280 of the Acts of 1918, and the statute with minor modifications is now in effect in every state in the country except Louisiana. The Act's provisions are intended to govern the determination of essentially all questions arising out of the formation and operation of limited partnerships. The rule that statutes in derogation of the common law are to be strictly construed is expressly made inapplicable to the Uniform Act.

Decisions interpreting the Uniform Act recognize that a limited partnership consists of general partners who conduct the business and who have unlimited liability to creditors for its obligations, and of limited partners who have no right to participate in the management of the business, and whose liability is limited to the amount of their capital contribution. [citation] As the Official Comment to §1 of the Uniform Act makes clear, a limited partner, though so called by custom, is not "in any sense" either a partner or a principal in the business or transactions of the partnership; his liability, except for known false statements in the certificate of partnership, is to the partnership, and not to its creditors. See 6 Uniform Laws Annotated, Uniform Limited Partnership Act § 1 (Master ed. 1969). Succinctly put, a limited partnership interest in a business is in the nature of an investment. [ULPA §17] delineates the extent of the limited partner's investment in the business; it makes him liable to the partnership:

"(1) For the difference between his contribution as actually made and that stated in the certificate as having been made; and

"(2) For any unpaid contribution which he agreed in the certificate to make in the future at the time and on the conditions stated in the certificate."

The creation of a limited partnership is not a mere private, informal, voluntary agreement as in the case of a general partnership, but is a public and formal proceeding which must follow the statutory requirements of the Uniform Act. ... The Act prescribes, [ULPA §2(2)], that a limited partnership is formed "if there has been substantial compliance in good faith" with the requirements contained in [ULPA §2(1)(a)]. That subsection mandates that a certificate of partnership be signed by the parties, acknowledged, and recorded with the clerk of the court. It requires that the certificate set forth 14 designated partnership details, including the name of the partnership, the character and location of the business, the identity of the general and limited partners, the term of the partnership, the cash contributions made by the limited partners, and such additional contributions, if any, which the limited partners have agreed to make in the future. The certificate is a statutory prerequisite to creation of a limited partnership and until it is filed, the partnership is not formed as a limited partnership. The principal function of the certificate is to give third persons notice of the essential features of the limited partnership. Of course, whether a limited partnership has been formed is of particular importance in determining whether a person has achieved the status of a limited partner with the attendant limitation of his liability to third persons dealing with the partnership [citations].

. . .

The receiver contends that the lower court erred in concluding that a condition precedent to any obligation on the part of the appellees to pay their capital contributions under the partnership documents was the sale of all 25 limited partnership units. He argues that failure of full subscription to the partnership units sought to be sold did not release those who did subscribe since there was no contractual commitment to full subscription and no appropriate reservation in either the original or the revised partnership documents. We agree.

The partnership agreement defines a "Limited Partnership Unit" in terms of the required initial and additional capital contributions, and provides that "The capital of the Partnership shall consist of a maximum of two (2) General Partnership Units and twenty-five (25) Limited Partnership Units." While Fulton and Rinaldi may have contemplated the sale of all 25 units, and indeed needed the proceeds from these sales to finance the acquisition as originally planned, nothing in the partnership documents-the agreement or the certificate calls for the sale of all 25 units as a contractual precondition to the formation of the Limited Partnership.

The partnership agreement makes reference to limited partners "additional" to those executing the agreement; it also provides that the partnership would begin on the date the agreement was executed. The clear import of these provisions is that the Limited Partnership would commence, and the obligation to make the initial capital contributions would become effective, on the date of the agreement, even though all 25 units had not been sold at that time. It is true that the mortgage payment schedule originally attached to the agreement calculated future contributions of the limited partners on the basis of the sale of 25 units; however, the schedule did not condition the capital obligation on the sale of all units.

Neither the original nor the revised partnership certificate contained any condition that all units had to be sold before the limited partners would become obligated to pay their capital contributions. Indeed, the certificate made no reference to any number of partnership units to be sold, and did not contain any condition with respect to the obligation of the limited partners to make additional contributions, as required by [ULPA §2(1)(a)(VII)], if any such conditions were to be imposed.

As heretofore indicated, the purpose of recording the partnership certificate is to acquaint third persons dealing with the partnership with its essential features, including its capital structure. Obviously, to give effect to alleged conditions not set out in, or at variance with, the certificate and partnership agreement is to fatally undermine the operation of the Uniform Act.

The appellees urge that we apply the common law rule, recognized in *Wright v. Lewis*, 161 Md. 674, 158 A. 704 (1932), that an inherent condition of a pre-incorporation subscription is that the authorized share capital will be fully subscribed and a subscriber will not be held liable on his subscription contract until that condition is fulfilled. The rule was changed as to corporate subscriptions by § 2-202 of the Corporations Article. We think the common law rule is manifestly inapplicable to subscriptions to limited partnerships in view of the provisions of the Uniform Act, at least in the absence of enforceable qualifications to the subscription obligation contained in the partnership documents. As the receiver so cogently observes, unlike the corporation charter involved in *Wright*, the partnership documents contain no statement parallel to that of an authorized capital which could in any way be construed as a condition precedent to formation.

The receiver contends that the lower court was in error in its apparent holding that the failure of the general partners to make calls for the additional contributions upon the limited partners, as contemplated by the partnership documents, barred enforcement of those obligations.

Both the original and revised partnership agreement and certificate required additional contributions in accordance with a mortgage payment schedule to be provided by the general partners. The only difference between the original and revised versions is that the former required 4% of a specified mortgage debt, per limited partnership share, to a maximum of $15,298.06, while the latter required a 4% per share payment of an unspecified mortgage debt. No payment schedule relating to the Commercial Credit first mortgage or the Joint Venture second mortgage was ever provided to the limited partners, and no request or demand was ever made upon the limited partners prior to the foreclosure of the Commercial Credit mortgage. No calls were ever made, according to Whitehead, because the amounts that would have been realized from the limited partners could not have been sufficiently supplemented by the general partners to meet the partnership's obligations.

We think that the failure of the general partners to make calls for the additional contributions, even though contractually contemplated, cannot defeat the interests of creditors to enforce their obligations. ... The same rule is applicable by analogy to suits by receivers to recover unpaid capital obligations of limited partners in a limited partnership.

The receiver contends that the limited partners were bound by the recorded certificate of limited partnership, even though it was revised by the general partners and Whitehead without their consent, because the general partners and Whitehead were their agents with authority to revise and record the certificate on their behalf.

As we have already noted, a limited partner under the Uniform Act (see Official Comment to §1 thereof) is not "in any sense" either a partner or a principal in the business or transactions of the partnership. Rather, he is an investor in the partnership venture, without authority to participate in the management of the business; his liability is limited to the amount of his stated capital contribution. The relationship between the general and limited partner is a fiduciary one-a relation of trust-similar to that existing between a corporate director and a shareholder. See *Miller v. Schweickart*, 405 F.Supp. 366 (S.D. N.Y.1975); *Allen v. Steinberg*, 244 Md. 119, 223 A.2d 240 (1966); *Lichtyger v. Franchard Corp.*, 18 N.Y.2d 528, 277 N.Y.S.2d 377, 223 N.E.2d 869 (1966). Hence, the general rule would appear to be that the principal-agent relationship which exists between the parties of an ordinary partnership is not per se present between general and limited partners in a limited partnership. *Donroy, Ltd. v. United States*, 301 F.2d 200 (9th Cir.1962); *Lynn v. Cohen*, 359 F.Supp. 565 (S.D.N.Y.1973); 60 Am.Jur.2d Partnership § 379 (1972). Thus, authority not specifically delegated in the limited partnership agreement to general partners is presumed to be withheld. *Allen v. Steinberg*, 244 Md. 119, 223 A.2d 240 (1966); *Homestake Mining Co. v. Mid-Continent Exploration Co.*, 282 F.2d 787 (10th Cir.1960). These principles are consistent with the provisions of [ULPA §9], which delineate the rights and powers of a general partner in a limited partnership.[2]

The partnership agreement in the present case specified that the limited partners appointed the general partners as their attorney and agent to execute and record:

"(1) all certificates and other instruments . . . which the General Partner deems appropriate to qualify or continue the Partnership as a Limited Partnership . . . , (2) all instruments which the General Partner deems appropriate to effect a change or modification of the Partnership in accordance with the terms of this Agreement ...."

---

[2][ULPA §9] provides:

(1) A general partner shall have all the rights and powers and be subject to all the restrictions and liabilities of a partner in a partnership without limited partners, except that without the written consent or ratification of the specific act by all the limited partners, a general partner or all of the general partners have no authority to:

(a) Do any act in contravention of the certificate;

(b) Do any act which would make it impossible to carry on the ordinary business of the partnership;

(c) Confess a judgment against the partnership;

(d) Possess partnership property, or assign their rights in specific partnership property, for other than a partnership purpose;

(e) Admit a person as a general partner;

(f) Admit a person as a limited partner, unless the right so to do is given in the certificate; or

(g) Continue the business with partnership property on the death, retirement, or insanity of a general partner, unless the right so to do is given in the certificate.

Despite the broad sweep of the powers which the limited partners agreed to vest in the general partners under the partnership agreement, we hold that the general partners did not have actual authority to revise the partnership certificate and agreement absent the express consent of the limited partners. ... Considering the agreement in its entirety, it does not appear that the general partners were empowered to revise and record the certificate without the express consent of the limited partners.

Nor is there any basis for holding that the general partners were clothed with apparent authority to alter the documents. Apparent authority results from certain acts or manifestations by the alleged principal to a third party leading the third party to believe that an agent had authority to act. *Reserve Ins. Co. v. Duckett*, 240 Md. 591, 214 A.2d 754 (1965). See also *B.P. Oil Corp. v. Mabe*, 279 Md. 632, 370 A.2d 554 (1977). While the appellees did permit the general partners to handle the documents, generally the law will not imply authority to alter from an agency involving the mere handling of an instrument. ...

Neither were the appellees bound by the terms of the altered certificate simply because it was recorded. While the recording requirement was meant to protect the public, the Uniform Act does not hold a limited partner liable for any statement contained in a recorded certificate. [ULPA §6] provides:

"If the certificate contains a false statement, one who suffers loss by reliance on the statement may hold liable any party to the certificate who knew the statement to be false:

(a)(1) At the time he signed the certificate; or

(2) Subsequently, but within a sufficient time before the statement was relied upon to enable him to cancel or amend the certificate, or to file a petition for its cancellation or amendment as provided in Section 23."

It is thus clear that a limited partner bears responsibility for a false statement in a certificate only if he knew the statement to be false. *Walraven v. Ramsay*, 335 Mich. 331, 55 N.W.2d 853 (1952). There was no false statement as to the contribution of limited partners at the time the instruments of execution were signed by the appellees, nor is there any evidence that they subsequently became aware of the false statement before the creditors had relied upon the certificate, if in fact they did.

Nor was Whitehead the agent of the limited partners. He represented the general partners and the Limited Partnership. His actions with respect to the partnership agreement and certificate were not, therefore, those of an agent acting on behalf of the limited partners.

The receiver next argues that even if the general partners had no authority to revise the partnership documents, they were nevertheless enforceable according to their original tenor, and the limited partners are therefore liable to the Limited Partnership for the capital contributions which they originally agreed to make. The appellees claim, as the lower court held, that no limited partnership ever came into existence. They say that the receiver's cause of action was based upon the revised partnership agreement and certificate, that these documents resulted from the fraudulent, material alteration of the original partnership agreement and certificate, and significantly increased the business risk of the investing limited partners; as a consequence, the appellees claim that the partnership documents were void, and the receiver is barred from all recovery on behalf of the creditors of the Limited Partnership.

A partnership is, of course, a contractual relation to which the principles of contract law are fully applicable. *Collier v. Collier*, 182 Md. 82, 32 A.2d 469 (1943); *Abbott v. Hibbitts*, 142 Md. 7, 119 A. 650 (1922); 59 Am.Jur.2d Partnership §§ 19, 33 (1971). An agreement to form a partnership may be made by the parties but such an agreement does not of itself create a partnership. *Maxa v. Jones*, 148 Md. 459, 129 A. 652 (1925). One of the essential elements for formation of a contract is a manifestation of agreement or mutual assent by the parties to the terms thereof; in other words, to establish a contract the minds of the parties must be in agreement as to its terms. ... The failure to agree on or even discuss an essential term of a contract may indicate that the mutual assent required to make or modify a contract is lacking. *L & L Corp. v. Ammendale*, 248 Md. 380, 236 A.2d 734 (1968). Whether a partnership exists is always a matter of fact which must depend on the intention of the parties. ...

That the appellees intended to enter into a limited partnership to acquire the Joint Venture property for investment purposes is entirely clear. It was based upon the understanding, clear from the original proposed partnership documents, that the property would cost $450,000; that $175,000 was expected to be derived from sales of partnership units and this amount paid in cash at the time of settlement; and that a $265,000 mortgage would be carried on the property. By the terms of the original documents, it was understood that, in addition to their initial contribution of $9,000, the limited partners were each obligated to pay not more than $15,298 to service the $265,000 mortgage debt over the loan period. While nothing in the original partnership documents required the sale of all 25 limited partnership units as a precondition to the formation of the partnership, or guaranteed their sale so as to realize the necessary $175,000 cash payment required at the time of settlement, the contract of sale for the property, which the limited partners ratified, specified that should the Limited Partnership be unable to settle for the property in accordance with the terms of the contract, the $10,000 deposit would be forfeited as agreed liquidated damages and all liability of the buyer thereby terminated. As revised without the consent or knowledge of the limited partners, the capital structure of the venture was so altered that the originally contemplated partnership debt was almost doubled and the individual obligations of the limited partners substantially increased to a 4% share of a greater, unauthorized mortgage debt of $450,000. We think the revised partnership documents so altered the original proposal as to result in an undertaking substantially different from that which the limited partners had contemplated.

The provision of [ULPA §2(2)] that a limited partnership is formed only if there has been "substantial compliance in good faith" with the requirements of [§2(1)] implicates two separate and distinct matters, although "substantial compliance" and "good faith" are closely related and seldom will one exist without the other. Rowley on Partnership, supra, at § 53.2. That the revised certificate was in proper form and in substantial compliance with the statutory requirements is plain. As to the "good faith" requirement, Rowley indicates that it may be satisfied where the parties honestly attempt to follow the provisions of the Act to the end that third persons will have notice of the essential features of the limited partnership. Id. at § 53.2. Compliance with the "good faith" requirement of [§2(2)] does not require the literal truth of every statement in the certificate; indeed [ULPA §6] takes into account the making of false statements in the certificate, not by inhibiting formation of the limited partnership, but by providing that one who suffers loss by reliance on such a statement may hold liable any party to the certificate who knew the statement to be false when he signed it, or within sufficient time before the statement was relied on to have had the certificate cancelled or amended. Rowley further indicates, however, that "persons who sign, swear to, and file for record a certificate which in any important particular is knowingly false, are not acting in good faith ... [and that] no limited partnership should be deemed formed thereby." Id. at § 53.2.

We think the unauthorized changes in the substituted certificate were not mere false statements within the contemplation of [ULPA §6], but were of such a fundamental character as affected the formation of the limited partnership itself. We hold, therefore, that the filing of the revised certificate did not comply with the "good faith" requirement of [ULPA §2(2)] and that consequently no limited partnership was created under the statute.[3] In so concluding, we note that Fulton clearly realized that he had no authority to revise the partnership documents without the consent of the appellees since he told Whitehead that he would obtain their consent to the intended changes. That he did not do so, but instead arranged the loan through Commercial Credit, and presumably made the necessary accommodation with the Joint Venture, without informing the appellees, indicates that the certificate was not filed in the honest but mis-

[3]In 1976, the Commissioners on Uniform State Laws drafted a Revised Uniform Limited Partnership Act. Section 201 of the Revised Act eliminates the "good faith" requirement of [§2(2)] of the Uniform Act; it provides that a limited partnership is formed if there has been "substantial compliance" with the statutory requirements pertaining to the filing of the certificate of limited partnership. ...

taken belief that he had authority to file it without the consent of the limited partners.[4]

The Uniform Act does not provide an explicit rule of law which is ultimately dispositive of this controversy. Section [29] of the Act specifies, however, that "[i]n any case not provided for in this title the rules of law and equity, including the law merchant, shall govern." The Uniform Partnership Act, Title 9, §§ 9-109 through 9-703 of the Corporations Article, provides in § 9-101(f) that its provisions are applicable to limited partnerships "except insofar as the statutes relating to such partnerships are inconsistent with this title." Since §[4(2)] of the Uniform Partnership Act provides that "[t]he law of estoppel shall apply under this title," this provision is plainly applicable to limited partnerships. More specifically, [UPA §16(1)] entitled "Partner by estoppel" provides:

> "When a person, by words spoken or written or by conduct, represents himself, or consents to another representing him to anyone, as a partner in an existing partnership or with one or more persons not actually partners, he is liable to any such person to whom the representation has been made, who has, on the faith of the representation, given credit to the actual or apparent partnership, and if he has made the representation or consented to its being made in a public manner he is liable to such person, whether the representation has or has not been made or communicated to the person so giving credit by or with the knowledge of the apparent partner making the representation or consenting to its being made."

That there may be a partnership by estoppel as to third persons, even though the parties are not partners inter se, is well recognized by our cases. [citations]. Under these cases, the ground of liability of a person as a partner, who is not so in fact, is that he has held himself out to the world as such, or has permitted others to do so and, by reason thereof, is estopped from denying that he is a partner as against those who have, in good faith, dealt with the firm or with him as a member of it.

The lower court did not consider these estoppel principles in exonerating the appellees from all liability to the receiver. Of course, it had no occasion to do so because the receiver's action was based on the validity of the revised partnership documents, it not being known to the receiver or counsel for the appellees until trial that the original partnership documents were in existence. Whether Commercial Credit made its mortgage loan to the Limited Partnership on the

---

[4]We do not think that Anthony ratified the partnership documents, as revised, because of his subsequent election not to rescind his limited partnership subscription. While the notice of the asserted "right" to rescind supplied particularized information with respect to the changes made in the documents, it did not, in our opinion, provide information sufficiently full and complete to justify a conclusion that Anthony ratified the revised partnership agreement and certificate. ...

basis of the underlying collateral and the general liability of Fulton and Rinaldi, without regard to the participation of the limited partners, was not an issue in the case to which evidence was addressed at trial. The same is true with respect to the second mortgage of the Joint Venture. Although no such finding was necessary to its decision, the lower court expressed the belief that the Joint Venture, in extending credit, detrimentally relied upon a representation that the limited partners were members of the Limited Partnership, while Commercial Credit did not. In view of the pleadings and the posture of the case at trial, the receiver had no reason to anticipate a need to produce evidence of reliance upon the participation of the limited partners in the partnership venture, and he did not do so. Of course, the facts upon which to rest an estoppel must be proved; they will not be presumed. *Miller v. Salabes*, 225 Md. 53, 169 A.2d 671 (1961).

Under Maryland Rule 871a, if it appears to us "that the substantial merits of a case will not be determined by affirming, reversing or modifying the judgment from which the appeal was taken, or that the purposes of justice will be advanced by permitting further proceedings in the cause, either through amendment of the pleadings, introduction of additional evidence, making of additional parties, or otherwise," we may order the case remanded for further proceedings. We think that rule is appropriately invoked in this case to permit further proceedings "as may be necessary for determining the action upon its merits as if no appeal had been taken and the judgment from which the appeal was taken had not been entered ...." Rule 871a. Upon remand, the receiver is to be afforded the fullest opportunity to amend his pleadings, and adduce evidence in an effort to establish responsibility of the appellees for an amount equal to their capital contributions under any contract, estoppel, or other theory of liability arising from the appellees' execution of the partnership documents which is not inconsistent with the views herein expressed.

. . .

Case remanded without affirmance or reversal pursuant to Maryland Rule 871a for further proceedings in accordance with this opinion; costs to abide the result.

Notes

1. The *Klein* court is emphatic in asserting that a limited partnership is a creature of statute and cannot come into existence save by compliance with the mandatory provisions of the limited partnership act. What is the court's understanding of a rationale requiring that information be generated through compliance with §2 of the ULPA or §201 of the RULPA?

The RULPA was adopted in Maryland in 1981 and became effective on July 1, 1982. Does the elimination of the "good faith" requirement in the revised act suggest that these defendants would have been precluded from the "no formation" defense had these same facts arisen after July, 1982? The official comment to §201 gives no warning of such an intended change:

> The matters required to be set forth in the certificate of limited partnership are not different in kind from those required by Section 2 of the prior uniform law, although certain additional and deletions have been made and the description has been revised to conform with the rest of the Act. In general, the certificate is intended to serve two functions: first, to place creditors on notice of the facts concerning the capital of the partnership and the rules regarding additional contributions to and withdrawals from the partnership; second, to clearly delineate the time at which persons become general partners and limited partners. Sub-paragraph (b) which is based upon the prior uniform law, has been retained to make it clear that the existence of the limited partnership depends only upon compliance with this section. The continued existence is not dependent upon compliance with other provisions of this Act.

In 1988, Maryland further amended its statutory provisions respecting limited partnerships by adopting the 1985 Amendments and so drastically modified the scope and utility of the certificate required by §201. The official comment prepared by the Commissioners on Uniform State Laws explained these changes in a muted voice:

> The 1985 Act requires far fewer matters to be set forth in the certificate of limited partnership than did Section 2 of the 1916 Act and Section 201 of the 1976 Act. This is in recognition of the fact that the partnership agreement, not the certificate of limited partnership, has become the authoritative and comprehensive document for most limited partnerships, and that creditors and potential creditors of the partnership do and should refer to the partnership agreement and to other information furnished to them directly by the partnership and by others, not to the certificate of limited partnership, to obtain facts concerning the capital and finances of the partnership and other matters of concern. ...

Were the facts in *Klein v. Weiss* to arise under RULPA/85 Fulton and Rinaldi would have had no occasion to alter the terms of the certificate. What would be the fate of the "no formation" defense? Under RULPA/85 a third party inspecting the certificate would have utterly no idea of the capital structure of the partnership. Even the number of limited partners would be a mystery. Pondering the fate of the individuals who did sign the subscription agreement and the creditors, are you convinced by the protestations of the framers of the 1985 Amendments that the certificate lacks modern relevance? The framers suggest that this information can be obtained from the partnership agreement and "other information." However, none of that information is a matter of public record, and partnership existence is not dependent upon any concept of "substantial compliance."

2. In *Klein* the defendants could meet the creditor's accusation that the partnership had done business before the certificate was filed by pointing to the material alteration in the certificate between the signed document and the filed instrument. What if this defense were not available and a contract executed in the name of the partnership was formed prior to filing the certificate? Courts which attempted to

meet this problem within the context of the ULPA were divided.

Ruth v. Crane, 392 F.Supp. 733 (E.D.Pa. 1976), asserts what appears to be the majoritarian position:

> . . .Under Pennsylvania law, where parties intend to enter into a limited partnership, but fail to comply with the requirements of the Limited Partnership Act, such as recording a proper certificate, the limited partnership is not formed, but the parties are treated as general partners as to third parties and creditors, and the partners' obligations and liabilities are found under the Pennsylvania Uniform Partnership Act.

Accord, *Heritage Hills v. Zion's First National Bank*, 601 F.2d 1023, 1025-26 (9th Cir. 1976)(construing the substantive law of Arizona). Recent Texas decisions have produced the opposite conclusion, holding that the failure to file a limited partnership agreement with the Secretary of State did not result in formation of a general partnership. *Voudouris v. Walter E. Heller & Co.*, 506 S.W.2d 202 (Tex.Civ.App. 1977). No reasoning was advanced by the Texas court in support of its position.

Is it relevant that the third party creditor was unaware of the failure to file the certificate and, in fact, thought that she was dealing with a limited partnership? Again, contemporary construction of the ULPA is divided. In the cases which follow you will note two irreconcilable lines of judicial reasoning. One stresses the theme that limited partnerships are the creature of statutory law, and concludes that the benefits and protections of that association may be claimed only by those who have complied with the relevant statutes. The expectations of creditors are irrelevant since limited liability is not conferred by contract but results from a statutory status. The contrary authorities argue that creditor expectations, not abstract notions of public policy, should govern individual liability claims.

1. The consequences of defective formation:

DWINELL'S CENTRAL NEON v. COSMOPOLITAN CHINOOK HOTEL

Court of Appeals of Washington, 1978.
21 Wash.App. 929, 587 P.2d 191.

MCINTURFF, JUDGE. Cosmopolitan Chinook Hotel (Cosmopolitan) appeals from a summary judgment, holding it liable as a general partnership-and not as a limited partnership-in connection with an action brought by Dwinell's Central Neon (Dwinell's) for breach of contract.

On October 25, 1972, Cosmopolitan and Dwinell's entered into three separate agreements for the lease-sale of neon signs. Dwinell's was represented by one of its salesmen and Cosmopolitan was represented by two of its partners. The contracts contained an acceleration clause in the event of Cosmopolitan's default and a provision for a reduction in the monthly payment should Dwinell's fail to properly maintain the signs.

In October, 1976, Cosmopolitan was behind on its payments and Dwinell's brought suit to accelerate the balance due under the contract. The complaint averred that Cosmopolitan was a general partnership due to its failure to comply with the statutory filing requirements of the Limited Partnership Act. Cosmopolitan, on the other hand, claimed limited partnership status and stated that their status was known by Dwinell's at the time of contracting and was a matter of common knowledge in the community.

We are asked to consider whether summary judgment was proper in light of the following alleged factual issues left unresolved:

(1) Whether Dwinell's had actual knowledge of Cosmopolitan's limited partnership status at the time of contracting;

(2) Whether the court erred in concluding that Cosmopolitan was a general partnership;

(3) ...

(4) Whether the court improperly shifted the burden of proof to Cosmopolitan when Dwinell's was the moving party for summary judgment.

At the time Dwinell's and Cosmopolitan entered into the lease-sale agreements, Cosmopolitan had taken no steps to comply with the filing requirements of [ULPA §2]. It was not until February 1973, several months following execution of the contract with Dwinell's, that the certificate of limited partnership was filed. Cosmopolitan argues, however, that it was widely known in Yakima that a limited partnership had purchased the Chinook Hotel. Further, Cosmopolitan states that this fact was communicated to Dwinell's via its salesman. This information was allegedly communicated in the following manner-the word "partnership" was circled as identifying the "user" under the contract and the contract was signed, "Evan Bargman, V.P., R. Powers, President." According to Cosmopolitan, circling the word "partnership" best indicated its status as a limited partnership and the signatures clearly indicated that Bargman and Powers were not signing as general partners but as corporate officers of the general partnership.

. . .

[A] third party's knowledge regarding the status of a limited partnership is irrelevant when at the time of contracting, the partners have made no attempt to comply with the statutory information and filing requirements of the Limited Partnership Act, [§2(1)].

Limited partnerships were unknown at common law and are purely creatures of statute. Parties seeking the protection of limited liability within the context of a partnership must follow the statutory requirements. See *Frigidaire Sales Corp. v. Union Properties, Inc.*, 88 Wash.2d 400, 402, 562 P.2d 244 (1977). To form a limited partnership, a certificate of limited partnership must be drafted and filed with the county clerk pursuant to [ULPA §2(1)(a)(I)-(XIV)]. While our courts no longer require literal compliance with the statute at one's peril, *Rathke v. Griffith*, 36 Wash.2d 394, 400-04, 218 P.2d 757 (1950), the statute does contemplate at least "substantial compliance with the requirements." [§2(2)]. Here, there was no compliance with the statute at the time of contracting and the certificate of limited partnership was not filed until several months later. The object of statutory regulation of limited partnerships is to insure that limited partners do not find themselves exposed to the unlimited liability of a general partner.

The statute specifies the acts which must be performed by persons desiring to become limited partners. Cosmopolitan had not complied with any requirements of the statute at the time it entered into the contract with Dwinell's. Obviously, the purpose of the filing requirement was thwarted, that is, to acquaint third persons dealing with the partnership of the details of the partnership arrangement. A creditor has a right to rely upon there being substantial compliance with [§2] before the protection of its provisions are afforded to any member of a partnership. *Tiburon National Bank v. Wagner*, 265 Cal.App.2d 868, 71 Cal.Rptr. 832, 837 (1968). Here there was no compliance.

Cosmopolitan, relying on the case of *Stowe v. Merrilees*, 6 Cal.App.2d 217, 44 P.2d 368 (1935), contends that because [ULPA §2] is silent as to when the certificate must be filed, a reasonable time is implied. Cosmopolitan submits that it substantially complied with the requirements of the statute by filing a certificate of limited partnership some 90 days after the contract went into effect. Reliance on *Stowe v. Merrilees* is misplaced. There, the partners executed a partnership agreement but failed to file the certificate until 49 days later. The court held that the firm became a limited partnership as to third parties who extended credit subsequent to the act of filing. Cosmopolitan wants the effect of filing the certificate of limited partnership to relate back to a contract previously entered into. To adopt this reasoning would render the statutory requirement of [§2] meaningless and business relationships would be rendered unstable and unpredictable.

Thus, since there was no compliance with the Limited Partnership Act, the court was correct in holding as a matter of law that Cosmopolitan was liable as a general partnership on the contract with Dwinell's.

. . .

Nor do we believe that the court improperly shifted the burden of proof to Cosmopolitan. There is no dispute that the statutory requirements to establish a limited partnership were not complied with, nor was written notice given so as to trigger the liquidated damage provision. Cosmopolitan attempted to impute knowledge on the part of Dwinell's regarding limited partnership status without offering any factual evidence to support this assertion. Furthermore, the assertion was irrelevant insofar as establishing limited liability.

232

The judgment of the superior court is affirmed.

Notes

Not all courts would agree. In *Garrett v. Koepke, et al.*, 569 S.W.2d 568, 570-71 (Tex.Civ.App. 1978), a creditor commenced an action against limited partners seeking their contract liability for the unpaid balance on a sign sold to a limited partnership formed to operate the Longview Motor Inn. A limited partnership agreement, which denominated the defendants as limited partners, was signed in February of 1971. However, neither the agreement nor a certificate containing the information required by §2 of the ULPA was ever filed with the Secretary of State. Plaintiff admitted that he signed the agreement thinking that he was dealing with a limited partnership and with the general business understanding that limited partners were not generally obligated for the contract debts of such a firm. However, he denied that he had any knowledge of the failure to comply with §2 of the ULPA. The trial court refused to hold the defendants liable on the theory that, at the formation stage, plaintiff did not expect to have recourse against them personally if the limited partnership defaulted. On appeal the Texas Court of Civil Appeals affirmed stating:

> Appellees admit that they had failed to file a certificate of limited partnership as required by [§2 of the ULPA]. Appellants contend, therefore, that appellees are liable for the debt sued upon as general partners. We cannot agree with this contention. We see no logical reason to strip appellees of their limited liability under their partnership agreement merely because they failed to comply with [§2]. The purpose of the filing requirements under the act is to provide notice to third persons dealing with the partnership of the essential features of the partnership agreement. [citations] Since appellants knew that the entity with which they were dealing was a limited partnership, as well as the consequences of dealing with such an entity, they were in no way prejudiced by the failure to comply with the statute. We see no compelling policy reason here for holding that appellees became general partners by requiring technical compliance with these notice provisions. Indeed, such was not the intent of the legislature in enacting the statute; instead, its intent was to provide notice of limited liability of certain partners to third parties dealing with the partnership. *R.H. Sanders Corp. v. Haves*, 541 S.W.2d 262, 265 (Tex.Civ. App. Dallas 1976, no writ). The nature and legal existence of a partnership does not depend upon any filing required by a statute. *Tracy v. Tuffly*, 134 U.S. 206, 226, 10 S.Ct. 527, 33 L.Ed. 879 (1890). We hold, therefore, that where a party has knowledge that the entity with which he is dealing is a limited partnership, that status is not changed by failing to file under [§2]. Indeed, the Houston Court of Civil Appeals in *Voudouris v. Walter E. Heller & Co.*, 560 S.W.2d 202, 207 ... held that the failure to file the limited partnership agreement with the Secretary of State did not result in the formation of a general partnership.

Whatever the merit of the view being espoused in recent decisions by the intermediate courts of civil appeals in Texas, the statement that *Tracy v. Tuffly* stands for the proposition that "the nature and legal existence of a partnership does not depend upon any filing requirement by a statute" is flatly wrong. First, it is important to note that *Tracy* had its factual origin in the 1880's eighty years before Texas adopted the Uniform Limited Partnership Act. More to the point, in *Tracy* the trial court had found that:

> [t]he certificate of partnership contained, substantially, all that was required by article 3445. It was duly verified by the general partner and was duly registered in the proper office. The required certificate having been made, acknowledged, filed and recorded, and the required affidavit having been filed, the limited partnership was, under article 3449, to be deemed as formed.

The dispute was not about filing, but centered around compliance with a further provision of the then Texas statute which required publication of the "terms" of the limited partnership in a newspaper. It was undisputed that a legal notice had been published but it was contended that it did not fully disclose the terms. It was in this context that the first Mr. Justice Harlan stated:

> Without deciding whether the notice sufficiently disclosed the terms of the partnership, it is clear that the legal existence of the partnership did not depend upon the notice or its contents. The only effect of the failure to make the required publication was that "the partnership shall be deemed general."

134 U.S. at 226.

In the thirteen years since the decisions in *Dwinell's Central Neon* and *Garrett* both Washington and Texas have adopted the Revised Uniform Limited Partnership Act with the 1985 Amendments. Section 201(b) provides that:

> A limited partnership is formed at the time of the filing of the certificate of limited partnership in the office of the Secretary of State or at any later time specified in the certificate of limited partnership if, in either case, there has been substantial compliance with the requirements of this section.

Does this language resolve the debate?

The doctrine of "substantial compliance" where there has at least been a filing with the designated state official was considered at length in *Micheli Contracting Corp. v. Fairwood Associates*, 68 App.Div.2d 460, 418 N.Y.S.2d 164 (1979). The court affirmed a refusal to hold limited partners exposed to a creditor who complained about the form in which several signatures had been affixed to the limited partnership agreement.

> In view of the fact that the certificate of limited partnership omitted nothing of substance required to be contained therein by the statute, and there is no claim that anything contained therein is false, or that the defects complained of misled and injured respondent, it would appear that there was substantial compliance with the statute, and the limited partnership was validly formed.

In *Dwinell's*, *Garrett* and *Micheli* creditors sought a declaration that none of the purported limited partners had achieved limited liability. Suppose that a specific partner in any of those enterprises had become suspicious as to the soundness the formation of the partnership. Both the ULPA and the RULPA outline self-protective steps.

2. The fate of an investor in a defectively formed limited partnership:

VIDRICKSEN v. GROVER
United States Court of Appeals, Ninth Circuit, 1966.
363 F.2d 372.

CHAMBERS, CIRCUIT JUDGE: Dr. Vidricksen intended, when he turned over to Thom $25,000 in July, 1952, to become a limited partner with Thom, the general partner, in a Chevrolet car agency business at Dunsmuir, California. Thus, the shoemaker strayed from his last.

Articles of partnership were drawn up but no effort was made to comply with the California Statutory requirement of recording a certificate of limited partnership. [ULPA §2].

Bankruptcy overtook Thom in September, 1961. And the issue here is whether Dr. Vidricksen is a general partner for the purposes of bankruptcy. The referee held he was. On review, the district court sustained the referee. Here on appeal, we affirm.

Apparently the agency developed financial difficulties in March, 1961, and the doctor consulted successively two different lawyers. From them, although they could not represent him because of conflict of interest, he did learn he had a problem, to-wit, whether in his venture he had attained a real limited partnership and therefore limited liability under California law. The Uniform Limited Partnership Act has been adopted in California with some modification.

On the issue before us, no significant facts occurred until after August, 1961, when, through another set of attorneys, he filed a complaint against Thom which seemed to seek an accounting. In it Vidricksen said:

"That due to the lack of filing and recordation of [the] Limited Partnership Agreement, all as is required under law, ... said plaintiff [Vidricksen] and said defendant [Thom] have become general partners, insofar as their relationship with third party creditors is concerned."

On September 19, 1961, (eight days after the bankruptcy proceeding started) Dr. Vidricksen filed in the bankruptcy proceedings a renunciation under Section 15511 of the Corporations Code of California [§11 of the UPA]. That section reads as follows:

"A person who has contributed to the capital of a business conducted by a person or partnership erroneously believing that he has become a limited partner in a limited partnership, is not, by reason of his exercise of the rights of a limited partner, a general partner with the person or in the partnership carrying on the business, or bound by the obligations of such person or partnership; provided, that on ascertaining the mistake he promptly renounces his interest in the profits of the business, or other compensation by way of income."

Was such a renunciation timely? We think not.

Appellant would count the time on "promptly" in "promptly renounces" only from August 7, 1961, to September 19, 1961, or a period of 43 days. We disagree. In our view "promptly" began to run when he learned in March, 1961, that something was wrong with the organizational setup.

No California case is of help to us in construing the code section, so we must use our best judgment as to what California court would hold. We do not think Dr. Vidricksen needed a bonded opinion to start the time running. Knowledge that he was probably in trouble was enough. Thus, we conclude that six months from the time he had notice something was wrong until the actual renunciation is not a prompt renunciation. Even in August when he sued, the doctor was not renouncing, but was apparently accepting the fate of a general partner. It is possible that that action on his part could be held an abandonment of the limited partnership and acceptance of general partnership status. But we do not find it necessary to so hold. Certainly, though, the act went in the wrong direction. And we do not reach the question of his status had he renounced on August 7, 1961, when he instead affirmed general partnership. We simply hold the attempted renunciation was not timely. Thus, the doctor must be held to the pains of a general partner.

Affirmed.

Notes

California enacted the RULPA in 1983; four years later it adopted RULPA/85. What would be the consequences to Dr. Vidricksen's status had his case been adjudicated under §304 of the revised act?

Section 304. Person Erroneously Believing Himself a Limited Partner.

(a) Except as provided in subsection (b), a person who makes a contribution to a business enterprise and erroneously but in good faith believes that he has become a limited partner in the enterprise is not a general partner in the enterprise and is not bound by its obligations by reason of making the contribution, receiving distributions from the enterprise, or exercising any rights of a limited partner, if, on ascertaining the mistake he:

(1) causes an appropriate certificate of limited partnership or a certificate of amendment to be executed and filed; or

(2) withdraws from future equity participation in the enterprise.

(b) A person who makes a contribution of the kind described in subsection (a) is liable as a general partner to any third party who transacts business with the enterprise (i) before the person withdraws and an appropriate certificate is filed to show withdrawal, or (ii) before an appropriate certificate is filed to show his status as a limited partner and, in the case of an amendment, after expiration of the 30-day period for filing an amendment relating to the person as a limited partner under §202, but in either case only if the third party actually believed in good faith that the person was a general partner at the time of the transaction.

C. THE RELATIONSHIP INTER SE

Recall the picture of the limited partnership painted by the Court of Appeals of Maryland in *Klein v. Weiss*:

> . . .a limited partnership consists of general partners who conduct the business and who have unlimited liability to creditors for its obligations, and of limited partners who have no right to participate in the management of the business, and whose liability is limited to the amount of their capital contribution.

The fact patterns which follow center on the attempts of individuals to have the benefit of the prerogatives outlined in that statement while eluding the burdens described by the Maryland court. General partners will fret about their exposure to unlimited liability under §15 of the UPA and resent any conduct or attitudes by the limited partners that are thought to exacerbate that exposure. Limited partners will chafe at the posture of passivity depicted by the *Klein* court. Their concern will range from a desire to keep the general partner faithful to the terms of the partnership to the more ambitious quest for an influence over or participation in the affairs of the firm. In the most extreme case, the limited partners will "capture" the general by the expedient of using a corporate entity as the general partner. Control will be assured by their ownership of the stock in the general partner and their absolute personal dominion will be asserted in their capacity as directors and officers of that entity! Caught in these cross currents courts will strive to do "equity" by the litigants, keep "faith" with the statute, and fidelity to what some perceive as a social contract.

1. "No action at law prior to dissolution" rule:

The rule reviewed in *Pilch v. Milikin* has been held to have no application to limited partners. In *Wood v. Holiday Mobile Home Resorts, Inc.*, 128 Ariz. 274, 625 P.2d 337, 345 (1981), limited partners sought court ordered dissolution and an accounting alleging persistent failure on the part of the general partner to render accountings. The general partners counterclaimed for alleged intentional interference on the part of the limited partners with the contractual relationship. The trial court dismissed the counterclaims invoking the "no action against a partner prior to dissolution" rule. In reversing the dismissal the Supreme Court of Arizona declared:

> In this action Holiday Mobile and Dunkel filed counterclaims alleging that the limited partners had unlawfully interfered with the limited partnership's contractual relationships or its property. As to Holiday Mobile, the trial court

dismissed its counterclaim on the theory that prior to dissolution or accounting one party may not sue another for a transaction arising out of the partnership business. ...

In regard to the counterclaim of Holiday Mobile, it is clear in Arizona that insofar as a limited partnership is concerned, the rule applied by the trial court was correct. ... Whether this rule should be applied to limited partnerships is less clear.

Whatever the reasons underlying the rule as applied to general partnerships, we see no reason to extend that rule to limited partnerships. Limited partners may be added without affecting continuation of the partnership. ... Limited partners have no liability to creditors of the partnership. ... Limited partners have no right to control the business of the partnership and have limited rights in the partnership assets. ...

In short, the "oneness" associated with general partners certainly does not exist in a limited partnership. Seeing no reason to treat the members of a limited partnership differently from other litigants in civil actions, we conclude the trial court erred in dismissing Holiday Mobile's counterclaim solely on the basis of the status of the parties.

Do you find this reasoning convincing?

2. Prerogatives of the general partner(s):

Review Sections 7, 9, and 10 of the ULPA, and the contents of Article 4 of the RULPA/85. The *Klein* court suggested that control and management of the conduct of a limited partnership belong to the general partner. If there is more than one, the relationship between or among the general partners is governed by the Uniform Partnership Act. Their liability exposure is determined by §15. To what extent may express provisions of the partnership agreement alter these assumptions?

BROOKE v. MT. HOOD MEADOWS OREG., LTD.
Court of Appeals of Oregon, 1986.
81 Or.App. 387, 725 P.2d 925

BUTTLER, PRESIDING JUDGE. Plaintiffs are three of 18 limited partners in Mt. Hood Meadows, Oreg., Ltd., a limited partnership established to carry on the business of constructing and operating a winter sports development in the Hood River Meadows area of the Mt. Hood National Forest. They brought this action against the general partner, Mt. Hood Meadows Development Corp., and the partnership for money had and received and conversion. The conversion claim was dismissed on the pleadings; after a trial on the merits, the court awarded judgment to plaintiffs on their claim for money had and received. Defendants appeal, assigning as error the trial court's denial of their motion for judgment on the pleadings on the money had and received claim. ORCP 21B.

We reverse.

The question is whether plaintiffs, as limited partners, have a right to compel the general partner to distribute to them all of the profits allocated to them under the provisions of the partnership agreement. For the years in which profits were earned after 1974, the general partner's board of directors voted to distribute only 50 percent of the limited partners' taxable profits. The remaining profits were retained and reinvested in the business. The trial court held that the general partner had no authority to retain profits and ordered that it distribute annually to all limited partners cash equal to the profits allocated to them.

Article X of the limited partnership agreement provides:

"POWERS AND RESPONSIBILITIES, COMPENSATION

"Management and control of the partnership business shall be vested exclusively in the general partner, who, except as otherwise herein provided, shall have all the rights and powers and be subject to all the restrictions and liabilities of a general partner. The general partner shall have the power to borrow funds for the partnership's business and to pledge, mortgage, assign or otherwise hypothecate any or all properties of the partnership to secure such borrowings.

"None of the limited partners shall have any voice or take any part in the control or management of the business of the partnership nor shall any limited partner have any power or authority to act for or on behalf of the partnership in any respect whatever; provided that nothing herein contained shall in any way affect the rights of the limited partners to dissolve the partnership as provided in Article XI hereof."

That section directs that all management decisions of the partnership be the responsibility of the general partner and that the limited partners have no right to take part in the control of the business. That provision protects the limited partners from becoming liable as general partners. Former [RULPA §303].[1]

---

[1] ORS 69.150 to ORS 69.530 were repealed, Or.Laws 1985, ch. 677, 69, effective July 1, 1986, and replaced by ORS 70.005 to ORS 70.490. [The changes referenced by the court reflect the repeal of ULPA, the enactment of RULPA and the subsequent enactment of the 1985 Amendments. The fact pattern in *Brooke* is governed by Oregon's non-uniform enactment of the 1976 Revised Uniform Limited Partnership Act. ed.] *Former* ORS 69.280 provided:

"(1) A limited partner shall not become liable as a general partner unless, in addition to the exercise of rights and powers as a limited partner, the limited partner takes part in the control of the business.

"(2) A limited partner shall not be considered as taking part in the control of the business by virtue of possessing or exercising a power, specified in the certificate or partnership agreement, to vote upon matters affecting the basic structure of the partnership, including the following matters or others of a similar nature:

"(a) The dissolution and winding up of the partnership;

Management of the business necessarily includes decisions regarding the management of profits, unless the parties have specified otherwise in the limited partnership agreement.

Article VII of the agreement defines the partners' interest in the *capital* of the partnership:

> "The partners' interest in the capital of the partnership shall be in the proportions in which the agreed capital contributions of each, increased by his share of profits, gains, credits, and additional capital contributions and decreased by his share of losses, expenses, deductions and withdrawals bears to the aggregate capital contributions of all partners so increased or decreased, as the case may be."

Article VI of the agreement describes each limited partner's interest in the profits.

> "Each limited partner shall be entitled to a portion of the remainder of the profits after payment to the general partner as specified above, which bears the same ratio to such remainder as such limited partner's capital contribution bears to the total capital contribution of the limited partners."

A partner's interest in the capital of the partnership is made up of the partner's capital contributions and, in part, his share of undistributed profits. That is what, in accounting terms, constitutes a partner's capital account. Although Article VI, the only section of the agreement that addresses the partners' right to profits, describes the percentage of profits to which each partner is "entitled," it does not address the distribution of profits; it merely provides the method of calculating and allocating profits. We conclude that the agreement contains no provision expressly directing the general partner to distribute profits to the limited partners.

"(b) The sale, exchange, lease, mortgage, pledge or other transfer of all or substantially all the assets of the partnership other than in the ordinary course of business;

"(c) Incurring of indebtedness by the partnership other than in the ordinary course of business;

"(d) A change in the nature of the business of the partnership;

"(e) The election or removal of a general partner;

"(f) The amendment of the partnership agreement; or

"(g) The continuation of the partnership as provided in ORS 69.360.

"(3) A limited partner does not participate in the control of the business within the meaning of subsection (1) of this section solely by participating in a derivative action as provided in ORS 69.475.

"(4) The statement of powers set forth in subsections (2) and (3) of this section shall not be construed as exclusive or as indicating that any other powers possessed or exercised by a limited partner shall be sufficient to cause the limited partner to be considered taking part in the control of the business within the meaning of subsection (1) of this section."

Plaintiffs argue that the authority to retain profits is one that must be granted expressly to the general partner and that, in the absence of a grant, is presumed to have been withheld. That proposition is too broad. With certain exceptions and unless otherwise agreed, a broad grant of authority to manage a business, such as that applicable here, includes the authority to conduct all affairs reasonably necessary or incidental to the expressly authorized business. *Beeson et al. v. Hegstad et al.*, 199 Or. 325, 330, 261 P.2d 381 (1953); *see Restatement (Second) Agency* 189, § 73 (1958). Decisions regarding the management, including the distribution, of profits fall within that broad authority.

Profit is an accounting concept; its allocation takes place in the partnership books, and it may bear little or no relationship to cash on hand. Each partner is taxed on his distributable share of the profits, regardless of whether cash is actually distributed or whether it is available for distribution. For that reason, the partnership agreement must specify how the profits are to be allocated. The availability of cash for distribution, however, depends strictly on management's operation of the business. The business' future cash needs are also determined by management. That is why the decision as to how much, if any, of a limited partner's share of the profits is to be distributed is a management decision. If a limited partner were to take part in that aspect of the control of the business, the partner would risk the loss of his limited liability. *Former* ORS 69.280 [RULPA §303].

. . .

Plaintiffs' final assertion meriting discussion is that the accumulation of profits in their capital accounts increased their liability. Plaintiffs' liability was not increased beyond that provided in Article VIII of the limited partnership agreement, under which their liability is limited to their "interest in the capital of the partnership."[3] It is not limited to their "capital contribution." Although it is true that their interest in the capital of the partnership increased with the increase in undistributed profits, they agreed in Article VII that undistributed profits be a component of their interest in the capital of the partnership and agreed in Article VIII that their liability be limited to that amount.

---

[3]Article VIII provides:
"LIMITED LIABILITY

"Except to the extent of his or its interest in the capital of the partnership and to the extent of his or its unpaid capital contribution, a limited partner shall have no liability for or on account of any of the losses of the partnership. To the extent that losses of the partnership exceed its assets plus any unpaid balance of the limited partner's capital contributions, such losses shall be borne solely by the general partner."

A limited partner's position is analogous to that of a corporate shareholder, whose role is that of an investor with limited liability, *former* ORS 69.280 [RULPA §303](1), and with no voice in the operation of the enterprise. *See Lichtyger v. Franchard Corp.*, 18 N.Y.2d 528, 277 N.Y.S.2d 377, 223 N.E.2d 869 (1966). With limited exceptions, which do not include control over the distribution of profits, a limited partner who takes part in the control of the business may be held liable as a general partner. Former ORS 69.280 [RULPA §303]. A general partner's relationship to the limited partners is analogous to the relationship of a corporate board of directors to the corporate shareholders; the general partner functions as a fiduciary with a duty of good faith and fair dealing. *Bassan v. Investment Exchange Corp.*, 83 Wash.2d 922, 524 P.2d 233 (1974); see *Iwasaki v. Iwasaki Bros., Inc.*, 58 Or.App. 543, 547, 649 P.2d 598 (1982). Like the corporate director's fiduciary responsibility to the shareholders for the declaration of dividends, the general partner's duty to the limited partners in the distribution of profit is discharged by decisions made in good faith that reflect legitimate business concerns. See *Iwasaki v. Iwasaki Bros., Inc.*, supra. There is no contention here that the general partner acted in bad faith in failing to distribute all of the profits. The limited partners' right to a share of the profits of the partnership under former ORS 69.240(2) [ULPA §10(2)][4] is unrestricted; however, in the absence of a provision to the contrary in the partnership agreement, the right to a distribution of that share is subject to the good faith judgment of the general partner. The agreement is not ambiguous and contains no provision that would give plaintiffs the right to demand payment for undistributed profits. Accordingly, the trial court erred in denying defendants' motion for judgment on the pleadings. Given that conclusion, we need not address defendants' other assignments of error.

Reversed and remanded for entry of judgment for defendants.

Notes

In *Brooke* the disenchanted limited partners resorted to litigation in an effort to coerce the decision of the general partner. Suppose that they were to resort to self-help measures within the context of the partnership by seeking to interfere in management decisions or, issuing orders to partnership employees which contradict the instructions of the general. Both the ULPA and the RULPA define circumstances in which such participation in control and management may expose the active limited partners to liability for firm debts and obligations under §15 of the UPA. May the aggrieved general partner seek this reclassification?

---

[4]*Former* ORS 69.240(2) provided:

"A limited partner shall have the right to receive a share of the profits or other compensation by way of income, and to the return of his contribution as provided by ORS 69.270 and 69.230."

In *Weil v. Diversified Properties*, 319 F.Supp. 778 (D.D.C. 1970), the court examined §7 of the ULPA, the terms of the partnership agreement, and the fact that the limited partners had not sought to become active until the business affairs of the partnership were in a crisis. It declared:

> Cases relating to whether or not limited partners have taken part in control of the business and are thus to be treated as general partners involve claims by creditors against the partners.... No case has been found where a general partner has invoked §7 of the Act against his own limited partners. The purpose of §7 is to protect creditors:

> > The Act proceeds on the assumption that no public policy requires a person who contributes to the capital of a business, acquires an interest in its profits, and some degree of control over the conduct of the business to become bound for the obligations of the business, provided creditors have no reason to believe that when their credits were extended that such persons were so bound. (William Draper Lewis, 65 U.Pa.L.Rev. at 715 (1917)).

Abendroth v. Van Dolsen, 131 U.S. 66, 9 S.Ct. 619, 33 L.Ed. 57 (1889) although decided under a New York statute which preceded the Uniform [Limited] Partnership Act, is closely in point:

> [T]he statute, in fixing this liability on account of noncompliance with its provisions, does not change his special partnership into a general one, but simply makes him liable as a general partner to creditors. All his relations to his copartners, and their obligations growing out of their relation to him as a special partner, remain unimpaired. 131 U.S., at 73. ...

The remedy of a general partner who faces interference from his limited partners is to dissolve the partnership under §31 of the Uniform Partnership Act. ... So long as the partnership continues, he is in a relationship of trust with his colleagues, *Meinhard v. Salmon*, 249 N.Y. 458, 164 N.E. 545 (1928). He may not invoke the provisions of the Act to enlarge the liability of his partners.

Even if a general partner might hold his limited partners to account as a general partners under certain circumstances, Weil cannot do so on the facts of this case. Weil considers himself still a general partner and recognizes that the written partnership agreement by its terms is a bona fide limited partnership under the Code. As between themselves, partners may make any agreement they wish which is not barred by prohibitory provisions of statutes, by common law, or by considerations of public policy. Whatever may be the obligations of the limited partners as against creditors or third parties, Weil may not prevail against them if they have not breached the terms of the agreement. Having entered into the partnership agreement with advice of counsel, an agreement made largely for his own benefit in a field where he was especially experienced, he is bound by its terms. Accordingly, the initial inquiry must be to determine whether the limited partners have in any way violated the terms of the written agreement.

Paragraph 11 of the Diversified Properties agreement. . .provides in pertinent part as follows with respect to the management of the business of the partnership:

> *Management of Business.* The day-to-day management of the business of this partnership shall be conducted by the general partner through whatever entity the partnership by majority votes decides to establish. No limited partner (in his or other capacity as a limited partner) shall have or exercise any rights in connection with the day-to-day management of the partnership business. The general partner, so long as Martin L. Weil is the general partner, shall receive from the partnership. . .the total sum of Thirty-five Thousand ($35,000) Dollars per year as salary and shall in turn manage all of the partnership properties. All decisions which are not in the normal day-to-day course of business shall be made by the partnership and with respect to any such decision, and except as is herein provided, a majority vote shall govern. ...

Thus it is apparent that the partners contemplated the general partner would receive a substantial salary and have the day-to-day management of the properties. ... After May 1, 1969, the partnership operation became a matter of salvaging what could be salvaged in the enterprise as it then existed. This naturally involved refinancing and sale of properties and other matters not in the normal course of day-to-day business. As to these nonroutine matters, the limited partners by the very terms of their agreement had a majority vote, and were certainly authorized to comment upon them. Weil believes he should have had exclusive say as to how and what bills were to be paid with any money available beyond immediate operating needs, but under the prevailing conditions this clearly was not a normal day-to-day business question; it involved the very ability of the enterprise to survive. ...

Assuming that Diversified Properties was on the verge if not in fact insolvent, was the interest of creditors served in denying the aggrieved general partner a right to seek reclassification of the limiteds? Isn't the general partner in the best position to provide evidence of the degree to which the limited partners have taken part in the control and management of the firm? We will turn to the circumstances in which the limited partners may lose their shield of limited liability after we consider the variety of techniques which they may use to discipline the action or inaction of a general partner.

3. Disciplining the general partner:

Whether viewed from the vantage point of the common law or the perspective of modern statutes, it is clear that the relationship of a general to the limited partners is influenced by three factors: (1) the mandatory settlement imposed by statute; (2) the terms of a specific partnership agreement; and (3) fiduciary standards. In *Allen v. Steinberg*, 244 Md. 119, 223 A.2d 240 (1966), the court asserted that the prerogatives of the general partner are to be ascertained from the partnership agreement. "It is also generally held that power and authority not

specifically delegated in a partnership agreement is presumed to be withheld."
In *Boxer v. Husky Oil Co.*, 429 A.2d 995, 997 (Del. Super. 1981), the court
elaborated on this theme:

> The complaint alleges a breach of a fiduciary duty on the part of the
> general partner as a basis for equity jurisdiction. The Uniform Limited Partner-
> ship Act, which has been adopted in both Delaware and Colorado, provides that
> a general partner has all the rights and powers and is subject to all the restric-
> tions and liabilities of a partner in a partnership without limited partners. Section
> 9 of the Uniform Limited Partnership Act provides:

> Rights, powers and liabilities of a general partner

> A general partner shall have all the rights and powers and be subject to all
> the restrictions and liabilities of a partner in a partnership without limited part-
> ners, except that without the written consent or ratification of the specific act by
> all the limited partners, a general partner or all of the general partners have no
> authority to:

> (1) Do any act in contravention of the certificate;
> (2) Do any act which would make it impossible to carry on the ordinary
> business of the partnership;
> (3) Confess a judgment against the partnership;
> (4) Possess partnership property, or assign their rights in specific partner-
> ship property, for other than a partnership purpose;
> (5)　Admit a person as a general partner, unless the right so to do is given
> in the certificate;
> (6)　Admit a person as a limited partner, unless the right so to do is given
> in the certificate;
> (7)　Continue the business with partnership property on the death, retire-
> ment, bankruptcy, or mental illness of a general partner, unless the right so
> to do is given in the certificate.

> The Uniform Partnership Act. . . makes a partner accountable as a fiducia-
> ry. Section 21 of the Uniform Partnership Act provides in part:

> Partner accountable as a fiduciary

> (a) Every partner must account to the partnership for any benefit, and
> hold as trustee for it any profits derived by him without the consent of the
> other partners from any transaction connected with the formation, conduct,
> or liquidation of the partnership or from any use by him of its property.

> When the provisions of the Uniform Partnership Act and the Uniform
> Limited Partnership Act are read together, it is clear that the general partner in
> a limited partnership owes a fiduciary duty to the limited partners. [citations] It
> is also clear that a partner owes a fiduciary duty to the other partners at common
> law. [citations]

> The duty of the general partner in a limited partnership to exercise the
> utmost good faith, fairness, and loyalty is often compared to that of corporate

directors:

> "Furthermore, the fiduciary duty of fair dealing by a general partner to a limited partner is no less than that owed by a corporate director to a shareholder. The form of the enterprise does not diminish the duty of fair dealing by those in control of the investments." *Miller v. Schweickart*, S.D. N.Y., 405 F.Supp. 366 (1975).

Both the statutory and common law predicates recited in *Boxer* were invoked by the Supreme Court of Alabama in *Cox v. F & S*, 489 So.2d 516 (1986). What makes *Cox* interesting is that the limited partnership, Second Monclair Company, featured two general partners, Joseph Cox and F & S, a partnership. Each of the general partners held a one-third equity participation in the limited partnership. The remaining one-third equity interest was held in equal shares by eleven limited partners. Over the course of the years, F & S became increasingly suspicious respecting the business practices employed by Cox in the management of an office building belonging to the partnership. Ultimately, an action was commenced by F & S seeking the dissolution and liquidation of the partnership, cancellation of the management agreement between the partnership and a corporation controlled by Joseph Cox, and an award of compensatory and punitive damages against Cox as a disloyal general partner. Faced with proof that Cox had violated the terms of the management contract, charged unrelated business expenses to the partnership account, refused to share information with the other general and the limited partners, and misappropriated partnership assets, the trial court granted judgment in favor of the partnership in full conformity with the complaint. It also forbade Cox from the use of partnership assets to pay for his legal defense of his stewardship as a general partner.

The fact that the relief sought in *Cox* was pursued in the name of the partnership, and the recovery available to the claims of third parties in the course of the court ordered dissolution, permitted the Alabama court to avoid many of the difficult conceptual questions surrounding litigation within the partnership which may impact adversely upon the claims of contract creditors and tort victims of the partnership business. As the following cases illustrate, while there is no debate over the proposition that the general partner is a fiduciary, there is considerable discord over the question of whether that duty is owed to the limited partnership, the limited partners collectively, or individual limited partners. Depending upon one's position on this question it is possible to sort out questions of standing and the appropriate nature of remedies for breach of the fiduciary duty.

a. A conceptual basis for litigation against the general partner(s):

WYLER v. FEUER
California District Court of Appeal, 1978.
85 Cal.App.3d 392, 149 Cal.Rptr. 626

FLEMING, ASSOCIATE JUSTICE.   Claiming fraud and failure of consideration plaintiff Leopold S. Wyler sued to rescind a limited partnership agreement, under which as limited partner he invested $1.5 million in the production of a motion picture on the early life of French singer Edith Piaf. The jury found for the defendants, and the trial judge awarded them $125,000 in attorney's fees. Wyler appeals the adverse jury verdict. ...

FACTS

Defendants Cy Feuer and Ernest Martin, associated as Feuer and Martin Productions, Inc. (FMPI), have been successful producers of Broadway musical comedies since 1948.[1] Their first motion picture, "Cabaret," produced by Feuer in conjunction with Allied Artists and American Broadcasting Company, received eight Academy Awards in 1973. Plaintiff Wyler is president and largest shareholder of Tool Research and Engineering Corporation, a New York Stock Exchange Company based in Beverly Hills. Prior to 1972 Wyler had had no experience in the entertainment industry.

In 1969 Simone Berteaut wrote a best-selling book about her early life with her half-sister Edith Piaf. Martin became interested in the book as a possible motion picture, and in August 1972 FMPI acquired worldwide motion picture and television rights to the book for $50,000, plus a percentage of motion picture profits. This was the first motion picture defendants attempted to finance themselves, "Cabaret" having been financed by Allied Artists and ABC. Because defendants desired to avoid studio financing with its burdensome overhead and loss of artistic control, they sought to finance the Piaf picture through a combination of: (a) private investment under a standard agreement whereby investors receive 50 percent of profits in return for 100 percent of financing, and (b) production financing. Production financing consists of advance sales of distribution rights prior to completion of the motion picture, for sums certain, payable on delivery of the film to the distributor. If both producer and distributor are favorably known in the motion picture world, the producer can obtain a bank loan, discounted at a high rate of interest and secured by the distributor's promised payment for distribution rights.

In November 1972 Feuer went to Paris to audition actresses for the lead role of Piaf, and there he discovered Bridgette Ariel, an unknown bilingual French actress who closely resembled Piaf. He also met Wyler in Paris, and the two discussed the Piaf motion picture and the financing of its budget of $1 million for a French-language version of the picture. Wyler expressed interest in the project. In January 1973 defendants decided to film French and English-speaking versions of the motion picture simultaneously, which raised their estimated

---

[1] Over a twenty-year span Feuer and Martin produced ten Broadway musicals, which include "Where's Charlie?", "Guys and Dolls", "Can-Can", and the Pulitzer Prize winning "How to Succeed in Business Without Really Trying." These musicals were financed by investor contributions of five, ten, and fifteen thousand dollars.

budget from $1 million for the French version to $1.5 million for both French and English versions. In February 1973 Wyler and Feuer met in New York, and Wyler offered to provide $750,000 of the proposed $1.5 million budget. However, Wyler rejected the standard ratio of 25 percent profits for 50 percent financing and demanded 371/2 percent of profits. Defendants' secretary interrupted this meeting to announce that "Cabaret" had been nominated for 10 Academy Awards.

On February 19 Martin and FMPI's attorney, Irving Cohen, met Wyler in Beverly Hills and told him they could not accept his money until they had commitments for 100 percent of the needed financing. Wyler offered to finance the entire $1.5 million budget for 50 percent of profits, subject to the following conditions: defendants would obtain up to $750,000 production financing outside the United States; for each $100,000 production financing so obtained defendants would receive an additional 12/3 percent of profits; if defendants raised all the $1.5 million through production financing, Wyler would still receive 25 percent of profits for his original commitment. The parties resumed negotiations the next day with Leon Kaplan in attendance as Wyler's adviser. Kaplan, a prominent entertainment attorney, asked that Wyler be given the right to approve the final screenplay, the final budget, the completion bond surety, and United States distribution arrangements, and expressed his opinion that defendants' estimate of $750,000 from production financing outside the United States was realistic, since he thought $250,000 to $300,000 could be raised from distribution rights in France alone. At that meeting Kaplan recalled that Warner Brothers had some motion picture rights to the Piaf story. Martin, who had been employed at Warner Brothers in 1970, replied the risk of copyright infringement would be minimal, since defendants' motion picture would be based on Berteaut's book and not on any Piaf material owned by the studio; at Warner Brothers he (Martin) had discussed the subject with Warner executives, who had not objected to his project; in any event defendants would obtain an errors-and-omissions policy to insure against liability for copyright infringement.

On 1 March 1973 a Deal Memorandum preliminary to the final LIMITED PARTNERSHIP agreement was executed. In addition to the foregoing terms and conditions it included a provision inserted at Cohen's request that failure to raise production financing would not constitute a default but would reduce defendants' $150,000 producer's fee (payable from initial distribution receipts) by $10,000 for each $100,000 of the $750,000 not raised through production financing, down to a minimum fee of $75,000.[3]

---

[3]". . . (ii) FMPI agrees to obtain not less than Seven Hundred Fifty Thousand Dollars ($750,000) of production financing by means of outright sales or non-returnable advances against distribution as herein set forth; provided that FMPI's failure to obtain all or part of said Seven Hundred Fifty Thousand Dollars ($750,000) shall not be a default hereunder but in such case the Production Fee shall be reduced by an amount equal to ten percent (10%)

On 13 July 1973 the parties simultaneously executed a LIMITED PART-NERSHIP agreement and a modifying memorandum which increased the proposed budget to. $1.6 million and the proposed production financing to $850,000 in order to take into account the appreciation of the French franc. These documents followed the terms of the Deal Memorandum and declared that Wyler would provide, interest free, 100 percent financing, consisting of $350,000 already advanced plus 5 million francs (approximately $1,250,000), and that defendants would obtain $850,000 in production financing outside the United States by September 30. Defendants further agreed to defer their producer's fee until Wyler's capital contribution had been repaid. With respect to defendants' obligation to obtain production financing, the agreement provided:

> "(Defendants) agree to obtain not less than ($850,000) of production financing in the form of nonreturnable loans repayable solely out of proceeds from distribution of the Picture or in the form of outright sales, solely from territories outside of the United States, on or before September 30, 1973. . . . If (defendants have) not raised the aforementioned sum by September 30, 1973 (defendants) shall continue to be under an obligation to raise such sum after said date. *[Defendants'] failure to raise the minimum sum of ($850,000) of production financing by September 30, 1973 shall not be deemed a breach of this agreement, it being agreed that the consequences set forth in Paragraph X hereof (dealing with reduction in the producer's fee) shall be (Wyler's) sole remedy . . .*" (Italics ours.)

Despite their acclaimed success in "Cabaret," defendants at the time of execution of the limited partnership agreement were experiencing difficulties in obtaining distributor commitments and knew it would be unlikely they could obtain any production financing by the September 30 deadline. Their difficulties arose from their overestimation of the attractiveness of the Piaf subject-matter, from the unknown leading actress, and from the scheduling of photography during the summer months when most Europeans go on vacation.

Filming of the motion picture began July 23 and ended October 9. By that time Wyler had advanced $1.25 million and defendants had failed to obtain any production financing. The completed cost of the picture was $1,512,000.

Early in October, Feuer met Wyler in Paris and requested an extension of the deadline for production financing to December 30, so that defendants could take advantage of distributor negotiations in process and recoup their profit percentage and their producer's fee. Wyler said he had already financed the picture and refused to extend the deadline, thereby maintaining his profit percentage at 50

---

of the difference between the amount of production financing actually so obtained and the sum of Seven Hundred Fifty Thousand Dollars ($750,000); it is agreed that the maximum amount of the reduction of the production fee shall be Seventy-Five Thousand Dollars ($75,000) as aforesaid."

percent.

At this same meeting Wyler, on Feuer's advice, rejected a distribution offer by United Artists of $100,000 cash against a 35-percent distributor share for distribution rights in France, in favor of a French distributor's offer of nothing down but only a 20-percent distributor share. From September through December 1973 defendants actually obtained worldwide distribution contracts totalling $265,000 in firm commitments, of which $24,000 in cash had been received by March 1974. Defendants did not notify Wyler of these other distribution contacts, nor did they attempt to obtain production financing on them. Defendants attributed their inaction to two factors: (1) many of the contracts were not "bankable" because they were subject to such contingencies as a country's censorship approval or the requirement that the motion picture be dubbed in another language; (2) high rates of discount (14 percent) made it uneconomic to bank these contracts in late 1973 when the motion picture was scheduled to open in early 1974. On advice of counsel defendants treated the $24,000 in hand and all subsequent proceeds from the $265,000 in distributor commitments as distribution receipts, which entitled them to deduct distribution expenses before reimbursing Wyler for his investment.

In March 1974 defendants previewed the French and English versions of the Piaf motion picture for Wyler in Beverly Hills. While the French version was generally acclaimed by all parties, the English version, which presented English translations of the Piaf songs, was not. At a meeting in Kaplan's office a decision was made to replace the English translations with French originals. Wyler demanded that the $24,000 received from distribution commitments be turned over to him as production financing, but this issue was not resolved.

The motion picture premiered in Paris in April 1974. On June 26 Warner Brothers filed in New York a lawsuit which sought damages for copyright infringement and an injunction against United States distribution of the Piaf film. The present action was filed by Wyler on July 22. Although a producer's representative and a publicity man for United States distribution were hired in August 1974, and although the Warner Brothers suit was settled in November 1974, the Piaf film has never been released in the United states, either for theatrical exhibition or for television. In 1975 defendants proposed a distribution contract, which was turned down by Wyler as totally unreasonable. As of 31 December 1975 the Piaf motion picture had enjoyed less than overwhelming success, with total receipts of $478,000 from distribution outside the United States, of which $313,500 went to Wyler as reimbursement for his investment.

Wyler's action sought rescission of the agreement and recovery of his investment on theories of fraud and failure of consideration, and, alternatively, sought damages for mismanagement of the business of the limited partnership.

DISCUSSION

After Wyler rested his case-in-chief the trial court nonsuited Wyler's cause of action which sought $1.5 million damages for defendants' mismanagement of the limited partnership business. The mismanagement cause of action pleaded misrepresentations about marketability and production financing, plaintiff's reliance on defendants' misrepresentations and promises, and the trust and confidence reposed in defendants by plaintiff. As specifications for the charge of mismanagement Wyler alleged excessive costs of production for the French version of the motion picture, failure to produce a marketable English version, improvident selection of actors, unseasonable scheduling of photography, failure to obtain production financing, and procurement of disadvantageous distribution contracts.

To support his mismanagement theory of liability plaintiff cites cases holding that a hired professional owes a duty of reasonable care in exercising his expertise for the benefit of the person who hired him.[4] But those cases do not support plaintiff's theory of liability, in that defendants were not hired or employed by plaintiff in any rational sense of the words. Existence of liability for mismanagement depends here on the partnership relation of the parties.

A limited partnership affords a vehicle for capital investment whereby the limited partner restricts his liability to the amount of his investment in return for surrender of any right to manage and control the partnership business. [ULPA §7]. In a limited partnership the general partner manages and controls the partnership business. [ULPA §9(1)]. In exercising his management functions the general partner comes under a fiduciary duty of good faith and fair dealing toward other members of the partnership. [UPA §21; *Laux v. Freed* (1960) 53 Cal.2d 512, 522, 2 Cal. Rptr. 265, 348 P.2d 873; *Dennis v. Gordon* (1912) 163 Cal. 427, 433, 125 P. 1063.)

These characteristics limited investor liability, delegation of authority to management, and fiduciary duty owed by management to investors are similar to those existing in corporate investment, where it has long been the rule that directors are not liable to stockholders for mistakes made in the exercise of honest business judgment (*Findley v. Garrett* (1952) 109 Cal.App.2d 166, 174, 178, 240 P.2d 421; *Marsili v. Pacific Gas & Electric Co.* (1975) 51 Cal.App.3d 313, 324, 124 Cal.Rptr. 313), or for losses incurred in the good faith performance of their duties when they have used such care as an ordinarily prudent person would use. (Corp.Code, § 309(a).) By this standard a general partner may not be held liable for mistakes made or losses incurred in the good faith exercise of reasonable business judgment.

---

[4]*Coberly v. Superior Court* (1965) 231 Cal.App.2d 685, 689, 42 Cal.Rptr. 64 (duty of corporate trustee); *Gagne v. Bertran* (1954) 43 Cal.2d 481, 489, 275 P.2d 15 (general duty of experts and professionals); *Estate of Beach* (1975) 15 Cal.3d 623, 635, 125 Cal.Rptr. 570, 542 P.2d 994 (duty of corporate executor).

According all due inferences to plaintiff's evidence, as we do on review of a nonsuit, we agree with the trial court that plaintiff did not produce sufficient evidence to hold defendants liable for bad business management.

Plaintiff's evidence showed that the Piaf picture did not make money, was not sought after by distributors, and did not live up to its producers' expectations. The same could be said of the majority of motion pictures made since the invention of cinematography. No evidence showed that defendants' decisions and efforts failed to conform to the general duty of care demanded of an ordinarily prudent person in like position under similar circumstances.[5] The good faith business judgment and management of a general partner need only satisfy the standard of care demanded of an ordinarily prudent person, and will not be scrutinized by the courts with the cold clarity of hindsight. The trial court correctly granted a nonsuit on the mismanagement cause of action.

The judgment is affirmed.

b. The fiduciary duties of general partners and the analogy to corporate directors:

Brooke v. Mt. Hood Meadows and *Boxer v. Husky Oil* analogized the status of a general partner to that of a corporate director. There is more than a surface attraction in the comparison for each is a steward of what Brandeis termed "other people's money." Such a parallel has potentially far reaching consequences including the identification of two cardinal fiduciary duties and the suggestion that they run to the business enterprise rather than the equitable owners. See, *Abeloff v. Barth*, 119 F.R.D. 332 (D.Mass. 1988). It may also be the source of a powerful defense in the hands of a general partner targeted by disenchanted limiteds.

The duties in question are of loyalty and care. The duty of loyalty requires that in all dealings the director seek the advantage of the corporate entity. The duty of care is a negligence standard and, assuming that there has been fidelity duty of loyalty, has rarely formed the basis for successful litigation. In *Wyler* the court imports from decisions affecting corporate directors the "business judgment rule" to insulate from judicial review ". . .mistakes made in the exercise of honest business judgment. . .or for losses incurred in the good faith

---

[5] The 1975 Legislative Comment to the business judgment standard of Corporations Code section 309 stated:

"The reference to 'ordinarily prudent person' emphasizes long traditions of the common law, in contrast to standards that might call for some undefined degree of expertise, like 'ordinarily prudent businessman'; the phrase is not intended to establish the preservation of assets as a priority for the corporate director, but, rather, to recognize the need for innovation as an essential of profit orientation and, in short, to focus on the basic director attributes of common sense, practical wisdom and informed judgment."

performance of their duties when they have used such care as an ordinarily prudent person would use."

Not all courts agree that the "business judgment rule" should be available to a general partner. If a limited partner conceptualizes his grievance as a breach of a contract of association formed with the general partner, at least one recent decision has concluded that the business judgment rule may not be invoked as a defense. In *Roper v. Thomas*, 60 N.C.App. 64, 298 S.E.2d 424 (1982), the limited partner brought an action against the general partners to recover his capital contribution in a limited partnership formed for the construction of an apartment complex.

In November, 1972, the plaintiff and 21 other people became limited partners with the defendants, Edward H. Thomas and Jesse M. Waller. The parties executed a limited partnership agreement (hereinafter referred to as "LPA"). The partnership was formed to provide for the construction and opera- tion of a 208-unit apartment complex. ... Prior to the execution of the LPA, all of the partners were furnished with a Private Placement Memorandum (herein- after referred to as "PPM") outlining the proposed project and its potential risks, profits, and tax consequences. Plaintiff invested a total of $31,200, purchasing two units in the partnership.

. . .

The construction project encountered difficulties from the beginning, including weather, soil problems, withdrawal of subcontractors, escalating costs and interest rates. When completed, the project had a cost overrun, which the general partners were obligated to pay and did not. A soft rental market added to the woes, and at no time was the project more than 51 per cent occupied. Rental income was approximately $18,000 less per month than what was re- quired to pay the monthly operating expenses plus principal and interest pay- ments on the projected permanent loan. The general partners were unable to obtain permanent financing, which they were obligated to do under the PPM and LPA. Although the construction loan was extended six months by the lender, the loan was foreclosed subsequently, and plaintiff lost his total investment of $31,200. ...

. . .

Defendants contend that a general partner may be likened to a corporate director who may be personally liable for gross neglect of his duties, misman- agement, fraud and deceit resulting in loss to a third person, but not for error of judgment made in good faith. ... Defendants' arguments are meritless. The judge, recognizing the defendants as general partners in the project, concluded defen- dants were jointly and severally liable for such damages the plaintiff may have suffered as a proximate result of defendants' breach of the PPM and LPA. In effect, the judge treated the matter as a negligent breach of contractual obliga- tions. ...

Defendants breached their obligations under the partnership agreement. They pursued a course of conduct that an ordinary person may reasonably have foreseen as injurious to others. They were negligent in performance of the contract with the plaintiff. ...

Not only did the *Roper* court preclude the assertion of the "business judgment rule," but it also permitted the aggrieved limited partner a direct recovery against the general partners. If the fiduciary or contract duties of a general partner are properly regarded as running to the limited partners, what would have prevented all 21 investors in the failed apartment complex from asserting their cause of action as a class? Recent authorities are divided.

The analogy of the general partner or partners to corporate directors should not obscure the structural differences in their status. Corporate directors serve terms fixed in the articles or incorporation and limited by statute. In states like California their terms cannot exceed one year, and in even the most permissive states the term limit is three years. While a director may be re-elected, she must still seek renewal of her status on a fairly frequent basis. By contrast, in the typical limited partnership the general partner or partners usually retain their control and management for the duration of the business vehicle. They do not face periodic retention election. There is another important difference. In a corporate setting there is no contemplation that the directors will be secondarily liable for the debts and obligations of the enterprise. On the contrary, there is an expectation of limited liability for both managers and investors. In a limited partnership, the general partner or partners have secondary liability under §15 of the UPA. Should the fact that they run such a risk entitle general partners to greater judicial sympathy than would be shown corporate directors in a like business setting?

c.   A class action seeking a direct recovery by disgruntled limited partners:

Alpert v. Haimes, 64 Misc.2d 608, 315 N.Y.S.2d 332 (1970), allowed limited partners to commence a class action seeking a direct recovery from the general partner. The prejudice to third party creditors from such litigation is obvious. It is difficult to imagine that such an action would be sought unless the business affairs of the limited partnership were in chaos if not bankruptcy. If limited partners are successful in a class action, the recovery realized against the general partner directly diminishes the resources that general partner would have to assume secondary liability to creditors and tort victims under §15 of the UPA.

Such litigation was forbidden in *Phillips v. KULA 200 II*, 4 Hawaii App. 350, 667 P.2d 261, 265 (1983):

. . .we conclude that the general partner's fiduciary duty is owed to the limited partnership, not the limited partners.

The resulting question is whether a limited partner can maintain an individual action against the general partner for breach of the fiduciary duty owed by the general partner to the limited partnership. As did Judge Friendly in *Klebanow v. New York Produce Exchange*, 344 F.2d 294 (2d Cir. 1965), we find corporate law to be analogous. Under the corporate law, "in no case can the stockholder bring suit for himself and in his own right on a cause of action belonging to the corporation." [citation] We think the same rule should be applied with respect to limited partnerships. Consequently, we hold that a limited partner may not bring suit for himself and in his own right on a cause of action belonging to the limited partnership.

d. Limited partner's interest as a security:

While securities law is an area of specialization, there is no mystery about what constitutes a "security." In *SEC v. W.J. Howey Co.*, 328 U.S. 293, 66 S.Ct. 1100, 90 L.Ed. 1244 (1946), the Court laid down a test which has been aptly recast as follows: "If A gives his money to B and thereafter looks for a return on that placement solely to B's efforts, the arrangement is a security." Subsequent cases have indicated that the term "solely" need not be taken literally. The fact that A is not totally passive does not defeat the notion that his investment vehicle was a security. See, *SEC v. Glenn Turner Enterprises, Inc.*, 474 F.2d 476 (9th Cir. 1973). Given the *Howey* test you can easily see that an investment in a limited partnership interest is a classical security. As such, the sale is subject to both federal and state regulation. Federal statutory law and the federal Securities and Exchange Commission obtain jurisdiction whenever the offer to sell a security crosses state lines or involves the use of interstate means of communication. If the offering is contained within the jurisdiction of a single state it may evade federal regulation but will surely be the target of that state's securities law. A common objective of both federal and state regulation is to proscribe the making of any "untrue statements of material fact."

In *Shinn v. Thrust IV, Inc.*, 56 Wash.App. 827, 786 P.2d 285 (1990), the court surveyed recent federal and state decisions and concluded that the offering of limited partnership interests to multiple investors would qualify as the offer to sell a security. By contrast, a one-on-one negotiation between a prospective general and a single or a few prospective limited partners might lack the "promotional characteristics" classically associated with the need for state regulation.

The advantage to a limited partner if she can qualify her investment as a "security" is that rescission and recovery of the purchase price is a common remedy if the sale was influenced by misstatements or omissions of material facts.

e. Derivative litigation against the general partner(s):

MOORE V. 1600 DOWING STREET, LTD.
Colorado Court of Appeals, 1983.
668 P.2d 16.

BERMAN, JUDGE. In a derivative action by a limited partner, plaintiff, Robert Moore, appeals the summary judgment entered for defendants. Because we find that there are genuine issues of material fact to be determined, we reverse and remand to the trial court.

This limited partnership derivative action was filed by Moore, a limited partner having a 6% interest, on behalf of himself and on behalf of the limited partnership, 1600 Dowing Street, Ltd. Moore later conceded both in his appellate briefs and at oral argument that he was not pursuing any claims on his own behalf; rather, it was purely a derivative action. The claims include mismanagement, misrepresentation, and breaches of fiduciary duties by the general partners and third parties.

A number of motions to dismiss were filed by defendants, but were denied by the trial court. After an affidavit and additional factual materials were presented to the court, many of the same issues raised by the motions to dismiss were renewed in summary judgment motions. These motions asserted that a limited partnership derivative action may not be maintained in Colorado, that Moore's sole remedy is a return of his capital contribution, and that, in the alternative, if a limited partnership derivative action is permitted in Colorado, Moore did not fairly and adequately represent the interests of those similarly situated. Moore contested all of the above grounds, and also maintained that the denial of defendants' motions to dismiss was the law of the case as to all issued raised by those motions.

Summary judgment was granted, and this appeal followed. Because no on reason was given for the trial court's ruling, we assume that it considered each of the grounds asserted in support of the motions, as well as Moore's counter arguments; thus, we discuss each separately here.

. . .

Moore argues that if the trial court's basis for granting summary judgment was a refusal to recognize the right of limited partners to sue derivatively, the court was in error. We agree.

Preliminarily, we note that this limited partners was formed in 1973. Hence, the provision of the Uniform Limited Partnership Act, as reenacted in 1981 [RULPA], which specifically permits a derivative action by a limited partner, [RULPA §§1001–1004], is not applicable; rather the action is governed by the Uniform Limited Partnership Law. . .and the common law.

Beginning with the landmark decision of *Klebanow v. New York Produce Exchange*, 344 F.2d 294 (2nd Cir. 1965), the majority of jurisdictions to have considered the issue have concluded that, *under the common law,* a limited partner may bring a derivative action against the general partners for breach of fiduciary duty to the management of the affairs of the partnership if the general partners refuse to or are unable to bring such an action. See, *e.g., Riviera Congress Associates v. Yassky*, 18 N.Y.2d 540, 277 N.Y.S.2d 386, 223 N.E.2d 876 (1966); ...

256

The rationale behind permitting such suits was stated succinctly by the New York Court of Appeals:

"There can be no question that a managing or general partner of a limited partnership is bound in a fiduciary relationship with the limited partners . . . and that the latter are, therefore, *cestuis que trustent*[sic] . . . . It is fundamental to the law of trusts that *cestuis* have the right 'upon the general principles of equity' . . . and 'independently of [statutory] provisions . . . to sue for the benefit of the trust on a cause of action which belongs to the trust if the trustees refuse to perform their duty in that respect."

Riviera Congress Associates v. Yassky, supra (brackets in original).

. . .

The third issue raised during hearings on the summary judgment motions was whether a limited partner's sole remedy is the return of his contribution with interest. We hold such remedy to be nonexclusive.

Defendants rely on *Gundelach v. Gollechon*, 42 Colo.App. 437, 598 P.2d 521 (1979) and [ULPA §16] to argue that the trial court should have awarded Moore his contribution with interest, in lieu of permitting a derivative suit. However, the *Gundelach* court specifically recognized that a general partner owes a fiduciary duty to a limited partner, and recognized that the *minimum* amount of damages for such a beach is a return of contribution. It in no way limited the amount of damages recoverable, nor did it touch on the question of whether a suit seeking such damages was limited to one brought by a limited partner in his individual capacity, or included one brought on behalf of the business entity in the form of a derivative suit.

. . .

Moore's final argument is that he fairly and adequately represents the partnership members similarly situated. We hold that the record has not been adequately developed on this factual issue; thus, summary judgment was not proper. C.R.C.P. 56(c); *Discovery Land & Development Co. v. Colorado-Aspen Development Corp.*, 40 Colo.App. 292, 577 P.2d 1101 (1977).

C.R.P.C. 23.1 governs "derivative action[s] brought by one or more shareholders or members to enforce a right of a corporation or of an unincorporated association . . ..." and provides that a "derivative action may not be maintained if it appears that the plaintiff does not fairly and adequately represent the interests of the shareholders or members similarly situated in enforcing the right of the corporation or association." The record reveals that approximately 47 of the other limited partners, at the behest of defendants, submitted letters wherein they stated that they did not believe that Moore represented their interests in this lawsuit. In addition, one limited partner submitted an affidavit to that effect. However, it appears from the record that at least six limited partners have not expressed their opinion on this issue. The trial court must determine, on remand, whether any of the six limited partners are similarly dissatisfied with the actions of the general partners. See *Clemons v. Wallace*, 42 Colo.App. 17, 592 P.2d 14 (1978).

If the court finds that one or more other limited partners are similarly dissatisfied, the court must consider, in addition to the extent of support shown by the members plaintiff seeks to represent, the following factors:

> "economic antagonisms between representative and class; the remedy sought by plaintiff in the derivative action; indications that the named plaintiff was not the driving force behind the litigation; plaintiff's unfamiliarity with the litigation; other litigation pending between the plaintiff and defendants; the relative magnitude of plaintiff's personal interests as compared to his interest in the derivative action itself; [and] plaintiff's vindictiveness toward the defendants . ..."

Davis v. Comed, Inc., 619 F.2d 588 (6th Cir. 1980).

. . .

The judgment is reversed and the cause is remanded for further proceedings, including such evidentiary hearings as may be appropriate, consistent with this opinion.

Notes

Review Article 10 of RULPA. The 1985 Amendments made no significant changes. Do the provisions of the statute settle the issue of whether a limited partner may litigate in the name of the partnership if the majority of the limited partners are opposed to such a suit? Their indisposition may be motivated by numerous factors which only begin with a differing view of the merits of the claim. What if the claim has legal merit, but the opposition of the majority of the limited partners is predicated upon such pragmatic grounds as the disruption, adverse publicity and morale problems which such a suit would cause within the partnership workforce or the community? What about the general partner or partners? In *Moore* they are the named defendants, and the futility of a demand that they commence an action against themselves is fairly obvious. See RULPA and RULPA/85 §1003. Suppose a limited partnership with five general partners in which only two were implicated in the alleged wrong. Would a decision by the three non-implicated general partners to reject the demand by a limited partner under §1003, preclude the litigation?

In *Caley Investments I v. Lowe Family Associates, Ltd. v. Walters*, 754 P.2d 793 (Colo.App. 1988), the court which had decided *Moore* began to provide answers to some of these critical questions. In a fact pattern now governed by Colorado's adoption of RULPA, the court rejected the standing of limited partners to bring a direct cause of action for injury to partnership assets allegedly caused by the misdeeds of the general partners. Lowe and LFA were the two limited partners in the Caley partnerships. They had sought to assert such grievances as counterclaims when faced with actions commenced by the limited partnerships.

Prior to Lowe and LFA's investment in the Caley partnerships, Walters, allegedly acting on his own behalf, obtained a $26,000,000 line of credit from third-party defendant Manufacturers Hanover Trust Company (MHTC). The line of credit was secured by two promissory notes and deeds of trust on property owned by the Caley partnerships. Before this transaction, Walters, and allegedly the then limited partner, executed authorization and indemnification agreements purporting to authorize him to encumber the partnerships' property. At the time these encumbrances were established, neither Lowe nor LFA had any interest in the Caley partnerships.

Lowe and LFA's fourth counterclaim sought a judgment declaring the two deeds of trust and the authorization agreements invalid, on the grounds that they were executed without the express consent of the limited partners. Lowe and LFA also sought a declaratory judgment that neither Lowe, LFA, Caley I, nor Caley II are obligated to repay the $26,000,000 indebtedness to MHTC. In bringing this counterclaim, Lowe and LFA joined Walters, MHTC, and Jo Fleming, as the Public Trustee for Arapahoe County, as third-party defendants. The Public Trustee has disclaimed. Upon MHTC's motion, the trial court dismissed Lowe and LFA's fourth counterclaim as to all parties. The trial court held that Lowe and LFA failed to state a claim upon which relief may be granted. The trial court further held that Lowe and LFA "improperly raised claims belonging to the plaintiff partnerships, and have failed to set forth any facts showing that a present controversy exists and that they are entitled to relief in their individual capacities." The trial court then certified this order pursuant to C.R. C.P. 54(b) and Lowe and LFA now appeal. Lowe's and LFA's counterclaims for breach of fiduciary duty, indemnification, and declaration of contractual rights remain pending and are not the subject of this appeal.

Defendants contend that the trial court erred in dismissing their fourth counterclaim; that defendants had standing to assert claims belonging to the Caley partnerships; and that a present controversy exists entitling them to a declaratory judgment. We disagree.

In order to have standing, a plaintiff must suffer an injury in fact to a legally protected interest as contemplated by statute or constitutional provision. *Wimberly v. Ettenberg*, 194 Colo. 163, 570 P.2d 535 (1977); *East Grand County School District No. 2 v. Town of Winter Park*, 739 P.2d 862 (Colo.App.1987). If a person suffers no injury in fact or suffers injury in fact but not from the violation of a protected interest, no relief can be afforded, and the case should be dismissed for lack of standing. Initially, therefore, we consider whether Lowe and LFA would arguably suffer injury in fact should the declaratory relief they seek be denied, and the encumbrances allowed to stand. Secondly, we consider whether the potential injury to Lowe and LFA stems from the violation of a legal right, which violation may be afforded judicial relief.

Limited partners are generally not liable to third-party creditors for obligations of the partnership. [ULPA §7 and RULPA §303]; *Silvola v. Rowlett*, 129 Colo. 522, 272 P.2d 287 (1954).

A limited partner may become individually liable only when he takes part in control or operation of the partnership. [ULPA §7 and RULPA §303]; *Roeschlein v. Watkins*, 686 P.2d 1347 (Colo.App. 1983).

Further, limited partners own an interest in a legal entity, but hold no title or property right to the partnership assets. See *Evans v. Galardi*, 128 Cal.Rptr. 25, 546 P.2d 313 (1976); *Maxco, Inc. v. Volpe*, 247 Ga. 212, 274 S.E.2d 561 (1981). A limited partner is a capitalist or investor only, placing his money into a partnership without becoming a general partner or risking anything in the business except the capital originally subscribed. *Silvola v. Rowlett*, supra. See also *Klein v. Weiss*, 284 Md.App. 36, 395 A.2d 126 (1978).

Here, any injury which Lowe and LFA could suffer as a result of the encumbrances would be indirect, resulting from a diminution in value of their investment in the Caley partnerships. We conclude that, as to a limited partnership interest, such injury is not the type of direct injury required to satisfy the first prong of the Wimberly standing test.

As to the second prong of the Wimberly standing test, Lowe and LFA do not have a legal right to sue the general partner and third-party creditors directly; rather, they are restricted to bringing a derivative action. See C.R.C.P. 23.1; [RULPA §1001 to 1003]; *Moore v. 1600 Downing Street, Ltd.*, 668 P.2d 16 (Colo.App. 1983). The rationale behind this restriction is that the interests of individual limited partners are not necessarily the interests of the partnership as a whole. If a limited partner were allowed to proceed with an individual action, the limited partnership's interests could be harmed, and the entity would be subject to multiple suits by parties not joined in the action. See *R.S. Ellsworth v. Amfac Financial Corp.*, 65 Haw. 345, 652 P.2d 1114 (1982).

Therefore, Lowe and LFA have no standing to bring suit on behalf of the Caley partnerships absent compliance with the procedural requirements for derivative actions. Lowe and LFA's interests do not necessarily reflect those of the Caley partnerships. Lowe and LFA, thus, under their fourth counterclaim as drafted, have no legal right which may be afforded judicial remedy. The second prong of the standing test is, therefore, not satisfied.

Lowe and LFA further assert that the fourth counterclaim, while not in strict compliance with the procedural requirements for derivative actions, nonetheless was properly brought as such. We disagree. C.R.C.P. 23.1 delineates the requirements for commencing a derivative action. These requirements are paralleled by those in [RULPA §1001]. C.R.C.P. 23.1 mandates that: (1) the complaint be verified; (2) the claim alleges that plaintiff was a member of the association at the time of the transaction of which he complains, or that his membership thereafter devolved upon him by operation of law; (3) the claim alleges with particularity the efforts made, if any, by the complaining party to obtain the action he desires from the directors or comparable authority; and (4) the complaint states the reasons for the complaining party's failure to obtain the relief or for not making the effort.

Similarly, [RULPA §1001] requires that: (1) the general partners with authority to do so have refused to bring the action or that an effort to cause those general partners to bring the action is not likely to succeed; (2) the general partners decision not to sue constitutes an abuse of discretion or involves a conflict of interest that prevents an unprejudiced exercise of judgment; and (3) the complaining party was a limited partner at the time of the transaction of which he complains or his status as a limited partner had devolved upon him by operation of law or pursuant to the terms of the partnership agreement from a person who was a partner at the time of the transaction.

Compliance with C.R.C.P. 23.1 is mandatory in derivative actions against corporations and must be shown on the face of the complaint. *Bell v. Arnold*, 175 Colo. 277, 487 P.2d 545 (1971); *Van Schaack v. Phipps*, 38 Colo.App. 140, 558 P.2d 581 (1976). The purpose underlying the requirements of this rule is to avoid the possibility of a multiplicity of lawsuits by individual members of an association, or small groups of members of an association. *Bell v. Arnold*, supra. We conclude that the requirements set forth in [RULPA §1001] further this same purpose. Therefore, compliance with C.R.C.P. 23.1 and [RULPA §1001] is also mandatory when initiating derivative actions by limited partners. We therefore do not agree with Lowe and LFA that the form of the fourth counterclaim should be disregarded, and that they should be allowed to proceed as parties to a derivative action. The fourth counterclaim as drafted does not meet those requirements, and Lowe and LFA made no attempt to amend their counterclaim.

. . .

The provisions of Colorado's rule of civil procedure are in substance the same as the contents of Rule 23.1 of the Federal Rules of Civil Procedure. The distinction between a direct a derivative action, and an application of the pleading and exhaustion requirements applicable to a plaintiff who would litigate in the name and interest of a limited partnership are further explored in *Abeloff, et al. v. Barth, et al.*, 119 F.R.D. 332 (D.Mass. 1988).

I do not agree with the defendants' argument that the plaintiffs need allege or demonstrate that they adequately represent the interests of all the persons holding limited partnership interests to survive a motion to dismiss pursuant to Rule 12(b)(6). F.R.Civ.P. Rule 23.1, does not require such an allegation, and cases have held that the burden is on the defendant to prove that the plaintiffs will not adequately represent all persons holding interests in the limited partnerships. As one district court ruled:

> ... [I]t is the defendants who must bear the burden of showing "that a serious conflict exists and that plaintiff could not be expected to act in the interests of the other shareholders because doing so would harm his other interests."

Ohio-Sealy Mattress Manufacturing Co. v. Kaplan, 90 F.R.D. 21, 25 (N.D.Ill., 1980) quoting from Wright & Miller, 7A Federal Practice and Procedure, P 1833 at 393 (1972 ed.).

f. Ouster and replacement of the offending general partner(s):

From the vantage point of the limited partners the preceding cases have afforded relief only at the price of destroying the limited partnership and, with it, their investment vehicle. What if the aggrieved limited partners seek to expel the offending general partner and replace him with an individual deemed more able, trustworthy or agreeable?

LESESNE ET AL. v. MAST PROPERTY MANAGEMENT, INC.
Supreme Court of Georgia, 1983.
251 Ga. 550, 307 S.E.2d 661.

MARSHALL, PRESIDING JUSTICE. The present imbroglio arises from a dispute between limited and general partners of Island Retreat, Ltd., which is a limited partnership organized for the purpose of constructing and managing an apartment project on St. Simons Island, Georgia.

The limited partnership was organized in 1978 by an investment adviser named Lesesne. This litigation began when Lesesne, as a limited partner of Island Retreat, filed a complaint against Mast Property Management, Inc., which manages the apartment project under written agreement with the limited partnership. Mast is, in turn, owned by Baer, who is one of the two general partners of Island Retreat.

Under one section of the parties' limited partnership agreement, the limited partners whose aggregate percentages of interest exceed 50% may remove the general partners (or either of them) and select a person(s) or corporation(s) experienced in the real estate business to become the successor of the general partners and to take over and assume the operations of the partnership.

Under another section of the agreement, if limited partners whose aggregate percentages of interests equal or exceed 30% notify the general partners that they wish to propose, among other things, (i) termination of any contract between the partnership and the general partners, or their affiliates; or (ii) removal of the general partners and appointment of a successor to the general partners, the general partners shall, within 30 days after such notice, mail to the limited partners a notice describing the proposal and a form to be returned indicating whether they oppose or approve the proposal.

Under the foregoing provisions of the limited partnership agreement, Baer has sent out such notices and the limited partners have voted unanimously to approve a proposal for termination of the management agreement between the limited partnership and Mast, as well as a proposal for the removal of Baer as general partner and the appointment of Lesesne as a successor general partner.

Baer argues, among other things, that the limited partners' votes for these proposals were obtained by fraud and misrepresentation on Lesesne's part. This alleged fraud and misrepresentation consists of statements by Lesesne that the partners were not receiving any return on their investments because Mast was mismanaging the property, as well as statements by Lesesne concerning the real estate experience of Brandon Management Co., a company which is controlled by Lesesne and which was recommended by Lesesne to the other limited partners as a new property manager. Baer has filed a countersuit against Lesesne based on this alleged fraud and misrepresentation.

The superior court has entered an order granting interlocutory injunctive relief to Baer and, thus, temporarily restraining removal of him as general partner and enjoining Lesesne from assuming management of the partnership's operations. This appeal is from that order. *Held:* We reverse for the following reasons.

. . .

The question of law here is whether the fraud and misrepresentation claim asserted by Baer against Lesesne would authorize the setting aside of the limited partners' vote removing Baer as general partner and appointing Lesesne as successor general partner.

The only authority on this question to which we have been cited is *Consortium Management Co v. Mutual America Corp.*, 246 Ga. 346, 271 S.E.2d 488 (1980), as well as the line of cases represented by *Ga. Power Co. v. Busbin*, 242 Ga. 612, 250 S.E.2d 442 (1978).

In *Consortium Management*, supra, Mutual America, which held the majority interest in a limited partnership, exercised its right under the partnership agreement to remove the general partners and replace them with itself. When other partners refused to execute the amendment to the certificate of limited partnership effectuating the change, suit was brought in order to have the clerk of the court record such amendment. On appeal from a judgment entered in Mutual America's favor, we held that personal service of process on one of the former general partners was not necessary to maintenance of the action. 246 Ga., supra, at pp. 347, 348, 271 S.E.2d 488. No question was raised concerning the legal efficacy of Mutual America's decision to remove the general partners.

Busbin, supra, and the cases cited therein, hold that, although an employment terminable at will gives no rise to a cause of action against the employer for wrongful termination, an action may be maintained against a third person for tortious interference with the employment relationship.

In our opinion, the closest analogy to the present situation is found in *Busbin*. Here, the limited partners with the requisite aggregate percentages of interest had the right, for whatever reason, to remove Baer as general partner, replace him with Lesesne as successor general partner, and terminate the management agreement with Mast. As previously stated, the discharged employee in *Busbin* may have had a claim against a third person for tortious interference with his employment, but he had no claim against the employer for the wrongful termination thereof. By a similarity of reasoning, Baer has no right to be reinstated as general partner of Island Retreat, although he may or may not have a claim against Lesesne for tortious interference with whatever employment relationship he had with Island Retreat.

Judgment reversed.

Notes

Georgia adopted RULPA/85 in 1988. Does §303(b)(6)(v) extend as far as the common law right recognized by the *Lesesne* court? Examine §402(3). What if the partnership agreement did not contain a provision for the removal of a general partner? In *Mahon v. Harst*, 738 P.2d 1190 (Colo.App. 1987) the court was confronted with proof that an oral agreement called for the creation of a formal written partnership agreement which would include machinery for the removal of a general partner. The formal instrument was never created. Notwithstanding, the court concluded that the oral agreement among the partners was sufficient to enable removal by the agreed majority vote.

4. Dissolution at the behest of aggrieved limited partners:

Article 8 of the RULPA for the first time provides statutory coverage of dissolution of a limited partnership. Under the ULPA the topic was covered by reference to the Uniform Partnership Act. Article 8 distinguishes between "nonjudicial" and "judicial" dissolution.

Section 802. Judicial Dissolution

> On application by or for a partner the [here designate the proper court] court may decree dissolution of a limited partnership whenever it is not reasonably practicable to carry on the business in conformity with the partnership agreement.

Would this section have been useful to an aggrieved general partner such as Weil? Would it extend relief to the aggrieved limited partners in the following case?

BLOCK v. DARDANES, ET AL.
Appellate Court of Illinois, 1980.
83 Ill.App.3d 819, 39 Ill.Dec. 216, 404 N.E.2d 807.

SULLIVAN, PRESIDING JUSTICE. Defendant George Dardanes, a general partner in a limited partnership known as Wildfire Investments, appeals from an order granting plaintiff, his limited partner, an accounting and judgment for $105,400.54. On review, Dardanes contends that the trial court erred in denying his motion to dismiss at the close of plaintiff's case on grounds that (1) plaintiff failed to establish a prima facie case; and (2) plaintiff "did not come to the court with clean hands."

Many of the essential facts in this case are uncontradicted, inasmuch as defendants called no witnesses to testify. It appears that in January of 1973 plaintiff, a physician, was introduced to Dardanes by a common friend, Tony Dicharinti. Plaintiff and Dardanes became interested in the purchase of the Adria restaurant in unincorporated Lake County, and they entered into a written limited partnership agreement whereby Dardanes, who had experience in the restaurant business and at that time owned and managed the Sir George's restaurant, was the general partner, and plaintiff was the limited partner. The purpose was to finance and operate the anticipated new restaurant and, pursuant to the terms of the agreement, Dardanes was to be responsible for the actual management of the business, including the keeping of partnership records and accounts.

The seller of the Adria restaurant wanted $550,000 for the property—$50,000 of which was required as a down payment; $200,000 of which was to be paid in cash "under the table"; and the partnership was to obtain a mortgage for the remaining $300,000. Plaintiff, Dardanes and Dicharinti each agreed to furnish one-third of the cash needed for the down payment and the "under the table" money, although Dicharinti was not mentioned in the written partnership agreement.

It is somewhat unclear from the record exactly how plaintiff provided his share of the cash. He testified that he promptly gave Dardanes $3,333.33, representing one-third of the $10,000 earnest money; that in order to pay his share of the $200,000 "under the table" money he removed $46,000 in cash from his safety deposit box at the Old Orchard Bank; that he and Dicharinti took this money to his (plaintiff's) house and counted it; that they placed it in an attache case and brought it to Dardanes at Sir George's restaurant; that Dardanes said plaintiff was short by $1,070; that approximately one week later he gave Dardanes two watches (valued at $740) and $330 in cash to make up this deficit; that in order to pay his share of the $50,000 down payment, he withdrew $5,500 from his account at Home Federal Savings and Loan and $3,000 from his account at Continental Illinois National Bank and Trust; that he also sold some stock for $5,455 and wrote a check payable to "cash" for $4,000; and that he gave these sums to Dardanes. However, plaintiff's wife (Louise Block), who is also a physician and practices with plaintiff, testified that plaintiff originally removed $18,400 from the safety deposit box; that she later witnessed him counting $38,760 in cash, which he had taken from the box; that she gave plaintiff $1,600 from their office account and later gave him an additional $2,000 from office funds to invest in the partnership. Finally, plaintiff's income tax return for 1973 indicates that he invested $21,000 in the business.

In any event, it is clear that the partnership secured a mortgage, under which it was to pay approximately $3,000 per month and, in April of 1973, the purchase of the property was finalized. A corporation (Wildfire, Inc.) was set up as the owner of the business, and plaintiff personally paid $4,000 of a $12,000 charge by an architect who was hired to plan the new restaurant. Plaintiff made 20 to 25 visits to the restaurant before it opened on May 1, 1974, under the name "Wildfire."

Subsequent to the opening, Bruce Block (plaintiff's son), who had worked for Dardanes at Sir George's restaurant, began working at Wildfire and Dicharinti, together with an individual named Frank DeMarie, also became involved. Plaintiff testified that they were considered partners, even though their names did not appear in the limited partnership agreement. Plaintiff also testified that when Dicharinti suggested DeMarie's sons (Frank, Jr. and Salvatore) would be helpful at the restaurant, Dardanes agreed that they should be hired. Plaintiff and his son testified that Salvatore took over the day-to-day management of Wildfire. Plaintiffs son also testified that Sal kept two sets of books—one which was shown to anyone asking information, while the other was "private"; and that he (Bruce) told plaintiff of the two sets of books and reported the actual daily receipts to plaintiff.

It appears evident from the record that Dardanes did not involve himself in the operation of the restaurant to the extent contemplated in the limited partnership agreement. Plaintiff testified that he never saw any income statements of Wildfire Investments; that on several occasions during the period from July to September, 1974, he had requested of Dardanes some indication as to the partnership income, but he never received any such information; and that Dardanes never furnished plaintiff with an accounting.

Dardanes, called to testify under section 60 of the Civil Practice Act (Ill.Rev. Stat.1977, ch. 110, par. 60), stated that while he was at the Wildfire approximately ten times in May of 1974, he was never there during the period of June to September, 1974; that he "never operated personally the Wildfire"; that he did not have a key; that he never had anything to do with Wildfire from the beginning; that he never kept the partnership books; that his inactivity at Wildfire resulted because the DeMaries forcibly took over the business a few months after it opened; that Sal and Frank DeMarie Jr. threatened his life; and that they and Bruce Block were in total control of Wildfire. On the other hand, plaintiff testified that Frank DeMarie did not threaten him or Dardanes in order to become involved in Wildfire. Bruce Block testified that the relationship between Sal DeMarie and Dardanes was amicable and that he never observed any quarreling between the two, and that he never heard Frank DeMarie Sr. threaten Dardanes although, on occasions, one of the DeMaries had kept a revolver in his desk.

Dardanes testified that he tried to render an accounting, stating that he had hired Norman Diamond, an accountant, to do so and that the DeMaries brought various vouchers and receipts to his (Dardanes's) home, which he in turn delivered to Diamond. Diamond testified that during the period of May to October, 1974, he received books from Dardanes; that he (Diamond) also visited Wildfire and requested and received various documents from Frank DeMarie. It was conceded at the oral arguments here that no accounting was in fact ever completed.

In October, 1974, plaintiff filed the instant suit against Dardanes, Sal and Frank DeMarie, Jr., and Wildfire, Inc., seeking essentially a dissolution, accounting, and termination of the limited partnership. Dardanes filed an appearance and answer and, although the DeMaries were served with summons, they did not appear. At trial, plaintiff's witnesses testified as related above and, in addition, Dardanes testified that the restaurant was in serious financial difficulty during the period of June through September, 1974; that in November, he orally agreed to sell the premises to an individual named George Christopulous; that under the agreement, Christopulous was to pay the outstanding bills and take over the mortgage; that three or four days after the agreement was reached, Christopulous gave Dardanes $20,000 in cash and later gave him an additional $17,500; that he neither gave nor received a written document of any kind; that the sale was never consummated; and that Christopulous sued him and recovered a judgment of $47,000. The record is not clear as to whether plaintiff was actually apprised of the proposed sale. In any event, Dardanes testified that he did not have to report it to plaintiff since he "seemed to know everything" but that he did in fact tell plaintiff of the sale during a telephone conversation; that plaintiff told him "to go right ahead and sell it" and then hung up on him; that plaintiff refused to talk to him and that he thus never had a chance to tell him that Christopulous had paid $37,500; and that he never gave plaintiff any part of that payment. It also appears from the testimony that a foreclosure suit was filed against the partnership in December 1974 for default of mortgage payments.

Plaintiff also testified that he personally paid many of the partnership debts, including the mortgage payments for March, April and May of 1974; that he paid the real estate taxes; that he loaned Dardanes $1,500; and that his "out-of--pocket" loss is over $118,000 as a result of the partnership effort.

At the close of plaintiffs case, Dardanes moved to dismiss on the grounds that plaintiff had failed to establish a prima facie case and that he came into court with unclean hands. The motion was denied, and Dardanes chose to stand on the motion and not introduce any evidence in his behalf. A default judgment order was then entered against the DeMaries for $105,400.54 and, subsequently, the court entered judgment against Dardanes in the same amount, with findings that plaintiff paid $105,400.54 to Dardanes in reliance upon his representations that it would be used in furtherance of the partnership; that Dardanes failed to fully and fairly account to plaintiff; that Dardanes failed to perform the duties and obligations incumbent upon him as general partner; that Dardanes failed to manage the business and thereby caused a waste of the assets of the partnership; and that there is due and owing from Dardanes the sum of $105,400.54. The trial court then entered a final order consolidating the two judgment orders, stating that Dardanes and the DeMaries were to be held jointly and severally liable for the amount of the judgment. Dardanes' motion for a new trial was denied, and this appeal was from the judgment against him.

OPINION

The seminal question here is whether the trial court erred in denying Dardanes' motion to dismiss at the close of plaintiff's evidence. In order to address this issue properly, we would first point out that the briefs of both parties center on the question of whether plaintiff was entitled to an "accounting." However, in view of the fact that plaintiff was apparently awarded the return of his capital contribution, it appears that at the request of plaintiff, the trial court in fact ordered a dissolution of Wildfire, followed by an accounting and termination. We find it proper for a trial court to grant all such relief in a single action. See *Rudnick v. Delfino* (1956), 140 Cal.App.2d 260, 294 P.2d 983; 60 Am.Jur.2d *Partnership* § 270 (1972).

Dissolution is defined in the Uniform Partnership Act as "the change in the relation of the partners caused by any partner ceasing to be associated in the carrying on as distinguished from the winding up of the business." [UPA §29] Under the Uniform Limited Partnership Act, a limited partner has the same rights as a general partner to have dissolution and winding up by decree of court. (*Curtis v. Johnson* (1968), 92 Ill.App.2d 141, 234 N.E.2d 566; [ULPA §10(1)(c)]. Such decree of dissolution may be sought under the numerous circumstances set forth in section 32 of the Uniform Partnership Act. ... Section 32(1)(d), which is relevant here, allows dissolution whenever:

> "A partner wilfully or persistently commits a breach of the partnership or agreement, or otherwise so conducts himself in matters relating to the partnership business that it is not reasonably practicable to carry on the business in partnership with him," [UPA §32(d)].

Also see 60 Am.Jur.2d *Partnership* § 191 (1972). Furthermore, a limited partner has the right to a formal account of partnership affairs whenever circumstances render it just and reasonable [ULPA §10(1)(b)], and failure to account is grounds for an order of dissolution (*Fisher v. Fisher* (1967), 352 Mass. 592, 227 N.E.2d 334; *Schroer v. Schroer* (Mo.1952), 248 S.W.2d 617).

In applying the above law to the facts of the instant case, we note that under the terms of the written limited partnership agreement, Dardanes was responsible for the operation and management of the restaurant. However, plaintiff testified that he never received any income statements for the partnership and, although he requested of Dardanes some indication of the partnership income several times during the period of July to September, 1974, the information was never provided. On his section 60 examination, Dardanes testified that he was never at the restaurant during the period of June to September, 1974; that he did not keep books; that he did not have a key to the premises; and that he never had anything to do with Wildfire from the beginning. Further, plaintiff testified that he personally paid some of the partnership debts and also loaned money to Dardanes. In view of the above testimony that Dardanes failed to render an accounting when requested and that he persistently breached the partnership agreement, we feel the evidence tended to establish a cause of action for dissolution.

We see no merit in any of the arguments made by Dardanes in support of his contention that plaintiff failed to establish a prima facie case. He first points out that he hired Diamond in order to satisfy plaintiffs demand for an accounting. We find this unpersuasive, however, in view of the fact the Dardanes's attorney admitted at the oral arguments in this case that no statements or results of any accounting were ever given to plaintiff.

Second, Dardanes refers us to his section 60 testimony that he could not manage the partnership affairs as required in the agreement because of the DeMaries' hostility toward him, and he urges that this testimony destroyed plaintiff's prima facie case for dissolution. Dardanes testified that he read the partnership agreement and understood his responsibilities under it and that he had been to the restaurant about ten times in May, but was not there in June, July, August and September, 1974, although he did pay some liquor bills in July and August. Dardanes also stated that the DeMaries had taken over the operation of the restaurant, and he was afraid to do anything in connection with it because they had threatened his life. We note, however, that there was other testimony indicating that this alleged animosity between Dardanes and the DeMaries did not exist. Specifically, plaintiff testified that Frank DeMarie did not threaten him or Dardanes in order to become active in the restaurant, and Bruce Block testified that the relationship between Sal DeMarie and Dardanes was amicable and that he never observed any quarreling between the two. Since the trial court was required to consider all the testimony, we cannot agree with Dardanes that a prima facie case was not established because of his testimony that he was prevented from managing the restaurant. Furthermore, Dardanes's counsel admitted at oral arguments that Dardanes was nevertheless charged with the obligations of a general partner up until the time the DeMaries allegedly took over the restaurant a few months after it opened. His inactivity during this initial time, without anything else, tended to establish neglect of his partnership obligations.

. . .

We turn then to the contention of Dardanes that the trial court should have granted his motion to dismiss because plaintiff "did not come to the court with clean hands." He points out that plaintiff testified he participated in paying the seller of the restaurant a portion of the purchase price "under the table" and that plaintiff was aware of the fact that Sal DeMarie kept two sets of books. We are not persuaded, however, that plaintiff's conduct in this regard prevented him from obtaining the equitable relief granted. We recognize that "[ilt is a fundamental rule that one seeking equitable relief cannot take advantage of his own wrong or, as otherwise stated, he who comes into equity must come with clean hands." (*Metcalf v. Altenritter* (1977), 53 Ill.App. 3d 904, 908, 12 Ill.Dec. 1, 4, 369 N.E.2d 498, 501.) However, as stated in *Mascenic v. Anderson* (1977), 53 Ill.App.3d 971, 972, 11 Ill.Dec. 718, 719, 369 N.E,2d 172, 173:

> "We deem it well settled that misconduct on the part of a plaintiff which will defeat a recovery in a court of equity under the doctrine of 'unclean hands' must have been conduct in connection with the very transaction being considered or complained of, and must have been misconduct, fraud, or bad faith toward the defendant making the contention."

Also see *Metcalf v. Altenritter; Illinois Power Co.v. Latham* (1973), 15 Ill. App.3d 156, 303 N.E.2d 448.) In addition, application of the doctrine of unclean hands is a matter for the sound discretion of the trial court. [citations].

In the case at bar, while the conduct to which Dardanes points may have been an attempt to conceal data from the Internal Revenue Service, there is nothing in the record to indicate that it was directed toward Dardanes, and we accordingly hold that the trial court did not abuse its discretion in refusing to deny plaintiff recovery on the basis of unclean hands.

For the reasons stated above, the judgment of the trial court is affirmed.

Affirmed.

Note

In *Wood v. Holiday Mobile Home Resorts, Inc.*, 128 Ariz. 274, 625 P.2d 337, 345 (1981), the court declared: ". . . the 'oneness' associated with general partners does not exist in a limited partnership." Compare the grounds for judicial dissolution in §802 of the RULPA with the more extensive grounds set forth in §32 (Dissolution by Decree of Court) of the Uniform Partnership Act. Under the UPA, §32 was the statutory foundation for a petition for dissolution whether lodged by an aggrieved limited or general partner. Section 1105 of the RULPA provides: "In any case not provided for in this Act the provisions of the Uniform Partnership Act govern." Should a court interpret this language as ousting the relevance of §32 of the UPA given the treatment of the subject in §802? If it were to look to a policy predicate for such an interpretation would it find it in *Wood*?

In *Mahon v. Harst*, 738 P.2d 1190 (Colo.App. 1987), the court was obliged to construe both the ULPA and RULPA's provisions with respect to court ordered dissolution at the behest of aggrieved limited partners. Prior to 1981 both plaintiffs and defendants had been shareholders, officers and directors of Western Health

Center, Inc., which owned and operated a nursing home. The pursuit of tax advantages caused them to dissolve the corporation and reorganize the enterprise as a limited partnership. The terms of the limited partnership agreement specified that the plaintiffs would be limited partners while Harst and Smith were to be the general partners in Mark V, Ltd.. Whatever the tax advantages, the new arrangement proved a source of internal strife. Eventually, the limited partners sought court ordered removal of the defendants as general partners, dissolution of the limited partnership, and an award of damages for breach of the partnership agreement. Their complaint alleged that:

> Defendants began paying themselves a monthly management fee of $3,750. Plaintiffs testified that they had never agreed to any such fee. Plaintiffs and defendants continually disagreed about the fees, and defendants refused to satisfy plaintiffs' demands for financial and management information about the nursing home.

In remanding the matter with directions, the appeals court addressed the issues of court ordered removal and dissolution:

> Where removal of a general partner is sought pursuant to a vote of the partners under the terms of a partnership agreement, the proper remedy in the event of a recalcitrant general partner is afforded by §7-61-126(3) and (4), C.R.S. (1986 Repl.Vol. 3A). This section empowers the court to issue an order directing the recordation of an amendment of the certificate of limited partnership to reflect removal of a general partner and the substitution of a limited partner in his place. See *Consortium Management Co. v. Mutual America Corp.*, 246 Ga. 346, 271 S.E.2d 488 (1980); *Brown v. Panish*, 99 Cal.App.3d 429, 160 Cal.Rptr. 282 (1979).

> However, plaintiffs' complaint did not seek to amend the certificate, but instead sought judicial dissolution of the partnership pursuant to [UPA § 32(1)], a right granted to limited partners by [ULPA § 10(1)(c)]. Section [UPA 32(1)] provides that a court shall decree the dissolution of a partnership if:

> > "(c) A partner has been guilty of such conduct as tends to affect prejudicially the carrying on of business;

> > "(d) A partner willfully or persistently commits a breach of the partnership agreement or otherwise so conducts himself in matters relating to the partnership business that it is not reasonably practicable to carry on the business in partnership with him;

> > "(f) Other circumstances render a dissolution equitable."

The findings of fact made by the trial court were sufficient to support a decree of dissolution under [UPA § 32(1)(c), (d), and (f)].

> The court found that defendants, pursuant to their administration of the partnership business, permitted the nursing home to be operated for nearly a year without a licensed nursing home administrator. This represented a violation of § 12-39-102, C.R.S. (1985 Repl.Vol. 5) and exposed the partnership to loss of

its hospital license and to potential third-party liability. Hence, defendants' conduct tended to affect prejudicially the carrying on of the partnership business and was grounds for dissolution under [UPA § 32(1)(c)].

The court also found that defendants willfully refused to furnish plaintiffs with financial information relating to operation of the nursing home, thus depriving plaintiffs of their right to true and full information under [ULPA § 10(1)(b)]. Defendants' refusal to furnish such information also justified a decree of dissolution under [UPA § 32(1)(d)]. See *Saballus v. Timke*, 122 Ill.App.3d 109, 77 Ill.Dec. 451, 460 N.E.2d 755 (1983); *Lau v. Wong*, 1 Hawaii App. 217, 616 P.2d 1031 (1980).

Judicial dissolution under [UPA §32(1)(2)] will also be granted if the evidence establishes substantial misconduct on a defendant partners' part. See *Master Garage, Inc. v. Bugdanowitz*, 690 P.2d 879 (Colo.App. 1984); see also *Fuller v. Brough*, 159 Colo. 147, 411 P.2d 18 (1966).

Here, the trial court further found that defendants breached their duty as fiduciaries by paying themselves an unauthorized management fee, that they failed to relinquish their positions as general partners when voted out, and that the further friction and discord between partners resulted in polarization of the parties. Based on these facts, the court could reasonably have concluded that defendants had engaged in such substantial misconduct in matters relating to the partnership business that it was no longer reasonably practicable for plaintiffs to carry on the business in partnership with them. See *May v. Flowers*, 106 A.D.2d 873, 483 N.Y.S.2d 551 (1984), appeal dismissed, 64 N.Y.2d 611, 491 N.Y.S.2d 1025, 480 N.E.2d 749, (1985); *Saballus v. Timke*, supra; *Lau v. Wong*, supra; *Ferrick v. Barry*, 320 Mass. 217, 68 N.E.2d 690 (1946).

Furthermore, the circumstances between the limited and general partners were such that a dissolution decree would have been equitable under [UPA § 32(1)(f)]. See *Beals v. Tri-B Associates*, 644 P.2d 78 (Colo. App.1982). Hence, dissolution was an appropriate remedy.

Because judicial dissolution of the partnership was both available to plaintiffs and appropriate under the circumstances, the trial court erred in issuing an order to enforce defendants' removal as general partners pursuant to C.R.C.P. 106(a)(2), together with injunctive relief in aid thereof, when it should have granted plaintiffs' prayer for dissolution pursuant to § 7-60-132. Therefore, on remand, the court is directed to enter a decree dissolving the partnership.

. . .

D. LIABILITY TO THIRD PARTY CREDITORS

The functional reasons for the creation of the limited partnership as a business vehicle include the assurance to "limited partners" that only their investment is at risk in the enterprise. Unlike the general partner or partners, the limiteds have no §15 exposure under the UPA. Repeatedly, we have seen courts note the countervailing expectation that in exchange for the privilege of limited liability society expects passivity from the limited partners who are to concede control and management of the enterprise to the general partner(s). A quick review of the fact patterns at bar in the last section reveals the disinclination of limited partners to be content with that aspect of their bargain! In the cases which follow we will review classical and novel strategies designed to reshuffle the cards. For more than a half century the point of departure in this debate has been §7 of the ULPA: "A limited partner shall not become liable as a general partner unless, in addition to the exercise of his rights and powers as a limited partner, he takes part in the control of the business."

HOLZMAN v. De ESCAMILLA
California District Court of Appeal, 1948.
86 Cal.App.2d 858, 195 P.2d 833.

MARKS, JUSTICE.   This is an appeal by James L. Russell and H.W. Andrews from a judgment decreeing they were general partners in Hacienda Farms Limited, a limited partnership, from February 27 to December 1, 1943, and as such were liable as general partners to the creditors of the partnership.

Early in 1943, Hacienda Farms Limited was organized as a limited partnership (Civ.Code, §§ 2477 et seq.), with Ricardo de Escamilla as the general partner and James L. Russell and H.W. Andrews as limited partners.

The partnership went into bankruptcy in December, 1943, and Lawrence Holzman was appointed and qualified as trustee of the estate of the bankrupt. On November 13, 1944, he brought this action for the purpose of determining that Russell and Andrews, by taking part in the control of the partnership business, had become liable as general partners to the creditors of the partnership. The trial court found in favor of the plaintiff on this issue and rendered judgment to the effect that the three defendants were liable as general partners.

The findings supporting the judgment are so fully supported by the testimony of certain witnesses, although contradicted by Russell and Andrews, that we need mention but a small part of it. We will not mention conflicting evidence as conflicts in the evidence are settled in the trial court and not here.

De Escamilla was raising beans on farm lands near Escondido at the time the partnership was formed. The partnership continued raising vegetable and truck crops which were marketed principally through a produce concern controlled by Andrews.

The record shows the following testimony of de Escamilla:

"A. We put in some tomatoes. Q. Did you have a conversation or conversations with Mr. Andrews or Mr. Russell before planting the tomatoes? A. We always conferred and agreed as to what crops we would put in.. . . Q. Who determined that it was advisable to plant watermelons? A. Mr.Andrews.. . . Q.Who determined that string beans should be planted? A. All of us. There was never any planting done —except the first crop that was put into the partnership as an asset by myself, there was never any crop that was planted or contemplated in planting that wasn't thoroughly discussed and agreed upon by the three of us;

particularly Andrews and myself."

De Escamilla further testified that Russell and Andrews came to the farms about twice a week and consulted about the crops to be planted. He did not want to plant peppers or egg plant because, as he said, "I don't like that country for peppers or egg plant; no, sir," but he was overruled and those crops were planted. The same is true of the watermelons.

Shortly before October 15, 1943, Andrews and Russell requested de Escamilla to resign as manager, which he did, and Harry Miller was ' appointed in his place.

Hacienda Farms Limited maintained two bank accounts, one in a San Diego bank and another in an Escondido bank. It was provided that checks could be drawn on the signatures of any two of the three partners. It is stated in plaintiffs brief, without any contradiction (the checks are not before us) that money was withdrawn on 20 checks signed by Russell and Andrews and that all other checks except three bore the signatures of de Escamilla, the general partner, and one of the other defendants. The general partner had no power to withdraw money without the signature of one of the limited partners.

[ULPA §7] provides as follows:

"A limited partner shall not become liable as a general partner unless, in addition to the exercise of his rights and powers as a limited partner, he takes part in the control of the business,"

The foregoing illustrations sufficiently show that Russell and Andrews both took "part in the control of the business." The manner of withdrawing money from the bank accounts is particularly illuminating. The two men had absolute power to withdraw all the partnership funds in the banks without the knowledge or consent of the general partner. Either Russell or Andrews could take control of the business from de Escamilla by refusing to sign checks for bills contracted by him and thus limit his activities in the management of the business. They required him to resign as manager and selected his successor. They were active in dictating the crops to be planted, some of them against the wish of de Escamilla. This clearly shows they took part in the control of the business of the partnership and thus became liable as general partners. *Tyler v. Wilson*, 58 Cal.-App.2d 583 137 P.2d 33.

Judgment affirmed.

1. Predicate for reclassification—powers reserved or actually exercised?

A creditor seeking to reclassify a limited partner advances a liability vehicle akin to the partnership by estoppel doctrine reviewed in *Martin v. Peyton*. Recall that in *Martin* the written agreement provided the purported "lenders" with a variety of prerogatives whereby they could influence the direction if not the personnel of the brokerage house. In fact, few if any of these powers were ever employed by the defendants who had retired from the world of business. In the final analysis, a sympathetic court reviewed the liability question in light of the little that they had done rather than the far greater reserved power of participation. Such an analysis could not assist Russell or Andrews for it appears that they fully exercised the rights reserved in their agreement with de Escamilla and under the terms of banking arrangements. However, in *Plasteel Products Corp. v. Helman*, 271 F.2d 354 (1st Cir. 1959), the court interpreted §7 of the ULPA in a manner highly reminiscent of Judge Andrews' opinion in *Martin*.

There are very few cases which afford much assistance in the interpretation and application of §7. The cases applying statutes in force prior to the Uniform Limited Partnership Act cannot be relied on since the uniform act was drawn to overcome the strict interpretations which were frustrating the purpose of statutory limited partnerships.

The cases that do interpret and apply §7 contain some elements which aid in reaching a decision here. In *Rathke v. Griffith*, 1950, 36 Wash.2d 394, 218 P.2d 757, 18 A.L.R.2d 1349, the copartners had drawn by-laws that provided that the affairs of the partnership should be handled by a board of directors and named the defendant, a purported limited partner, as one of the directors. But in view of testimony that the defendant had never functioned as a director, the court refused to hold that this arrangement itself constituted participation in control of the business sufficient to make the defendant generally liable. In the instant case the only conduct relied on to charge appellees as general partners is the signing of the limited partnership agreement. By analogy to the Rathke case, this does not constitute participation such as to impose general liability.

2. Structural participation:

In both *Rathke* and *Helman* the partnership agreements had reserved powers of participation to the limited partners which they never exercised. A lawyer drafting such an agreement would do well to determine the likelihood of the client's use of such provisions before condemning an individual passive by nature to the pains of a reclassification bid. In the cases which follow, the structure of the limited partnerships was well tuned to the ambitions of the limited partners. Their goal was not only participation but complete dominion over the control and management of the partnership. Their strategy of choice: incorporate a minimally funded entity to function as the general partner and then conduct the business of the limited partnership in the guise of officers and directors of that wholly owned corporation! The very different reception accorded this strategy in Texas and Washington sees those jurisdictions exchange the positions they had taken on the issue of defective formation. Again, the contest is over statutory compliance vs. creditor reliance.

a. Discord under the Uniform Limited Partnership Act:

DELANEY v. FIDELITY LEASE LIMITED
Supreme Court of Texas, 1975.
526 S.W.2d 543.

DANIEL, JUSTICE. The question here is whether limited partners in a limited partnership become liable as general partners if they "take part in the control of the business" while acting as officers of a corporation which is the sole general partner of the limited partnership. The trial court, by summary judgment, held that under such circumstances the limited partners did not become liable as general partners. The court of civil appeals affirmed with a dissent and a concurring opinion. 517 S.W.2d 420. We reverse and remand the case for trial on the merits.

Fidelity Lease Limited is a limited partnership organized under the Texas Uniform Limited Partnership Act, Article 6132a, to lease restaurant locations. It is composed of 22 individual partners, and a corporate general partner, Interlease Corporation. Interlease's officers, directors and shareholders were W.S. Crombie, Jr., Alan Kahn, and William D. Sanders, who were also limited partners of Fidelity. In February of 1969, plaintiffs Delaney, et al. entered into an agreement with the limited partnership, Fidelity, acting by and through its corporate general partner, Interlease, to lease a fast-food restaurant to the partnership. In accordance therewith, plaintiffs built the restaurant, but Fidelity failed to take possession or pay rent.

Plaintiffs brought suit for damages for breach of the lease agreement, naming as defendants the limited partnership of Fidelity Lease Limited, its corporate general partner Interlease Corporation, and all of its limited partners. On plaintiffs' motion the cause against the limited partners individually, insofar as it relates to their personal capacities and liabilities, was severed from the cause against Fidelity and Interlease. In this severed cause, the trial court granted a take nothing summary judgment for the limited partners. Plaintiffs appealed only as to limited partners Crombie, Kahn, and Sanders. Plaintiffs sought to hold these three individuals personally liable under Section 8 of Article 6132a, alleging that they had become general partners by participating in the management and control of the limited partnership.

Pertinent portions of the Texas Uniform Limited Partnership Act, Article 6132a, provide:

"Sec. 8. [ULPA §7] A limited partner shall not become liable as a general partner unless, in addition to the exercise of his rights and powers as a limited partner, he *takes part in the control of the business.*

". . .

"Sec. 13. [ULPA §12](a) A person may be a general partner and a limited partner in the same partnership at the same time.

"(b) A person who is a general, and also at the same time a limited partner, shall have all the rights and powers and be subject to all the restrictions of a general partner; except that, in respect to his contribution, he shall have the rights against the other members which he would have had if he were not also a general partner." (Emphasis added.)

It was alleged by plaintiffs, and there is summary judgment evidence, that the three limited partners controlled the business of the limited partnership, albeit through the corporate entity. The defendant limited partners argue that they acted only through the corporation and that the corporation actually controlled the business of the limited partnership. In response to this contention, we adopt the following statements in the dissenting opinion of Chief Justice Preslar in the court of civil appeals:

"I find it difficult to separate their acts for they were at all times in the dual capacity of limited partners and officers of the corporation. Apparently the corporation had no function except to operate the limited partnership and Appellees were obligated to their other partners to so operate the corporation as to benefit the partnership. Each act was done then, not for the corporation, but for the partnership. Indirectly, if not directly, they were exercising control over the partnership. Truly 'the corporation fiction' was in this instance a fiction." 517 S.W.2d at 426-27.

Thus, we hold that the personal liability, which attaches to a limited partner when "he takes part in the control and management of the business," cannot be evaded merely by acting through a corporation. [citations].

The defendant limited partners also contend that the "control" test enumerated in [ULPA §7] for the purpose of inflicting personal liability should be coupled with a determination of whether the plaintiffs relied upon the limited partners as holding themselves out as general partners. Thus, they argue that, before personal liability attaches to limited partners, two elements must coincide: (1) the limited partner must take part in the control of the business; and (2) the limited partner must have held himself out as being a general partner having personal liability to an extent that the third party, or plaintiff, relied upon the limited partners' personal liability. [citations]. They observe that there is no question in this case but that the plaintiffs were in no way misled into believing that these three limited partners were personally liable on the lease, because the lease provided that the plaintiffs were entering into the lease with "Fidelity Lease, Ltd., a limited partnership acting by and through Interlease Corporation, General Partner."

We disagree with this contention. Section [7 of the ULPA] simply provides that a limited partner who takes part in the control of the business subjects himself to personal liability as a general partner. The statute makes no mention of any requirement of reliance on the part of the party attempting to hold the limited partner personally liable.

Crombie, Kahn, and Sanders argue that, since their only control of Fidelity's business was as officers of the alleged corporate general partner, they are insulated from personal liability arising from their activities or those of the corporation. This is a general rule of corporate law, but one of several exceptions in which the courts will disregard the corporate fiction is where it is used to circumvent a statute. ... That is precisely the result here, for it is undisputed that the corporation was organized to manage and control the limited partnership. Strict compliance with the statute is required if a limited partner is to avoid liability as a general partner. See Hamilton on *Business Organizations*, 19 Texas Practice § 215, at p. 206. *See also* "The Limited Partnership With a Corporate General Partner. . .", Comment, 24 S.W.Law J. 285, 291-292 (1970). It is quite clear that there can be more than one general partner. Assuming that Interlease Corporation was a legal general partner, a question which is not before us and which we do not decide, this would not prevent Crombie, Kahn, and Sanders from taking part in the control of the business in their individual capacities as well as their corporate capacities. In no event should they be permitted to escape the statutory liability which would have devolved upon them if there had been no attempted interposition of the corporate shield against personal liability. Otherwise, the statutory requirement of at least one general partner with general liability in a limited partnership can be circumvented or vitiated by limited partners operating the partnership through a corporation with minimum capitalization and therefore minimum liability. We hold that the trial court erred in granting summary judgment for the defendants, Crombie, Kahn, and Sanders. If, upon trial on the merits it is found from a preponderance of the evidence that either of these three limited partners took part in the control of the business, whether or not in his capacity as an officer of Interlease Corporation, he should be adjudged personally liable as a general partner.

In affirming the trial court, the majority opinion of the court of civil appeals stated:

"It is permissible in this State to form a limited partnership where a corporation is the only general partner, provided that the purpose to be carried out by the limited partnership is lawful." 517 S.W.2d at 423.

The court had no point of error before it requiring such statement to be made. Its accuracy depends upon the scope of the corporate charter, *Luling Oil & Gas Co. v. Humble Oil & Refining Co.*, 144 Tex. 475, 191 S.W.2d 716 (1945), and upon whether we should extend our holding in *Port Arthur Trust Co. v. Muldrow*, 155 Tex. 612, 291 S.W.2d 312 (1956), to sanction corporations acting as general partners in a statutory limited partnership. We reserve any decision on these questions until they are properly presented for our determination.

Accordingly, the cause of action against the defendants Crombie, Kahn, and

Sanders is severed, and as to that portion of the case the judgments of the lower courts are reversed and such cause as to them is remanded for trial in accordance with this opinion. As to the remainder of the case, the judgment of the trial court is affirmed.

FRIGIDAIRE SALES CORP. v. UNION PROPERTIES, INC.
Court of Appeals of Washington, 1976.
14 Wash.App. 634, 544 P.2d 781.

CALLOW, JUDGE. The plaintiff, Frigidaire Sales Corporation, appeals from a superior court judgment dismissing its claim against defendants Leonard Mannon and Raleigh Baxter. The sole issue presented on appeal is whether individuals who are limited partners become liable as general partners when they also serve as active officers or directors, or are shareholders of a corporation which is the managing general partner of the limited partnership.

The parties agreed on the facts. On January 15, 1969, Frigidaire Sales Corporation entered into a contract with Commercial Investors, a limited partnership, for the sale of appliances to Commercial. The contract was signed on behalf of Commercial Investors by defendants Mannon and Baxter in their respective capacities as president and secretary-treasurer of Union Properties, Inc., the corporate general partner of Commercial Investors. Mannon and Baxter were also directors of Union Properties, Inc., and each owned 50 percent of the outstanding shares of Union Properties, Inc. In their capacities as directors and officers of Union Properties, Inc., the defendants exercised the day-to-day management and control of Union Properties, Inc. Both defendants also held one limited partnership unit out of a total of 52 outstanding partnership investment units in Commercial Investors.

Frigidaire Sales Corporation, as the creditor, instituted this action against the general partner Union Properties, Inc. and the defendants Mannon and Baxter individually when Commercial Investors, as the debtor and as the purchaser of the appliances, failed to pay the November 1970 installment and all subsequent installments due on the contract. The trial court entered judgment for the plaintiff against Union Properties, Inc., but dismissed the plaintiff's claim against Mannon and Baxter. The plaintiff appeals the dismissal of the individual defendants.

LIMITED PARTNERSHIPS

A limited partnership is a statutory form of business organization defined as "a partnership formed by two or more persons. . . having as members one or more general partners and one or more limited partners." [ULPA §1]; J. Crane & A. Bromberg, *Law of Partnership* § 26 (1968). It is provided by a section of the uniform partnership act (RCW 25.04) that the provisions of that act apply to limited partnerships except when inconsistent. RCW25.04.060(3). A partnership is defined by [UPA §6(1)] as "an association of two or more persons to carry on as co-owners a .business for profit." Since a corporation is included within the definition of the term "person" under [UPA §2], it follows that a corporation can enter into a limited partnership as a general or limited partner, [citations]. RCW 25.08.070(2)(a) [Washington's non-uniform content of ULPA §7] assumes that a corporation can be a general partner of a limited partnership when it states that a limited partner shall not be deemed to take part in control by possessing or exercising the power to vote on the transfer of a majority of the voting stock of a "corporate general partner." Cf. *Basson v.Investment Exch. Corp.*, 83 Wash.2d 922, 524 P.2d 233 (1974). With this premise in mind, we note that [ULPA §12] provides:

(1) A person may be a general partner and a limited partner in the same partnership at the same time.

(2) A person who is a general, and also at the same time a limited partner, shall have all the rights and powers and be subject to all the restrictions of a general partner; except that, in respect to his contribution, he shall have the rights against the other members which he would have had if he were not also a general partner.

IS THE DOMINANT CONSIDERATION CREDITOR RELIANCE OR PROHIBITED CONTROL?

The plaintiff contends that the defendants, as limited partners, controlled the business because they were (1) sole shareholders of Union Properties, Inc., the general partner; (2) on the board of directors of Union Properties, Inc. ; (3) president and secretary of Union Properties, Inc. ; and (4) exercised the day-to-day management of Union Properties, Inc. The defendants contend, on the other hand, that the limited partnership was controlled by its general partner Union Properties, Inc., a distinct and separate legal entity, and not by the defendants in their individual capacities.

The precise issue has not been previously raised in Washington, and the term "control" as used in [ULPA §7] has not been defined with the present problem in mind. ...

The issue recently received attention in Texas. In *Delaney v.Fidelity Lease Ltd.*, 526 S.W.2d 543 (Tex.1975), the limited partners controlled the business of the limited partnership as officers, directors and stockholders of the corporate general partner. The Texas Supreme Court held at 545:

[Tlhat the personal liability, which attaches to a limited partner when "he takes part in the control and management of the business," cannot be evaded merely by acting through a corporation.

The opinion overrules the decision of the Texas Court of Civil Appeals, in which it had been stated:

The logical reason to hold a limited partner to general liability under the control prohibition of the Statute is to prevent third parties from mistakenly assuming that the limited partner is a general partner and to rely on his general liability. However, it is hard to believe that a creditor would be deceived where he knowingly deals with a general partner which is a corporation. That in itself is a creature specifically devised to limit liability. The fact that certain limited partners are stockholders, directors or officers of the corporation is beside the point where the creditor is not deceived.

Delaney v. Fidelity Lease Ltd., 517 S.W.2d 420, 425 (Tex.Civ.App,1974).

The Supreme Court opinion in *Delaney* was concerned that the statutory requirements of at least one general partner with general liability in a limited partnership could be circumvented by limited partners operating the partnership through the corporation with minimum capitalization and, therefore, with limited liability. The fear is, however, not peculiar to a limited partnership with a corporate general partner. An individual may form a corporation with limited capitalization and thereby attempt to avoid personal liability. When one acts in such fashion, however, the inadequate capitalization is a factor in determining whether to disregard the corporate entity. See W. Fletcher, *Private Corporations* § 44.1 (M. Wolf 1974 rev.vol.); H. Henn, *Law of Corporations* §§ 146, 147 (2d ed. 1970). If a corporate general partner in a limited partnership is organized without sufficient capitalization so that it was foreseeable that it would not have sufficient assets to meet its obligations, the corporate entity could be disregarded to avoid injustice. We find no substantive difference between the creditor who does business with a corporation that is the general partner in a limited partnership and a creditor who simply does business with a corporation. In the absence of fraud or other inequitable conduct, the corporate entity should be respected. [citations].

We note that the decision of the Supreme Court of Texas in *Delaney* relies upon the reasoning of the dissent filed in the Texas Court of Civil Appeals. We believe that the dissent, however, is based in part upon the incorrect premise that a corporation may not be a general partner under the Uniform Limited Partnership Act. We have shown that this is not so under the Washington act. Moreover, the dissent based its reasoning upon the assumption that, because the limited partners acted as officers of the corporate general partner, they "were obligated to their other partners to so operate the corporation as to benefit the partnership." 517 S.W.2d at426. We find no inherent wrong in this. Persons in the position of the individual defendants in this case would be bound to act in the best interests of both the corporate general partner and the limited partners under the guidelines of RCW 25.08.120. The dual capacities are not inimical as asserted.

Apparently prior to the filing of the Texas Supreme Court decision in *Delaney. . .*, a law review article discussing the Texas Civil Court of Appeals decision. . .appeared in 6 Texas Tech.L.Rev. 1171 (1974). Therein the author observed at 1175-76:

> In *Delaney* the court was confronted squarely with the choice of adopting a creditor reliance test or imposing personal liability because of the statutory control prohibition, even though the plaintiff originally did not require the defendant's personal guaranty in the execution of the lease. By adopting the creditor reliance test the court has expanded the permissible forms of business organizations. Texas businessmen now can combine the advantages of both the partnership and the corporation. The desirability of the court's decision is demonstrated by the fact that under such an arrangement the limited partners may enjoy the conduit theory of income taxation as well as complete protection from personal liability. The additional benefit flowing from the *Delaney* decision is that the businessman now can take advantage of these previously existing benefits without forfeiting managerial control of the organization.

(Footnote omitted.) See also J. Barrett & E. Seago, *Partners and Partnerships, Law and Taxation* ch. 13, § 1.3 at 491 (1956).

Moreover, a literal reading of RCW 25.08,070 that disregards the existence of the corporate entity as a general partner is not justified. The consideration of the issue must inquire not only whether a limited partner has participated in a forbidden control, but also whether the corporate entity should be regarded or disregarded. In Horowitz, *Disregarding the Entity of Private Corporations*, 15 Wash.L.Rev. 1, 11 (1940), certain principles are suggested for testing whether corporate entities should be acknowledged or disregarded. The principles, pertinent to our inquiry, were stated to be:

> (a) If there is an overt intention to regard or disregard the corporate entity, effect will be given thereto unless so to do will violate a duty owing.

> (b) The overt intention is that of the corporation whose entity is sought to be disregarded or of the person or persons owning its stock and sought to be visited with the consequence of regard or disregard of the corporate entity.

> (c) The duty owing must be owing to the person seeking to invoke the doctrine, and such duty may arise from common law and equity, contract or statute.

Here, there was an overt intention to regard the corporate entity and no showing of the violation of any duty owing to the creditor. The creditor dealt with the corporate general partner in full awareness of the corporate status of the general partner. There is no showing of any fraud, wrong or injustice perpetrated upon the creditor, merely that RCW 25.08,070 provides that a limited partner becomes liable as a general partner if he takes part in the control of the business. See *Rohda v. Boen*, 45 Wash.2d 553, 558, 276 P.2d 586 (1954). When these are the circumstances, we hold that the corporate entity should be upheld rather than the statute applied blindly with no inquiry as to the purpose it seeks to achieve. ...

. . .

A limited partner is made liable as a general partner when he participates in the "control" of the business in order to protect third parties from dealing with the partnership under the mistaken assumption that the limited partner is a general partner with general liability. See Feld, *The "Control" Test for Limited Partnerships*, 82 Harv.L.Rev. 1471, 1479 (1969). If a limited partnership certificate pursuant to RCW 25.08.020(2) is properly prepared and filed and the limited partner does not participate in the control of the business, it is unlikely that third parties will be misled as to the limited liability of the limited partners. The underlying purpose of the control prohibition of [ULPA §7] is not furthered, however, by prohibiting limited partners from forming a corporation to act as the sole general partner in a limited partnership. A third party dealing with a corporation must reasonably rely on the solvency of the corporate entity. It makes little difference if the corporation is or is not the general partner in a limited partnership. In either instance, the third party cannot justifiably rely on the solvency of the individuals who own the corporation.

We hold that limited partners are not liable as general partners simply because they are active officers or directors, or are stockholders of a corporate general partner in a limited partnership.

Affirmed.

b. Safe harbor under Revised Uniform Limited Partnership Act:

MOUNT VERNON SAVINGS AND LOAN ASSOCIATION, et al.
v.
PARTRIDGE ASSOCIATES, et al.
United States District Court, D. Maryland, 1987.
679 F.Supp. 522

MOTZ, DISTRICT JUDGE. Plaintiff in this action is the Federal Savings and Loan Insurance Corporation ("FSLIC"), the receiver for the original plaintiff, Mount Vernon Savings and Loan Association, which has been declared insolvent. Defendants are Partridge Associates, a limited partnership, and American Housing, Inc. and MIW Investors of Washington ("MIW"), its general partner and one of its limited partners. FSLIC asserts a contract claim against Partridge Associates for failing to pay for 2.6 million dollars of mortgages which FSLIC contends were turned over by Mount Vernon to Partridge Associates pursuant to a Memorandum of Understanding between them dated January 19, 1982. FSLIC seeks to hold MIW liable on this claim on the ground that MIW, although nominally a limited partner, took part in the control of the partnership's business.

Partridge Associates, American Housing and MIW have all filed counterclaims. Partridge Associates and American Housing allege that Mount Vernon breached a contract which it had made to provide permanent financing to Partridge Associates. MIW alleges that Mount Vernon committed fraud by representing to MIW that there was a balance outstanding on one of the mortgage loans transferred by Mount Vernon to Partridge Associates when, in fact, the loan had been paid off and Mount Vernon had wrongfully retained the proceeds. The parties have moved for summary judgment as to all of the claims which they have asserted against one another.

BACKGROUND

In 1971, MIW sold to one David Dreyfuss an apartment project in Columbia, Maryland known as Partridge Courts. As part of that transaction, MIW took a note from Dreyfuss in the amount of $4,826,000. Over the next ten years Dreyfuss paid off only $3,000 on the principal amount of the loan, and the note became an unproductive asset in MIW's portfolio. In 1981 MIW entered into an agreement with Dreyfuss whereunder MIW repurchased Partridge Courts by assuming the outstanding balance of $4,823,000 on the note and paying certain other consideration not relevant here.

MIW's plan was to convert Partridge Courts into a condominium complex. In October 1981 Partridge Associates was formed for that purpose. MIW was one of two limited partners and owned a 50% interest in the partnership; Friendship Services, Inc., a subsidiary of Friendship Savings and Loan Association, was the other limited partner and owned a 48% interest; American Housing was the general partner and owned a 2% interest. Only $2,000 in capital was contributed to Partridge Associates by the partners (in amounts proportionate to their respective shares).

MIW assigned to Partridge Associates its rights under the repurchase agreement with Dreyfuss. MIW also agreed to lend $6,000,000 to Partridge Associates. $4,823,000 of this loan was used by Partridge Associates to purchase from MIW the 1971 Dreyfuss note. The remainder of the loan proceeds were to be used to fund construction. The principal amount of the loan was to be repaid from release fees generated by the sale of the individual condominium units at Partridge Courts. The interest rate on the $6,000,000 loan was substantially greater than the interest rate had been on the 1971 Dreyfuss note, and MIW therefore contemplated that it would benefit from what was in effect the exchange of the two notes. The $6,000,000 loan was not to be secured by a deed of trust on Partridge Courts but by various negotiable home mortgage notes unrelated to Partridge Courts. Friendship Savings guaranteed to MIW that it would pledge $2,600,000 of such notes. Another $4,300,000 of such notes were obtained by Partridge Associates from Dominion Federal Savings and Loan Association in exchange for an assignment of the Dreyfuss note and its supporting deed of trust on Partridge Courts.

In late 1981, E. Mitchell Fry, Jr.—who with one Anthony Koones controlled the Friendship defendants and American Housing—approached James F. Russell,

II, the president of Mount Vernon, about participating in the Partridge transaction. His purpose was to have Mount Vernon enter into an agreement with Partridge Associates similar to the $4,300,000 Dominion Federal transaction, whereby Partridge Associates would purchase $2,600,000 in negotiable residential mortgage notes from Mount Vernon. These notes were to replace the notes which Friendship had agreed to pledge to MIW.

For reasons which are not clear, Russell agreed to Fry's proposal.[3] On January 19, 1982, Fry, on behalf of American Housing, Partridge Associates and Friendship Services, and Russell, on behalf of Mount Vernon, signed a Memorandum of Understanding under which Mount Vernon agreed to make a $2,600,000 loan to Partridge to be used for the purchase of 2.6 million dollars worth of residential mortgage loans. Two days later, Russell delivered to Fry mortgages in that face amount, and subsequently MIW agreed to accept these mortgages as substitute collateral for the similar Friendship notes.

Mount Vernon was never paid a single penny for its mortgages, and no loan documents between Partridge Associates and Mount Vernon were ever executed. Subsequently, the Partridge transaction turned sour, and, in November 1982, MIW sent Partridge Associates a notice of default under the $6,000,000 loan. When MIW sought to foreclose upon the Mount Vernon notes, Mount Vernon instituted an action in the District of Columbia against Riggs National Bank (which was holding the notes as custodian), seeking an injunction to prevent their turnover to MIW. When Mount Vernon's motion for a preliminary injunction was denied, MIW foreclosed upon the notes. As a result, Mount Vernon suffered a $2,600,000 loss.

DISCUSSION

FSLIC'S Claim Against MIW

FSLIC contends that MIW has unlimited liability for Partridge Associates' obligations because MIW took part in the control of the business of the partnership. Theoretically, a threshold question is presented whether this case is gov-

---

[3]Even if Mount Vernon had ultimately been paid for the mortgages which it turned over to Partridge Associates, the transaction did not make economic sense from Mount Vernon's point of view. The interest on its loan was simply to be the weighted average of the interest rates on the mortgages which were turned over by Mount Vernon to Partridge Associates. Moreover, although Friendship Services assigned to Mount Vernon a 50% interest in the profits (if any) which it was to receive from Partridge Associates, the financial structure of the Partridge project was such that it was highly unlikely that the limited partners would earn any such profits. It appears that what might have motivated Russell into signing the Memorandum of Understanding was that he needed Friendship Savings' participation in an unrelated deal to which Mount Vernon was committed in an amount beyond its lending authority under governing regulations. At approximately the same time, Mount Vernon made a below interest personal loan to Fry in the amount of $50,000.

erned by the "old" Uniform Limited Partnership Act, which was in effect in Maryland when Partridge Associates was formed and which governed Partridge Associates at the time of the occurrence of the events giving rise to this action, or under the "new" Revised Uniform Limited Partnership Act, which became applicable to partnerships formed under the old Act on July 1, 1985. See Md. Corps. & Ass'ns Code Ann., Section 10-1104(2) (Michie Supp.1987). However, this Court believes that insofar as the statutory provisions here involved are concerned, the new Act merely clarifies what was inchoate in the old. Therefore, this threshold question need not be resolved.

Section 7 of [ULPA] provided as follows:

A limited partner shall not become liable as a general partner unless, in addition to the exercise of his rights and powers as a limited partner, he takes part in the control of the business.

Some courts held that, under this section, a limited partner could not be held liable as a general partner unless he had led the plaintiff to believe that he was a general partner. *See, e.g., Western Camps, Inc. v. Riverway Ranch Enterprises*, 70 Cal.App.3d 714, 138 Cal.Rptr. 918 (1977); *Outlet Co. v. Wade*, 377 So.2d 722 (Fla.Dist.Ct.App.1979); *Frigidaire Sales Corp. v. Union Properties, Inc.*, 88 Wash.2d 400, 562 P.2d 244 (1977) (en banc). These cases drew support from an official comment to Section 1 of [RULPA] that "no public policy requires a person who contributes to the capital of a business ... to become bound for the obligations of the business; provided creditors have no reason to believe that the times their credits were extended that such person was so bound." At least one other court held, however, that reliance by the plaintiff was not an element of control under the old Act. *See Delaney v. Fidelity Lease Ltd.*, 526 S.W.2d 543, 545 (Tex.1975). ...

Although undoubtedly in conflict with one another, these two dichotomous lines of authority can be explained by recognizing that the different courts had different focuses. Those which required reliance as an element of control were concentrating upon the external relationship between the plaintiff and the limited partner, and were concerned with the equities arising from that relationship. The Delaney Court, in contrast, appears to have been concerned about the broader public policy of requiring those who choose to accept the benefits of the limited partnership form to preserve the integrity of the partnership's internal relationships. This distinction is made explicit in the new Act. Under [RULPA §303(a)], a limited partner who disregards the limited partnership form to such an extent that he becomes substantially the same as a general partner has unlimited liability regardless of a plaintiff's knowledge of his role. At the same time, a limited partner may have unlimited liability for exercising less than a general partner's power if the fact that he acted as more than a limited partner was actually known to the plaintiff.

Against this background it is too facile simply to say that "control" is a question of fact which must be resolved by the fact-finder. . . .Such an approach begs the question of what "control" means. Rather, analysis must first proceed by asking whether Mount Vernon had actual knowledge that MIW was acting as something more than a limited partner. FSLIC has presented no evidence to prove that fact. There is no indication whatsoever that Russell was led into the Partridge transaction by knowledge of MIW's participation in the partnership, and Donald Eversoll, the then chairman of the Board of Mount Vernon, has testified that he did not learn of the Partridge transaction until November, 1982, long after Mount Vernon had entered the Memorandum of Understanding and turned over the mortgages. Furthermore, the documents promoting the Partridge venture to which FSLIC points as mentioning MIW's participation clearly identify MIW as a limited partner.

Therefore, it must then be asked, as phrased in the new Act, whether MIW's "participation in the control of ... [Partridge Associates] ... was substantially the same as the exercise of the powers of a general partner." As to this question, FSLIC properly maintains that the record is clear that MIW originated the basic concept of Partridge Associates in order to breathe life into a dormant loan. Further, the affidavit of Michael J. Ferraguto, Jr., the president of an American Housing subsidiary which did construction for the Partridge project, does establish that MIW's president attended and participated in periodic operational meetings concerning the progress of the project. However, the law does not confine the role of a limited partner to that of a passive investor, as in a conventional syndication. To the contrary, as is expressly recognized in the new Act, see [RULPA §303(b)], and as was implicit in the old, see *Silvola v. Rowlett*, 129 Colo. 522, 272 P.2d 287 (1954) (en banc), a limited partner may be actively involved in the day to day operation of the partnership's affairs, provided that he does not have ultimate decision making responsibility. Thus, the question is not whether MIW provided advice and counsel to Partridge Associates (which, undoubtedly, it did in light of its long association with the Partridge project) but whether it exercised at least an equal voice in making partnership decisions so as, in effect, to be a general partner. On that issue FSLIC has presented no evidence, and summary judgment against it is therefore proper.

Note

Examine the fate of §303 as revised by the 1985 Amendments. Does it suggest any theory as to the identity of the forces which have sought change in the law governing limited partnerships?

APPENDIX A

THE OFFICIAL TEXT OF THE UNIFORM PARTNERSHIP ACT

PART I
PRELIMINARY PROVISIONS

§ 1. Name of Act

This act may be cited as Uniform Partnership Act.

§ 2. Definition of Terms

In this act, "Court" includes every court and judge having jurisdiction in the case.

"Business" includes every trade, occupation, or profession.

"Person" includes individuals, partnerships, corporations, and other associations.

"Bankrupt" includes bankrupt under the Federal Bankruptcy Act or insolvent under any state insolvent act.

"Conveyance" includes every assignment, lease, mortgage, or encumbrance.

"Real property" includes land and any interest or estate in land.

§ 3. Interpretation of Knowledge and Notice

(1) A person has "knowledge" of a fact within the meaning of this act not only when he has actual knowledge thereof, but also when he has knowledge of such other facts as in the circumstances shows bad faith.

(2) A person has "notice" of a fact within the meaning of this act when the person who claims the benefit of the notice:

(a) States the fact to such person, or

(b) Delivers through the mail, or by other means of communication, a written statement of the fact to such person or to a proper person at his place of business or residence.

§ 4. Rules of Construction

(1) The rule that statutes in derogation of the common law are to be strictly construed shall have no application to this act.

(2) The law of estoppel shall apply under this act.

(3) The law of agency shall apply under this act.

(4) This act shall be so interpreted and construed as to effect its general purpose to make uniform the law of those states which enact it.

(5) This act shall not be construed so as to impair the obligations of any

contract existing when the act goes into effect, nor to affect any action or proceedings begun or right accrued before this act takes effect.

§ 5. Rules for Cases Not Provided for in This Act

In any case not provided for in this act the rules of law and equity, including the law merchant, shall govern.

PART II

NATURE OF A PARTNERSHIP

§ 6. Partnership Defined

(1) A partnership is an association of two or more persons to carry on as co-owners a business for profit.

(2) But any association formed under any other statute of this state, or any statute adopted by authority, other than the authority of this state, is not a partnership under this act, unless such association would have been a partnership in this state prior to the adoption of this act; but this act shall apply to limited partnerships except in so far as the statutes relating to such partnerships are inconsistent herewith.

§ 7. Rules for Determining the Existence of a Partnership

In determining whether a partnership exists, these rules shall apply:

(1) Except as provided by section 16 persons who are not partners as to each other are not partners as to third persons.

(2) Joint tenancy, tenancy in common, tenancy by the entireties, joint property, common property, or part ownership does not of itself establish a partnership, whether such co-owners do or do not share any profits made by the use of the property.

(3) The sharing of gross returns does not of itself establish a partnership, whether or not the persons sharing them have a joint or common right or interest in any property from which the returns are derived.

(4) The receipt by a person of a share of the profits of a business is prima facie evidence that he is a partner in the business, but no such inference shall be drawn if such profits were received in payment:

(a) As a debt by installments or otherwise,

(b) As wages of an employee or rent to a landlord,

(c) As an annuity to a widow or representative of a deceased partner,

(d) As interest on a loan, though the amount of payment vary with the profits of the business,

(e) As the consideration for the sale of a good-will of a business or other property by installments or otherwise.

§ 8. Partnership Property

(1) All property originally brought into the partnership stock or subsequently acquired by purchase or otherwise, on account of the partnership, is partnership

property.

(2) Unless the contrary intention appears, property acquired with partnership funds is partnership property.

(3) Any estate in real property may be acquired in the partnership name. Title so acquired can be conveyed only in the partnership name.

(4) A conveyance to a partnership in the partnership name, though without words of inheritance, passes the entire estate of the grantor unless a contrary intent appears.

PART III
RELATIONS OF PARTNERS TO PERSONS DEALING WITH THE PARTNERSHIP

§ 9. Partner Agent of Partnership as to Partnership Business

(1) Every partner is an agent of the partnership for the purpose of its business, and the act of every partner, including the execution in the partnership name of any instrument, for apparently carrying on in the usual way the business of the partnership of which he is a member binds the partnership, unless the partner so acting has in fact no authority to act for the partnership in the particular matter, and the person with whom he is dealing has knowledge of the fact that he has no such authority.

(2) An act of a partner which is not apparently for the carrying on of the business of the partnership in the usual way does not bind the partnership unless authorized by the other partners.

(3) Unless authorized by the other partners or unless they have abandoned the business, one or more but less than all the partners have no authority to:

(a) Assign the partnership property in trust for creditors or on the assignee's promise to pay the debts of the partnership,

(b) Dispose of the good-will of the business,

(c) Do any other act which would make it impossible to carry on the ordinary business of a partnership,

(d) Confess a judgment,

(e) Submit a partnership claim or liability to arbitration or reference.

(4) No act of a partner in contravention of a restriction on authority shall bind the partnership to persons having knowledge of the restriction.

§ 10. Conveyance of Real Property of the Partnership

(1) Where title to real property is in the partnership name, any partner may convey title to such property by a conveyance executed in the partnership name; but the partnership may recover such property unless the partner's act binds the partnership under the provisions of paragraph (1) of section 9, or unless such property has been conveyed by the grantee or a person claiming through such grantee to a holder for value without knowledge that the partner, in making the conveyance, has exceeded his authority.

(2) Where title to real property is in the name of the partnership, a conveyance

executed by a partner, in his own name, passes the equitable interest of the partnership, provided the act is one within the authority of the partner under the provisions of paragraph (1) of section 9.

(3) Where title to real property is in the name of one or more but not all the partners, and the record does not disclose the right of the partnership, the partners in whose name the title stands may convey title to such property, but the partnership may recover such property if the partners' act does not bind the partnership under the provisions of paragraph (1) of section 9, unless the purchaser or his assignee, is a holder for value, without knowledge.

(4) Where the title to real property is in the name of one or more or all the partners, or in a third person in trust for the partnership, a conveyance executed by a partner in the partnership name, or in his own name, passes the equitable interest of the partnership, provided the act is one within the authority of the partner under the provisions of paragraph (1) of section 9.

(5) Where the title to real property is in the names of all the partners a conveyance executed by all the partners passes all their rights in such property.

§ 11. Partnership Bound by Admission of Partner

An admission or representation made by any partner concerning partnership affairs within the scope of his authority as conferred by this act is evidence against the partnership.

§ 12. Partnership Charged with Knowledge of or Notice to Partner

Notice to any partner of any matter relating to partnership affairs, and the knowledge of the partner acting in the particular matter, acquired while a partner or then present to his mind, and the knowledge of any other partner who reasonably could and should have communicated it to the acting partner, operate as notice to or knowledge of the partnership, except in the case of a fraud on the partnership committed by or with the consent of that partner.

§ 13. Partnership Bound by Partner's Wrongful Act

Where, by any wrongful act or omission of any partner acting in the ordinary course of the business of the partnership or with the authority of his co-partners, loss or injury is caused to any person, not being a partner in the partnership, or any penalty is incurred, the partnership is liable therefor to the same extent as the partner so acting or omitting to act.

§ 14. Partnership Bound by Partner's Breach of Trust

The partnership is bound to make good the loss:

(a) Where one partner acting within the scope of his apparent authority receives money or property of a third person and misapplies it; and

(b) Where the partnership in the course of its business receives money or property of a third person and the money or property so received is misapplied by any partner while it is in the custody of the partnership.

§ 15. Nature of Partner's Liability

All partners are liable

(a) Jointly and severally for everything chargeable to the partnership under sections 13 and 14.

(b) Jointly for all other debts and obligations of the partnership; but any partner may enter into a separate obligation to perform a partnership contract.

§ 16. Partner by Estoppel

(1) When a person, by words spoken or written or by conduct, represents himself, or consents to another representing him to any one, as a partner in an existing partnership or with one or more persons not actual partners, he is liable to any such person to whom such representation has been made, who has, on the faith of such representation, given credit to the actual or apparent partnership, and if he has made such representation or consented to its being made in a public manner he is liable to such person, whether the representation has or has not been made or communicated to such person so giving credit by or with the knowledge of the apparent partner making the representation or consenting to its being made.

(a) When a partnership liability results, he is liable as though he were an actual member of the partnership.

(b) When no partnership liability results, he is liable jointly with the other persons, if any, so consenting to the contract or representation as to incur liability, otherwise separately.

(2) When a person has been thus represented to be a partner in an existing partnership, or with one or more persons not actual partners, he is an agent of the persons consenting to such representation to bind them to the same extent and in the same manner as though he were a partner in fact, with respect to persons who rely upon the representation. Where all the members of the existing partnership consent to the representation, a partnership act or obligation results; but in all other cases it is the joint act or obligation of the person acting and the persons consenting to the representation.

§ 17. Liability of Incoming Partner

A person admitted as a partner into an existing partnership is liable for all the obligations of the partnership arising before his admission as though he had been a partner when such obligations were incurred, except that this liability shall be satisfied only out of partnership property.

PART IV
RELATIONS OF PARTNERS TO ONE ANOTHER

§ 18. Rules Determining Rights and Duties of Partners

The rights and duties of the partners in relation to the partnership shall be determined, subject to any agreement between them, by the following rules:

(a) Each partner shall be repaid his contributions, whether by way of capital or advances to the partnership property and share equally in the profits and surplus remaining after all liabilities, including those to partners, are satisfied; and must contribute towards the losses, whether of capital or otherwise, sustained by the partnership according to his share in the profits.

(b) The partnership must indemnify every partner in respect of payments made and personal liabilities reasonably incurred by him in the ordinary and proper conduct of its business, or for the preservation of its business or property.

(c) A partner, who in aid of the partnership makes any payment or advance beyond the amount of capital which he agreed to contribute, shall be paid interest from the date of the payment or advance.

(d) A partner shall receive interest on the capital contributed by him only from the date when repayment should be made.

(e) All partners have equal rights in the management and conduct of the partnership business.

(f) No partner is entitled to remuneration for acting in the partnership business, except that a surviving partner is entitled to reasonable compensation for his services in winding up the partnership affairs.

(g) No person can become a member of a partnership without the consent of all the partners.

(h) Any difference arising as to ordinary matters connected with the partnership business may be decided by a majority of the partners; but no act in contravention of any agreement between the partners may be done rightfully without the consent of all the partners.

§ 19. Partnership Books

The partnership books shall be kept, subject to any agreement between the partners, at the principal place of business of the partnership, and every partner shall at all times have access to and may inspect and copy any of them.

§ 20. Duty of Partners to Render Information

Partners shall render on demand true and full information of all things affecting the partnership to any partner or the legal representative of any deceased partner or partner under legal disability.

§ 21. Partner Accountable as a Fiduciary

(1) Every partner must account to the partnership for any benefit, and hold as trustee for it any profits derived by him without the consent of the other partners from any transaction connected with the formation, conduct, or liquidation of the partnership or from any use by him of its property.

(2) This section applies also to the representatives of a deceased partner engaged in the liquidation of the affairs of the partnership as the personal representatives of the last surviving partner.

§ 22. Right to an Account

Any partner shall have the right to a formal account as to partnership affairs:

(a) If he is wrongfully excluded from the partnership business or possession of its property by his co-partners,

(b) If the right exists under the terms of any agreement,

(c) As provided by section 21,

(d) Whenever other circumstances render it just and reasonable.

§ 23. Continuation of Partnership Beyond Fixed Term

(1) When a partnership for a fixed term or particular undertaking is continued after the termination of such term or particular undertaking without any express agreement, the rights and duties of the partners remain the same as they were at such termination, so far as is consistent with a partnership at will.

(2) A continuation of the business by the partners or such of them as habitually acted therein during the term, without any settlement or liquidation of the partnership affairs, is prima facie evidence of a continuation of the partnership.

PART V

PROPERTY RIGHTS OF A PARTNER

§ 24. Extent of Property Rights of a Partner

The property rights of a partner are (1) his rights in specific partnership property, (2) his interest in the partnership, and (3) his right to participate in the management.

§ 25. Nature of a Partner's Right in Specific Partnership Property

(1) A partner is co-owner with his partners of specific partnership property holding as a tenant in partnership.

(2) The incidents of this tenancy are such that:

(a) A partner, subject to the provisions of this act and to any agreement between the partners, has an equal right with his partners to possess specific partnership property for partnership purposes; but he has no right to possess such property for any other purpose without the consent of his partners.

(b) A partner's right in specific partnership property is not assignable except in connection with the assignment of rights of all the partners in the same property.

(c) A partner's right in specific partnership property is not subject to attachment or execution, except on a claim against the partnership. When partnership property is attached for a partnership debt the partners, or any of them, or the representatives of a deceased partner, cannot claim any right under the homestead or exemption laws.

(d) On the death of a partner his right in specific partnership property vests in the surviving partner or partners, except where the deceased was the last surviving partner, when his right in such property vests in his legal representative. Such surviving partner or partners, or the legal representative of the last surviving partner, has no right to possess the partnership property for any but a partnership purpose.

(e) A partner's right in specific partnership property is not subject to dower, curtesy, or allowances to widows, heirs, or next of kin.

§ 26. Nature of Partner's Interest in the Partnership

A partner's interest in the partnership is his share of the profits and surplus, and the same is personal property.

§ 27. Assignment of Partner's Interest

(1) A conveyance by a partner of his interest in the partnership does not of itself dissolve the partnership, nor, as against the other partners in the absence of agreement, entitle the assignee, during the continuance of the partnership, to interfere in the management or administration of the partnership business or affairs, or to require any information or account of partnership transactions, or to inspect the partnership books; but it merely entitles the assignee to receive in accordance with his contract the profits to which the assigning partner would otherwise be entitled.

(2) In case of a dissolution of the partnership, the assignee is entitled to receive his assignor's interest and may require an account from the date only of the last account agreed to by all the partners.

§ 28. Partner's Interest Subject to Charging Order

(1) On due application to a competent court by any judgment creditor of a partner, the court which entered the judgment, order, or decree, or any other court, may charge the interest of the debtor partner with payment of the unsatisfied amount of such judgment debt with interest thereon; and may then or later appoint a receiver of his share of the profits, and of any other money due or to fall due to him in respect of the partnership, and make all other orders, directions, accounts and inquiries which the debtor partner might have made, or which the circumstances of the case may require.

(2) The interest charged may be redeemed at any time before foreclosure, or in case of a sale being directed by the court may be purchased without thereby causing a dissolution:

(a) With separate property, by any one or more of the partners, or

(b) With partnership property, by any one or more of the partners with the consent of all the partners whose interests are not so charged or sold.

(3) Nothing in this act shall be held to deprive a partner of his right, if any, under the exemption laws, as regards his interest in the partnership.

PART VI

DISSOLUTION AND WINDING UP

§ 29. Dissolution Defined

The dissolution of a partnership is the change in the relation of the partners caused by any partner ceasing to be associated in the carrying on as distinguished from the winding up of the business.

§ 30. Partnership not Terminated by Dissolution

On dissolution the partnership is not terminated, but continues until the winding up of partnership affairs is completed.

§ 31. Causes of Dissolution

Dissolution is caused:

(1) Without violation of the agreement between the partners,

(a) By the termination of the definite term or particular undertaking specified in the agreement,

(b) By the express will of any partner when no definite term or particular undertaking is specified,

(c) By the express will of all the partners who have not assigned their interests or suffered them to be charged for their separate debts, either before or after the termination of any specified term or particular undertaking,

(d) By the expulsion of any partner from the business bona fide in accordance with such a power conferred by the agreement between the partners;

(2) In contravention of the agreement between the partners, where the circumstances do not permit a dissolution under any other provision of this section, by the express will of any partner at any time;

(3) By any event which makes it unlawful for the business of the partnership to be carried on or for the members to carry it on in partnership;

(4) By the death of any partner;

(5) By the bankruptcy of any partner or the partnership;

(6) By decree of court under section 32.

§ 32. Dissolution by Decree of Court

(1) On application by or for a partner the court shall decree a dissolution whenever:

(a) A partner has been declared a lunatic in any judicial proceeding or is shown to be of unsound mind,

(b) A partner becomes in any other way incapable of performing his part of the partnership contract,

(c) A partner has been guilty of such conduct as tends to affect prejudicially the carrying on of the business,

(d) A partner wilfully or persistently commits a breach of the partnership agreement, or otherwise so conducts himself in matters relating to the partnership business that it is not reasonably practicable to carry on the business in partnership with him,

(e) The business of the partnership can only be carried on at a loss,

(f) Other circumstances render a dissolution equitable.

(2) On the application of the purchaser of a partner's interest under sections 28 or 29 [should read 27 or 28];

(a) After the termination of the specified term or particular undertaking,

(b) At any time if the partnership was a partnership at will when the interest was assigned or when the charging order was issued.

§ 33. General Effect of Dissolution on Authority of Partner

Except so far as may be necessary to wind up partnership affairs or to complete transactions begun but not then finished, dissolution terminates all authority of any partner to act for the partnership,

(1) With respect to the partners,

(a) When the dissolution is not by the act, bankruptcy or death of a partner; or

(b) When the dissolution is by such act, bankruptcy or death of a partner, in cases where section 34 so requires.

(2) With respect to persons not partners, as declared in section 35.

§ 34. Right of Partner to Contribution from Co-partners after Dissolution

Where the dissolution is caused by the act, death or bankruptcy of a partner, each partner is liable to his co-partners for his share of any liability created by any partner acting for the partnership as if the partnership had not been dissolved unless

(a) The dissolution being by act of any partner, the partner acting for the partnership had knowledge of the dissolution, or

(b) The dissolution being by the death or bankruptcy of a partner, the partner acting for the partnership had knowledge or notice of the death or bankruptcy.

§ 35. Power of Partner to Bind Partnership to Third Persons after Dissolution

(1) After dissolution a partner can bind the partnership except as provided in Paragraph (3).

(a) By any act appropriate for winding up partnership affairs or completing transactions unfinished at dissolution;

(b) By any transaction which would bind the partnership if dissolution had not taken place, provided the other party to the transaction

(I) Had extended credit to the partnership prior to dissolution and had no knowledge or notice of the dissolution; or

(II) Though he had not so extended credit, had nevertheless known of the partnership prior to dissolution, and, having no knowledge or notice of dissolution, the fact of dissolution had not been advertised in a newspaper of general circulation in the place (or in each place if more than one) at which the partnership business was regularly carried on.

(2) The liability of a partner under Paragraph (1b) shall be satisfied out of partnership assets alone when such partner had been prior to dissolution

(a) Unknown as a partner to the person with whom the contract is made; and

(b) So far unknown and inactive in partnership affairs that the business reputation of the partnership could not be said to have been in any degree due to his connection with it.

(3) The partnership is in no case bound by any act of a partner after dissolution

(a) Where the partnership is dissolved because it is unlawful to carry on the business, unless the act is appropriate for winding up partnership affairs; or

(b) Where the partner has become bankrupt; or

(c) Where the partner has no authority to wind up partnership affairs; except by a transaction with one who

(I) Had extended credit to the partnership prior to dissolution and had no knowledge or notice of his want of authority; or

(II) Had not extended credit to the partnership prior to dissolution, and, having no knowledge or notice of his want of authority, the fact of his want of authority has not been advertised in the manner provided for advertising the fact of dissolution in Paragraph (1b II).

(4) Nothing in this section shall affect the liability under Section 16 of any person who after dissolution represents himself or consents to another representing him as a partner in a partnership engaged in carrying on business.

§ 36. Effect of Dissolution on Partner's Existing Liability

(1) The dissolution of the partnership does not of itself discharge the existing liability of any partner.

(2) A partner is discharged from any existing liability upon dissolution of the partnership by an agreement to that effect between himself, the partnership creditor and the person or partnership continuing the business; and such agreement may be inferred from the course of dealing between the creditor having knowledge of the dissolution and the person or partnership continuing the business.

(3) Where a person agrees to assume the existing obligations of a dissolved partnership, the partners whose obligations have been assumed shall be discharged from any liability to any creditor of the partnership who, knowing of the agreement, consents to a material alteration in the nature or time of payment of such obligations.

(4) The individual property of a deceased partner shall be liable for all obligations of the partnership incurred while he was a partner but subject to the prior payment of his separate debts.

§ 37. Right to Wind Up

Unless otherwise agreed the partners who have not wrongfully dissolved the partnership or the legal representative of the last surviving partner, not bankrupt, has the right to wind up the partnership affairs; provided, however, that any partner, his legal representative or his assignee, upon cause shown, may obtain winding up by the court.

§ 38. Rights of Partners to Application of Partnership Property

(1) When dissolution is caused in any way, except in contravention of the partnership agreement, each partner, as against his co-partners and all persons claiming through them in respect of their interests in the partnership, unless otherwise agreed, may have the partnership property applied to discharge its liabilities, and the surplus applied to pay in cash the net amount owing to the respective partners. But if dissolution is caused by expulsion of a partner, bona fide under the partnership agreement and if the expelled partner is discharged from all partnership

liabilities, either by payment or agreement under section 36(2), he shall receive in cash only the net amount due him from the partnership.

(2) When dissolution is caused in contravention of the partnership agreement the rights of the partners shall be as follows:

(a) Each partner who has not caused dissolution wrongfully shall have,

I. All the rights specified in paragraph (1) of this section, and

II. The right, as against each partner who has caused the dissolution wrongfully, to damages for breach of the agreement.

(b) The partners who have not caused the dissolution wrongfully, if they all desire to continue the business in the same name, either by themselves or jointly with others, may do so, during the agreed term for the partnership and for that purpose may possess the partnership property, provided they secure the payment by bond approved by the court, or pay to any partner who has caused the dissolution wrongfully, the value of his interest in the partnership at the dissolution, less any damages recoverable under clause (2a II) of this section, and in like manner indemnify him against all present or future partnership liabilities.

(c) A partner who has caused the dissolution wrongfully shall have:

I. If the business is not continued under the provisions of paragraph (2b) all the rights of a partner under paragraph (1), subject to clause (2a II), of this section,

II. If the business is continued under paragraph (2b) of this section the right as against his co-partners and all claiming through them in respect of their interests in the partnership, to have the value of his interest in the partnership, less any damages caused to his co-partners by the dissolution, ascertained and paid to him in cash, or the payment secured by bond approved by the court, and to be released from all existing liabilities of the partnership; but in ascertaining the value of the partner's interest the value of the good-will of the business shall not be considered.

§ 39. Rights Where Partnership is Dissolved for Fraud or Misrepresentation

Where a partnership contract is rescinded on the ground of the fraud or misrepresentation of one of the parties thereto, the party entitled to rescind is, without prejudice to any other right, entitled,

(a) To a lien on, or a right of retention of, the surplus of the partnership property after satisfying the partnership liabilities to third persons for any sum of money paid by him for the purchase of an interest in the partnership and for any capital or advances contributed by him; and

(b) To stand, after all liabilities to third persons have been satisfied, in the place of the creditors of the partnership for any payments made by him in respect of the partnership liabilities; and

(c) To be indemnified by the person guilty of the fraud or making the representation against all debts and liabilities of the partnership.

§ 40. Rules for Distribution

In settling accounts between the partners after dissolution, the following rules shall be observed, subject to any agreement to the contrary:

(a) The assets of the partnership are:

I. The partnership property,

II. The contributions of the partners necessary for the payment of all the liabilities specified in clause (b) of this paragraph.

(b) The liabilities of the partnership shall rank in order of payment, as follows:

I. Those owing to creditors other than partners,

II. Those owing to partners other than for capital and profits,

III. Those owing to partners in respect of capital,

IV. Those owing to partners in respect of profits.

(c) The assets shall be applied in the order of their declaration in clause (a) of this paragraph to the satisfaction of the liabilities.

(d) The partners shall contribute, as provided by section 18(a) the amount necessary to satisfy the liabilities; but if any, but not all, of the partners are insolvent, or, not being subject to process, refuse to contribute, the other partners shall contribute their share of the liabilities, and, in the relative proportions in which they share the profits, the additional amount necessary to pay the liabilities.

(e) An assignee for the benefit of creditors or any person appointed by the court shall have the right to enforce the contributions specified in clause (d) of this paragraph.

(f) Any partner or his legal representative shall have the right to enforce the contributions specified in clause (d) of this paragraph, to the extent of the amount which he has paid in excess of his share of the liability.

(g) The individual property of a deceased partner shall be liable for the contributions specified in clause (d) of this paragraph.

(h) When partnership property and the individual properties of the partners are in possession of a court for distribution, partnership creditors shall have priority on partnership property and separate creditors on individual property, saving the rights of lien or secured creditors as heretofore.

(i) Where a partner has become bankrupt or his estate is insolvent the claims against his separate property shall rank in the following order:

I. Those owing to separate creditors,

II. Those owing to partnership creditors,

III. Those owing to partners by way of contribution.

§ 41. Liability of Persons Continuing the Business in Certain Cases

(1) When any new partner is admitted into an existing partnership, or when any partner retires and assigns (or the representative of the deceased partner assigns) his rights in partnership property to two or more of the partners, or to one or more of the partners and one or more third persons, if the business is continued without liquidation of the partnership affairs, creditors of the first or dissolved partnership are also creditors of the partnership so continuing the business.

(2) When all but one partner retire and assign (or the representative of a deceased partner assigns) their rights in partnership property to the remaining

300

partner, who continues the business without liquidation of partnership affairs, either alone or with others, creditors of the dissolved partnership are also creditors of the person or partnership so continuing the business.

(3) When any partner retires or dies and the business of the dissolved partnership is continued as set forth in paragraphs (1) and (2) of this section, with the consent of the retired partners or the representative of the deceased partner, but without any assignment of his right in partnership property, rights of creditors of the dissolved partnership and of the creditors of the person or partnership continuing the business shall be as if such assignment had been made.

(4) When all the partners or their representatives assign their rights in partnership property to one or more third persons who promise to pay the debts and who continue the business of the dissolved partnership, creditors of the dissolved partnership are also creditors of the person or partnership continuing the business.

(5) When any partner wrongfully causes a dissolution and the remaining partners continue the business under the provisions of section 38(2b), either alone or with others, and without liquidation of the partnership affairs, creditors of the dissolved partnership are also creditors of the person or partnership continuing the business.

(6) When a partner is expelled and the remaining partners continue the business either alone or with others, without liquidation of the partnership affairs, creditors of the dissolved partnership are also creditors of the person or partnership continuing the business.

(7) The liability of a third person becoming a partner in the partnership continuing the business, under this section, to the creditors of the dissolved partnership shall be satisfied out of partnership property only.

(8) When the business of a partnership after dissolution is continued under any conditions set forth in this section the creditors of the dissolved partnership, as against the separate creditors of the retiring or deceased partner or the representative of the deceased partner, have a prior right to any claim of the retired partner or the representative of the deceased partner against the person or partnership continuing the business, on account of the retired or deceased partner's interest in the dissolved partnership or on account of any consideration promised for such interest or for his right in partnership property.

(9) Nothing in this section shall be held to modify any right of creditors to set aside any assignment on the ground of fraud.

(10) The use by the person or partnership continuing the business of the partnership name, or the name of a deceased partner as part thereof, shall not of itself make the individual property of the deceased partner liable for any debts contracted by such person or partnership.

§ 42. Rights of Retiring or Estate of Deceased Partner When the Business is Continued

When any partner retires or dies, and the business is continued under any of the conditions set forth in section 41(1, 2, 3, 5, 6), or section 38(2b) without any settlement of accounts as between him or his estate and the person or partnership continuing the business, unless otherwise agreed, he or his legal representative as against such persons or partnership may have the value of his interest at the date of dissolution ascertained, and shall receive as an ordinary creditor an amount equal to the value of his interest in the dissolved partnership with interest, or, at his option or at the option of his legal representative, in lieu of interest, the profits attributable to the use of his right in the property of the dissolved partnership; provided that the creditors of the dissolved partnership as against the separate creditors, or the representative of the retired or deceased partner, shall have priority on any claim arising under this section, as provided by section 41(8) of this act.

§ 43. Accrual of Actions

The right to an account of his interest shall accrue to any partner, or his legal representative, as against the winding up partners or the surviving partners or the person or partnership continuing the business, at the date of dissolution, in the absence of any agreement to the contrary.

PART VII

MISCELLANEOUS PROVISIONS

§ 44. When Act Takes Effect

This act shall take effect on the _____ day of _____ one thousand nine hundred and _____ .

§ 45. Legislation Repealed

All acts or parts of acts inconsistent with this act are hereby repealed.

APPENDIX B

OFFICIAL TEXT OF THE UNIFORM LIMITED PARTNERSHIP ACT

§ 1. Limited partnership defined

A limited partnership is a partnership formed by two or more persons under the provisions of Section 2, having as members one or more general partners and one or more limited partners. The limited partners as such shall not be bound by the obligations of the partnership.

§ 2. Formation

(1) Two or more persons desiring to form a limited partnership shall

(a) Sign and swear to a certificate, which shall state

I. The name of the partnership,

II. The character of the business,

III. The location of the principal place of business,

IV. The name and place of residence of each member; general and limited partners being respectively designated,

V. The term for which the partnership is to exist,

VI. The amount of cash and a description of and the agreed value of the other property contributed by each limited partner,

VII. The additional contributions, if any, agreed to be made by each limited partner and the times at which or events on the happening of which they shall be made,

VIII. The time, if agreed upon, when the contribution of each limited partner is to be returned,

IX. The share of the profits or the other compensation by way of income which each limited partner shall receive by reason of his contribution,

X. The right, if given, of a limited partner to substitute an assignee as contributor in his place, and the terms and conditions of the substitution,

XI. The right, if given, of the partners to admit additional limited partners,

XII. The right, if given, of one or more of the limited partners to priority over other limited partners, as to contributions or as to compensation by way of income, and the nature of such priority,

XIII. The right, if given, of the remaining general partner or partners to continue the business on the death, retirement or insanity of a general partner, and

XIV. The right, if given, of a limited partner to demand and receive property other than cash in return for his contribution.

(b) File for record the certificate in the office of [here designate the proper office].

(2) A limited partnership is formed if there has been substantial compliance in

good faith with the requirements of paragraph (1).

§ 3. Business which may be carried on

A limited partnership may carry on any business which a partnership without limited partners may carry on, except [here designate the business to be prohibited].

§ 4. Character of limited partner's contribution

The contributions of a limited partner may be cash or other property, but not services.

§ 5. A name not to contain surname of limited partner; exceptions

(1) The surname of a limited partner shall not appear in the partnership name, unless

(a) It is also the surname of a general partner, or

(b) Prior to the time when the limited partner became such the business had been carried on under a name in which his surname appeared.

(2) A limited partner whose name appears in a partnership name contrary to the provisions of paragraph (1) is liable as a general partner to partnership creditors who extend credit to the partnership without actual knowledge that he is not a general partner.

§ 6. Liability for false statements in certificate

If the certificate contains a false statement, one who suffers loss by reliance on such statement may hold liable any party to the certificate who knew the statement to be false.

(a) At the time he signed the certificate, or

(b) Subsequently, but within a sufficient time before the statement was relied upon to enable him to cancel or amend the certificate, or to file a petition for its cancellation or amendment as provided in Section 25(3).

§ 7. Limited partner not liable to creditors

A limited partner shall not become liable as a general partner unless, in addition to the exercise of his rights and powers as a limited partner, he takes part in the control of the business.

§ 8. Admission of additional limited partners

After the formation of a limited partnership, additional limited partners may be admitted upon filing an amendment to the original certificate in accordance with the requirements of Section 25.

§ 9. Rights, powers and liabilities of a general partner

(1) A general partner shall have all the rights and powers and be subject to all the restrictions and liabilities of a partner in a partnership without limited partners, except that without the written consent or ratification of the specific act by all the limited partners, a general partner or all of the general partners have no authority to

(a) Do any act in contravention of the certificate,

(b) Do any act which would make it impossible to carry on the ordinary business of the partnership,

(c) Confess a judgment against the partnership,

(d) Possess partnership property, or assign their rights in specific partnership property, for other than a partnership purpose,

(e) Admit a person as a general partner,

(f) Admit a person as a limited partner, unless the right so to do is given in the certificate,

(g) Continue the business with partnership property on the death, retirement or insanity of a general partner, unless the right so to do is given in the certificate.

§ 10. Rights of a limited partner

(1) A limited partner shall have the same rights as a general partner to

(a) Have the partnership books kept at the principal place of business of the partnership, and at all times to inspect and copy any of them.

(b) Have on demand true and full information of all things affecting the partnership, and a formal account of partnership affairs whenever circumstances render it just and reasonable, and

(c) Have dissolution and winding up by decree of court.

(2) A limited partner shall have the right to receive a share of the profits or other compensation by way of income, and to the return of his contribution as provided in Sections 15 and 16.

§ 11. Status of person erroneously believing himself a limited partner

A person who has contributed to the capital of a business conducted by a person or partnership erroneously believing that he has become a limited partner in a limited partnership, is not, by reason of his exercise of the rights of a limited partner, a general partner with the person or in the partnership carrying on the business, or bound by the obligations of such person or partnership; provided that on ascertaining the mistake he promptly renounces his interest in the profits of the business, or other compensation by way of income.

§ 12. One person both general and limited partner

(1) A person may be a general partner and a limited partner in the same partnership at the same time.

(2) A person who is a general, and also at the same time a limited partner, shall have all the rights and powers and be subject to all restrictions of a general partner; except that, in respect to his contribution, he shall have the rights against the other members which he would have had if he were not also a general partner.

§ 13. Loans and other business transactions with limited partner

(1) A limited partner also may loan money to and transact other business with the partnership, and, unless he is also a general partner, receive on account of

resulting claims against the partnership, with general creditors, a pro rata share of the assets. No limited partner shall in respect to any such claim

(a) Receive or hold as collateral security any partnership property, or

(b) Receive from a general partner or the partnership any payment, conveyance, or release from liability, if at the time the assets of the partnership are not sufficient to discharge partnership liabilities to persons not claiming as general or limited partners,

(2) The receiving of collateral security, or a payment, conveyance, or release in violation of the provisions of paragraph (1) is a fraud on the creditors of the partnership.

§ 14. Relation of limited partners inter se

Where there are several limited partners the members may agree that one or more of the limited partners shall have a priority over other limited partners as to the return of their contributions as to their compensation by way of income, or as to any other matter. If such an agreement is made it shall be stated in the certificate, and in the absence of such a statement all the limited partners shall stand upon equal footing.

§ 15. Compensation of limited partner

A limited partner may receive from the partnership the share of the profits or the compensation by way of income stipulated for in the certificate; provided, that after such payment is made, whether from the property of the partnership or that of a general partner, the partnership assets are in excess of all liabilities of the partnership except liabilities to limited partners on account of their contributions and to general partners.

§ 16. Withdrawal or reduction of limited partner's contribution

(1) A limited partner shall not receive from a general partner or out of partnership property any part of his contribution until

(a) All liabilities of the partnership, except liabilities to general partners and to limited partners on account of their contributions, have been paid or there remains property of the partnership sufficient to pay them,

(b) The consent of all members is had, unless the return of the contribution may be rightfully demanded under the provisions of paragraph (2), and

(c) The certificate is canceled or so amended as to set forth the withdrawal or reduction.

(2) Subject to the provisions of paragraph (1) a limited partner may rightfully demand the return of his contribution

(a) On the dissolution of a partnership, or

(b) When the date specified in the certificate for its return has arrived, or

(c) After he has given six months' notice in writing to all other members, if no time is specified in the certificate either for the return of the contribution or for the dissolution of the partnership,

(3) In the absence of any statement in the certificate to the contrary or the consent of all members, a limited partner, irrespective of the nature of his contribution, has only the right to demand and receive cash in return for his contribution.

(4) A limited partner may have the partnership dissolved and its affairs wound up when

(a) He rightfully but unsuccessfully demands the return of his contribution, or

(b) The other liabilities of the partnership have not been paid, or the partnership property is insufficient for their payment as required by paragraph (1a) and the limited partner would otherwise be entitled to the return of his contribution.

§ 17. Liability of limited partner to partnership

(1) A limited partner is liable to the partnership

(a) For the difference between his contribution as actually made and that stated in the certificate as having been made, and

(b) For any unpaid contribution which he agreed in the certificate to make in the future at the time and on the conditions stated in the certificate.

(2) A limited partner holds as trustee for the partnership

(a) Specific property stated in the certificate as contributed by him, but which was not contributed or which has been wrongfully returned, and

(b) Money or other property wrongfully paid or conveyed to him on account of his contribution.

(3) The liabilities of a limited partner as set forth in this section can be waived or compromised only by the consent of all members; but a waiver or compromise shall not affect the right of a creditor of a partnership who extended credit or whose claim arose after the filing and before a cancellation or amendment of the certificate, to enforce such liabilities.

(4) When a contributor has rightfully received the return in whole or in part of the capital of his contribution, he is nevertheless liable to the partnership for any sum not in excess of such return with interest, necessary to discharge its liabilities to all creditors who extended credit or whose claims arose before such return.

§ 18. Nature of limited partner's interest in partnership

A limited partner's interest in the partnership is personal property.

§ 19. Assignment of limited partner's interest

(1) A limited partner's interest is assignable.

(2) A substituted limited partner is a person admitted to all the rights of a limited partner who has died or has assigned his interest in a partnership.

(3) An assignee, who does not become a substituted limited partner, has no right to require any information or account of the partnership transactions or to inspect the partnership books; he is only entitled to receive the share of the profits or other compensation by way of income, or the return of his contribution, to which his assignor would otherwise be entitled.

(4) An assignee shall have the right to become a substituted limited partner if

all the members (except the assignor) consent thereto or if the assignor, being thereunto empowered by the certificate, gives the assignee that right.

(5) An assignee becomes a substituted limited partner when the certificate is appropriately amended in accordance with Section 25.

(6) The substituted limited partner has all the rights and powers, and is subject to all the restrictions and liabilities of his assignor, except those liabilities of which he was ignorant at the time he became a limited partner and which could not be ascertained from the certificate.

(7) The substitution of the assignee as a limited partner does not release the assignor from liability to the partnership under Sections 6 and 17.

§ 20. Effect of retirement, death or insanity of a general partner

The retirement, death or insanity of a general partner dissolves the partnership, unless the business is continued by the remaining general partners

(a) Under a right so to do stated in the certificate, or

(b) With the consent of all members.

§ 21. Death of limited partner

(1) On the death of a limited partner his executor or administrator shall have all the rights of a limited partner for the purpose of settling his estate, and such power as the deceased had to constitute his assignee a substituted limited partner.

(2) The estate of a deceased limited partner shall be liable for all his liabilities as a limited partner.

§ 22. Rights of creditors of limited partner

(1) On due application to a court of competent jurisdiction by any judgment creditor of a limited partner, the court may charge the interest of the indebted limited partner with payment of the unsatisfied amount of the judgment debt; and may appoint a receiver, and make all other orders, directions, and inquiries which the circumstances of the case may require.

> In those states where a creditor on beginning an action can attach debts due the defendant before he has obtained a judgment against the defendant it is recommended that paragraph (1) of this section read as follows:

> On due application to a court of competent jurisdiction by any creditor of a limited partner, the court may charge the interest of the indebted limited partner with payment of the unsatisfied amount of such claim; and may appoint a receiver, and make all other orders, directions, and inquiries which the circumstances of the case may require.

(2) The interest may be redeemed with the separate property of any general partner, but may not be redeemed with partnership property.

(3) The remedies conferred by paragraph (1) shall not be deemed exclusive of others which may exist.

(4) Nothing in this act shall be held to deprive a limited partner of his statutory

exemption.

§ 23. Distribution of assets

(1) In settling accounts after dissolution the liabilities of the partnership shall be entitled to payment in the following order:

(a) Those to creditors, in the order of priority as provided by law, except those to limited partners on account of their contributions, and to general partners,

(b) Those to limited partners in respect to their share of the profits and other compensation by way of income on their contributions,

(c) Those to limited partners in respect to the capital of their contributions,

(d) Those to general partners other than for capital and profits,

(e) Those to general partners in respect to profits,

(f) Those to general partners in respect to capital.

(2) Subject to any statement in the certificate or to subsequent agreement, limited partners share in the partnership assets in respect to their claims for capital and in respect to their claims for profits or for compensation by way of income on their contributions respectively, in proportion to the respective amounts of such claims.

§ 24. When certificate shall be canceled or amended

(1) The certificate shall be canceled when the partnership is dissolved or all limited partners cease to be such.

(2) A certificate shall be amended when

(a) There is a change in the name of the partnership or in the amount or character of the contribution of any limited partner,

(b) A person is substituted as a limited partner,

(c) An additional limited partner is admitted,

(d) A person is admitted as a general partner,

(e) A general partner retires, dies or becomes insane, and the business in continued under Section 20,

(f) There is a change in the character of the business of the partnership,

(g) There is a false or erroneous statement in the certificate,

(h) There is a change in the time as stated in the certificate for the dissolution of the partnership or for the return of a contribution,

(i) A time is fixed for the dissolution of the partnership, or the return of a contribution, no time having been specified in the certificate, or

(j) The members desire to make a change in any other statement in the certificate in order that it shall accurately represent the agreement between them.

§ 25. Requirements for amendment and for cancellation of certificate

(1) The writing to amend a certificate shall

(a) Conform to the requirements of Section 2(1a) as far as necessary to set forth clearly the change in the certificate which it is desired to make, and

(b) Be signed and sworn to by all members, and an amendment substituting a limited partner or adding a limited or general partner shall be signed also by the member to be substituted or added, and when a limited partner is to be substituted, the amendment shall also be signed by the assigning limited partner.

(2) The writing to cancel a certificate shall be signed by all members.

(3) A person desiring the cancellation or amendment of a certificate, if any person designated in paragraphs (1) and (2) as a person who must execute the writing refuses to do so, may petition the [here designate the proper court] to direct a cancellation or amendment thereof.

(4) If the court finds that the petitioner has a right to have the writing executed by a person who refuses to do so, it shall order the [here designate the responsible official in the office designated in Section 2] in the office where the certificate is recorded to record the cancellation or amendment of the certificate; and where the certificate is to be amended, the court shall also cause to be filed for record in said office a certified copy of its decree setting forth the amendment.

(5) A certificate is amended or canceled when there is filed for record in the office [here designate the office designated in Section 2] where the certificate is recorded

(a) A writing in accordance with the provisions of paragraph (1), or (2) or

(b) A certified copy of the order of court in accordance with the provisions of paragraph (4).

(6) After the certificate is duly amended in accordance with this section, the amended certificate shall thereafter be for all purposes the certificate provided for by this act.

§ 26. Parties to actions

A contributor, unless he is a general partner, is not a proper party to proceedings by or against a partnership, except where the object is to enforce a limited partner's right against or liability to the partnership.

§ 27. Name of act

This act may be cited as The Uniform Limited Partnership Act.

§ 28. Rules of construction

(1) The rule that statutes in derogation of the common law are to be strictly construed shall have no application to this act.

(2) This act shall be so interpreted and construed as to effect its general purpose to make uniform the law of those states which enact it.

(3) This act shall not be so construed as to impair the obligations of any contract existing when the act goes into effect, nor to affect any action or proceedings begun or right accrued before this act takes effect.

§ 29. Rules for cases not provided for in this act

In any case not provided for in this act the rules of law and equity, including the law merchant, shall govern.

§ 30. Provisions for existing limited partnerships

(1) A limited partnership formed under any statute of this state prior to the adoption of this act, may become a limited partnership under this act by complying with the provisions of Section 2; provided the certificate sets forth

(a) The amount of the original contribution of each limited partner, and the time when the contribution was made, and

(b) That the property of the partnership exceeds the amount sufficient to discharge its liabilities to persons not claiming as general or limited partners by an amount greater than the sum of the contributions of its limited partners.

(2) A limited partnership formed under any statute of this state prior to the adoption of this act, until or unless it becomes a limited partnership under this act, shall continue to be governed by the provisions of [here insert proper reference to the existing limited partnership act or acts], except that such partnership shall not be renewed unless so provided in the original agreement.

§ 31. Act (acts) repealed

Except as affecting existing limited partnerships to the extent set forth in Section 30, the act (acts) of [here designate the existing limited partnership act or acts] is (are) hereby repealed.

APPENDIX C

REVISED UNIFORM LIMITED PARTNERSHIP ACT (1976) WITH 1985 AMENDMENTS

ARTICLE 1

GENERAL PROVISIONS

§ 101. Definitions

As used in this [Act], unless the context otherwise requires:

(1) "Certificate of limited partnership" means the certificate referred to in Section 201, and the certificate as amended or restated.

(2) "Contribution" means any cash, property, services rendered, or a promissory note or other binding obligation to contribute cash or property or to perform services, which a partner contributes to a limited partnership in his capacity as a partner.

(3) "Event of withdrawal of a general partner" means an event that causes a person to cease to be a general partner as provided in Section 402.

(4) "Foreign limited partnership" means a partnership formed under the laws of any state State other than this State and having as partners one or more general partners and one or more limited partners.

(5) "General partner" means a person who has been admitted to a limited partnership as a general partner in accordance with the partnership agreement and named in the certificate of limited partnership as a general partner.

(6) "Limited partner" means a person who has been admitted to a limited partnership as a limited partner in accordance with the partnership agreement and named in the certificate of limited partnership as a limited partner.

(7) "Limited partnership" and "domestic limited partnership" mean a partnership formed by two or more persons under the laws of this State and having one or more general partners and one or more limited partners.

(8) "Partner" means a limited or general partner.

(9) "Partnership agreement" means any valid agreement, written or oral, of the partners as to the affairs of a limited partnership and the conduct of its business.

(10) "Partnership interest" means a partner's share of the profits and losses of a limited partnership and the right to receive distributions of partnership assets.

(11) "Person" means a natural person, partnership, limited partnership (domestic or foreign), trust, estate, association, or corporation.

(12) "State" means a state, territory, or possession of the United States, the District of Columbia, or the Commonwealth of Puerto Rico.

§ 102. Name

The name of each limited partnership as set forth in its certificate of limited partnership:

(1) shall contain without abbreviation the words "limited partnership";

(2) may not contain the name of a limited partner unless (i) it is also the name of a general partner or the corporate name of a corporate general partner, or (ii) the business of the limited partnership had been carried on under that name before the admission of that limited partner;

(3) may not contain any word or phrase indicating or implying that it is organized other than for a purpose stated in its certificate of limited partnership;

(4) (3) may not be the same as, or deceptively similar to, the name of any corporation or limited partnership organized under the laws of this State or licensed or registered as a foreign corporation or limited partnership in this State; and

(5) (4) may not contain the following words [here insert prohibited words].

§ 103. Reservation of Name

(a) The exclusive right to the use of a name may be reserved by:

(1) any person intending to organize a limited partnership under this [Act] and to adopt that name;

(2) any domestic limited partnership or any foreign limited partnership registered in this State which, in either case, intends to adopt that name;

(3) any foreign limited partnership intending to register in this State and adopt that name; and

(4) any person intending to organize a foreign limited partnership and intending to have it register in this State and adopt that name.

(b) The reservation shall be made by filing with the Secretary of State an application, executed by the applicant, to reserve a specified name. If the Secretary of State finds that the name is available for use by a domestic or foreign limited partnership, he [or she] shall reserve the name for the exclusive use of the applicant for a period of 120 days. Once having so reserved a name, the same applicant may not again reserve the same name until more than 60 days after the expiration of the last 120-day period for which that applicant reserved that name. The right to the exclusive use of a reserved name may be transferred to any other person by filing in the office of the Secretary of State a notice of the transfer, executed by the applicant for whom the name was reserved and specifying the name and address of the transferee.

§ 104. Specified Office and Agent

Each limited partnership shall continuously maintain in this State:

(1) an office, which may but need not be a place of its business in this State, at which shall be kept the records required by Section 105 to be maintained; and

(2) an agent for service of process on the limited partnership, which agent must be an individual resident of this State, a domestic corporation, or a foreign corporation authorized to do business in this State.

§ 105. Records to be Kept

(a) Each limited partnership shall keep at the office referred to in Section 104(1) the following:

(1) a current list of the full name and last known business address of each partner set forth, separately identifying the general partners (in alphabetical order) and the limited partners (in alphabetical order;);

(2) a copy of the certificate of limited partnership and all certificates of amendment thereto, together with executed copies of any powers of attorney pursuant to which any certificate has been executed,;

(3) copies of the limited partnership's federal, state and local income tax returns and reports, if any, for the three most recent years, and;

(4) copies of any then effective written partnership agreements and of any financial statements of the limited partnership for the three most recent years; and

(5) unless contained in a written partnership agreement, a writing setting out:

(i) the amount of cash and a description and statement of the agreed value of the other property or services contributed by each partner and which each partner has agreed to contribute;

(ii) the times at which or events on the happening of which any additional contributions agreed to be made by each partner are to be made;

(iii) any right of a partner to receive, or of a general partner to make, distributions to a partner which include a return of all or any part of the partner's contribution; and

(iv) any events upon the happening of which the limited partnership is to be dissolved and its affairs wound up.

(b) Those records Records kept under this section are subject to inspection and copying at the reasonable request and at the expense of any partner during ordinary business hours.

§ 106. Nature of Business

A limited partnership may carry on any business that a partnership without limited partners may carry on except [here designate prohibited activities].

§ 107. Business Transactions of Partner With Partnership

Except as provided in the partnership agreement, a partner may lend money to and transact other business with the limited partnership and, subject to other applica-

316

ble law, has the same rights and obligations with respect thereto as a person who is not a partner.

ARTICLE 2

FORMATION; CERTIFICATE OF LIMITED
PARTNERSHIP

§ 201. Certificate of Limited Partnership
(a) In order to form a limited partnership, ~~two or more persons must execute~~ a certificate of limited partnership. ~~The certificate shall be~~ <u>must be executed and</u> filed in the office of the Secretary of State<u>. and</u> ~~and~~ <u>The certificate shall</u> set forth:
(1) the name of the limited partnership;
~~(2) the general character of its business;~~
~~(3)~~<u>(2)</u> the address of the office and the name and address of the agent for service of process required to be maintained by Section 104;
~~(4)~~<u>(3)</u> the name and the business address of each <u>general</u> partner ~~(specifying separately the general partners and limited partners)~~;
~~(5) the amount of cash and a description and statement of the agreed value of the other property or services contributed by each partner and which each partner has agreed to contribute in the future;~~
~~(6) the times at which or events on the happening of which any additional contributions agreed to be made by each partner are to be made;~~
~~(7) any power of a limited partner to grant the right to become a limited partner to an assignee of any part of his partnership interest, and the terms and conditions of the power;~~
~~(8) if agreed upon, the time at which or the events on the happening of which a partner may terminate his membership in the limited partnership and the amount of, or the method of determining, the distribution to which he may be entitled respecting his partnership interest, and the terms and conditions of the termination and distribution;~~
~~(9) any right of a partner to receive distributions of property, including cash from the limited partnership;~~
~~(10) any right of a partner to receive, or of a general partner to make, distributions to a partner which include a return of all or any part of the partner's contribution;~~
~~(11) any time at which or events upon the happening of which the limited partnership is to be dissolved and its affairs wound up;~~
~~(12) any right of the remaining general partners to continue the business on the happening of an event of withdrawal of a general partner; and~~
<u>(4) the latest date upon which the limited partnership is to dissolve; and</u>
~~(13)~~<u>(5)</u> any other matters the <u>general</u> partners determine to include therein.

(b) A limited partnership is formed at the time of the filing of the certificate of limited partnership in the office of the Secretary of State or at any later time specified in the certificate of limited partnership if, in either case, there has been substantial compliance with the requirements of this section.

§ 202. Amendment to Certificate

(a) A certificate of limited partnership is amended by filing a certificate of amendment thereto in the office of the Secretary of State. The certificate shall set forth:

    (1) the name of the limited partnership;

    (2) the date of filing the certificate; and

    (3) the amendment to the certificate.

(b) Within 30 days after the happening of any of the following events, an amendment to a certificate of limited partnership reflecting the occurrence of the event or events shall be filed:

    (1) a change in the amount or character of the contribution of any partner, or in any partner's obligation to make a contribution;

    (2)(1) the admission of a new general partner;

    (3)(2) the withdrawal of a general partner; or

    (4)(3) the continuation of the business under Section 801 after an event of withdrawal of a general partner.

(c) A general partner who becomes aware that any statement in a certificate of limited partnership was false when made or that any arrangements or other facts described have changed, making the certificate inaccurate in any respect, shall promptly amend the certificate; but an amendment to show a change of address of a limited partner need be filed only once every 12 months.

(d) A certificate of limited partnership may be amended at any time for any other proper purpose the general partners determine.

(e) No person has any liability because an amendment to a certificate of limited partnership has not been filed to reflect the occurrence of any event referred to in subsection (b) of this Section section if the amendment is filed within the 30-day period specified in subsection (b).

    (f) A restated certificate of limited partnership may be executed and filed in the same manner as a certificate of amendment.

§ 203. Cancellation of Certificate

A certificate of limited partnership shall be canceled upon the dissolution and the commencement of winding up of the partnership or at any other time there are no limited partners. A certificate of cancellation shall be filed in the office of the Secretary of State and set forth:

    (1) the name of the limited partnership;

(2) the date of filing of its certificate of limited partnership;

(3) the reason for filing the certificate of cancellation;

(4) the effective date (which shall be a date certain) of cancellation if it is not to be effective upon the filing of the certificate; and

(5) any other information the general partners filing the certificate determine.

§ 204. Execution of Certificates

(a) Each certificate required by this Article to be filed in the office of the Secretary of State shall be executed in the following manner:

(1) an original certificate of limited partnership must be signed by all general partners ~~named therein~~;

(2) a certificate of amendment must be signed by at least one general partner and by each other general partner designated in the certificate as a new general partner ~~or whose contribution is described as having been increased~~; and

(3) a certificate of cancellation must be signed by all general partners~~;~~.

(b) Any person may sign a certificate by an attorney-in-fact, but a power of attorney to sign a certificate relating to the admission~~, or increased contribution,~~ of a general partner must specifically describe the admission ~~or increase~~.

(c) The execution of a certificate by a general partner constitutes an affirmation under the penalties of perjury that the facts stated therein are true.

§ 205. ~~Amendment or Cancellation~~ Execution by Judicial Act

If a person required by Section 204 to execute ~~a~~ any certificate ~~of amendment or cancellation~~ fails or refuses to do so, any other ~~partner, and any assignee of a partnership interest,~~ person who is adversely affected by the failure or refusal~~,~~ may petition the [designate the appropriate court] to direct the ~~amendment or cancellation~~ execution of the certificate. If the court finds that ~~the amendment or cancellation is proper~~ it is proper for the certificate to be executed and that any person so designated has failed or refused to execute the certificate, it shall order the Secretary of State to record an appropriate certificate ~~of amendment or cancellation~~.

§ 206. Filing in Office of Secretary of State

(a) Two signed copies of the certificate of limited partnership and of any certificates of amendment or cancellation (or of any judicial decree of amendment or cancellation) shall be delivered to the Secretary of State. A person who executes a certificate as an agent or fiduciary need not exhibit evidence of his [or her] authority as a prerequisite to filing. Unless the Secretary of State finds that any certificate does not conform to law, upon receipt of all filing fees required by law he [or she] shall:

(1) endorse on each duplicate original the word "Filed" and the day, month, and year of the filing thereof;

(2) file one duplicate original in his [or her] office; and

(3) return the other duplicate original to the person who filed it or his [or her] representative.

(b) Upon the filing of a certificate of amendment (or judicial decree of amendment) in the office of the Secretary of State, the certificate of limited partnership shall be amended as set forth therein, and upon the effective date of a certificate of cancellation (or a judicial decree thereof, the certificate of limited partnership is canceled.

§ 207. Liability for False Statement in Certificate

If any certificate of limited partnership or certificate of amendment or cancellation contains a false statement, one who suffers loss by reliance on the statement may recover damages for the loss from:

(1) any person who executes the certificate, or causes another to execute it on his behalf, and knew, and any general partner who knew or should have known, the statement to be false at the time the certificate was executed; and

(2) any general partner who thereafter knows or should have known that any arrangement or other fact described in the certificate has changed, making the statement inaccurate in any respect within a sufficient time before the statement was relied upon reasonably to have enabled that general partner to cancel or amend the certificate, or to file a petition for its cancellation or amendment under Section 205.

§ 208. Scope of Notice

The fact that a certificate of limited partnership is on file in the office of the Secretary of State is notice that the partnership is a limited partnership and the persons designated therein as ~~limited~~ general partners are ~~limited~~ general partners, but it is not notice of any other fact.

COMMENT

Section 208 ~~is new~~ first appeared in the 1976 Act, and referred to the certificate's providing constructive notice of the status as limited partners of those so identified therein. The 1985 Act's deletion of any requirement that the certificate name limited partners required that Section 208 be modified accordingly.

By stating that the filing of a certificate of limited partnership only results in notice of the ~~limited~~ general liability of the ~~limited~~ general partners, ~~it~~ Section 208 obviates the concern that third parties may be held to have notice of special provisions set forth in the certificate. While this section is designed to preserve by implication the limited liability of limited partners, the ~~notice~~ implicit protection provided is not intended to change any liability of a limited partner which may be created by his action or inaction under the law of estoppel, agency, fraud, or the like.

§ 209. Delivery of Certificates to Limited Partners

Upon the return by the Secretary of State pursuant to Section 206 of a certificate marked "Filed", the general partners shall promptly deliver or mail a copy of the certificate of limited partnership and each certificate of amendment or cancellation to each limited partner unless the partnership agreement provides otherwise.

ARTICLE 3

LIMITED PARTNERS

§ 301. Admission of ~~Additional~~ Limited Partners

(a) A person becomes a limited partner:
    (1) at the time the limited partnership is formed; or
    (2) at any later time specified in the records of the limited partnership for becoming a limited partner.

~~(a)~~(b) After the filing of a limited partnership's original certificate of limited partnership, a person may be admitted as an additional limited partner:

    (1) in the case of a person acquiring a partnership interest directly from the limited partnership, upon compliance with the partnership agreement or, if the partnership agreement does not so provide, upon the written consent of all partners; and

    (2) in the case of an assignee of a partnership interest of a partner who has the power, as provided in Section 704, to grant the assignee the right to become a limited partner, upon the exercise of that power and compliance with any conditions limiting the grant or exercise of the power.

~~(b) In each case under subsection (a), the person acquiring the partnership interest becomes a limited partner only upon amendment of the certificate of limited partnership reflecting that fact.~~

§ 302. Voting

Subject to Section 303, the partnership agreement may grant to all or a specified group of the limited partners the right to vote (on a per capita or other basis) upon any matter.

§ 303. Liability to Third Parties

(a) Except as provided in subsection (d), a limited partner is not liable for the obligations of a limited partnership unless he [or she] is also a general partner or, in addition to the exercise of his [or her] rights and powers as a limited partner, he [or she] ~~takes part~~ participates in the control of the business. However, if the limited ~~partner's participation~~ partner participates in the control of the business ~~is not substantially the same as the exercise of the powers of a general partner~~, he [or she] is liable only to persons who transact business with the limited partnership ~~with actual knowledge of his participation in control~~ reasonably believing, based upon the limited partner's conduct, that the limited partner is a general partner.

(b) A limited partner does not participate in the control of the business within the meaning of subsection (a) solely by doing one or more of the following:

(1) being a contractor for or an agent or employee of the limited partnership or of a general partner or being an officer, director, or shareholder of a general partner that is a corporation;

(2) consulting with and advising a general partner with respect to the business of the limited partnership;

(3) acting as surety for the limited partnership or guaranteeing or assuming one or more specific obligations of the limited partnership;

(4) ~~approving or disapproving an amendment to the partnership agreement~~ taking any action required or permitted by law to bring or pursue a derivative action in the right of the limited partnership; ~~or~~

~~(5) voting on one or more of the following matters;~~

(5) requesting or attending a meeting of partners;

(6) proposing, approving, or disapproving, by voting or otherwise, one or more of the following matters:

(i) the dissolution and winding up of the limited partnership;

(ii) the sale, exchange, lease, mortgage, pledge, or other transfer of all or substantially all of the assets of the limited partnership ~~other than in the ordinary course of its business~~;

(iii) the incurrence of indebtedness by the limited partnership other than in the ordinary course of its business;

(iv) a change in the nature of the business; ~~or~~

(v) the admission or removal of a general partner;

(vi) the admission or removal of a limited partner;

(vii) a transaction involving an actual or potential conflict of interest between a general partner and the limited partnership or the limited partners;

(viii) an amendment to the partnership agreement or certificate of limited partnership; or

(ix) matters related to the business of the limited partnership not otherwise enumerated in this subsection (b), which the partnership agreement states in writing may be subject to the approval or disapproval of limited partners;

(7) winding up the limited partnership pursuant to Section 803; or

(8) exercising any right or power permitted to limited partners under this [Act] and not specifically enumerated in this subsection (b).

(c) The enumeration in subsection (b) does not mean that the possession or exercise of any other powers by a limited partner constitutes participation by him [or her] in the business of the limited partnership.

(d) A limited partner who knowingly permits his [or her] name to be used in the name of the limited partnership, except under circumstances permitted by Section 102(2), is liable to creditors who extend credit to the limited partnership without actual knowledge that the limited partner is not a general partner.

§ 304. Person Erroneously Believing Himself [or Herself] Limited Partner

(a) Except as provided in subsection (b), a person who makes a contribution to a business enterprise and erroneously but in good faith believes that he [or she] has become a limited partner in the enterprise is not a general partner in the enterprise and is not bound by its obligations by reason of making the contribution, receiving distributions from the enterprise, or exercising any rights of a limited partner, if, on ascertaining the mistake, he [or she]:

(1) causes an appropriate certificate of limited partnership or a certificate of amendment to be executed and filed; or

(2) withdraws from future equity participation in the enterprise by executing and filing in the office of the Secretary of State a certificate declaring withdrawal under this section.

(b) A person who makes a contribution of the kind described in subsection (a) is liable as a general partner to any third party who transacts business with the enterprise (i) before the person withdraws and an appropriate certificate is filed to show withdrawal, or (ii) before an appropriate certificate is filed to show his status as a limited partner and, in the case of an amendment, after expiration of the 30-day period for filing an amendment relating to the person as a limited partner under Section 202 that he [or she] is not a general partner, but in either case only if the third party actually believed in good faith that the person was a general partner at the time of the transaction.

§ 305. Information

Each limited partner has the right to:

(1) inspect and copy any of the partnership records required to be maintained by Section 105; and

(2) obtain from the general partners from time to time upon reasonable demand (i) true and full information regarding the state of the business and financial condition of the limited partnership, (ii) promptly after becoming available, a copy of the limited partnership's federal, state, and local income tax returns for each year, and (iii) other information regarding the affairs of the limited partnership as is just and reasonable.

ARTICLE 4

GENERAL PARTNERS

§ 401. Admission of Additional General Partners

After the filing of a limited partnership's original certificate of limited partnership, additional general partner, may be admitted only as provided in writing in the partnership agreement or, if the partnership agreement does not provide in writing for the admission of additional general partners, with the ~~specific~~ written consent of ~~each partner~~ all partners.

§ 402. Events of Withdrawal

Except as approved by the specific written consent of all partners at the time, a person ceases to be a general partner of a limited partnership upon the happening of any of the following events:

(1) the general partner withdraws from the limited partnership as provided in Section 602;

(2) the general partner ceases to be a member of the limited partnership as provided in Section 702;

(3) the general partner is removed as a general partner in accordance with the partnership agreement;

(4) unless otherwise provided in writing in the ~~certificate of limited~~ partnership agreement, the general partner: (i) makes an assignment for the benefit of creditors; (ii) files a voluntary petition in bankruptcy; (iii) is adjudicated a bankrupt or insolvent; (iv) files a petition or answer seeking for himself [or herself] any reorganization, arrangement, composition, readjustment, liquidation, dissolution or similar relief under any statute, law, or regulation; (v) files an answer or other pleading admitting or failing to contest the material allegations of a petition filed against him [or her] in any proceeding of this nature; or (vi) seeks, consents to, or acquiesces in the appointment of a trustee, receiver, or liquidator of the general partner or of all or any substantial part of his [or her] properties.

(5) unless otherwise provided in writing in the ~~certificate of limited~~ partnership agreement [120] days after the commencement of any proceeding against the general partner seeking reorganization, arrangement, composition, readjustment, liquidation, dissolution or similar relief under any statute, law, or regulation, the proceeding has not been dismissed, or if within [90] days after the appointment without his [or her] consent or acquiescence of a trustee, receiver, or liquidator of the general partner or of all or any substantial part of his [or her] properties, the appointment is not vacated or stayed or within [90] days after the expiration of any such stay, the appointment is not vacated;

(6) in the case of a general partner who is a natural person,

(i) his [or her] death; or

(ii) the entry of an order by a court of competent jurisdiction adjudicating him [or her] incompetent to manage his [or her] person or his [or her] estate;

(7) in the case of a general partner who is acting as a general partner by virtue of being a trustee of a trust, the termination of the trust (but not merely the substitution of a new trustee);

(8) in the case of a general partner that is a separate partnership, the dissolution and commencement of winding up of the separate partnership;

(9) in the case of a general partner that is a corporation, the filing of a certificate of dissolution, or its equivalent, for the corporation or the revocation of its charter; or

(10) in the case of an estate, the distribution by the fiduciary of the estate's entire interest in the partnership.

§ 403. General Powers and Liabilities

(a) Except as provided in this [Act] or in the partnership agreement, a general partner of a limited partnership has the rights and powers and is subject to the restrictions of a partner in a partnership without limited partners.

(b) Except as provided in this [Act], a general partner of a limited partnership has the liabilities of a partner in a partnership without limited partners to persons other than the partnership and the other partners. Except as provided in this [Act] or in the partnership agreement, a general partner of a limited partnership has the liabilities of a partner in a partnership without limited partners to the partnership and to the other partners.

§ 404. Contributions by General Partner

A general partner of a limited partnership may make contributions to the partnership and share in the profits and losses of, and in distributions from, the limited partnership as a general partner. A general partner also may make contributions to and share in profits, losses, and distributions as a limited partner. A person who is both a general partner and a limited partner has the rights and powers, and is subject to the restrictions and liabilities, of a general partner and, except as provided in the partnership agreement, also has the powers, and is subject to the restrictions, of a limited partner to the extent of his [or her] participation in the partnership as a limited partner.

§ 405. Voting

The partnership agreement may grant to all or certain identified general partners the right to vote (on a per capita or any other basis), separately or with all or any class of the limited partners, on any matter.

ARTICLE 5

FINANCE

§ 501. Form of Contribution

The contribution of a partner may be in cash, property, or services rendered, or a promissory note or other obligation to contribute cash or property or to perform services.

§ 502. Liability for Contribution

(a) A promise by a limited partner to contribute to the limited partnership is not enforceable unless set out in a writing signed by the limited partner.

(a)(b) Except as provided in the certificate of limited partnership agreement, a partner is obligated to the limited partnership to perform any <u>enforceable</u> promise to contribute cash or property or to perform services, even if he [or she] is unable to perform because of death, disability, or any other reason. If a partner does not make the required contribution of property or services, he [or she] is obligated at the option of the limited partnership to contribute cash equal to that portion of the value, as stated in the ~~certificate of limited~~ partnership <u>records required to be kept pursuant to Section 105</u>, of the stated contribution which has not been made.

~~(b)~~(c) Unless otherwise provided in the partnership agreement, the obligation of a partner to make a contribution or return money or other property paid or distributed in violation of this [Act] may be compromised only by consent of all partners. Notwithstanding the compromise, a creditor of a limited partnership who extends credit~~,~~ or ~~whose claim arises~~, <u>otherwise acts in reliance on that obligation</u> after the ~~filing of the certificate of limited partnership or an amendment thereto~~ <u>partner signs a writing</u> which~~, in either case,~~ reflects the obligation, and before the amendment or cancellation thereof to reflect the compromise, may enforce the original obligation.

§ 503. Sharing of Profits and Losses

The profits and losses of a limited partnership shall be allocated among the partners, and among classes of partners, in the manner provided <u>in writing</u> in the partnership agreement. If the partnership agreement does not so provide <u>in writing</u>, profits and losses shall be allocated on the basis of the value, as stated in the ~~certificate of limited~~ partnership <u>records required to be kept pursuant to Section 105</u>, of the contributions made by each partner to the extent they have been received by the partnership and have not been returned.

§ 504. Sharing of Distributions

Distributions of cash or other assets of a limited partnership shall be allocated among the partners and among classes of partners in the manner provided <u>in writing</u> in the partnership agreement. If the partnership agreement does not so provide <u>in writing</u>, distributions shall be made on the basis of the value, as stated in the ~~certificate of limited~~ partnership <u>records required to be kept pursuant to Section 105</u>, of the contributions made by each partner to the extent they have been received by the partnership and have not been returned.

ARTICLE 6

DISTRIBUTIONS AND WITHDRAWAL

§ 601. Interim Distributions

Except as provided in this Article, a partner is entitled to receive distributions from a limited partnership before his [or her] withdrawal from the limited partnership and before the dissolution and winding up thereof:

~~(1)~~ to the extent and at the times or upon the happening of the events specified in the partnership agreement; ~~and~~

~~(2) if any distribution constitutes a return of any part of his contribution under Section 608(c), to the extent and at the times or upon the happening of the events specified in the certificate of limited partnership.~~

§ 602. Withdrawal of General Partner

A general partner may withdraw from a limited partnership at any time by giving written notice to the other partners, but if the withdrawal violates the partnership agreement, the limited partnership may recover from the withdrawing general partner damages for breach of the partnership agreement and offset the damages against the amount otherwise distributable to him [or her].

§ 603. Withdrawal of Limited Partner

A limited partner may withdraw from a limited partnership at the time or upon the happening of events specified ~~in the certificate of limited partnership and in accordance with~~ in writing in the partnership agreement. If the ~~certificate~~ agreement does not specify in writing the time or the events upon the happening of which a limited partner may withdraw or a definite time for the dissolution and winding up of the limited partnership, a limited partner may withdraw upon not less than six months' prior written notice to each general partner at his [or her] address on the books of the limited partnership at its office in this State.

§ 604. Distribution Upon Withdrawal

Except as provided in this Article, upon withdrawal any withdrawing partner is entitled to receive any distribution to which he [or she] is entitled under the partnership agreement and, if not otherwise provided in the agreement, he [or she] is entitled to receive, within a reasonable time after withdrawal, the fair value of his [or her] interest in the limited partnership as of the date of withdrawal based upon his [or her] right to share in distributions from the limited partnership.

§ 605. Distribution in Kind

Except as provided in writing in the ~~certificate of limited~~ partnership agreement, a partner, regardless of the nature of his [or her] contribution, has no right to demand and receive any distribution from a limited partnership in any form other than cash. Except as provided in writing in the partnership agreement, a partner may not be compelled to accept a distribution of any asset in kind from a limited partnership to the extent that the percentage of the asset distributed to him [or her] exceeds a percentage of that asset which is equal to the percentage in which he [or she] shares in distributions from the limited partnership.

§ 606. Right to Distribution

At the time a partner becomes entitled to receive a distribution, he [or she] has the status of, and is entitled to all remedies available to, a creditor of the limited partnership with respect to the distribution.

§ 607. Limitations on Distribution

A partner may not receive a distribution from a limited partnership to the extent that, after giving effect to the distribution, all liabilities of the limited partnership, other than liabilities to partners on account of their partnership interests, exceed the fair value of the partnership assets.

§ 608. Liability Upon Return of Contribution

(a) If a partner has received the return of any part of his [or her] contribution without violation of the partnership agreement or this [Act], he [or she] is liable to the limited partnership for a period of one year thereafter for the amount of the returned contribution, but only to the extent necessary to discharge the limited partnership's liabilities to creditors who extended credit to the limited partnership during the period the contribution was held by the partnership.

(b) If a partner has received the return of any part of his [or her] contribution in violation of the partnership agreement or this [Act], he [or she] is liable to the limited partnership for a period of six years thereafter for the amount of the contribution wrongfully returned.

(c) A partner receives a return of his [or her] contribution to the extent that a distribution to him [or her] reduces his [or her] share of the fair value of the net assets of the limited partnership below the value, as set forth in the certificate of limited partnership records required to be kept pursuant to Section 105, of his contribution which has not been distributed to him [or her].

ARTICLE 7

ASSIGNMENT OF PARTNERSHIP INTERESTS

§ 701. Nature of Partnership Interest

A partnership interest is personal property.

§ 702. Assignment of Partnership Interest

Except as provided in the partnership agreement, a partnership interest is assignable in whole or in part. An assignment of a partnership interest does not dissolve a limited partnership or entitle the assignee to become or to exercise any rights of a partner. An assignment entitles the assignee to receive, to the extent assigned, only the distribution to which the assignor would be entitled. Except as provided in the partnership agreement, a partner ceases to be a partner upon assignment of all his [or her] partnership interest.

§ 703. Rights of Creditor

On application to a court of competent jurisdiction by any judgment creditor of a partner, the court may charge the partnership interest of the partner with payment of the unsatisfied amount of the judgment with interest. To the extent so charged, the judgment creditor has only the rights of an assignee of the partnership interest. This [Act] does not deprive any partner of the benefit of any exemption laws applicable to his [or her] partnership interest.

§ 704. Right of Assignee to Become Limited Partner

(a) An assignee of a partnership interest, including an assignee of a general partner, may become a limited partner if and to the extent that (1) (i) the assignor gives the assignee that right in accordance with authority described in the ~~certificate of limited~~ partnership <u>agreement</u> or (2)(ii) all other partners consent.

(b) An assignee who has become a limited partner has, to the extent assigned, the rights and powers, and is subject to the restrictions and liabilities, of a limited partner under the partnership agreement and this [Act]. An assignee who becomes a limited partner also is liable for the obligations of his [or her] assignor to make and return contributions as provided in ~~Article~~ <u>Articles 5 and</u> 6. However, the assignee is not obligated for liabilities unknown to the assignee at the time he [or she] became a limited partner ~~and which could not be ascertained from the certificate of limited partnership~~.

(c) If an assignee of a partnership interest becomes a limited partner, the assignor is not released from his [or her] liability to the limited partnership under Sections 207 and 502.

§ 705. Power of Estate of Deceased or Incompetent Partner

If a partner who is an individual dies or a court of competent jurisdiction adjudges him [or her] to be incompetent to manage his [or her] person or his [or her] property, the partner's executor, administrator, guardian, conservator, or other legal representative may exercise all the partner's rights for the purpose of settling his [or her] estate or administering his [or her] property, including any power the partner had to give an assignee the right to become a limited partner. If a partner is a corporation, trust, or other entity and is dissolved or terminated, the powers of that partner may be exercised by its legal representative or successor.

ARTICLE 8

DISSOLUTION

§ 801. Nonjudicial Dissolution

A limited partnership is dissolved and its affairs shall be wound up upon the happening of the first to occur of the following:

(1) at the time <u>specified in the certificate of limited partnership;</u>

<u>(2)</u> ~~or~~ upon the happening of events specified <u>in writing</u> in the ~~certificate of limited~~ partnership <u>agreement;</u>

(2)(3) written consent of all partners;

(3)(4) an event of withdrawal of a general partner unless at the time there is at least one other general partner and the ~~certificate of limited~~ written provisions of the partnership agreement ~~permits~~ permit the business of the limited partnership to be carried on the remaining general partner and that partner does so, but the limited partnership is not dissolved and is not required to be wound up by reason of any event of withdrawal, if, within 90 days after the withdrawal, all partners agree in writing to continue the business of the limited partnership and to the appointment of one or more additional general partners if necessary or desired; or

(4)(5) entry of a decree of judicial dissolution under Section 802.

§ 802. Judicial Dissolution

On application by or for a partner the [designate the appropriate court] court may decree dissolution of a limited partnership whenever it is not reasonably practicable to carry on the business in conformity with the partnership agreement.

§ 803. Winding Up

Except as provided in the partnership agreement, the general partners who have not wrongfully dissolved a limited partnership or, if none, the limited partners, may wind up the limited partnership's affairs; but the [designate the appropriate court] court may wind up the limited partnership's affairs upon application of any partner, his [or her] legal representative, or assignee.

§ 804. Distribution of Assets

Upon the winding up of a limited partnership, the assets shall be distributed as follows:

(1) to creditors, including partners who are creditors, to the extent permitted by law, in satisfaction of liabilities of the limited partnership other than liabilities for distributions to partners under Section 601 or 604;

(2) except as provided in the partnership agreement, to partners and former partners in satisfaction of liabilities for distributions under Section 601 or 604; and

(3) except as provided in the partnership agreement, to partners first for the return of their contributions and secondly respecting their partnership interests, in the proportions in which the partners share in distributions.

ARTICLE 9

FOREIGN LIMITED PARTNERSHIPS

§ 901. Law Governing

Subject to the Constitution of this State, (i) the laws of the state under which a foreign limited partnership is organized govern its organization and internal affairs and the liability of its limited partners, and (ii) a foreign limited partnership may not be denied registration by reason of any difference between those laws and the laws of this State.

§ 902. Registration

Before transacting business in this State, a foreign limited partnership shall register with the Secretary of State. In order to register, a foreign limited partnership shall submit to the Secretary of State, in duplicate, an application for registration as a foreign limited partnership, signed and sworn to by a general partner and setting forth:

(1) the name of the foreign limited partnership and, if different, the name under which it proposes to register and transact business in this State;

(2) the ~~state~~ State and date of its formation;

~~(3) the general character of the business it proposes to transact in this State;~~

(4)(3) the name and address of any agent for service of process on the foreign limited partnership whom the foreign limited partnership elects to appoint; the agent must be an individual resident of this ~~state~~ State, a domestic corporation, or a foreign corporation having a place of business in, and authorized to do business in, this State;

(5)(4) a statement that the Secretary of State is appointed the agent of the foreign limited partnership for service of process if no agent has been appointed under paragraph (4)(3) or, if appointed, the agent's authority has been revoked or if the agent cannot be found or served with the exercise of reasonable diligence;

(6)(5) the address of the office required to be maintained in the ~~State~~ state of its organization by the laws of that ~~State~~ state or, if not so required, of the principal office of the foreign limited partnership; ~~and~~

~~(7) if the certificate of limited partnership filed in the foreign limited partnership's state of organization is not required to include the names and business addresses of the partners, a list of the names and addresses.~~

(6) the name and business address of each general partner; and

(7) the address of the office at which is kept a list of the names and addresses of the limited partners and their capital contributions, together with an undertaking by the foreign limited partnership to keep those records until the foreign limited partnership's registration in this State is canceled or withdrawn.

§ 903. Issuance of Registration

(a) If the Secretary of State finds that an application for registration conforms to law and all requisite fees have been paid, he [or she] shall:

(1) endorse on the application the word "Filed," and the month, day and year of the filing thereof;

(2) file in his [or her] office a duplicate original of the application; and

(3) issue a certificate of registration to transact business in this State.

(b) The certificate of registration, together with a duplicate original of the application, shall be returned to the person who filed the application or his [or her] representative.

§ 904. Name

A foreign limited partnership may register with the Secretary of State under any name, whether or not it is the name under which it is registered in its state of organization, that includes without abbreviation the words "limited partnership" and that could be registered by a domestic limited partnership.

§ 905. Changes and Amendments

If any statement in the application for registration of a foreign limited partnership was false when made or any arrangements or other facts described have changed, making the application inaccurate in any respect, the foreign limited partnership shall promptly file in the office of the Secretary of State a certificate, signed and sworn to by a general partner, correcting such statement.

§ 906. Cancellation of Registration

A foreign limited partnership may cancel its registration by filing with the Secretary of State a certificate of cancellation signed and sworn to by a general partner. A cancellation does not terminate the authority of the Secretary of State to accept service of process on the foreign limited partnership with respect to [claims for relief] [causes of action] arising out of the transactions of business in this State.

§ 907. Transaction of Business Without Registration

(a) A foreign limited partnership transacting business in this State may not maintain any action, suit, or proceeding in any court of this State until it has registered in this State.

(b) The failure of a foreign limited partnership to register in this State does not impair the validity of any contract or act of the foreign limited partnership or prevent the foreign limited partnership from defending any action, suit, or proceeding in any court of this State.

(c) A limited partner of a foreign limited partnership is not liable as a general partner of the foreign limited partnership solely by reason of having transacted business in this State without registration.

(d) A foreign limited partnership, by transacting business in this State without registration, appoints the Secretary of State as its agent for service of process with respect to [claims for relief] [causes of action] arising out of the transaction of business in this State.

§ 908. Action by [Appropriate Official]

The [designate the appropriate official] may bring an action to restrain a foreign limited partnership from transacting business in this State in violation of this Article.

ARTICLE 10

DERIVATIVE ACTIONS

§ 1001. Right of Action

332

A limited partner may bring an action in the right of a limited partnership to recover a judgment in its favor if general partners with authority to do so have refused to bring the action or if an effort to cause those general partners to bring the action is not likely to succeed.

§ 1002. Proper Plaintiff

In a derivative action, the plaintiff must be a partner at the time of bringing the action and (i) <u>must have been a partner</u> at the time of the transaction of which he [or she] complains or (ii) his [or her] status as a partner ~~had~~ <u>must have</u> devolved upon him [or her] by operation of law or pursuant to the terms of the partnership agreement from a person who was a partner at the time of the transaction.

§ 1003. Pleading

In a derivative action, the complaint shall set forth with particularity the effort of the plaintiff to secure initiation of the action by a general partner or the reasons for not making the effort.

§ 1004. Expenses

If a derivative action is successful, in whole or in part, or if anything is received by the plaintiff as a result of a judgment, compromise or settlement of an action or claim, the court may award the plaintiff reasonable expenses, including reasonable attorney's fees, and shall direct him [or her] to remit to the limited partnership the remainder of those proceeds received by him [or her].

ARTICLE 11
MISCELLANEOUS

§ 1101. Construction and Application

This [Act] shall be so applied and construed to effectuate its general purpose to make uniform the law with respect to the subject of this [Act] among states enacting it.

§ 1102. Short Title

This [Act] may be cited as the Uniform Limited Partnership Act.

§ 1103. Severability

If any provision of this [Act] or its application to any person or circumstance is held invalid, the invalidity does not affect other provisions or applications of the [Act] which can be given effect without the invalid provision or application, and to this end the provisions of this [Act] are severable.

§ 1104. Effective Date, Extended Effective Date and Repeal

Except as set forth below, the effective date of this [Act] is _____ and the following acts [list ~~prior~~ existing limited partnership acts] are hereby repealed:

(1) The existing provisions for execution and filing of certificates of limited partnerships and amendments thereunder and cancellations thereof continue in effect until [specify time required to create central filing system], the extended effective date, and Sections 102, 103, 104, 105, 201, 202, 203, 204 and 206 are not effective until the extended effective date.

(2) Section 402, specifying the conditions under which a general partner ceases to be a member of a limited partnership, is not effective until the extended effective date, and the applicable provisions of existing law continue to govern until the extended effective date.

(3) Sections 501, 502 and 608 apply only to contributions and distributions made after the effective date of this [Act].

(4) Section 704 applies only to assignments made after the effective date of this [Act].

(5) Article 9, dealing with registration of foreign limited partnerships, is not effective until the extended effective date.

(6) Unless otherwise agreed by the partners, the applicable provisions of existing law governing allocation of profits and losses (rather than the provisions of Section 503), distributions to a withdrawing partner (rather than the provisions of Section 604), and distribution of assets upon the winding up of a limited partnership (rather than the provisions of Section 804) govern limited partnerships formed before the effective date of this [Act].

§ 1105. Rules for Cases Not Provided for in This [Act]

In any case not provided for in this [Act] the provisions of the Uniform Partnership Act govern.

§ 1106. Savings Clause

The repeal of any statutory provision by this [Act] does not impair, or otherwise affect, the organization or the continued existence of a limited partnership existing at the effective date of this [Act], nor does the repeal of any existing statutory provision by this [Act] impair any contract or affect any right accrued before the effective date of this [Act].

INDEX

References are to Pages

AGENCY
See also APPARENT AUTHORITY, AUTHORITY OF AGENT, FIDUCIARY CONCEPTS, PRINCIPAL
Creation in general, 22
Duration, 23
Fiduciary consequences, 23
Joint venture, consequences of, 190, 194, 198, 199
Partnership, consequences of:
Authority impasse in two member firm, 83
Burden of proof, 80
Creation of agency status in partners, 75
Section 9(1) creation of agency status, 65, 73
Section 9(1) liability for unauthorized act, 65
Section 9(1) real authority, 73, 76
Section 13 liability for tort of partner, 68, 82
Third person's knowledge, 65, 76, 79
Limited partnership:
Authority of general partner(s), 221, 222, 223
Negligent selection of unqualified independent contractor, 55, 61
Powers of, 25, 39
Servant agent, 25
Tort consequences: 43
Entrepreneur theory, 45, 54
Frolic vs. deviation, 56
Respondeat superior, 43
Scope of employment, 55
Servant vs. non-servant agent, 48

APPARENT AUTHORITY
Belief of third party:
Informed, reasonable person standard, 36, 38
Reasonable person standard, 32. 38
Relevance of subjective belief, 38
Burden of proof, 36, 80
Defined, 223

Liability:
Betrayed principal, 32, 39
Faithless agent, 39, 40
Of a general partner in a limited partnership, 223
Real authority distinguished, 33
Source:
Established by acts or omissions of principal, 32,36
Not established by acts or statements of agent, 36, 38

AUTHORITY OF AGENT
In general, 24, 32
Burden of proof, 36
Distinguished from apparent authority, 33
Express real authority: 25, 32, 33
Defined, 25, 33
Implied real authority: 25, 32, 33
Defined, 33
Distinguished from express real authority, 33
Source, 27
Liability of principal:
Power to bind principal for necessaries, 25
Warranty of agent, 41
Within general partnership:
Authority impasse in two member firm, 83
Burden of proof, 80
Section 9(1) liability for unauthorized act, 65
Section 9(1) real authority, 76
Section 13 liability for tort of partner, 68, 82
Third person's knowledge, 76, 79

BOOKS AND RECORDS
Access by limited partner,
Access within general partnership, 111

COMPENSATION
Default presumption against, 93
Express agreement to, 93

Implied agreement to, 93, 94
Partner's claim to, 92, 98
Quasi-contract as basis for, 100

CONCILIATION
As alternative to dissolution, 127

DISSOLUTION
As breach of partnership agreement, 97, 153,
    154, 164, 165
At will of any partner, 125, 152
Causes:
    Consequences of court order, 124, 125,
        132, 158
    Death of a partner, 160, 161, 168, 170
    Withdrawal of partner, 168
Consequences:
    Effect on authority of partner as agent, 97,
        168, 170
    Power of partner to bind firm, 97, 170
    Right to application of partnership proper-
        ty, 97, 147, 172
    Right to continue business, 159, 172, 173
    Right to wind up, 97, 147, 172, 173
Defined, 97, 167
Duty to account in wake of, 172
Estate of deceased partner:
    Agreement to use fixed figure, 185
    Agreement to use valuation formula, 180,
        182
    Consent to continuation of business, 176,
        178
    Liability, 176, 179
    Rights, 173, 181
    Status with respect to decedent's interest
        in specific partnership property, 137,
        142
    Valuation of interest, 173, 180, 183
Fiduciary duties attach, 152
Of joint venture, 158, 160
Of limited partnership, 269
    Under RULPA, 269
    Under ULPA, 269, 270
Partnership agreement, effect of, 122, 166
Rightful, 97
Winding up as duty of surviving partner, 168,
    170, 172
Wrongful:
    In general, 97
    Liability of wrongful partner, 173
    Rights of wronged partners:
        In general, 173
        Election to continue business, 159,
            173
    Rights of wrongful partner, 174

DURATION OF GENERAL PARTNER-
SHIP
In general, 148, 149
Fixed by implied agreement, 125, 126
    At sufferance or will of any partner, 126,
        151
        Stabilized by covenant not to compete,
            90, 122, 125, 126, 165, 166
    For a task, 149
    For a term, 149, 150

ENTREPRENEUR THEORY
    See AGENCY, TORT LIABILITY

ESTOPPEL
Source of liability for betrayed principal, 41

FIDUCIARY CONCEPTS
Agent and principal, 23
Joint venture, 104, 204
Limited partnership, 222, 244, 250, 251
Partners:
    Duty to account, 110
    Duty to disclose information, 106, 108
    Formation of partnership, 106, 107
    General nature, 104
    Misappropriation of partnership opportuni-
        ty as breach, 105, 109, 111
    Remedies:
        Accounting to aggrieved partners, 110
        Constructive trust, imposition of, 104,
            204
        Dissolution as precondition to damage
            action, 113, 121
        Exceptions, 114, 119, 120
    Principal and agent, 23
    Uniform Partnership Act and, 104

FORMATION OF GENERAL PARTNER-
SHIP
Defined, 7
De facto, 8
    Presumption rebutted, 14
    Presumptions, 9, 12
De jure, 14
Fiduciary concepts, 106, 107
Introduction and nature, 7
Role of intention, 9, 10, 14

GENERAL PARTNERSHIP
    See BOOKS AND RECORDS; CONCILI-
        ATION; DISSOLUTION; DURA-
        TION OF GENERAL PARTNER-
        SHIP; FIDUCIARY CONCEPTS;
        FORMATION OF GENERAL PART-

NERSHIP; PARTNERSHIP AGREE-
MENT; PARTNERSHIP PROPERTY;
RIGHTS OF PARTNER; WITHDRA-
WAL OF PARTNER

INDEPENDENT CONTRACTOR
See also, PRINCIPAL, TORT LIABILITY,
NON-SERVANT AGENT
Liability for negligent selection of, 55, 61

INFORMATION
Duty of partners to disclose, 106, 108, 113
Rights of limited partners to, 271
Section 20 of UPA, 108

JOINT VENTURE
In general, 189
Agency concepts within, 190, 194, 198, 199
Application of UPA to, 193
Control and management, 209
Corporate participation permitted, 189, 190
Dissolution, 158, 160, 209
Distinguished from partnership, 193
Fiduciary duties within, 104, 204, 209
Power of corporation to enter, 189, 190
Similarity to partnership, 193, 209
UPA Section 9(1) applicability of, 198
Use to share technology, 210

LIABILITY
See PARTNERSHIP AS PRINCIPAL

LIMITED PARTNERSHIP
In general, 211
Apparent authority of general partner, 223
Creature of statute, 218, 227, 230
Formation:
Certificate of limited partnership, 219, 220,
228
Abbreviation under RULPA/85, 228
Consequences of failure to file, 229, 231
Essential to formation, 219
Liability for false statement contained
within, 223
Defective formation:
Liability consequences, 229
Relevance of third party's knowledge,
229, 230, 232
Erroneous belief in formation, 233
Generally, 234
Under RULPA, 235
Under ULPA, 234
Substantial compliance, 225, 227, 233
General partners:
Agency powers of, 221, 222

Disciplining behavior of, 243
Derivative suit by limited partner, 254,
257
Exhaustion of intra-corporate
remedies, 259
Rule 23.1 Federal Rules of Civil
Procedure, 256
Standing requirements, 256, 257,
258, 260
Dissolution at behest of limited part-
ner, 269
"No action at law prior to dissolution",
rule inapplicable, 236
Ouster of general partner, 261, 263
Representative suit or class action by
limited partners, 253
Fiduciary duties to limited partners, 244,
250, 251, 252
Prerogatives of, 237, 244
Fixed by terms of partnership agree-
ment, 222, 238, 243
Strictly construed, 223, 243
Relation between or among general part-
ners, 237
History of, 211, 212, 213, 218
Liability to third parties:
General partners, 219, 271
Limited partners, 219, 272
Under RULPA, 282, 285
Under RULPA/85, 286
Under ULPA, 241, 272, 273, 275, 278
Limited partners:
Consequences of participation in control,
272
Relevance of creditor reliance, 272
Under RULPA, 282, 285
Under RULPA/85, 286
Under ULPA, 241, 272, 273, 275, 278
Contributions to capitalization of firm, 221
Obligations, 221
Status as investor, 219, 221, 250, 259
Rights, 239
Plight of person erroneously believing himself
limited partner:
Under RULPA, 235
Under ULPA, 234
Relationship between general and limited part-
ners, 236

PARTNER AS AGENT
Authority curtailed in wake of dissolution, 97
Authority to wind up, 97
Binding force of admission or representation,
69
Creation of agency status in partners, 75

Section 9(1) liability for unauthorized act, 65
Section 9(1) real authority, 76
Third person's knowledge, 76, 79
Stand-off in two member firm, 83

PARTNERSHIP AGREEMENT
Admission of new partner, 92
Amendment of, 89
Anti-competition clause, 90, 122, 125, 126
Compensation of partners, 92
Control and management of firm, 89
Default terms under UPA §18, 89, 92
Duration, 148, 149
Implied from conduct, 93, 99
Provision for executive committee, 89, 90
Regulating dissolution, 122
Valuation of deceased partner's interest, 180, 182, 185

PARTNERSHIP AS PRINCIPAL
Bound by admission of partner, 69
Burden of proof, 80
Liability for appearance of ordinary course of business, 79
Liable for authorized act, 68
Liable for torts, 68, 82
Misappropriation by a partner, 65

PARTNERSHIP BY ESTOPPEL
Generally, 13, 17, 21, 226
Liability consequences, 21

PARTNERSHIP PROPERTY
In general, 131
Distinguished from property of individual partners, 131
How created, 131, 135, 137
Impact of partner's death, 137
Presumed if acquired with partnership funds, 131, 139, 142
Rights and duties of surviving partner(s), 142, 143
Rights of partners with respect to specific partnership property, 146
Status of good will, 143

PRINCIPAL
Contract liability of, 39
Estoppel as source of liability, 41
Liable for negligent selection of unqualified agent, 55, 61
Partnership as principal:
  Bound by admission of partner, 69
  Burden of proof, 80
  Liability for appearance of ordinary course

of business, 79
  Liable for authorized act, 68
  Liable for torts, 68, 82
  Misappropriation by a partner, 65
Quasi-contract liability, 43
Ratification by, 42
Tort liability, 43, 68
  Defenses to:
    Frolic of agent, 56
    Non-servant status of agent, 48
    Scope of employment, 55
  Rationale of, 45
    Entrepreneur theory, 45
    Respondeat superior, 43, 47
      Control criteria, 49, 52

PROPERTY RIGHTS OF PARTNER
In general, 144, 146
Interest in profits and surplus, 146
Interest in specific partnership property, 146
Tenant in partnership, 147

QUASI-CONTRACT
Source of liability of betrayed principal, 43
Partner's compensation, 100

RATIFICATION
Express, 42
Implied, 42
Source of liability of betrayed principal, 42

RESPONDEAT SUPERIOR
See PRINCIPAL, TORT LIABILITY

RIGHTS OF PARTNER
Access to books and information, 111
Property rights, 131, 146
To accounting, 110, 112
To information respecting things affecting partnership, 106, 108, 113

SOLE PROPRIETORSHIP
Advantages, 2, 5
Disadvantages, 2, 6
Nature, 1
Taxation of, 6

TORT LIABILITY
In general, 43
Entrepreneur theory, 45, 54
Frolic vs. deviation, 56
Inherently dangerous task, 55
Negligent selection of unqualified independent contractor, 55, 61

Respondeat superior, 43
Scope of employment, 55
Servant vs. non-servant agent, 48

UNLIMITED LIABILITY OF PARTNERS
Joint and several, 65

WARRANTY OF AUTHORITY
By agent to third party, 41

WINDING UP OF PARTNERSHIP
   See DISSOLUTION

WITHDRAWAL OF PARTNER
Rightful, 125
Wrongful, 125